Genreflecting

Genreflecting Advisory Series

Diana Tixier Herald, Series Editor

Genreflecting

A Guide to Reading Interests in Genre Fiction

Fifth Edition

Diana Tixier Herald

2000
Libraries Unlimited, Inc.
Englewood, Colorado

To Rick for everything.

Libraries Unlimited, Inc.
P.O. Box 6633
Englewood, CO 80155-6633
1-800-237-6124
www.lu.com

Library of Congress Cataloging-in-Publication Data

Herald, Diana Tixier.
    Genreflecting : a guide to reading interests in genre fiction / Diana Tixier Herald.--5th ed.
        p. cm. -- (Genreflecting advisory series)
    Includes bibliographical references and index.
    ISBN 1-56308-638-7
    1. American fiction--Stories, plots, etc. 2. Popular literature--Stories, plots, etc. 3. English fiction--Stories, plots, etc. 4. Fiction genres--Bibliography. 5. Fiction--Bibliography. 6. Reading interests. I. Title. II. Series.

PS374.P63 H47 2000
016.813009--dc21

                                                                99-089778

Contents

Acknowledgments

The late Betty Rosenberg did more than anyone else to make the reading we do for fun acceptable in libraries and to legitimize it as an area of study for librarians. I (and other readers of popular genre fiction) owe her a debt of gratitude for validating our love of purely fun reading matter and giving genre fiction the status it well deserves.

I would like to thank Bonnie Kunzel, readers' advisor extraordinaire, for her assistance in finding wonderful new books to read. Thanks also go to Nathan Sundance Herald for assistance with this manuscript. Thanks to Joyce Saricks, Kristen Ramsdell, Tony Fonseca, June Michele Pulliam, and Michael Gannon for helping keep me on track and providing ideas for lots of new great stuff to read. Barbara Ittner provided invaluable insights and suggestions, as well as major hand-holding through the tough parts.

The online catalogs of Rio Grande (NM) Library District, Los Angeles (CA) Public Library, Johnson County (KS) Public Library, San Antonio (TX) Public Library, and Arapahoe County (CO) Library District were essential in the preparation of this book.

Acknowledgment must also be made of the vital online community of readers' advisors that meets daily on fiction_l, of Roberta Johnson for creating it in the first place, and of Natalya Fishman, who currently manages it. And last but not least, thanks to all the folks who recommend their favorite genre fiction to me wherever I go in my travels.

Preface to the Fifth Edition

Rosenberg's first law of reading:
"Never apologize for your reading tastes."

Genre fiction has been important to me my entire life. I started off conventionally enough with Nancy Drew and Tom Swift, rapidly moving on to Cherry Ames and Vicki Barr and then to the works of T. H. White, Zane Grey, Andre Norton, Anya Seton, and Frank Yerby before hitting my teens. I lived my life in genre fiction and fortunately moved often, finding new and exciting treasures in every new library about the time I would exhaust the resources of the old one. My book-a-day habit required that I read from several genres, which made me an omnivorous fan. For years I thought this propensity for compulsively losing myself in other worlds and other times was a defect—but then I came across the work of Betty Rosenberg, a pivotal point in my life. Betty's *Genreflecting* actually validated the type of reading I had been pursuing since primary school. When Ed Evans introduced *Genreflecting* to me in library school, I realized I was there for a purpose: to put people together with the books they wanted to read. This guide, then, is an attempt to help bring together readers and the books that will give them pleasure. Nothing else gives a readers' advisor—whether in the library, a bookstore, or in everyday life—the satisfaction of successfully playing cupid between a reader and a book.

Genre fiction is constantly evolving and changing, even though at its core it remains the same: a story in which something noticeable happens. Trends affect what is available in stores and libraries. Genres wax and wane. The current strength of mysteries makes it hard to believe that in the 1970s some experts were worrying about that genre's incipient demise. Westerns, once a genre section found in almost every public library, seem to be disappearing, as very few new titles are being published as Westerns. The major trend in the late 1990s was genre blending, a mixing of one genre with another. For example, Westerns, which at first glance seem to be fading, are turning up in romance, fantasy, and historical fiction. Romance now plays a greater role in science fiction and in fact in almost every genre. Strains of humor and detection are found in horror and science fiction. The combination of genres is endless. Genres, once so easy to codify that Jove published a series of generic genre fiction in the 1970s, are becoming increasingly difficult to pigeonhole. Where once the biggest decision was whether a specific work belonged in romantic suspense or suspenseful romance, now one may have to contend with a book that could fit into the genres of horror, romance, crime, and fantasy as well as being humorous.

The chapter on historical fiction (Chapter 1) is new to this volume. After debating whether to continue with the chapter on Westerns or integrate it into the historical chapter, it was decided to let it stand, at least for this edition. A few of the other changes include the addition of "Biothrillers" to "Adventure" (Chapter 4), "Literary Fantasy" to "Fantasy" (Chapter 7), "Virtual Reality" to "Science Fiction" (Chapter 6), and several more new subgenres. Of course, many new authors and titles have been added and those no longer in print or easily available in libraries have been deleted. To find information on older titles and reference works of historical interest, readers should consult previous editions of this book.

The importance of genre fiction in the lives of readers has been made more evident by the plethora of tools now available to help genre readers find the books they want. Several new guides, listed in the "Topics" section of each chapter, have been published. Libraries Unlimited has embarked on a bold new series of advisory guides that covers several different genres and fiction types. NoveList, now marketed by EBSCO, assists patrons with readers' advisory queries through the automated catalogs of libraries, and book shoppers in bookstores that have Syndetic Solutions Fiction Profiles or Muze Books kiosks find genre access there. As far as training for librarians who want to help with the patron's search for the right book at the right time, some library schools have recently added readers' advisory classes, and libraries, consortiums, library systems, and library organizations across the country are making available workshops and programs on genre fiction and readers' advisory. The Internet has made available the readers' services desks of several public libraries providing lists of book groupings and read-alikes. In addition to mailing list groups and newsgroups for specific genres, a mailing group called fiction_l now exists for librarians working with fiction questions. Here readers' advisors can get help, exchange information, answer difficult questions, and assemble read-alike lists. The professional review journals have been more accepting of genre fiction in recent years.

One can only hope that in the coming years these trends will continue, because as our awareness grows and new readers' advisory tools appear, we, as librarians or booksellers, can do our jobs more effectively. In the end, the satisfied reader is our greatest reward.

Introduction

What is not found in life—success, prestige, pleasure—is sought in reading material.

—Richard Baumberger
"Promoting the Reading Habit," *UNESCO Reports and Papers on Mass Communication* 72 (1975)

"But as for me, I find escapist literature the very thing for my woes big and small, and always have done. I write it to escape, and read it for the same reason ... Fiction tries to interpret ... truth, and escapist fiction tries to do that, and give it the best ending it can while it's at it. That's why I love it. What's so bad about feeling good?"

—Edith Layton in posting to RRA-L

The American Heritage® Dictionary of the English Language, Third Edition (© 1996 by Houghton Mifflin Company) defines genre as "a category of artistic composition, as in music or literature, marked by a distinctive style, form, or content." The term *genre fiction* is commonly used to discuss works of fiction that fall into the areas of mystery, suspense, thriller, adventure, romance, Western, science fiction, fantasy, and horror. The books usually described as genre fiction are books that have content that allows them to be easily categorized as belonging to a specific genre. Settings, whether the Old West, a distant planet in a distant time, a historical period on our planet, or a place where magic happens, are easily identifiable as one criterion for some types of genre fiction. Other times it is the plot—boy meets girl, boy loses girl, boy and girl come back together and live happily ever after. Death happens under unusual circumstances and a detective follows clues until the mystery is solved. Literary, mainstream, or substantial fiction—all terms used to define much of the fiction that is regarded as literature—is actually a genre of its own that is not ordinarily grouped with genre fiction. A full discussion of the literary genre can be found in Nancy Pearl's *Now Read This: A Guide to Mainstream Fiction, 1978–1998* (Libraries Unlimited, 1999).

It can be said that genre fiction, which tends to be the favorite form of fiction of the common reader, is the Rodney Dangerfield of literature. These books "get no respect." While critics, scholars, and even some librarians hope to elevate the tastes of the reading public, readers continue to read what they like.

The roots of genre fiction are in the distant past, when storytellers and bards held audiences enraptured by their tales and ballads of wondrous adventure, larger-than-life heroes and heroines, and magical beasts. While the literary quality may vary, the thrill of a strong plot, interesting dialog, and a satisfactory conclusion lead many individuals to read for pleasure.

The Nature of Genre Fiction

Genre fiction is constantly evolving, even though its essence remains the same—a tale of heroism in which the characters surmount obstacles to triumph. The scale of the heroism can be as large as a galaxy or as small and intimate as a pair of struggling lovers, but in genre fiction a character or characters are faced with an obstacle that is overcome through some strength of character, intelligence, or physical attribute. Genre fiction is plot-driven, but can also have masterful characterization and graceful prose.

In recent years genre fiction has undergone a metamorphosis that continues. Genreblending runs rampant. Genre fiction, once known for being formulaic, now stretches boundaries while trying to maintain its original appeal. Romance tales often include mysteries and murder that take place in futuristic societies. Faerie folk pop up in Westerns, while tales of horror and the occult go for the laughs. Any imaginable combination of genres has probably been attempted. This may be the most exciting era in history to be a reader of genre fiction or to be a librarian or bookseller helping readers to find suitable genre fiction.

Authors of genre fiction tend to be prolific, with continuing characters playing a large role in most genres. Characters are so important that often books are referred to by the names of the characters rather than by the name of the author or the book's title. Some characters seem so real that biographies have been written about them. Two excellent resources exist for finding the order of books in the series listed in this guide. They are *To Be Continued: An Annotated Guide to Sequels* (Oryx Press, 1995), by Merle L. Jacob and Hope Apple, and *Sequels: An Annotated Guide to Novels in Series* (American Library Association, 1997), by Janet G. Husband and Jonathan F. Husband. If you need to answer questions about genre fiction that is out of print or no longer easily available, *The Whole Story: 3000 Years of Sequels & Sequences* (Thorpe, 1998), compiled by John E. Simkin, is a good resource. This book can also help identify authors or titles when only the character name is known.

Who Is the Common Reader?

In recent years librarians, enamored with the possibilities of technology and anxious to justify their budgets and services, have increasingly cast themselves in the role of information professionals. Public libraries filled with glowing computer terminals link patrons to data in their local collections and beyond—to the global metadata available through the Internet. Indeed, the librarian as gatekeeper to the world of information is a position of power and importance—to governmental organizations and corporations, as well as to everyday citizens. From this lofty position it is sometimes difficult to consider the needs of the common reader who seeks the simple pleasure of books. As a gatekeeper, a librarian may question the value of dispensing the latest Stephen King horror novel or Catherine Coulter romance to eager patrons, or may wonder how to justify the expenditure of library funds on popular fiction. Yet it is in this capacity as a provider of genre fiction that librarians may be able to best serve their publics. Circulation figures consistently demonstrate that library users seek and use fiction collections as much or more than other parts of the library. At the North Carolina Central University Readers' Advisory Conference in 1999, it was noted that in North Carolina, two-thirds of public library circulation was fiction. It is clear that, to a large extent, our public is the common reader. But who are the common readers and what exactly do they want?

Simply put, common readers are the people who read. Common readers borrow from the library, or buy or trade books. Common readers read because they enjoy reading, entering another world with more excitement than the mundane, everyday world. These people know the difference between reality and fantasy, but choose to enjoy the age-old tradition of storytelling. Common readers are of any intellectual level and work in all jobs, professions, and careers. They fall into all economic levels of society. Common readers are our public and our customers.

Libraries and Genre Fiction

Earlier editions of *Genreflecting* discussed the controversy over maintaining collections of genre fiction in libraries. Rosenberg cited many articles criticizing popular reading as well as many articles promoting the library as a community resource for popular fiction. Even now, nearly 20 years after publication of the first edition of *Genreflecting,* where Rosenberg introduced her first law of reading—never apologize for your reading tastes—to the public, the controversy rages. The forum may have moved from library periodicals onto the Internet, but a lively exchange still ensued when a librarian asked a newsgroup for opinions regarding the purchase of a "not so good book" because a library user had made requests that it be purchased. Oh, the flames as accusations of censorship and wrong thinking were exchanged! In truth, while the American Library Association has recognized the value of a library's role as "popular reading center," some librarians continue to sniff disdainfully at genre fiction. Fortunately for the millions of library users, more librarians see their community's need for popular reading materials. While popular fiction collections are not funded in a ratio equivalent to their usage, libraries in the 1990s are making an effort to improve access to popular fiction.

Several library schools have added readers' advisory classes. In 1998 the Public Library Association conference offered an entire track of workshops on popular reading topics attended by standing-room-only audiences. Because of the popularity of the topic, PLA offered an additional symposium on this topic in 1999 and is offering the track again at its 2000 conference. Many libraries throughout the United States have staff training and in-service days devoted to learning more about genre fiction and how to help library patrons with their popular reading needs.

To further help patrons find genre fiction, easily identifiable genre fiction is often shelved separately in libraries. Historically, Westerns, mysteries, and science fiction have had their own sections or shelves in libraries. Some consider this unfair segregation, but most common readers (who know what they like and don't care about others' opinions of their reading tastes) like the chance to browse a manageable segment of the collection and find a number of books from their favorite genre all in one place. In large collections, separate shelving provides access to genre collections and also helps avoid information overload. Sharon L. Baker, who has written about information overload and fiction classification, has suggested that physically separating genre books from the general collection helps users of large collections select books without becoming overwhelmed. In addition to giving browsers a smaller and less intimidating set of books to choose from, it allows them to select from particular genres of interest. Spine labeling by genre is another widely used method to help readers in their quest for books they want to read.

Some libraries shelve paperbacks separately from hardcover books. One common practice is to shelve hardcover romance fiction with general fiction and to segregate the paperbacks of the genre in another area. This gives the impression that paperback romances are not "quite as good" as their hardcover counterparts. Avid readers of a particular genre want the story and are not particular about the format. In my experience as a librarian, most readers prefer that hardcover and paperback books be shelved together by genre. Paperbacks covered with self-adhesive plastic often hold up for more than 100 circulations at Mesa County (CO) Public Library. This defeats the argument that paperbacks cannot be treated like hardcover books because they physically do not last as long.

Shelving books by genre does create problems, especially in this era of genreblending. Should a science fiction romance be shelved with science fiction or with romance? Challenges in classification and organization, however, have yet to deter any self-respecting readers' advisory librarian from trying to organize the fiction collection in a manner that helps readers find the books they want.

Another improvement is access to genre fiction through the catalog. The GASFD classifications give users points of access for fiction other than merely title and author. Unfortunately, many libraries fail to catalog paperback fiction, which leaves huge segments of the collection read by common readers inaccessible except by serendipity. This presents problems, especially when an author's first several titles are paperback originals followed by hardcover releases. The reader wants early books in the series, but even when the library owns the paperbacks, they can't always be easily found, and there is no way of placing a hold or reserve on them through the public access catalog.

Readers' Advisory Service

Putting people together with the books they want to read is the purpose of a readers' advisory service. Knowing the literature, knowing the reader, and facilitating the meeting of the two are the key to being an effective readers' advisor.

Almost 20 years ago, John Naisbitt, in his best-selling book *Megatrends*, wrote about the importance of becoming "high touch" in a "high tech" world. As libraries become more and more high-tech, readers' advisory is one of the best ways for librarians to maintain a personal relationship with patrons. Readers' advisory may well be the library service that keeps libraries vital in the new century as current library users become more sophisticated at using the electronic resources that are moving out of libraries and into homes via personal computers.

A well-armed readers' advisor keeps an arsenal of resources at hand, including bibliographies and book lists in the form of bookmarks or pamphlets that many libraries provide. A helpful method, particularly for librarians who follow a reading plan, is to maintain a list of all titles read. Some librarians prefer to keep the list on index cards in a file, others use a database, and some keep a chronological list in their day planners. A short annotation and an indication of genre and type make the list extremely useful for readers' advisory service and also sharpen the librarian's writing skills. Many libraries maintain notebooks where staff reviews or annotations are on file, which gives greater access to the information. Even if one does not have the time to write annotations, however, it is very helpful to maintain at least an author/title listing of books read.

Reading plans, scorned by some, are simply ways of mapping out in advance a plan to sample various genres. Several years ago in libraries with a dedication to readers' advisory services (and the staff to support it), novice readers' advisors were assigned a variety of novels to read to become conversant in the different genres. An example of such a reading plan might be to read one book from each genre, then go back through the genres again, this time reading a book by a different author in each genre. Some reading plans were very specific; for example, to read a novel by Dorothy Sayers, followed by a novel by Zane Grey, then one by Isaac Asimov, and finally one by Grace Livingston Hill. A second pass in such a specific plan might call for novels by Raymond Chandler, Max Brand, Robert Silverberg, and Danielle Steel. This ensured that the readers' advisors became familiar with a diversity of authors within each genre. For an advisor who does not read romance, it can be quite eye-opening to read a Bertrice Small novel and an Avalon romance to see the diversity within the genre.

Guiding the Reader to the Next Book (Neal-Schuman, 1996), edited by Kenneth D. Shearer, features articles that not only provide a philosophical overview of readers' advisory but also includes articles on practical aspects of the art.

Joyce G. Saricks and Nancy Brown have written an excellent guide, *Readers' Advisory Service in the Public Library*, second edition (American Library Association, 1997). It is a must-read for anyone striving to perform readers' advisory service with any degree of excellence. The authors detail ways to determine the appeal of a book so that similar books can be found. Discovering "likes" comes only from reading the books themselves, not from reading a reference book about genres. Just because two books are similar by virtue of belonging to the same genre does not mean that they have similar appeal.

In her brief chapter "Advising the Reader" in *Romance Fiction: A Guide to the Genre* (Libraries Unlimited, 1999), Kristin Ramsdell shares some effective guidelines for advising readers in general. She notes that not all readers in need of assistance will ask for it, thus the need for passive readers' advisory. Passive readers' advisory includes shelving genre fiction separately, providing book lists and displays, and labeling spines. All these things, though not a substitute for an interview with a good readers' advisor, help readers to find books in the genres they like.

Readers' advisory pages are springing up on the World Wide Web. *Needle in a CyberStack* lists several at http://members.home.net/albeej/pages/Advisory.html.

Most are published by libraries and include book reviews, lists, and links to helpful fiction-related sites. Morton Grove Public Library maintains one of the best readers' advisory sites on the Web at http://www.webrary.org/rs/rslinks.html. Roberta Johnston, the originator of fiction_l, has posted information from her workshop, *Readers' Advisory on the Internet*, at http://www.fictional.org/index.html.

But perhaps the most important skills for readers' advisors are listening skills. Simply asking patrons about a book they enjoyed in the past reveals more about what they might enjoy in the future than all the reference books and reading lists put together.

Publishing Genre Fiction

Genre fiction is popular fiction that publishers continue to publish because it sells. At least half of the titles on the weekly best-seller lists (hardcover and paperback) are genre titles. Prolific and popular authors appear regularly—anything they publish, regardless of its quality, will sell. In the article "The Red & the Black: Hardcover Bestsellers" by Daisy Maryles in the March 29, 1999, issue of *Publishers Weekly Online*, she states that the books that were best sellers for the year were "predictable," "commercial," and had "name-brand recognition." The *Publishers Weekly* number one best seller was a legal thriller by John Grisham, who has held the number one spot for four years. In second place was a Tom Clancy technothriller, and in third a Stephen King horror novel. Out of the top 15 bestsellers, there were five crime novels, three romance novels (if one includes womanly fiction by Danielle Steel in romance), two horror novels, and one adventure novel. *Publishers Weekly* does not separate fiction from non-fiction for its mass market best seller list, but all eight titles that sold in excess of 2 million copies in 1998 were genre fiction, and of the 26 titles that sold between 1 and 2 million copies, 20 were genre fiction ("The Red & the Black: Paperback Bestsellers" by Mark Rotella, *Publishers Weekly Online*, March 29, 1999). Even the bestseller lists from the *New York Times Book Review*, a bastion of literary fiction, reflect that genre fiction is what people want to read. The May 16, 1999, Best Sellers Plus list of 35 books featured nine romance, six crime, three adventure, three science fiction, two fantasy, and two horror titles.

Genre fiction is published in all formats: hardcover, paperback, audiotape, compact disc, and over the Internet. The publishing industry has seen radical changes in the last couple of years. Giant publishing houses have merged, forming even larger houses. Bantam Doubleday Dell is now part of Random, Inc. Penguin and Putnam have become Penguin Putnam.

As the giants battle it out for supremacy on the best-seller lists by giving staggeringly huge contracts to the top grossing writers, they seem to be publishing less and less midlist fiction, which, of course, is necessary for the voracious appetites of readers.

At the same time, new technology gives small publishers and self-published authors opportunities never before seen. It is now possible for small publishing houses to make a go of it. Even self-published titles are garnering critical approval. These small presses are becoming a good resource for finding new authors. Write Way Publishing publishes approximately 10 original genre novels a year in hardcover. These are primarily mystery novels, but also include science fiction, fantasy, and horror. Intrigue Press, which specializes in mysteries, publishes seven to 10 original and reprint titles a year in both hardcover and paperback. Genesis Press began in 1993 by publishing African-American romances but now also publishes Latino, Asian, and interracial romances. Russell Like formed Brunswick Galaxy Publishing to publish his science fiction book *After the Blue,* which he bought back from a publisher who had placed it on a backburner. It has garnered critical praise as a highly entertaining book.

Reprint editions are of particular importance in genre fiction because so many titles go out of print so quickly. Readers often discover a "new" author, often of a series, and find that reprint editions are the only source for finding earlier titles. The large-print publishers have long been a great source for genre fiction reprints in both hardcover and trade paperback. Severn House publishes hardcover reprints of several genres. New on the scene is Five Star, which publishes both reprints and originals in Westerns and romance.

Women and Genre Fiction

Women have always written and been featured in genre fiction, but the 1980s saw a tremendous surge in the popularity of the woman's role. By the end of the decade, thrillers featuring women as private investigators or amateur investigators were appearing weekly. Who by now has not heard of V. I. Warshawski or Kinsey Millhone? The 1990s saw an explosion of secondary materials dealing with women in crime fiction, such as the titles *Detecting Women* and *By a Woman's Hand.* Women also gained recognition in science fiction and fantasy and no longer had to resort to male pseudonyms or only their initials. Many readers discovered for the first time that James Tiptree, Jr., Andre Norton, Julian May, and C. J. Cherryh were all women. It became more acceptable in those genres for authors to have first names like Margaret, Sherri, or Pamela. In the new millennium, genre fiction continues to grow and evolve, which makes it more difficult to define, but also builds excitement in the reading public. In this milieu, the role of the readers' advisor has expanded and become more complex. The core of our role, however, remains the same: as readers' advisors it is important first to read and enjoy, and second to share information.

Purpose and Scope of This Guide

The primary purpose of this guide is to put books and readers together by helping readers' advisors in libraries, bookstores, and academic institutions find the books their readers will enjoy reading. Offering a structured overview of genres, it can also be used as a textbook for courses in genre literature and readers' advisory to discuss popular genres of fiction.

Organization

Each chapter covers one of the popular genres. An overview of historical, Western, crime, adventure, romance, science fiction, fantasy, and horror is followed by descriptions of subgenres. Bibliographies for each subgenre list authors and titles important in the genre because of popularity or influence on the genre. Following the lists of authors and titles in each chapter, a topics section provides information on resources for more in-depth information on specific facets of the genre. The information varies by chapter depending on the specific character of the genre. Generally bibliographies, critical works, and organizations pertaining to the genre are included, but each chapter, like each genre, has unique characteristics. At the end of each chapter is a section called "D's Picks," a personal recommendation by the author.

Authors Included

Most of the authors included are prolific. It is not uncommon for genre authors to write dozens or even hundreds of books. Some authors are actually house names used by publishers or book packagers to put all titles in a series or sequence under one author, while in other instances the author has actually written all those books. The most amazing recent trend has been for authors to continue publishing for years after death. An example is V. C. Andrews, who is still wildly prolific, publishing four books in 1999, a decade after her death. Of course, another author is writing the books published under her name. Some authors are included who have written only a few novels that have made a tremendous impact on their specific genre or who are relatively new authors who are popular or show marked promise.

Titles Included

Title listings are not intended to be all-inclusive, but rather exemplary of a writer's work in print near the end of the millennium or available in public library collections.

Years Covered

The intent of *Genreflecting* is to identify titles enjoyed by the common reader rather than to provide comprehensive lists of genre fiction published within a certain time frame. Therefore, no specific time range is covered. The focus is on works that are widely available in libraries. Most of the titles were published or reprinted in the 1990s. This edition of *Genreflecting* features many new authors and titles published since the last edition was released.

Entries and Annotations

Ideally every title would be annotated, but that would make this guide too large and cumbersome for readers and their advisors to take to the shelves or stacks in search of the next good read. Selected titles are annotated to illustrate the subgenre or type. Most entries list the author and titles that fit into the subgenre under which they are listed. In order to provide as much coverage as possible but still be concise, some entries (particularly in crime, where many of the entries list the author and the detective) list only the author when that author writes primarily within a specific subgenre.

Suggestions for Use

There are many different ways to access the information in *Genreflecting*. Readers' advisors (in libraries and in bookstores) should read through the text and familiarize themselves with the genres and subgenres as well as authors and titles within each. They can also use the book to fill patron requests for fiction read-alikes. Many readers will enjoy using this book on their own. To find specific authors and titles, users can refer to the index. When looking for books similar to a known author or title, the user can check the other listings in the specific subgenre section identified by using the index to find where the known author is listed. The table of contents and the subject index can be used to find information on the genres and subgenres. Scholarly materials and reference sources can be found by consulting the topics section of each chapter. Librarians have also used previous editions of *Genreflecting* to select titles for displays or for separating genre collections from large general fiction collections.

Chapter 1

Historical

"What is history but a fable agreed upon?"
—Napoleon

The allure of the past as it never was is fascinating enough to make even the most reticent individuals express opinions as to which other time period they would have liked to live in. Much historical fiction, and the kind preferred by those who read it as genre fiction, presents a somewhat romanticized, sanitized view of the past. Focusing on the delights of bygone eras, these books make the past seem all the more attractive when compared to the perceived horrors of today. In fact, some definitions of historical fiction require that the settings be in a time before the birth of the author. Other readers, particularly teens, consider anything that happened before they were old enough to remember it an appropriate setting for historical fiction. In this guide historical fiction is considered stories that begin prior to the middle of the twentieth century.

Historical fiction offers much diversity, and not all of it will satisfy the common reader of popular fiction. Some is quite literary. Some is quite bleak. The historical fiction included in this guide concentrates on stories with strong plots in which the setting (time and place) also plays a prominent and integral role in the story rather than serving simply as a backdrop. Historical authenticity is not always the ultimate aim. Some works that fall into the genre of literary fiction are included in this chapter because they are titles that the historical genre reader may be familiar with and have an interest in.

Popular historical fiction is peopled by romantic heroes and heroines who face adventure and emerge triumphant. It follows the same model of other genre fiction in that a character faces and overcomes adversity. At its best, historical fiction makes the past come to life. It spins intriguing stories around dry dates and facts and imprints them indelibly on the memory. This author managed to score 99 out of 100 on a high school history final exam solely by using the knowledge gained through reading historical fiction as a teen.

Advising the Reader

Readers of historical fiction often prefer to stay with a specific time period or geographical location. This guide is arranged more or less chronologically and geographically (by setting) to help guide readers to the books they will enjoy.

As the popularity of historicals has increased, so has the number of resources related to the genre. Outstanding World Wide Web sites abound and some are listed in the "Topics" section of this chapter along with other resources for information about historical fiction.

History has become a more important element in other genres; thus readers have turned to historical fiction as a genre in and of itself. It can easily be argued that Westerns, in particular the traditional Westerns that were set between 1865 and 1910, fall into the category of historical fiction, but they also make up a genre of their own. Readers who enjoy the American West as a setting may also want to consult Chapter 2.

Historical settings abound in other genres, so they should be checked for the avid reader. Time travel takes readers of fantasy and science fiction into the past. Alternate history in science fiction shows a different view of how things might have been (see Chapter 6). Historical romances are included in the romance chapter (Chapter 5), historical nautical and military adventure are in the adventure chapter (Chapter 4), and the blending of mysteries and historical fiction will be found in the crime chapter (Chapter 3).

In addition to consulting the following listings under geographical location, readers should see the sections in this chapter on sagas and epics. Finally, some readers of historical fiction also enjoy nonfiction books about the same events and time periods they enjoy in fiction.

Why This Chapter?

Previous editions of this guide did not treat historical fiction as a separate genre. However, readers who read historicals are looking for the same thrill, the same sense of the heroic that exists in other genres. Also, as stated above, historical fiction has been growing in popularity. Yes, there are literary historical fiction novels, but that isn't the focus here. This guide only touches on some of the most popular and identifiable areas of historical fiction as a genre. Because of this, some areas seem to be underrepresented. Unfortunately, the bulk of historical fiction read in the United States focuses on U.S. and British settings. It is to be hoped that more popular titles will be forthcoming that will be set in South America, Central America, eastern Europe, Asia, Africa, and Australia. For most of this century the most visible historical novels were Westerns, which are treated in Chapter 2. Now that "genre blending" has become so prevalent, we see historical fiction popping up everywhere. Historical fiction is popular in romance and has established a firm following in science fiction and fantasy through time travel. Many of the titles in the adventure chapter, especially those that deal with daring on the high seas in the time of sail, are also historical fiction. And possibly the most popular kind of historical fiction, outside the romance, is historical mysteries, covered in the crime chapter (Chapter 3).

Because the sheer number of historical fiction titles (which would fill several volumes) precludes comprehensive coverage, the titles selected for inclusion in this book are those that have been popular in libraries. Most of them are actual answers to real readers' advisory inquiries, gleaned from years of library information desk duty. Because of this, coverage is not balanced through the eras, although a smattering of different places and times can be found. This chapter is intended to provide a sampling of the historical genre that will be expanded upon in future editions.

Themes and Types

Historical settings are found in all genres of fiction, from romances, to historical mysteries, to medieval fantasy, to time travel science fiction. The titles in this chapter may have elements of those other genres but the focus is on the historical context. This is a rich and extensive category, and the titles listed are only the tip of the iceberg. The emphasis is on U.S. settings because they seem to be the most published in the United States, followed by British settings.

Prehistoric Epics, Ancient Civilizations, and Precontact Native Americans

The prehistoric epic has become very popular since the 1980 publication of Jean Auel's *Clan of the Cave Bear*, the first in her Earth's Children series. Readers want to know what life was like before our civilization and before there was a written record of how society lived. The dawn of humanity's tenure on this planet offers many venues for action-packed adventure and romantic encounters. The settings, drawn from archaeological and anthropological research, provide a distant and romantic arena for the action. Often, even though the settings, costumes, and tools are scientifically correct, the heroine or hero exhibits traits and follows social mores belonging more in the late twentieth century than in prehistoric times. Tales set in ancient civilizations provide a sense of lost wonders and settings that seem more exotic than those in eras with well-documented history.

Allan, Margaret

Spirits Walking Woman. Ancient Olmec culture.

Mammoth trilogy. The first two titles deal with Maya, exiled from her southwestern peoples to acquire a stone of great power and be trained by a shaman. The third book follows the quest of a descendant of Maya's to find the Mammoth stone.

The Mammoth Stone.

Keeper of the Stone.

The Last Mammoth.

Auel, Jean

Earth's Children series. Ayla, a contemporary-style woman born in the Upper Paleo-lithic, domesticates horses and discovers romance.

Clan of the Cave Bear.

The Mammoth Hunters.

The Valley of Horses.

The Plains of Passage.

Bradshaw, Gillian

The Beacon at Alexandria. Fourth century.

Bruchac, Joseph

Dawn Land. Young Hunter and his faithful dog companions set out on a quest to save his people from destruction.

Long River. Young Hunter is now married. The story deals with the necessity of maintaining a balance with nature 10,000 years ago.

Cockrell, Amanda

Deer Dancers.

Daughter of the Sky.

Wind Caller's Children.

The Long Walk.

Conley, Robert J.

Real People series. The first few books are set in precontact America. Others in the series are listed in the "Native American" section in the Western chapter (Chapter 2).

The Dark Way.

The Way of the Priests.

Diamant, Anita

The Red Tent. Biblical.

Gear, W. Michael, and Kathleen O'Neal Gear

The First North Americans series. Written by a couple of archaeologists, each title is a stand-alone set at a cusp that decides the future of a culture.

People of the Wolf. Alaska and Northwest Canada, approximately 13,000–10,000 B.C.

People of the Fire. Central Rockies and Great Plains, approximately 5000 B.C.

People of the Earth. Northern Plains, approximately 5000 B.C.

People of the River. Mississippi Valley, approximately ninth–thirteenth centuries.

People of the Sea. California, approximately 13,000–10,000 B.C.

People of the Lakes. Great Lakes area, approximately 100 A.D.

People of the Lightning. Florida, approximately thirteenth century.

People of the Silence. Twelfth-century Southwest.

People of the Mist. Approximately fourteenth century, Chesapeake Bay area.

People of the Masks. Upstate New York, eleventh century.

Gedge, Pauline
Hera series. Ancient Egypt.

George, Margaret
The Memoirs of Cleopatra: A Novel.

Gray, Robert Steele
Survivor. North American Plains, approximately 200 A.D.

Harrison, Sue
Aleutian trilogy.

      Mother Earth, Father Sky. Chagak, a young woman who has made an epic journey, comes of age at the end of the last Ice Age, approximately 9,000 years ago.

      My Sister the Moon. Both of Chagak's sons vie for the love of Kiin.

      Brother Wind. Kiin and another widow struggle for survival.

      Song of the River. Alaska, seventh century B.C.

Jacq, Christian
Ramses series.

      The Son of Light.

      The Eternal Temple.

      The Battle of Kadesh.

      The Lady of Abu Simbel.

      Under the Western Acacia.

Jennings, Gary
      Aztec.

      Aztec Autumn.

Lambert, Joan Dahr
      Circles of Stone. Three strong women named Zena in three different prehistoric eras.

Mackey, Mary
      The Year the Horses Came. Matriarchal European society in 4372 B.C.

      The Horses at the Gate.

      The Fires of Spring.

McCullough, Colleen
Masters of Rome series.

      The First Man in Rome.

      The Grass Crown.

      Fortune's Favorite.

      Caesar's Women.

      Caesar.

Prentiss, Charlotte

Children of the Ice.

People of the Mesa.

Children of the Sun.

The Island Tribe. Approximately 10,000 B.C.

Ocean Tribe.

Pressfield, Steven

Gates of Fire: An Epic Novel of the Battle of Thermopylae. 480 B.C.

Rofheart, Martha

The Alexandrian. Cleopatra.

Sarabande, William

The First Americans. Series about prehistoric humans crossing a land bridge to the Americas.

Beyond the Sea of Ice. Torka, Umak, and Lonit embark on a quest to hunt down the mammoth that destroyed their clan.

Corridor of Storms.

Forbidden Land.

Walkers of the Wind.

Sacred Stones.

Thunder in the Sky.

Edge of the World.

Shadow of the Watching Star.

Face of the Rising Sun.

Time Beyond Beginning.

Shuler, Linda Lay

Time Circle quartet. Thirteenth-century Southwest.

She Who Remembers. An Anasazi woman becomes special after traveling with the god Kokopelli.

Voice of the Eagle.

Let the Drum Speak.

Smith, Wilbur

The River God. Ancient Egypt.

The Seventh Scroll. Ancient Egypt.

Tarr, Judith

Ancient Egypt.

Lord of the Two Lands.

Throne of Isis.

King and Goddess.

Thomas, Elizabeth Marshall

Realistic tales of a young Siberian woman in a hunting-gathering society about 20,000 years ago.

      Reindeer Moon.

      The Animal Wife.

Waltari, Mika

      The Egyptian.

      The Etruscan.

      The Roman.

Wolf, Joan

      Daughter of the Red Deer. Southern Europe, Paleolithic era.

      Horsemasters.

      Reindeer Hunters.

Asia, Africa, and the Antipodes

Buck, Pearl S.

      Imperial Woman.

      Peony. China, nineteenth century.

Campion, Jane

      The Piano. Nineteenth-century New Zealand.

Clavell, James

      Shogun. Seventeenth-century Japan.

      Gai-Jin. Nineteenth-century Japan.

Holland, Cecelia

      Jerusalem. The Crusader kingdom in the twelfth-century Holy Land.

      Valley of the Kings. King Tutankhamen and an early twentieth-century British archaeologist.

Lord, Betty Bao

      The Middle Heart. China during the Communist Revolution.

Maalouf, Amin

      Leo Africanus. Fifteenth century.

Malouf, David

      The Conversations at Curlow Creek. Nineteenth-century Australia.

      Remembering Babylon. Nineteenth-century Australia.

      Fly Away Peter. World War I Australians.

McCullough, Colleen

Ladies of Missalonghi. Early twentieth-century Australia.

Shaw, Patricia

The Feather and the Stone. Nineteenth-century Australia.

Shute, Nevil

Several titles set in Australia following World War II.

Smith, Wilbur

Birds of Prey.

Monsoon.

Europe

Readers who enjoy tales of Arthur, Finn MacCool, and Robin Hood may also be interested in titles included in the "Saga, Myth, and Legend" section of the fantasy chapter (Chapter 7).

Baer, Ann

Down the Common. A woman's life in medieval England.

Benson, Ann

The Plague Tales.

The Burning Road. Fourteenth-century France and twenty-first-century America.

Buckley, Fiona

Elizabethan mysteries.

To Shield the Queen.

The Doublet Affair.

Queen's Ransom.

Cody, Denee

The Court of Love. A romance that brings the court of Eleanor of Aquitaine vividly to life.

Cornwell, Bernard

The Richard Sharpe series. Set during the Peninsular War against Napoleon. Titles are listed in the adventure chapter (Chapter 4).

Cowell, Stephanie

The Physician of London. Seventeenth-century England.

Delderfield, R. F.

God Is an Englishman. Victorian England.

Dukthas, Ann

Time travel mysteries dealing with actual historical events.

The Time of Murder at Mayerling. Nineteenth-century Austria.

In the Time of the Poisoned Queen. Tudor England.

The Prince Lost to Time. France, early nineteenth century.

A Time for the Death of a King. Mary, Queen of Scots.

Dunnett, Dorothy

Arguably the most popular writer of historical fiction in the 1990s, Dunnett writes books filled with adventure.

Francis Crawford Lyman series. Sixteenth-century Scotsman.

The Game of Kings.

Queen's Play.

The Disorderly Knights.

Pawn in Frankincense.

The Ringed Castle.

Checkmate.

House of Niccolo series. Fifteenth-century merchant prince.

Niccolo Rising.

The Spring of the Ram.

Race of Scorpions.

Scales of Gold.

The Unicorn Hunt.

To Lie with Lions.

Caprice and Rondo.

Eco, Umberto

The Name of the Rose. Fourteenth-century Italy.

Emerson, Kathy Lynn

Elizabethan-era mysteries.

Face Down in the Marrow-Bone Pie.

Face Down upon an Herbal.

Face Down Among the Winchester Geese.

Fitzgerald, Penelope.

Blue Flower. Eighteenth-century Germany. Literary.

Follett, Ken

Pillars of the Earth. Twelfth-century England.

Fowles, John

The French Lieutenant's Woman. Victorian. Literary.

Garwood, Haley Elizabeth

Warrior Queens series.

    The Forgotten Queen. Twelfth-century England.

    Swords Across the Thames. Tenth-century England.

Gordon, Noah

The Physician. Eleventh century. England and Persia.

Haasse, Hella S.

In a Dark Wood Wandering: A Novel of the Middle Ages.

Threshold of Fire: A Novel of Fifth Century Rome.

Scarlet City: A Novel of 16th Century Italy.

Harrison, Kathryn

Poison. Seventeenth-century Spain. Literary.

Holland, Cecelia

Great Maria. Twelfth-century Italy.

Howatch, Susan

The Wheel of Fortune. Nineteenth-century Wales.

Koen, Karleen

Through a Glass Darkly. London and Paris in the early eighteenth century.

Now Face to Face. The sequel to *Through a Glass Darkly.* Takes place in Colonial Virginia and London.

Laker, Rosalind

The Golden Tulip. Holland, seventeenth century.

Banners of Silk. Napoleonic France.

Circle of Pearls. Seventeenth-century England.

Pargeter, Edith

The Brothers of Gwynedd: Comprising, Sunrise in the West, the Dragon at Noonday, the Hounds of Sunset, Afterglow, and Nightfall. Medieval Wales.

Pears, Iain

An Instance of the Fingerpost. Seventeenth-century murder mystery set in England.

Penman, Sharon Kay

Here Be Dragons. King John of England.

The Sunne in Splendour. King Richard III of England.

Falls the Shadow. Simon de Montfort.

Peters, Ellis
Brother Cadfael mystery series. Twelfth-century Britain.

Riley, Judith Merkle
The Oracle Glass. Highly entertaining tale of fraud in seventeenth-century France.

The Serpent Garden. A touch of the occult in Renaissance France.

Saramago, José
Baltasar and Blimunda. Portugal, 1711.

Smiley, Jane
The Greenlanders. Fourteenth-century Greenland.

Stone, Irving
The Agony and the Ecstasy. Fictionalized biography of Michelangelo.

Willis, Connie
The Doomsday Book. While this is science fiction time travel, the accurately depicted England of the fourteenth century is a favorite of historical fiction fans.

The "Royals"

Biography of royal personages has long been a popular type of publication. Many historical novels, treating history in terms of a country's rulers, have been at least partially biographies of rulers.

Barnes, Margaret Campbell
The Passionate Brood.

The King's Bed.

The Tudor Rose.

Within the Hollow Crown.

Brief Gaudy Hour. Anne Boleyn.

King's Fool.

Mary of Carisbrooke. Charles I.

My Lady of Cleves. Anne of Cleves.

George, Margaret
Autobiography of Henry VIII: With Notes by His Fool, Will Somers: A Novel.

Mary Queen of Scotland and the Isles: A Novel.

Harrod-Eagles, Cynthia
I, Victoria.

Hill, Pamela
Tsar's Woman. Catherine I of Russia.

Holt, Victoria

(Holt also wrote as Jean Plaidy and Philippa Carr.)

The Queen's Confession. Marie Antoinette.

Kay, Susan

Legacy. Elizabeth I of England.

Keyes, Frances Parkinson

I, the King. Philip IV of Spain and Isabel de Borbón of Spain.

Lambton, Anthony

Elizabeth & Alexandra. Queen Victoria's granddaughters: Alix, married to Czar Nicholas II; Ella, married to Grand Duke Serge.

Maxwell, Robin

The Secret Diary of Anne Boleyn.

The Queen's Bastard. Queen Elizabeth I of England.

Meyerson, Evelyn Wilde

Princess in Amber. Queen Victoria's daughter, Princess Beatrice.

Pargeter, Edith

A Bloody Field by Shrewsbury. Henry IV of England.

Plaidy, Jean

Plaidy also wrote novels on Isabella of Spain, Catherine of Aragon, and Mary of Scotland.

Georgian saga.

Queen in Waiting.

The Princess of Celle. Sophia Dorothea, divorced wife of George I of England.

Caroline the Queen (and others).

Victorian saga.

The Captive of Kensington Palace.

Victoria in the Wings.

The Queen and Lord M.

The Queen's Husband.

The Widow of Windsor.

Victoria Victorious.

Tannahill, Reay

Fatal Majesty: A Novel of Mary, Queen of Scots.

The Americas

New frontiers and unexplored lands offer a broad canvas for fiction. Frontiers, whether Australia or the American West or other locales, focus on the clash of "civilization" and the taming of the wilderness. The lure of a place far from crowds, jobs, and schools offers instead freedom, danger, and excitement. Readers who like frontier fiction also will often like sagas because many of them deal with families or individuals who move to a new land and how they establish themselves. Many of the books in the Western chapter (Chapter 2) will also be appealing.

North America to 1800

Self-reliance and the strength to survive are some of the traits of the characters in this type of book. Man against nature, hewing out a home and livelihood from the wilderness while battling great odds just for survival, is typical. Often conflict arises from "civilization" trying to take over the wilderness and end the independence of early settlers.

Bristow, Gwen
Deep Summer.
Celia Garth. South Carolina, American Revolution.

Chase-Riboud, Barbara
Sally Hemmings. Sixty years in the life of Jefferson's mistress.

Conde, Maryse
I, Tituba, Black Witch of Salem. Massachusetts, late seventeenth century.

Cornwell, Bernard
Redcoat. American Revolution, Philadelphia.

Coyle, Harold
Savage Wilderness. French and Indian Wars.

Donati, Sara
Into the Wilderness. Romantic tale related to James Fenimore Cooper's *Leatherstocking Tales,* set in eighteenth-century upstate New York.
Dawn on a Distant Shore.

Fast, Howard
April Morning. American Revolution.

Follett, Ken
A Place Called Freedom. Eighteenth-century Scottish immigrant.

Giles, Janice Holt
Hannah Fowler. Kentucky.
The Kentuckians.

Grey, Zane

Betty Zane. Eighteenth-century Allegheny Mountains.

Grimes, Roberta

My Thomas: A Novel of Martha Jefferson's Life.

Hodge, Jane Aiken

Judas Flowering. American Revolution in the South.

Jekel, Pamela

Deepwater. Carolinas.

Lawrence, Margaret

Romantic mysteries set in Maine following the American Revolution.

Hearts and Bones.

Blood Red Roses.

The Burning Bride.

Mason, F. Van Wyck

Rascals Heaven. Georgia.

The Sea Venture.

The Young Titan. New England and Maine.

Wild Horizon. American Revolution.

Meyers, Maan

The Dutchman. Annotated in the crime chapter (Chapter 3).

Receveur, Betty Layman

Kentucky Home.

Robson, Lucia St. Clair

Mary's Land. Maryland, seventeenth century.

Seton, Anya

Devil Water. Virginia, eighteenth century.

Snelling, Lauraine

Red River of the North series. A Norwegian family, the Bjorklunds, sail to the New World to take up the backbreaking task of carving a farm out of the vast northern prairie. Inspirational.

An Untamed Land.

A New Day Rising.

A Land to Call Home.

Stone, Irving

Those Who Love. Abigail and John Adams.

The President's Lady. Rachel and Andrew Jackson.

Thane, Elswyth
> **Dawn's Early Light.** American Revolution, Williamsburg, Virginia.

Thom, James Alexander
> **Follow the River.** The harrowing tale of Mary Ingles's escape from the Shawnee and epic journey home.

Vidal, Gore
> **Burr.** Carefully researched fictional memoir of Aaron Burr.

Nineteenth Century

Aldrich, Bess Streeter
> **A Lantern in Her Hand.** Nebraska.

Barrett, Andrea
> **The Voyage of the Narwhal.** A nineteenth-century Arctic voyage.

Bristow, Gwen
> **The Handsome Road.** Civil War.
>
> **Calico Palace.**

Brown, Rita Mae
> **Dolley: A Novel of Dolley Madison and Love and War.**
>
> **High Hearts.** A young woman disguises herself to follow her love to war.

Cather, Willa
> **Death Comes for the Archbishop.** New Mexico.
>
> **My Antonia.** Nebraska.
>
> **Oh, Pioneers!** Nebraska.

Coleman, Lonnie
> **Beulah Land.**
>
> **Look Away, Beulah Land.**
>
> **Legacy of Beulah Land.**

Cornwell, Bernard
> *Nate Starbuck series.*
>> **Rebel.**
>>
>> **Copperhead: A Novel of the Civil War.**
>>
>> **Battle Flag.**
>>
>> **The Bloody Ground.**

Coyle, Harold W.
> **Look Away.**
>
> **Until the End.** Civil War.

Dallas, Sandra
> **The Diary of Mattie Spenser.** Colorado.

Eberhart, Mignon Good.
> **Bayou Road.** New Orleans, Civil War suspense.
> **Family Fortune.** West Virginia, Civil War suspense.

Eulo, Elena Yates
> **Southern Women.**

Fowler, Robert
> **Voyage to Honor.** War of 1812.

Frazier, Charles
> **Cold Mountain.** Civil War, North Carolina. A literary award winner and best seller.

Gear, W. Michael
> **The Morning River.**

Gordon, Noah
> **The Shaman.** Romantic tale of doctoring on the frontier.

Holland, Cecelia
> **The Bear Flag.** California.
> **Pacific Street.** San Francisco.

Jakes, John
> **North and South.**
> **Love and War.**
> **Heaven and Hell.**
> **Homeland.**

Kantor, MacKinlay
> **Andersonville.** Civil War. Literary.

Mitchell, Margaret
> **Gone with the Wind.** Classic romantic tale of Scarlett O'Hara, the Civil War, and its aftermath.

Morrison, Toni
> **Beloved.** Literary.

Nevin, David
> **1812.**

Osborn, Karen
> **Between Earth and Sky.** Epistolary novel about two sisters who separated after the Civil War, one to stay in Virginia and the other to venture forth to New Mexico.

Price, Eugenia

The Waiting Time. Antebellum Georgia from the viewpoint of a feminist and abolitionist who inherits a plantation and a hundred slaves.

Richter, Conrad

Awakening Land (omnibus edition title for the following books).

The Trees.

The Fields.

The Town.

Shaara, Michael

Killer Angels. Civil War. Literary.

Styron, William

The Confessions of Nat Turner. 1830s slave rebellion.

Thoene, Brock

The Legend of Storey County. The tale of a 100-year-old African-American born into slavery.

Vidal, Gore

Lincoln. Literary.

Willis, Connie

Lincoln's Dreams. See the fantasy chapter (Chapter 7).

Yerby, Frank

The Foxes of Harrow.

The Vixens.

Zollinger, Norman

Chapultepec. Mexico's struggle for independence.

Sagas

The saga series, spanning decades or centuries, have been around for a long time but they really took off when a book packager, the late Lyle Engel of Book Creations, started marketing several series that became immensely popular. Sagas and epics are generally lengthier and offer the reader an opportunity to know the families involved and to become immersed in their lives and times. Most involve a great deal of romance as well as adventure. Fans of sagas should also consult the saga sections in the romance and Western chapters (Chapters 5 and 2, respectively).

Anand, Valerie

Bridges over Time.

The Proud Villeins. Eleventh century.

The Ruthless Yeoman.

Women of Ashdon.

The Faithful Lovers. Seventeenth century.

The Cherished Wives. Eighteenth century.

Belle, Pamela

St. Barbe family, seventeenth-century Britain.

Wintercombe.

Herald of Joy.

A Falling Star.

Treason's Gift.

Cookson, Catherine

Several titles and series.

The Desert Crop.

Mallen trilogy.

Tilly Trotter trilogy.

De la Roche, Mazo

The Whiteoak Saga. Published between 1927 and 1960, the tales of the Whiteoak family and Jalna, their family estate in Canada, still circulate in some libraries.

Dengler, Sandy

Australian Destiny series. Christian saga.

Code of Honor.

The Power of Pinjarra.

Taste of Victory.

East of the Outback.

Fletcher, Inglis

Carolina series.

Roanoke Hundred.

Bennet's Welcome.

Men of Albemarle.

Lusty Wind for Carolina.

Cormorant's Brood.

The Scotswoman.

Toll of the Brave.

Raleigh's Eden.

The Queen's Gift.

Harrod-Eagles, Cynthia

Kirov Saga. Russia and England, nineteenth and early twentieth centuries.

    Anne.

    Fleur.

    Emily.

Jakes, John

The Kent Family chronicles. Originally called the American Bicentennial series. A Lyle Engel creation.

    The Bastard.

    The Rebels.

    The Seekers.

    The Furies.

    The Titans.

    The Warriors.

    The Lawless.

    The Americans.

Jordan, Robert, writing as Reagan O'Neal

Fallon series.

    Fallon Blood.

    Fallon Pride.

    Fallon Legacy.

Lofts, Norah

The adventures of the Reed family of Suffolk, England, are followed from 1496 to the twentieth century.

    The Town House: The Building of the House.

    The House at Old Vine.

    The House at Sunset.

Long, William Stewart

The Australians series. A Lyle Engel creation.

    The Exiles.

    The Settlers.

    The Traitors.

    The Explorers.

    The Adventures.

    The Colonists.

    The Gold Seekers.

    The Gallant.

    The Empire Builders.

Mahfouz, Naguib

The Harafish. Egypt.

Cairo trilogy.

> **Palace Walk.**
>
> **Palace of Desire.**
>
> **Sugar Street.**

McCullough, Colleen

The Thorn Birds.

McMurtry, Larry

Lonesome Dove saga. Listed in chronological, not publication, order.

> **Dead Man's Walk.**
>
> **Lonesome Dove.**
>
> **Comanche Moon.**
>
> **The Streets of Laredo.**

Park, Ruth

Australian family saga. Late nineteenth and early twentieth centuries.

> **Missus.**
>
> **The Harp in the South.**
>
> **12½ Plymouth Street.**

Porter, Donald Clayton

White Indian series, also called the Colonization of America series. Volume 28 was published in 1996.

Price, Eugenia

Florida trilogy. Florida history through the lives of three families.

> **Don Juan McQueen.**
>
> **Maria.**
>
> **Margaret's Story.**

Georgia trilogy. Antebellum Georgia.

> **Bright Captivity.**
>
> **Where Shadows Go.**
>
> **Beauty from Ashes.**

Savannah quartet. Antebellum Georgia.

> **Savannah.**
>
> **To See Your Face Again.**
>
> **Before the Darkness Falls.**
>
> **Stranger in Savannah.**

Ross, Dana Fuller

Wagons West series. A Lyle Engel creation.

The Holts: An American Dynasty series.

Seton, Anya

Hearth and the Eagle.

Smith, Wilbur

Ballantyne Family. Africa.

Flight of the Falcon.

Men of Men.

The Angels Weep.

The Leopard Hunts in Darkness.

The Courtneys.

When the Lion Feeds.

The Roar of Thunder.

A Sparrow Falls.

The Burning Shore.

Power of the Sword.

Rage.

A Time to Die.

Golden Fox.

Summers, Rowena

Cornish Clay series.

Thane, Elswyth Beebe

Williamsburg series.

Dawn's Early Light.

Yankee Stranger.

Ever After.

The Light Heart.

Kissing Cousin.

This Was Tomorrow.

Homing.

Epics

The epic historical novel covers centuries or even millennia and is focused on a specific geographical location. These large-scale tapestries woven from written words are best typified by James Michener's works.

Michener, James
> **The Source.** The Holy Land.
>
> **Centennial.** Colorado.
>
> **Alaska.**
>
> **Chesapeake.**
>
> **Texas.**
>
> **Caribbean.**
>
> **Hawaii.**
>
> **The Covenant.** South Africa.
>
> **Texas.**
>
> **Mexico.**
>
> **Poland.**

Rutherfurd, Edward
> **Sarum.** Ten thousand years of history, centered on five families from the Salisbury Plain.
>
> **London.** The 2,000 years of the great city's history, told from the viewpoints of several families.
>
> **Russka.** Four families and 1,800 years shape the history of Russia.

Topics

Classics of Historical Fiction

The following early prototypes are still available in reprint.

Cooper, James Fenimore
The Leatherstocking Tales.
> **The Pioneers.**
>
> **The Last of the Mohicans.**
>
> **The Prairie.**
>
> **The Pathfinder.**
>
> **The Deerslayer.**

Dumas, Alexandre
> **Three Musketeers.** Includes a spy/espionage plot.
>
> **The Count of Monte Cristo.**

Fast, Howard
Prolific.

Forester, C. S.
Hornblower series. Annotated in the adventure chapter (Chapter 4).

Graves, Robert
    I Claudius.
    Claudius, the God.

Heyer, Georgette
    The Spanish Bride.
    An Infamous Army.
    Lord John.
    The Nonsuch.

Hope, Anthony
    The Prisoner of Zenda (1894).

Kipling, Rudyard
    Captains Courageous.

Oldenbourg, Zoe
    The World Is Not Enough.
    The Cornerstone. Medieval France.

Orczy, Baroness
    The Scarlet Pimpernel (1905). French Revolution.

Renault, Mary
    The King Must Die. Theseus's Cretan adventure.
    The Last of the Wine.

Sabatini, Rafael
    Scaramouche. Adventure and the French Revolution.

Scott, Sir Walter
    Ivanhoe.
    Rob Roy.

Sutcliff, Rosemary
    Many adult readers of historical fiction were hooked at an early age by the prolific Sutcliff, who wrote dozens of titles for children and young adults. Her series of books about Roman Britain—*The Eagle of the Ninth, The Silver Branch,* and *The Lantern Bearers*—remains popular.

Tranter, Nigel

Tranter is the one to read for historicals set in Scotland. All have recently been reprinted.

The James V trilogy.

The Riven Realm.

James, by the Grace of God.

Rough Wooing.

The Stewart trilogy.

Lords of Misrule.

A Folly of Princes.

The Captive Crown.

The Bruce trilogy.

The Steps to the Empty Throne.

The Path of the Hero King.

The Price of the Kings Peace.

Undset, Sigrid

Kristin Lavransdatter. Fourteenth-century Scandinavia, a massive epic in several volumes by the 1928 Nobel Prize winner. Many different editions are currently in print.

Yourcenar, Marguerite

The Memoirs of Hadrian. Second-century Roman Empire, mostly in the form of letters from Hadrian to Marcus Aurelius. Originally published in 1951, it was most recently reprinted in 1995.

Bibliographies and Encyclopedias

Adamson, Lynda G. *Literature Connections to American History.* Libraries Unlimited, 1997.

———. *Literature Connections to World History.* Libraries Unlimited, 1998.

———. *World Historical Fiction: An Annotated Guide to Novels for Adults and Young Adults.* Oryx Press, 1998. Lists over 6,000 titles organized by geographic setting and time period. Extensive indexes. Succinct annotations for each title. Award winners and titles suitable for young adults are listed.

Adamson, Lynda G., and A. T. Dickinson. *American Historical Fiction: An Annotated Guide to Novels for Adults and Young Adults.* Oryx Press, 1998. Lists 3,000 titles. Indexed by author, title, genre, subject, and geographic setting.

Burt, Daniel *S. What Historical Novel Do I Read Next?* Gale Research, 1997.

Gerhardstein, Virginia Brokaw. *Dickinson's American Historical Fiction,* 5th ed. Scarecrow Press, 1986. Over 3,000 historical novels covering European colonization to 1984 are annotated and classified.

Hartman, Donald K., and Gregg Sapp. *Historical Figures in Fiction*. Oryx Press, 1994. Lists 4,200 novels organized by 1,500 significant historical characters.

VanMeter, Vandelia L. *America in Historical Fiction: A Bibliographic Guide*. Libraries Unlimited, 1997. Includes 1,168 annotated entries. Subject index. Arranged by time periods: "The Age of Exploration and the Colonization of America, 1492–1775"; "The American Revolution: The War and Its Causes, 1776–1783"; "The Age of Expansion, 1783–1860"; "The Civil War, 1861–1865"; "The Expanding Frontier, 1866–1899"; "Progressive Era, Twenties, and Depression, 1900–1939"; "World War II, 1939–1945"; "The Late Twentieth Century, 1945–1995"; "Epic Novels"; and additional titles arranged by state. It mostly covers titles that are appropriate for high school students.

Vasudevan, Aruna, and Lesley Henderson, eds. *Twentieth-Century Romance & Historical Writers*. St. James Press, 1994.

Writers' Manuals

Martin, Rhona. *Writing Historical Fiction*. Talman, 1995.

Oliver, Marina. *Writing Historical Fiction: How to Create Authentic Historical Fiction and Get It Published*. Trans-Atlantic, 1998.

Woolley, Persia. *How to Write and Sell Historical Fiction*. Writer's Digest Books, 1997.

Publishers

All the major trade publishers publish historical fiction. Some long-out-of-print historical novels are now being reprinted, most notably by Buccaneer Books, Inc., and Hodder & Stoughton.

Awards

Historical novels are frequently considered for and awarded literary prizes. There is one award, however, that is specifically awarded to a work of historical fiction set in the Americas for young adults or children, the Scott O'Dell award. A listing of winners can be found at the Writerswrite.com Web site: http://www.writerswrite.com/books/awards/odell.htm (accessed 19 January 2000).

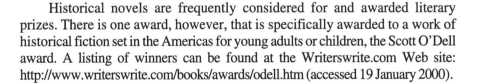

Online Resources

Newsgroups

rec.arts.books.hist-fiction (accessed 19 January 2000). Recent postings included a discussion of the 100 best historical novels, Web sites of novelists who write historical fiction, read-alikes, and queries about identifying books.

Web Sites

Canterbury, New Zealand Public Library. If You Like Historical Fiction Page, http://www.ccc.govt.nz/Library/IfYouLike/histfiction.asp (accessed 19 January 2000).

Evanston Library, http://www.evanston.lib.il.us/library/bibliographies/bdl3.html (accessed 19 January 2000). Lists authors of historical fiction by era.

Internet School Library Media Center, while primarily for children's and young adult works, also contains some information of interest to adult readers of historical fiction. Web site http://falcon.jmu.edu/~ramseyil/historical.htm (accessed 19 January 2000).

Los Angeles Public Library Historical Fiction, http://www.colapublib.org/services/advisory/historical.html (accessed 19 January 2000).

Soon's Historical Fiction Site, http://uts.cc.utexas.edu/~soon/histfiction/index.html (accessed 19 January 2000), lists many authors, some with titles, some with links to Web sites, specific newsgroups, or other locations that have additional information.

The Historical Novel Society, http://www.historical-novel-society.freeserve.co.uk/ (accessed 19 January 2000).

D's Historical Picks

Cody, Denée. *The Court of Love.*

Donati, Sara. *Into the Wilderness.*

Richter, Conrad. *Awakening Land.*

Shuler, Linda Lay. *She Who Remembers.*

Willis, Connie. *The Doomsday Book.*

Chapter 2

Western

"By the early 1990s, the traditional, male, shoot-'em-up hardcover western, if it wasn't quite pushing up daisies in Boot Hill, was riding into the sunset, heavily wounded."

—John Mort, *Booklist* (March 1, 1999)

Westerns, for decades one of the most popular genres, are evolving and changing. While some have bemoaned the death of the genre, it is in actuality alive and well, although evolving and appearing under other names. Many publishers are now publishing what would have been called Westerns a decade ago as historical or frontier fiction. Unfortunately, even though many publishers still print classics such as those by Zane Grey or Louis L'Amour as Westerns, and the well-respected Forge imprint continues to label their Westerns as "Western," the term has been more or less expropriated by marketers of softcore porn, who publish series like Lone Star and Long Arm. Betty Rosenberg, the originator of *Genreflecting*, was a devout fan of Westerns, as evidenced by the detailed coverage of them in earlier editions of this guide.

Betty aptly summed up their appeal in the second edition of *Genreflecting*:

> The appeal of this genre is worldwide, based in a dream of freedom in a world of unspoiled nature, a world independent of the trammels of restraining society. The hero dominates the western: competent, self-reliant, and self-sufficient, whether in conflict with nature, with man, or with himself. This most enduring of genres appeals to readers of all cultures, even those far removed geographically from the West of the United States, even those to whom its history and life modes are alien. For example, there was a Wild West in Asia in the nineteenth century. Not content with translations of U.S. westerns, the Germans (Karl May in the nineteenth century), Scandinavians, and Britons write their own. Why this universal appeal?

The simplest reason may be that it is just a good story, strong on adventure and thrilling action, having readily defined characters, supplying a satisfying resolution of conflicts in terms of simple blacks and whites (good and evil, right and wrong—the black and white Stetson hats of hero and villain), and even supplying a minor plot of romance. Add to this the characters and setting of the West. For example, the motion picture *Star Wars,* which has been labeled a horse opera in space; its saloon scene is immediately recognized as the classic western movie saloon. The Japanese motion picture *The Seven Samurai* appealed to fans of the western (not just because of the horses) and was later adapted by Hollywood as an American western.

Many of the Westerns found on library and bookstore shelves are decades old, proving the lasting affection of the public for the genre. Because newer titles are seldom published as Westerns, they tend to disappear into the general fiction stacks. Several librarians in public libraries have stated that the population that made Westerns such a beloved genre is dying off. Indeed, that is true for the authors of the traditional type. Browsing the shelves, the reader will find few contemporary authors of traditional Westerns. (An attempt has been made to provide the birth years for authors listed in the "Topics" section at the end of this chapter.) Even though the number of authors has drastically declined, and the titles published under the "Western" designation have also decreased, novels dealing with the West continue to be published.

In 1998 the most popular of the living authors were Larry McMurtry, whose titles are not published as Westerns; Elmer Kelton; and Terry C. Johnston. The Western best-seller lists are dominated by "dead guys." Louis L'Amour titles account for fully 25 percent of Western best sellers on both the Barnes and Noble and Amazon.com best-seller lists. Trevanian, known for his best-selling thrillers still popular after many years, has turned his pen to creating a Western, which may indicate a resurgence in their popularity yet to come.

One of the most active areas for publishing of new Westerns is in the young adult and juvenile categories. This may be a clever ploy on the part of Western writers. In an editorial in *Roundup,* Joan Lowery Nixon wrote of the resurgence of popularity in mysteries a few years after authors in that genre made a concerted effort to attract the young adult and juvenile market and suggested that the same could be done in the Western genre. Unfortunately, the adults who want to read Westerns are not readily finding them if they are shelved in the children's or YA sections of libraries and bookstores. University presses have become active in publishing Westerns, especially those set in their respective states. The evangelical publishers have found the West to be a fertile setting for their historicals, with Bethany House, Crossway, and Multnomah leading the pack.

Advising the Reader

Many readers of Westerns will find the elements that appeal to them in other works of historical fiction, particularly those with frontier settings. Many novels published for young adults will also appeal to those who like the traditional Westerns.

Readers who like contemporary Westerns will find some in the crime and romance chapters of this guide (Chapters 3 and 5). Some readers who enjoy the action in Westerns will also enjoy adventure novels (see Chapter 4).

Themes and Types

Native Americans

The history of indigenous peoples has been full of trials and tribulations. The indigenous characters in books and film have historically been portrayed in stereotypical terms, whether the derogatory Tonto model or the "noble savage." The best of the tales about Native peoples are those told with respect. Many deal with the depredations of the invading culture and the conflict between the two groups. Also included here are titles that deal with Indian captives. Some of the older titles unfortunately evidence the stereotypes found in the early days of the genre.

Readers may also find many of the titles listed in the "Prehistoric Epics, Ancient Civilizations, and Precontact Native Americans" section of the historical fiction chapter (Chapter 1) of interest.

Arnold, Elliott
Blood Brother. Source of the motion picture *Broken Arrow*.

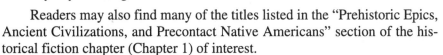

Baker, Will
Track of the Giant.

Blakely, Mike
Comanche Dawn. Born on the day the Comanche first discover horses, a young man comes of age to become a leader and warrior as his people become the great horsemen of the plains in this well-researched work.

Blevins, Win
Stone Song: A Novel of the Life of Crazy Horse.

Capps, Benjamin
The White Man's Road.

Carter, Forrest
Cry Geronimo. Also called *Watch for Me on the Mountain*.

Coldsmith, Don
The *Spanish Bit Saga* (see "Sagas" section of this chapter).

Comfort, Will L.
Apache.

Conley, Robert J.

Conley writes respectfully and sensitively.

Nickajack.

Crazy Snake.

Geronimo, an American Legend.

Mountain Windsong: A Novel of the Trail of Tears.

The Dark Island.

Real People series. Follows the history of the Cherokee.

The Way of the Priests.

The Dark Way.

The White Path.

The Way South.

The Long Way Home.

The War Trail North.

War Woman.

The Peace Chief.

Cooke, John Byrne

Between the Worlds.

Crawford, Max

Lords of the Plain.

Fast, Howard

The Last Frontier.

Fisher, Clay

Niño.

Garcia y Robertson, R.

American Woman.

Gear, Kathleen O'Neal

This Widowed Land. Huron.

Glancy, Diane

Pushing the Bear: A Novel of the Trail of Tears.

Haseloff, Cynthia

The Kiowa Verdict.

Man Without Medicine.

Henry, Will

From Where the Sun Now Stands.

Jackson, Helen Hunt
Ramona.

Jones, Douglas C.
Gone the Dreams and Dancing.

Johnson, Dorothy M.
The Hanging Tree and Other Stories.

La Farge, Oliver
Laughing Boy.

L'Amour, Louis
Hondo.

Lutz, Giles A.
The Magnificent Failure.

Patten, Lewis B.
Bones of the Buffalo.

Riefe, Barbara
Mohawk Woman.

Schlesier, Karl H.
Josanie's War.

Smith, C. W.
Buffalo Nickel.

Stratham, Frances Patton
Trail of Tears.

Thom, James Alexander
Panther in the Sky. Fictionalized account of Chief Tecumseh.

Vernam, Glenn R.
Indian Hater.

Waldo, Anna Lee
Sacajawea.

Welch, James
Fools Crow.

Indian Captives

Popular since colonial times, these tales about individuals captured by Indians who are often adopted into the tribes and about those who search for them have a great appeal.

Berger, Thomas
Little Big Man.

Blake, Michael
Dances with Wolves.

Capps, Benjamin
A Woman of the People.

Eidson, Tom
The Last Ride.

Haseloff, Cynthia
Satanta's Woman.
The Chains of Sarai Stone.

Horsley, Kate
Crazy Woman.

Johnson, Dorothy M.
Indian Country. Source of the motion picture *A Man Called Horse*.

Johnston, Terry C.
Cry of the Hawk.
Ride the Moon Down.

Jones, Douglas C.
Season of Yellow Leaf.

LeMay, Alan
The Unforgiven. Source of the motion picture by the same name.

Richter, Conrad
The Light in the Forest.

Riefe, Barbara
The Woman Who Fell from the Sky.
Desperate Crossing.

Robson, Lucia St. Clair
Ride the Wind: The Story of Cynthia Ann Parker and the Last Days of the Comanches.

Mountain Men

The earliest non-native group to invade the West were the mountain men and trappers, who often took on Indian ways and married Indian women.

Blevins, Win
The Misadventures of Silk and Shakespeare.
Charbonneau.

Fergusson, Harvey
Wolf Song.

Fisher, Vardis
Mountain Man. Source for the motion picture *Jeremiah Johnson*.

Guthrie, A. B.
The Big Sky.
The Way West.
These Thousand Hills.

2

Hotchkiss, Bill
The Medicine Calf: A Novel. Mountain man adopted by Indians.

Johnston, Terry C.
Carry the Wind. Titus Bass.
Border Lords.
One-Eyed Dream.
Dance on the Wind.
Buffalo Palace.
Crack in the Sky.
Ride the Moon Down.

Johnstone, William W.
Battle of the Mountain Men.

Sherman, Jory
The Medicine Horn.

Wagons West and Early Settlement

The westward journey, fraught with perils and hazards, placed ordinary people in extraordinary circumstances that tested their grit. The long and arduous journey from the East was often undertaken by family groups, who faced disease, disaster, and disaffection.

Haycox, Ernest
The Earthbreakers.
The Adventurers.

Hough, Emerson
The Covered Wagon.

Jones, Douglas C.
Roman Hasford. Originally published as *Roman*.

Kelton, Elmer
    Bitter Trail.

Ledbetter, Suzanne
    Redemption Trail.

Lee, Wendi
    The Overland Trail.

Mead, Robert Douglas
    Heartland.

Quarles, Johnny
    Spirit Trail.

Reynolds, Clay
    Franklin's Crossing.

Riefe, Barbara
    Against All Odds: The Lucy Scott Mitchum Story.

Taylor, Robert Lewis
    The Travels of Jaimie McPheeters. Pulitzer Prize winner; a long, picaresque adventure.

Thompson, David
    Northwest Passage.

Wheeler, Richard S.
    Flint's Gift. A newspaperman in an Arizona frontier town.

Merchants and Teamsters

For the West to be opened up, goods and supplies had to be brought in.

Haycox, Ernest
    Canyon Passage. Mule-train freight line in the Pacific Northwest.

Kelton, Elmer
    Bitter Trail.

Reese, John
    Sure Shot Shapiro. A Jewish traveling salesman in California's Mojave Desert.

Wheeler, Richard S.
    Sierra: A Novel of the California Gold Rush.

Mines and Mining

The lure of gold and silver brought many unlikely individuals together and brought out the best and the worst in them. The legends of lost mines and mother lodes drew many individuals to seek their fortunes.

Broomall, Robert W.
    California Kingdoms.

Henry, Will
    MacKenna's Gold.

L'Amour, Louis
    The Empty Land.

Myers, John Myers
    Dead Warrior.

Nye, Nelson
    The White Chip.

Shirreffs, Gordon D.
    The Manhunter.
    Hell's Forty Acres.

Thoene, Brock, and Bodie Thoene
    Riders of the Silver Rim.

Trevanian
    Incident at Twenty Mile.

Wheeler, Richard S.
    Fool's Coach. Three people try to escape the Gold Rush and the road agents, who try to waylay anyone who leaves Virginia City, Montana.

Law and Lawmen

The frontier was a haven for the lawless, so tales of those who oppose them, trying to impose order on the chaos, take on a greater significance.

Bennett, Dwight
    Legend in the Dust.

Clark, Walter Van Tilburg
    The Ox-Bow Incident.

Cook, Will
    Shotgun Marshal. Sometimes to be found under the pseudonym Wade Everett.

Hackenberry, Charles
Friends.

Hall, Oakley
Warlock. Recently reprinted by the University of Nevada Press.

Hart, Matthew S.
Cody's Law series.

Haycox, Ernest
Trail Town.

Jones, Douglas C.
A Spider for Loco Shoat.

Leonard, Elmore
Valdez Is Coming. Mexican town constable.

Paine, Lauran
Cache Cañon.

Patten, Lewis B.
Death of a Gunfighter.

Portis, Charles
True Grit. Basis of the movie with the same name.

Bad Men and Good

The color of the Stetson does not tell it all. Bad men may have a hidden core of goodness, while those on the side of the law may be evil through and through.

Brand, Max
Destry Rides Again. Not like the classic motion picture that took the title.

Carter, Forrest
Josey Wales: Two Westerns. Omnibus edition of *Gone to Texas*. Source of the motion picture *The Outlaw Josey Wales*.

Vengeance Trail of Josey Wales.

Doctorow, E. L.
Welcome to Hard Times.

Eidson, Tom
St. Agnes' Stand.

Estleman, Loren D.
Bloody Season. Tombstone, Arizona, and the OK Corral.
Gun Man.

Grey, Zane
Lone Star Ranger.

Hall, Oakley
The Coming of the Kid.
Warlock.

Haycox, Ernest
"Stage to Lordsburg." *The* classic short-story Western, source for *the* classic motion picture *Stagecoach*. Can be found in Haycox's *By Rope and Lead.*

Matheson, Richard
Journal of the Gun Years.

Rhodes, Eugene Manlove
Pasó por Aquí.

Schaefer, Jack
Shane. Still a Western best seller in 1998.

Svee, Gary D.
Sanctuary.

Swarthout, Glendon
The Shootist.

Trevanian
Incident at Twenty Mile.

Army in the West

The Indian wars and the presence of ex-soldiers in the aftermath of the Civil War brought an often lawless military presence to the West.

Ames, John Edward
The Unwritten Order.

Blake, Michael
Marching to Valhalla.

Brown, Dee
Action at Beecher Island.

Burks, Brian
Soldier Boy. Even though this was published as a young adult novel, it is turning up in the Western sections of bookstores.

Camp, Will
  Santa Fe Run.

Englade, Ken
  The Tribes.

Haycox, Ernest
  Border Trumpet.
  Bugles in the Afternoon.

Oliver, Chad
  Broken Eagle.

Olsen, Theodore V.
  Arrow in the Sun.

Short, Luke
  Ambush.

Texas and Mexico

The border country and the American settlement of Mexican lands provide an arena for heroics.

Brown, Sam
  The Long Season.

Camp, Will
  Blood of Texas.

Kelton, Elmer
  After the Bugles.

Lea, Tom
  The Brave Bulls.
  The Wonderful Country.

LeMay, Alan
  The Unforgiven.

Long, Jeff
  Empire of Bones.

Sanders, Leonard
  Star of Empire.

Worcester, Don
  Gone to Texas.

Hired Man on Horseback

Cowboys are the quintessential understated Western heroes, but if they spent their real lives like the cowboys in fiction, ranching could never have survived.

Adams, Andy
>The Log of a Cowboy.

Borland, Hal
>The Seventh Winter.

Brown, Sam
>The Big Lonely.
>Devil's Rim.

Decker, William
>To Be a Man.

Kelton, Elmer
>The Good Old Boys.
>The Smiling Country.
>The Man Who Rode Midnight.

Mulford, Clarence E.
>Hopalong Cassidy.

Schaefer, Jack
>Monte Walsh.

Wister, Owen
>The Virginian.

Cattle Drives

Driving cattle to a railhead provides the opportunity for adventures involving problems caused by both nature (stampedes, lightning, floods) and humans (rustlers, outlaws, Indians).

Adams, Andy
>The Log of a Cowboy. The classic cattle-drive story, first published in 1903.

Capps, Benjamin
>The Trail to Ogallala.

Flynn, Robert
>North to Yesterday.

Grey, Zane
> **Trail Driver.**
>
> **Wilderness Trek.** An Australian cattle drive.

Kelton, Elmer
> **The Far Canyon.**

McMurtry, Larry
> **Lonesome Dove.** Pulitzer Prize winner in 1986 and still a Western best seller in 1999.

Cattle Kingdoms

Although railroad barons dominated the country in the West, individuals tried to build their own fiefdoms based on huge ranges full of cattle.

Fergusson, Harvey
> **Grant of Kingdom.**

Guthrie, A. B.
> **These Thousand Hills.**

Richter, Conrad
> **The Sea of Grass.**

Range Wars

The battle for free range and to keep the West unfenced provides a scenario rife with possibilities.

Blakely, Mike
> **Shortgrass Song.**
>
> **Too Long at the Dance.** A cowboy troubadour from Texas experiences the range wars and land grabs of the West.

Clarke, Richard
> **The Homesteaders.**

Grey, Zane
> **To the Last Man.**

Henry, Will
> **Free Grass.**

Hoffman, Lee
> **West of Cheyenne.**

Johnstone, William W.
> **Battle of the Mountain Men.**

Vories, Eugene
>The Man from Colorado.
>
>Saddle a Whirlwind.

Sheepmen

Cattlemen were not the only ones who moved West looking for wide-open land, leading to bitter conflicts between those who raised sheep and those who raised cattle.

Doig, Ivan
>Dancing at the Rascal Fair.

Grey, Zane
>To the Last Man.

Land Rush

The lure of free land brought the homesteaders west in droves.

Blakely, Mike
>Shortgrass Song.
>
>Too Long at the Dance.

Ferber, Edna
>Cimarron. Also a classic motion picture.

Railroads

Ribbons of steel opened up the West to new waves of settlers and opportunists.

Grey, Zane
>U. P. Trail.

Haycox, Ernest
>Trouble Shooter.

Spearman, Frank
>Whispering Smith.

Buffalo Runners

In just a few years abundant herds of millions of buffalo were decimated almost to the point of extinction.

Estleman, Loren D.
> **The Hider.**

Grove, Fred
> **The Buffalo Runners.**
> **Buffalo Spring.**

Kelton, Elmer
> **Slaughter.** Spur Award winner.
> **Far Canyon.** Jeff Layne and Crow Feather try to turn to ranching in this sequel to *Slaughter*.
> **Buffalo Wagons.**

Unromanticized

These Westerns reveal the ugly underbelly of the West, with the patina of a glamorized frontier rubbed away to give a grim, uncompromising view of the area and times.

Askew, Rilla
> **The Mercy Seat.**

Dexter, Pete
> **Deadwood.**

Estleman, Loren D.
> **Journey of the Dead.**

Jones, Robert F.
> **Deadville.**

Matthews, Greg
> **Heart of the Country.**

McCarthy, Cormac
> **Blood Meridian.**

Swarthout, Glendon
> **The Homesman.**

Picaresque

In this type of story a roguish protagonist, clever and often amoral, is depicted in an episodic series of incidents. Frequently these stories are humorous and satirical.

Berger, Thomas
> **Little Big Man.**
> **The Return of Little Big Man.**

Combs, Harry
>**Brules.** Gritty tale of mountain man, Indian fighter, and outlaw Cat Brules, by an octogenarian first novelist.

Culp, John H.
>**The Bright Feathers.**

O'Rourke, Frank
>**The Swift Runner.**

Shrake, Edwin
>**Blessed McGill.**

Taylor, Robert Lewis
>**The Travels of Jaimie McPheeters.** Pulitzer Prize winner.

Comedy and Parody

Those who have read extensively in the genre and recognize the unique conventions and traditional devices will derive the most enjoyment from and find the most humor in the following titles.

Bickham, Jack
>**The Apple Dumpling Gang.**

Brand, Max
>**The Gentle Desperado.**

Evans, Max
>**The Rounders.**

Gulick, Bill
>**The Hallelujah Train.**

Matthews, Greg
>**Sassafras.**

McNab, Tom
>**The Fast Men.**

Myers, John Myers
>**Dead Warrior.**

O'Rourke, Frank
>**The Bride Stealer.**

Pronzini, Bill
>**The Last Days of Horse-Shy Halloran.**

Purdum, Herbert R.
    A Hero for Henry.

Reese, John
    Horses, Honor and Women.

Ross, Ann B.
    The Pilgrimage.

Coming of Age

Traditionally in this genre, coming of age could be described as boy into man, but now protagonists of both genders are experiencing the trials and travails of the journey from childhood to adult on a harsh frontier.

Blakely, Mike
    Comanche Dawn.

Blevins, Win
    The Misadventures of Silk and Shakespeare.

Conley, Robert J.
    The Dark Island. Squani, half Indian, half Spanish, confronts his identity.

Estleman, Loren D.
    Sudden Country.

Kelton, Elmer
    Pumpkin Rollers.

L'Amour, Louis
    Chancy.
    Down the Long Hills.

Laxalt, Robert
    Dust Devils.

Matthews, Greg
    The Further Adventures of Huckleberry Finn.

McMurtry, Larry
    Horseman Pass By. Source of the motion picture *Hud*.

Reilly, Shauna
    Freedom in My Soul.

Schaefer, Jack
    Shane. Still a Western best seller in 1998.

Celebrity Characters

The names of legendary western personages continue to evoke the spirit of the Wild West.

Brown, Dee
    Wave High the Banner. Davy Crockett.

Burns, Walter Noble
    The Saga of Billy the Kid.
    The Robin Hood of El Dorado. Joaquin Murieta.
    Tombstone. Wyatt Earp.

Camp, Deborah
    Belle Star: A Novel of the Old West.

Cooke, John Bryne
    South of the Border. Butch Cassidy and Charlie Siringo; 1919 movie set.

Eickhoff, Randy Lee, and Leonard C. Lewis
    Bowie. The legend of Big Jim Bowie.

Estleman, Loren D.
    Aces and Eights. Wild Bill Hickock.

    Billy Gashade. A 16-year-old fleeing the New York draft riots of 1863 becomes a piano player in the West and meets the famous and infamous, including George Armstrong Custer, Billy the Kid, Wild Bill Hickock, Oscar Wilde, and others, over the next several decades.

    This Old Bill. Buffalo Bill Cody.

Garfield, Brian
    Manifest Destiny. Teddy Roosevelt in the Badlands.

Irving, Clifford
    Tom Mix and Pancho Villa.

Kesey, Ken, and Ken Babbs
    Last Go Round: A Dime Western. John Muir makes an appearance.

McMurtry, Larry
    Anything for Billy. Billy the Kid.
    Buffalo Girls. Calamity Jane.

Swarthout, Glendon
    The Old Colts. Bat Masterson and Wyatt Earp, now old, get together in 1916.

Zollinger, Norman
    Meridian: A Novel of Kit Carson's West.

African-Americans in the West

Even though cowboys are most often portrayed as white, in truth there were many who were Hispanic and black. African-American soldiers were seen frequently enough that Native Americans created a name for them, "buffalo soldiers." Holloway House (http://www.hollowayhousebooks.com) is a small press that publishes African-American titles, including Westerns.

Burchardt, Bill
    Black Marshal.

Evans, Max
    Faraway Blue.

Fackler, Elizabeth
    Breaking Even. African-American sisters in the Southwest.

Garfield, Brian
    Tripwire.

Goodman, Charles R.
    Buffalo Soldier.

Henry, Will
    One More River to Cross.

Hotchkiss, Bill
    The Medicine Calf: A Novel. Black mountain man adopted by Indians.

Jones, Robert F.
    Deadville.

Keaton, Rina
    Revenge of June Daley.

Kelton, Elmer
    The Wolf and the Buffalo.

Kluge, P. F.
    Season for War. African-American soldiers go from fighting the Apache in Arizona to the Philippines to fight in the Spanish-American War.

Myers, Walter Dean
    The Righteous Revenge of Artemis Bonner. This humorous, picaresque novel is enjoyed by adults even though it was written for young teens.

Poston, Jeffrey
    A Man Called Trouble.

Proctor, George W.

> **Walks Without a Soul.** Nate Wagoner hunts the Comanches who killed his baby and kidnapped the rest of his family.

Willard, Tom

> **Buffalo Soldiers.** Former slave Augustus Sharps rises through the Army ranks in the West following the Civil War. This is the first book in the Black Sabre Chronicles, a series about a family of African-American military men.

Mormons

All well-defined groups who headed west became subjects of Westerns. The large group of controversial families traveling with Brigham Young, the extremes of polygamy some practiced, and the activities of the notorious Danites make this group a favorite element in Westerns. Often they are portrayed in a very unflattering light.

Card, Orson Scott

> **A Woman of Destiny.** Also published as *Saints*.

Grey, Zane

> **Riders of the Purple Sage.**

Johnston, Terry C.

> **Cry of the Hawk.**

Wells, Marian

> **The Wedding Dress.**

Wormser, Richard

> **Battalion of Saints.** The Mormon Battalion marching to the war with Mexico.

Singular Woman

In early Westerns women played lesser roles than horses. Fortunately this has changed in recent years, with strong, independent women playing prominent roles.

Alter, Judy

> **Mattie.**
>
> **Libbie.**
>
> **Jessie.**

Banis, V. J.

> **San Antone.**

Bonner, Cindy

    Lily.

    Looking After Lily.

    The Passion of Dellie O'Barr.

Carroll, Lenore

    One Hundred Girl's Mother. A female missionary works with Chinese women in San Francisco.

Charbonneau, Eileen

    Rachel Lemoyne.

Cooke, John Bryne

    The Snowblind Moon.

Downing, Sybil

    Fire in the Hole. The Ludlow Massacre.

Eidson, Tom

    All God's Children. A blind Quaker widow faces down a lynch mob.

Fackler, Elizabeth

    Breaking Even. African-American sisters in the Southwest.

    Badlands.

    Texas Lily.

Grey, Zane

    Woman of the Frontier. Published previously in a cut version as *30,000 on the Hoof.*

Kirkpatrick, Jane

    A Sweetness to the Soul.

Lehrer, Kate

    Out of Eden.

Levy, JoAnn

    Daughter of Joy: A Novel of Gold Rush California. A young Chinese woman in Gold Rush California.

Olsen, Theodore V.

    Arrow in the Sun.

Portis, Charles

    True Grit. Basis for the movie of the same name.

Richter, Conrad

    Tacey Cromwell.

Smiley, Jane
    The All-True Travels and Adventures of Lidie Newton: A Novel.

Stratham, Frances Patton
    Trail of Tears. Features a Cherokee schoolteacher.

Webster, Jan
    Muckle Annie.

Whitson, Stephanie Grace
    Walks the Fire. Christian emphasis.

Williams, Jeanne
    Home Mountain.

Williamson, Penelope
    Heart of the West.

Romance

    Wide-open landscapes, towering mountain ranges, and vivid sunsets make the West a natural setting for romantic fiction. The strong individuals who settled the area also make for engaging romantic leads. The western setting and heroes have become extremely popular in romance; the sheer abundance of cowboys in romance publishing making it appear that all American men are cowboys (or at least the good-looking, romantic ones). Readers who like Western romances should also check the romance chapter (Chapter 5).

Aldrich, Bess Streeter
    Spring Came on Forever.

Bittner, Rosanne
    She has more than 50 titles, published as romance.

Dailey, Janet
    Calder series.

Durham, Marilyn
    The Man Who Loved Cat Dancing.

Grey, Zane
    The Light of Western Stars.

Kelton, Elmer
    Smiling Country.

Lane, Elizabeth
    Apache Fire.

Oke, Janette
Her Christian tales of the prairie are sometimes read as Westerns.

Williams, Jeanne
> **The Valiant Women.**

Young Adult Westerns

The following Westerns may have been written for teens, but adults enjoy them, too.

Burks, Brian
> **Soldier Boy.**

Hardeman, Ric
> **Sunshine Rider: The First Vegetarian Western.**

Karr, Kathleen
> **Oh, Those Harper Girls!: Or Young and Dangerous.**

Myers, Walter Dean
> **The Righteous Revenge of Artemis Bonner.**

Patrick, Denise Lewis
> **The Adventures of Midnight Son.**
> **The Longest Ride.**

Stone, Gerald Eugene Nathan
> **Rockhand Lizzie.**

The West Still Lives

The qualities that make Western heroes popular are still inherent in the children of the West today. The following list demonstrates some of the cultural diversity of the region and the changes that have occurred in the twentieth century.

Abbey, Edward
> **The Brave Cowboy.**
> **Fire on the Mountain.**
> **The Monkey Wrench Gang.**
> **Hayduke Lives!**

Alexie, Sherman.
> **The Lone Ranger and Tonto Fistfight in Heaven.**
> **Reservation Blues.** Native American.

Anaya, Rudolfo.
  Alburquerque.
  Bless Me, Ultima. Hispanic.

Bradford, Richard.
  Red Sky at Morning.
  So Far from Heaven.

Doig, Ivan
  Ride with Me, Mariah Montana.

Dorris, Michael
  A Yellow Raft in Blue Water. Native American.

Evans, Max
  Bluefeather Fellini.
  Bluefeather Fellini in the Sacred Realm.
  The Hi-Lo Country.

Flynn, Robert
  Wanderer Springs.

Freeman, Judith
  Chinchilla Farm.
  Set for Life.
  A Desert of Pure Meaning.

Hillerman, Tony
  Many mystery titles featuring Jim Chee and Joe Leaphorn. Native American.

Hyson, Dick T.
  The Calling. Native American.

King, Thomas
  Medicine River.
  Green Grass, Running Water. Native American.

Kingsolver, Barbara
  Animal Dreams.
  Bean Trees.
  Pigs in Heaven.

McCarthy, Cormac
  The Border trilogy.
      All the Pretty Horses.
      The Crossing.
      Cities of the Plain.

McMurtry, Larry
The Last Picture Show.

Texasville.

Owens, Louis
The Sharpest Sight.

Bone Game.

Nightland.

Dark River.

Parks, Mary Anderson
The Circle Leads Home. Native American.

Power, Susan
The Grass Dancer. Native American.

Salisbury, Ralph
The Last Rattlesnake Throw.

Two-Rivers, E. Donald.
Survivor's Medicine.

Wheeler, Richard S.
The Buffalo Commons.

Eccentric Variations

While the traditional Western seems to be on the wane, the Western setting is finding its way into horror and fantasy as well as mystery and romance.

Foster, Alan Dean
Cyber Way. A futuristic, Hillerman-type mystery.

Hays, Clark, and Kathleen McFall
The Cowboy and the Vampire: A Very Unusual Romance. A contemporary Wyoming cowboy must fight for the woman he loves, who just may be the next queen of the vampires.

L'Amour, Louis
The Haunted Mesa. A breach in the universe opens parallel worlds.

Murphy, Pat
Nadya. A young female werewolf goes west.

Snyder, Midori
The Flight of Michael McBride. Pursued by evil denizens of Faerie, a railroad baron's son heads west to the end of the tracks.

Sagas

Bittner, Roseanne

Savage Destiny series. Seven volumes filled with romance take Abbie from a young woman in 1845 to a time when her grandson engages in a forbidden affair with a rancher's daughter. Through the Civil War, the coming of the railroads, and conflicts with homesteaders, Abbie loves Lone Eagle.

Coldsmith, Don

Tall Grass. An epic tale of Kansas that starts in the sixteenth century and continues in **South Wind.**

The Spanish Bit saga. Published in hardcover and reprinted in paperback.

Trail of the Spanish Bit.

Buffalo Medicine.

The Elk-Dog Heritage.

Follow the Wind.

Man of the Shadows.

Daughter of the Eagle.

Moon of Thunder.

The Sacred Hills.

Pale Star.

River of Swans.

Return to the River.

The Medicine Knife.

The Flower in the Mountains.

Trail from Taos.

Song of the Rock.

Fort De Chastaigne.

Quest for the White Bull.

Return of the Spanish.

Bride of the Morning Star.

Walks in the Sun.

Thunderstick.

Track of the Bear.

Child of the Dead.

Bearer of the Pipe.

Medicine Hat.

Cooke, John Byrne

The Snowblind Moon.

Dennis, Adair, and Janet Rosenstock
The Story of Canada.

Doig, Ivan
Dancing at the Rascal Fair.

English Creek.

Ride with Me, Mariah Montana.

James, Leigh Franklin
Saga of the Southwest series. A Lyle Engel creation.

Johnstone, William W.
Eagles series. Follows the MacCallister family.

Eyes of Eagles.

Dreams of Eagles.

Talons of Eagles.

Scream of Eagles.

L'Amour, Louis
Sackett Family series. Seventeen novels; several titles continue to be best-selling Westerns. L'Amour also wrote a guide to the series titled *The Sackett Companion: The Facts Behind the Fiction* (Bantam, 1988).

McCord, John S.
The Baynes Clan.

McMurtry, Larry.
Lonesome Dove saga. Listed in chronological, not publication, order.

Dead Man's Walk.

Lonesome Dove.

Comanche Moon. The fourth book to be published in the series, but the third chronologically, this was the undisputed number one best-selling Western of 1998.

The Streets of Laredo.

Ross, Dana Fuller
Wagons West series. A Lyle Engel creation.

The Holts: An American Dynasty series.

Sherman, Jory
Baron Family of Texas series.

The Barons of Texas.

Grass Kingdom.

The Baron Range.

Snelling, Lauraine
Red River of the North series. Christian.

Stegner, Wallace
Angle of Repose.

Thoene, Brock, and Bodie Thoene
Saga of the Sierras. Christian.
The Man from Shadow Ridge.
Riders of the Silver Rim.
Gold Rush Prodigal.
Sequoia Scout.
Cannons of the Comstock.
The Year of the Grizzly.
Shooting Star.
Flames on the Barbary Coast.

Zollinger, Norman
New Mexico.
Corey Lane.
Rage in Chupadera.
Not of War Only.

Series

One of the curiosities about Western series is that two very divergent styles appear together in them. Many of the inspirational, evangelical, or Christian Westerns appear as series, as do the "adult" Westerns featuring explicit violence and sex.

Bly, Stephen
Stuart Brannon series. Christian emphasis.

Cameron, Lou
Stringer series. Features Stringer MacKail, journalist.

Combs, Harry
Brules. Picaresque, gritty tale of mountain man, Indian fighter, and outlaw Cat Brules, by an octogenarian first novelist.
The Scout. Sequel to the best-selling *Brules.* A third title, *The Legend of the Painted Horse,* although about Steven Cartwright (who appeared in the first two novels), is not a Western.

Dawson, Clay
Long Rider series. Twenty-seven titles; adult.

Edson, J. T.
Floating Outfit series. Fifty-five titles.

Ellis, Wesley
Lone Star series. Has 150 titles; adult.

Estleman, Loren D.
Page Murdock series. "A lawless lawman, taming the frontier territory by territory for the federal court of Harlan A. Blackthorne." http://www.cyberzone-inc.net/ws/dmorgan/page.htm (accessed 10 November 1999).

City of Widows.

Murdock's Law.

Stamping Ground.

The High Rocks.

The Stranglers.

Evans, Tabor
Longarm series. Has 246 adult titles.

Fackler, Elizabeth
Seth Strummer series.

Blood Kin.

Backtrail.

Road from Betrayal.

Hart, Matthew S.
Cody's Law series.

Lacy, Al
Several Christian series:

Fort Bridger series.

Angel of Mercy series.

Journey of the Stranger series.

Battles of Destiny series.

Lacy, Al, and Joanna Lacy
Two Christian series:

Mail Order Brides series.

Hannah of Fort Bridger series.

Logan, Jake
Slocum series. Adult.

Nelson, Lee
Storm Testament series. Christian emphasis.

Pike, Charles R.
Jubal Cade series.

Rivers West series. Ongoing series by different authors.

The Yellowstone, by Win Blevins.

The Smoky Hill, by Don Coldsmith.

The Colorado, by Gary McCarthy.

Powder River, by Win Blevins.

The Russian, by Gary McCarthy.

The Columbia, by Jory Sherman.

The American River, by Gary McCarthy.

The Snake River, by Win Blevins.

The Two Medicine River, by Richard S. Wheeler.

The Gila River, by Gary McCarthy.

The Humboldt River, by Gary McCarthy.

The Pecos River, by Frederic Bean.

The South Platte, by Jory Sherman.

The Red River, by Frederic Bean.

The Cimarron River, by Gary McCarthy.

The High Missouri, by Win Blevins.

The Brazos, by Jory Sherman (1999).

Sharpe, Jon
Trailsman series. Adult.

Canyon O'Grady series. Adult.

Shirreffs, Gordon D.
Dave Hunter, treasure seeker.

Walker, Jim
Wells Fargo series. Christian.

Topics

Classic Authors of Westerns

Most of the classic authors remain in print, largely in paperback. The following authors have endured, either with one or a few titles, or, as with Brand and Grey, with all their titles.

Adams, Andy (1859–1935). His **The Log of a Cowboy** (1903) is the classic and authentic story of a trail drive from the Mexican border to Montana.

Brand, Max (1992–1944). Pseudonym of Frederick Faust. Used 13 (or more) pseudonyms and wrote 215 Westerns, publishing the first in 1919. His three top sellers (over two million copies) are **Destry Rides Again, Fightin' Fool,** and **Singing Guns.** Twenty-seven of his novels were made into motion pictures. A great many of his titles are currently in paperback, with all of the pseudonyms now appearing as Max Brand.

Burnett, W. R. (1899–1982). A writer of 60 filmed screenplays. Some of his crime novels remain in print but some of his Westerns remain in libraries.

Burroughs, Edgar Rice (1875–1950). Better known for his Tarzan series and science fiction adventures. Two of his Westerns were reprinted in the Gregg Press Western Fiction series: **The War Chief** and **Apache Devil** (both serialized in 1927 and 1928 before publication in book form).

Capps, Benjamin (1922–). Several of his books remain in print.

Fergusson, Harvey (1890–1971). The native New Mexican was considered a true chronicler of the Spanish Southwest.

Fisher, Vardis (1895–1968). Fisher is the subject of **Tiger on the Road: The Life of Vardis Fisher,** a biography by Tim Woodward.

Garfield, Brian (1939). Also known for his adventure novels.

Grey, Zane (1872–1939). From 1903 to his death in 1939 he wrote 89 books, including nonfiction. Westerns have been issued since 1939 "from the estate of Zane Grey" by Harpers, but the earlier titles are the classic ones. He appeared on the best-seller list in 1915 with **The Lone Star Ranger** and again each year from 1917 to 1924. Over 40 novels became motion pictures.

Gulick, Bill (1916–). Some consider his sense of humor to be his most important contribution to western fiction.

Guthrie, A. B. (1901–). **Big Sky** is one of the top-selling Westerns of all time.

Harte, Bret (1836–1902). Immortalized the miners, gamblers, and good-hearted fancy ladies of the West of the 1860s in "The Luck of Roaring Camp" and "The Outcasts of Poker Flat."

Haycox, Ernest (1899–1950). Haycox is important as a touchstone in the criticism of the Western: his writings, in style and characterization, set standards for the genre that have influenced others writing in the genre.

Henry, Will (1912–). Also published as Clay Fisher.

Hough, Emerson (1857–1923). **The Covered Wagon** set a pattern for the Oregon Trail Western.

Johnson, Dorothy M. (1905–1984). Several of her stories were turned into films including *A Man Called Horse* and *The Man Who Shot Liberty Valance.*

Kelton, Elmer (1926–). **The Day the Cowboys Quit** and **The Time It Never Rained** were named by the Western Writers of America as two of the "best Western novels of all time."

Knibbs, H. H. (1874–1934). **The Ridin' Kid from Powder River** (1919) is a classic boy-into-man Western.

L'Amour, Louis (1908–1988). When he died, sales of his 101 books, almost all Westerns, were nearing the 200 million mark. Forty-five of his novels were made into movies or television shows. In 1998 he had more than twice as many titles on lists of top 50 best-selling Westerns as any other author. "The Homer of the oaters."—*Time*.

LeMay, Alan (1899–1964). LeMay was popular in his time, but his racist depictions of Indians are now passé.

Mulford, Clarence E. (1883–1956). **Hopalong Cassidy** (1910) became immortal in a long-running series on the Bar-20 Ranch, appearing in novels, in motion pictures, and on television.

Olsen, Theodore V. His *Arrow in the Sun* was made into the movie *Soldier Blue*.

Raine, William MacLeod (1871–1954). He wrote about 85 Westerns, his first published in 1908, and they are still being reprinted in large print.

Rhodes, Eugene Manlove (1869–1934) "The Hired Man on Horseback" whose romantic Western heroes, frequently at odds with the law, were, as his first book affirmed, **Good Men and True** (1910). Most remember him for **Pasó por Aquí** (1926), with its tag line "We are all decent people." His typical humor is evoked by the compiler W. H. Hutchinson in *The Rhodes Reader: Stories of Virgins, Villains and Varmints* (University of Oklahoma Press, 1957).

Schaefer, Jack (1907–). **Shane** is one of the top-selling Westerns and became a classic motion picture.

Short, Luke (1908–1975). In some 57 novels, he covered most of the themes in the genre.

Twain, Mark (1835–1910). Twain brought welcome humor to the Western scene in "The Celebrated Jumping Frog of Calaveras County" (1867) and **Roughing It** (1872).

White, Stewart Edward (1873–1946). A prolific writer on the Western scene, White is chiefly remembered for **Arizona Nights** (1904), stories of the range, and a trilogy (1913–1915) gathered as **The Story of California.**

Wister, Owen (1860–1938). **The Virginian,** on the best-seller list in 1902 and 1903 and never out of print, set the pattern for the popular cowboy Western, with a hero, a heroine (the schoolmarm), rustlers, a shoot-out at sundown, and other incidents. It gave the genre its classic line: "When you call me that, *smile!*"

Short Stories

Since 1953 the Western Writers of America has edited an annual anthology, each volume on a theme of the Western story. All stories are by members, and each volume is a good introduction to the writers in the genre. A few of the anthology titles reveal the use of themes: *Badman and Good, The Fall Roundup, Holsters and Heroes, Branded West, The Wild Horse Roundup, Wild Streets, Trails of Adventure, Rawhide Men, They Opened the West, Iron Men and Silver Stars, Hoof Trails and Wagon Tracks, Rivers to Cross.*

Brown, Bill. *Reading the West: An Anthology of Dime Westerns.* Bedford Books, 1997.

Gorman, Ed, ed. *The Fatal Frontier.* Carroll & Graf, 1997. Western stories by crime writers.

Gorman, Ed, and Martin H. Greenberg, eds. *The Best of the American West: Outstanding Frontier Fiction.* Berkley, 1998.

Greenberg, Martin H., ed. *Great Stories of the American West.* Jove, 1996.

———. *Great Stories of the American West II.* Berkley, 1997.

Jakes, John, and Martin H. Greenberg, eds. *New Trails: Twenty-Three Original Stories of the West from Western Writers of America.* Bantam, 1994.

Kittredge, William, ed. *The Portable Western Reader.* Penguin USA, 1997.

Knight, Damon, ed. *Westerns of the 40s: Classics from the Great Pulps.* Bobbs-Merrill, 1977.

Lenniger, August, ed. *Western Writers of America: Silver Anniversary Anthology.* Ace, 1977.

Muller, Marcia, and Bill Pronzini, eds. *She Won the West: An Anthology of Western and Frontier Stories by Women.* Morrow, 1985. Fourteen stories by authors such as B. M. Bower, Gertrude Atherton, Willa Cather, Mary Austin, Eleanor Gates, Dorothy M. Johnson, Mari Sandoz, Ann Ahlswede, Carla Kelly, and Jeanne Williams.

Piekarski, Vicki, ed. *Westward the Women: An Anthology of Western Stories by Women.* Doubleday, 1984.

Pronzini, Bill, and Martin H. Greenberg, eds. *Best of the West: Stories That Inspired Classic Western Films.* New American Library, 1986.

———. *Christmas out West.* Doubleday, 1990.

———. *The Western Hall of Fame: An Anthology of Classic Western Stories Selected by the Western Writers of America.* Morrow, 1984. The 17 stories do warrant the "Hall of Fame" label. Includes Haycox's "Stage to Lordsburg" and two classic novellas, Schaefer's *Stubby Pringle's Christmas* and Rhodes's *Pasó por Aquí.*

Schaefer, Jack, ed. *Out West: An Anthology of Stories*. Houghton, 1955.

Short, Luke, ed. *Cattle, Guns and Men*. Bantam, 1955.

Stone, Ted, ed. *100 Years of Cowboy Stories*. Red Deer College Press, 1995.

Thomas, James, and Denise Thomas, eds. *Best of the West 4: New Stories from the Wide Side of the Missouri*. W. W. Norton, 1991. Contemporary Western stories.

Tuska, Jon, ed. *The American West in Fiction*. Mentor/NAL, 1982. An interpretive grouping of authors: "The East Goes West" (Mark Twain, Bret Harte, Stephen Crane, Frederic Remington, Owen Wister); "Where West Was West" (Dorothy M. Johnson, Willa Cather, John G. Neihardt, Eugene Manlove Rhodes, Ernest Haycox); "The West of the Storytellers" (Zane Grey, Max Brand, Louis L'Amour, James Warner Bellah, Luke Short); and "The West in Revision" (Elmer Kelton, Will Henry, Benjamin Capps, Walter Van Tilburg Clark, Max Evans). There are bibliographies or suggested further readings, including fiction in three groupings: "Formulary Westerns" (18 authors), "Romantic Historical Reconstructions" (16 authors), and "Historical Reconstruction" (18 authors).

———. *Shadow of the Lariat*. Carroll & Graf, 1995.

———. *The Western Story: A Chronological Treasury*. University of Nebraska Press, 1997.

Tuska, Jon, and Vicki Piekarski, eds. *The Morrow Anthology of Great Western Short Stories*. William Morrow, 1997.

Walker, Dale L., ed. *The Western Hall of Fame Anthology*. Berkley, 1997. A dozen stories by authors selected by the Western Writers of America.

Work, James C., ed. *Gunfight! Thirteen Western Stories*. University of Nebraska Press, 1996.

Bibliographies and Encyclopedias

Barton, Wayne. *What Western Do I Read Next?: A Reader's Guide to Recent Western Fiction*. Gale, 1998.

Drew, Bernard A. *Western Series and Sequels*. Garland, 1993. Lists 700 works that have one or more sequels. Includes frontier fiction.

Tuska, Jon, and Vicki Piekarski, eds. *Encyclopedia of Frontier and Western Fiction*. McGraw-Hill, 1983. Over 300 authors are discussed.

Vinson, James, and D. L. Kirkpatrick, eds. *Twentieth Century Western Writers*. Preface by C. L. Sonnichsen. London: Macmillan, 1982. Brief biography, bibliography, and critical essay for 310 authors.

History and Criticism

Allmendinger, Blake. *Ten Most Wanted: The New Western Literature*. Routledge Kegan Paul, 1998.

Emmert, Scott. *Loaded Fictions: Social Critique in the Twentieth-Century Western*. University of Idaho Press, 1997.

Erisman, Fred, and Richard W. Etulain, eds. *Fifty Western Writers*. Greenwood, 1982.

Tompkins, Jane P. *West of Everything: The Inner Life of Westerns*. Oxford University Press, 1992.

Yates, Norris W. *Gender and Genre: An Introduction to Women Writers of Formula Westerns, 1900–1950*. University of New Mexico Press, 1995.

Organizations

Western Writers of America. The Western Writers of America has a membership of writers of Western fact and Westerns (fiction). It publishes (since 1953) a monthly journal, *The Roundup*, which includes book reviews and is available for subscription by libraries. At its annual convention, "Spur" Awards are given in several categories, and the Golden Saddleman Award is given for an "outstanding contribution to the history and legend of the West." The Western Writers of America has a book club, which is managed by Doubleday.

Women Writing the West. This nonprofit organization promotes the women's West through a newsletter, an annual conference, a catalog, and taking their information on the road to booksellers' conferences.

Awards

The major awards for Westerns are awarded by the Western Writers of America and the Cowboy Hall of Fame.

Spur Awards

The Western Writers of America established the Spur Award in 1953, making it the oldest annual genre fiction award still in existence. When it started, it was awarded in the divisions of novel, historical novel, juvenile, short story, and reviewer. In 1998 the categories were Best Western Novel (under 90,000 words), Best Novel of the West (over 90,000 words), Original Western Paperback, Nonfiction Historical, Nonfiction Contemporary, Nonfiction Biography, Juvenile Fiction, Juvenile Nonfiction, Short Fiction, Short Nonfiction, Story Teller Award (for best illustrated children's literature), Medicine Pipe Bearer Award (Best First Novel), Documentary Screenplay, and Drama Screenplay. At one time there were categories for best TV script and best short subject. The broad categories demonstrate the interest of fans of Westerns in all facets of the western experience.

Western Novel

1954	*Lawman*, by Lee Leighton
1955	*The Violent Land*, by Wayne D. Overholser
1956	*Somewhere They Die*, by L. P. Holmes
1957	*High Gun*, by Leslie Ernenwein
1958	*Buffalo Wagons*, by Elmer Kelton
1959	*Short Cut to Red River*, by Noel Loomis
1960	*Long Run*, by Nelson Nye
1961	*The Nameless Breed*, by Will C. Brown
1962	*The Honyocker*, by Giles Lutz
1963	*Comanche Captives*, by Fred Grove
1964	*Follow the Free Wind*, by Leigh Brackett
1965	*The Trail to Ogallala*, by Benjamin Capps
1966	*Sam Chance*, by Benjamin Capps
1967	*My Brother John*, by Herbert R. Purdum
1968	*The Valdez Horses*, by Lee Hoffman
1969	*Down the Long Hills*, by Louis L'Amour
1970	*Tragg's Choice*, by Clifton Adams
1971	*The Last Days of Wolf Garnett*, by Clifton Adams
1972	*The Day the Cowboys Quit*, by Elmer Kelton
1973	*A Killing in Kiowa*, by Lewis B. Patten
1974	*The Time It Never Rained*, by Elmer Kelton
1975	*A Hanging in Sweetwater*, by Stephen Overholser
1976	*The Shootist*, by Glendon Swarthout
1977	*The Spirit Horses*, by Lou Cameron, and *The Court Martial of George Armstrong Custer*, by Douglas C. Jones
1978	*The Great Horse Race*, by Fred Grove
1979	*Riders to Cibola*, by Norman Zollinger
1980	*The Holdouts*, by William Decker
1981	*The Valiant Women*, by Jeanne Williams
1982	*Eye of the Hawk*, by Elmer Kelton, and *Horizon*, by Lee Head
1983	*Match Race*, by Fred Grove
1984	*Leaving Kansas*, by Frank Roderus
1985	*Gone the Dreams and Dancing*, by Douglas C. Jones
1986	*Lonesome Dove*, by Larry McMurtry

1987   *The Blind Corral*, by Ralph Robert Beer

1988   *Skinwalkers*, by Tony Hillerman

1989   *Mattie*, by Judy Alter

1990   *Fool's Coach*, by Richard Wheeler

1991   *Sanctuary*, by Gary Svee

1992   *Journal of the Gun Years*, by Richard Matheson

1993   *Nickajack*, by Robert J. Conley

1994   *Friends*, by Charles Hackenberry

1995   *St. Agnes' Stand*, by Tom Edison

1996   *The Dark Island*, by Robert Conley

1997   *Blood of Texas*, by Preston Lewis writing as Will Camp

1998   *The Kiowa Verdict*, by Cynthia Haseloff

1999   *Journey of the Dead*, by Loren D. Estleman

Novel of the West

1954   *The Wheel and the Hearth*, by Lucia Moore

1955   *Journey by the River*, by John Prescott

1956   no award

1957   *Generations of Men*, by John Clinton Hunt

1958   *Silver Mountain*, by Dan Cushman

1959   *The Fancher Train*, by Amelia Bean

1960   *The Buffalo Soldiers*, by John Prebble

1961   *From Where the Sun Now Stands*, by Will Henry

1962   *The Winter War*, by William Wister Haines

1963   *Moon Trap*, by Don Berry

1964   *Gates of the Mountains*, by Will Henry

1965   *Indian Fighter*, by E. E. Halloran

1966   *Gold in California*, by Todhunter Ballard, and *Mountain Man*, by Vardis Fisher

1967   *Hellfire Jackson*, by Garland Roark and Charles Thomas

1968   *The Wolf Is My Brother*, by Chad Oliver

1969   *The Red Sabbath*, by Lewis Patten

1970   *The White Man's Road*, by Benjamin Capps

1971–1972   no award

1973   *Chiricahua*, by Will Henry

1974–1977   no award

1978   *Swimming Man Burning*, by Terrence Kilpatrick

1979–1981   no award

1982   *Aces and Eights*, by Loren D. Estleman

1983   *Ride the Wind*, by Lucia St. Clair Robson

1984   *Sam Bass*, by Bryan Woolley

1985   no award

1986   *The Snowblind Moon*, by John Byrne Cook

1987   *Roman*, by Douglas C. Jones

1988   *Wanderer Springs*, by Robert Flynn

1989   *The Homesman*, by Glendon Swarthout

1990   *Panther in the Sky*, by James Alexander Thom

1991   *Home Mountain*, by Jeanne Williams

1992   *The Medicine Horn*, by Jory Sherman

1993   *Slaughter*, by Elmer Kelton

1994   *Empire of Bones*, by Jeff Long

1995   *The Far Canyon*, by Elmer Kelton

1996   *Stone Song: A Novel of the Life of Crazy Horse*, by Win Blevins

1997   *Sierra*, by Richard S. Wheeler

1998   *Comanche Moon*, by Larry McMurtry

1999   *The All-True Travels and Adventures of Lidie Newton*, by Jane Smiley

Western Heritage Award or the Wrangler Award

The National Cowboy Hall of Fame selects specific works in several different media categories that their judges feel "helped preserve the spirit of the West." The award is called the Western Heritage Award or the Wrangler Award. The books that have won the award for "Outstanding Novel" are listed here.

1962   Horan, James David. *The Shadow Catcher*

1963   Abbey, Edward. *Fire on the Mountain*

1964   Roripaugh, Robert. *Honor Thy Father*

1965   Berger, Thomas. *Little Big Man*

1966   Fisher, Vardis. *Mountain Man*

1967   Gulick, Bill. *They Came to a Valley*

1968   Flynn, Robert. *North to Yesterday*

1969   Grove, Fred. *The Buffalo Runners*

1970   Capps, Benjamin. *The White Man's Road*

1971   Guthrie, A. B. *Arfive*

1972   Waters, Frank. *Pike's Peak: A Family Saga*

1973   Henry, Will. *Chiricahua*

1974   Kelton, Elmer. *The Time It Never Rained*

1975   Michener, James A. *Centennial*

1978   Johnson, Dorothy M. *Buffalo Woman*

1979   Kelton, Elmer. *The Good Old Boys*

1980   Hill, Ruth Beebe. *Hanta Yo*

1984   Calkins, Frank. *The Long Riders' Winter*

1985   Doig, Ivan. *English Creek*

1986   Guthrie, A. B. *Playing Catch-up*

1987   Matthews, Greg. *Heart of the Country*

1988   Kelton, Elmer. *The Man Who Rode Midnight*

1989   Swarthout, Glendon. *The Homesman*

1990   Oliver, Chad. *Broken Eagle*

1991   McMurtry, Larry. *Buffalo Girls*

1992   Freeman, Judith, *Set for Life*

1993   McCarthy, Cormac. *All the Pretty Horses*

1994   Kingsolver, Barbara. *Pigs in Heaven*

1995   Evans, Max. *Bluefeather Fellini in the Sacred Realm*

1996   Kirkpatrick, Jane. *A Sweetness to the Soul*

1997   Lehrer, Kate. *Out of Eden*

1998   Askew, Rilla. *The Mercy Seat*

1999   Estleman, Loren D. *Journey of the Dead*

Publishers

Many of the large-type publishers are issuing reprints in both hardcover and paperback. Five Star is publishing several hardcover traditional Westerns each year, approximately 34 per year including originals, previously unpublished works by classic authors, and works that originally appeared only in serialized form. Forge is publishing hardcover and paperback originals. Several university presses are also publishing in this area, including University of Nebraska, publisher of *The Collected Stories of Max Brand,* which includes his short fiction in other genres as well. Some university presses, including the University of Oklahoma, are reprinting classic Westerns. Gunsmoke Large Print Westerns publishes three Westerns per month. Thorndike has a large-print Western series, as does Linsford. Roundup and Sagebrush also publish

Westerns in large print. Severn House often reprints paperback originals as hardcovers. Leisure publishes 60 paperback Western titles per year, originals and reprints, all set before 1900. A number of religious publishers, including Bethany House, Harvest, Word, Crossways, Multnomah, and Council Press, publish Westerns. Many of the Westerns found on the mass market racks are reprints.

Online Resources

The National Cowboy Hall of Fame and Western Heritage Center, http://www.cowboyhalloffame.org (accessed 19 January 2000).

The Salt Lake County Library System, http://www.slco.lib.ut.us/spur.htm (accessed 19 January 2000), lists all the Spur Awards from the Western Writers of America.

The Western Writers of America, http://www.westernwriters.org/western.html (accessed 19 January 2000).

Women Writing the West, http://www.womenwritingthewest.com (accessed 19 January 2000).

D's Western Picks

Alexie, Sherman. *Reservation Blues.*

Conley, Robert J. *Nickajack.*

Doig, Ivan. *Dancing at the Rascal Fair.*

Hardeman, Ric. *Sunshine Rider: The First Vegetarian Western.*

Nye, Nelson. *The White Chip.*

Chapter 3

Crime

"It is just possible that the tensions in a novel of murder are the simplest and yet most complete pattern of the tensions on which we live in this generation."
—Raymond Chandler

"The mystery form is like gymnastic equipment: you can grasp hold of it and show off what you can do."
—Mickey Friedman

"What the detective story is about is not murder but the restoration of order."
—P. D. James

History of the Genre

Although stories of crime and punishment have been around for centuries, the crime novel as we know and love it traces its roots back to Edgar Allan Poe. The so-called golden age of the mystery was in the 1920s and 1930s, the years between the two world wars, with well-mannered mysteries the norm and women writers, most particularly Agatha Christie and Dorothy L. Sayers, reigning. The 1940s and 1950s saw the rise of the hard-boiled detective, an American invention, featuring independent, solitary, taciturn men and the mean streets of major cities. With the emergence of hard-boiled, noir, or Black Mask mysteries, as they were sometimes called, male writers began to dominate the mystery scene. In the 1960s and 1970s gothic and romantic suspense involving crime became popular, but they had closer ties and better publishing options in romance, leaving the mystery scene dominated by the male hard-boiled detective and police procedural. During 1970s there was much discussion about the decline of mysteries, and at one point the Mystery Writers of America embarked on a campaign to target young readers, which some credit with revitalizing the genre. By the 1980s it was apparent that women were having a much more difficult time being published in crime fiction than men and several women authors, including Sara Paretsky, formed Sisters in Crime to promote women's efforts in the field. From the mid- 1980s through the end of the twentieth century, women writers gained ascendance in the mystery field, with a trend toward somewhat cozier mysteries placing more emphasis on the sleuth's interpersonal relationships.

The trends in the 1990s were toward diversity. Detectives can now be male or female, gay or straight, of any age or ethnic background. Settings are all over the globe and throughout time: past, present, future. Genre blending has introduced elements from romance, science fiction, and historicals into the mystery genre. All of these trends have contributed to the immense popularity and success of the genre in the 1990s.

Themes and Types

Crime novels include detective stories, mysteries, crime capers, suspense, and courtroom dramas. The driving force in these novels is crime, most commonly murder, but theft, assault, and confidence games are also popular. Spy and espionage novels, although considered by some (citizens of the "targeted" country) to be crime novels, revolve more around the adventure aspects of their plots and are thus treated in Chapter 4, "Adventure."

The murder mystery, or detective novel, has long been a staple in the book world. It makes up the largest of genre collections in most public libraries and approximately 20 percent of titles on best-seller lists.

Crime fiction allows the reader to experience danger and suspense vicariously while safely ensconced in a comfortable chair away from real crime. Michael Seidman, in a posting to the e-mail list DorothyL (5 September 1995), wrote "… in a mystery we never know more than the sleuth; in a suspense novel, we rarely know more than the bad guy. Mystery novels have to have suspense; there's a mystery in many suspense novels. But the mystery is more of a game between reader and author; who is going to get to the end first." Crime fiction engages the reader's mind, and one facet of its appeal is the challenge of trying to solve the crime before the sleuth in the pages does. In the case of detective fiction, readers become very attached to the characters of particular detectives.

Detective Story and Detectives

Tales of detection that involve solving a puzzle, finding the culprit, and bringing him or her to justice are the most popular or at least the most prolific of crime stories. The focus is on the detective and the process he or she uses to solve the crime. Frequently terms such as *hard-boiled, soft-boiled,* and *cozy* are used to describe the different types within this category.

Hard-boiled, noir, and *Black Mask* are terms used to describe mysteries in which the protagonist, usually a male private investigator, working for the most part alone, explores the dark underbelly of a major city while trying to solve the crime. The detective usually has no close personal relationships. The crimes, often depicted in vivid and gory detail, can be described as "gritty." James Ellroy is currently writing in this vein, and past masters include Raymond Chandler, Dashiell Hammett, and Jim Thompson, all of whose books continue to be read.

Soft-boiled and *cozy* are often used interchangeably, although it can be argued that soft-boiled falls between hard-boiled and cozy. In this category, interpersonal relationships are more important. The sleuths do have families and friends, who often play a role in the story. In this type of mystery the community is often smaller or rural as opposed to the urban scenes found in hard-boiled stories. The detective, instead of meeting a series of strangers in pursuit of answers, interacts with people known to him or her in the community. Often the sleuths have no official standing, being amateurs who just seem to be at the right (or perhaps the wrong) place at the right time. The murders often occur "offstage" or, if conducted in full view, are more genteelly described, rather than graphically as in hard-boiled detection.

3

The detective series seems to have become the rule rather than merely being very common. New mysteries frequently identify the sleuth on the cover, even if it is his or her first appearance. Many detective series that start off as paperback originals eventually move into hardcover publication as the sleuth becomes popular.

Professional Detectives

For most of the last 50 years, the detective who solves crime for a living was the most prevalent type of character, with amateur detectives only recently challenging their dominance. The two major types of professional detectives are the police detective and the private investigator. Insurance investigators could also be considered professional detectives. Until recent years the focus was completely on the detective and how he or she solved the crime. Now the detectives have relationships and families that help define them and add multiple levels to the tale of the detective and the crime.

Police Detectives

Mysteries involving police detectives often include several characters from a squad or division. Even the series that feature independent sleuths who are on a police force have to work within the constraints imposed by the organization and stay within the law they are trying to uphold. A new trend features one-person police departments, thus giving the sleuth much in common with independent private investigators. Frequently the plot will involve several crimes, requiring the detective to work more than one case at a time or to consult on other cases. The stories of police detectives became popular with the rise of organized police forces in the United States, Great Britain, and France.

Police procedurals are very much like crime blotters. A group of police officers solves crimes as they come up. Joseph Wambaugh and Ed McBain wrote the prototypes in this area.

The detective in the police procedural must function within the rules of the police department; he or she lacks the freedom of the private detective. Although the pattern may vary because of the personality of the detective, most police detectives work as part of a team (as opposed to the private detective, who is often a loner). Two plot patterns are common. One uses a single murder (or several linked murders) or mystery for the basic plot. The other, in effect, uses the police blotter: Every case followed up by the police station staff is observed in varying degrees, although one case is the focus of detection and, often, the other cases are ingeniously linked to the main crime. Television series such as *NYPD Blue* and *Homicide* are good examples of the composite stories and cast of characters found in police procedural novels.

Detection novels featuring police detectives can be either hard-boiled or cozy. The best indication of which category a book falls into is usually the size of the community in which the detective functions. Those set in New York, Los Angeles, and Chicago tend to be more hard-boiled, while those set in places like the fictional Maggody, Arkansas, where Chief Arly Hanks is the sum total of the local police force, are dealing with more cozy crimes.

The following authors are listed by the country to which the police detective belongs. Great Britain is further subdivided, with Scotland Yard detectives grouped separately from those in the rest of Great Britain. Under the United States heading the grouping is by state.

Australia

Cleary, Jon (Detective Sergeant Scobie Malone)

McNab, Claire (Detective Inspector Carol Ashton, lesbian)

Upfield, Arthur (Inspector Napoleon "Bony" Bonaparte, half-aborigine)

Belgium

Freeling, Nicolas (Henri Castang)

Bosnia

Fesperman, Dan (Detective Inspector Vlado Petric in *Lie in the Dark*)

Brabt (fictional European state)

Rathbone, Julian (Commissioner Jan Argand)

Brazil

Fish, Robert L. (Captain José da Silva)

Canada

Craig, Alisa (Madoc Rhys, Royal Canadian Mounted Police)

Gough, Laurence (Detectives Jack Willows and Claire Parker, Vancouver)

Reeves, John (Inspector Andrew Coggin and Sergeant Fred Stemp, Toronto)

Sale, Medora (Detective Inspector John Sanders, Toronto)

Wood, Ted (Reid Bennett, Murphy's Harbor, Ontario)

Wright, Eric (Charlie Salter, Toronto)

Wright, L. R. (Staff Sergeant Karl Aberg, Royal Canadian Mounted Police, British Columbia)

Young, Scott (Inspector Matteesie, Royal Canadian Mounted Police)

China

Van Gulik, Robert (Judge Dee, eighth century)

Czechoslovakia

Skvoreck, Josef (Lieutenant Boruvka)

3

Denmark

Nielsen, Torben (Superintendent Archer)

Orum, Poul (Detective Inspector Jonas Morck, Copenhagen)

Finland

Joensuu, Matti (Detective Timo Harjunpaa, SUOPO)

France

Freeling, Nicolas (Henri Castang)

Hebden, Mark (Inspector Evariste Clovis Désiré Pel, Burgundy)

Jacquemard, Yves, and Jean-Michel Sénécal (Superintendent Dullac)

Janes, J. Robert (Inspectors Jean-Louis St-Cyr of the French police and Hermann Kohler of the German police, World War II occupied France)

McConnor, Vincent (Francois Vidocq, founder of the Sûreté, nineteenth century)

Simenon, Georges (Inspector Maigret)

Great Britain: Scotland Yard

Barnard, Robert (Superintendent Percy Trethowan and Superintendent Sutcliffe)

Butler, Gwendoline (Inspector Coffin)

Crombie, Deborah (Superintendent Duncan Kincaid and Sergeant Gemma James)

Garve, Andrew (Chief Inspector Charles Grant)

Grimes, Martha (Detective Superintendent Richard Jury and amateur Melrose Plant)

Hare, Cyril (Inspector Mallett)

Harrison, Ray (Sergeant Bragg and James Morton, London City Police, 1890s)

Heyer, Georgette (Chief Inspectors Hannasyde and Hemingway)

Hilton, John Buxton (Inspector Kenworthy)

Hunter, Alan (Chief Superintendent George Gently)

Inchbald, Peter (Francis Corti, Art and Antiques Squad)

Innes, Michael (Inspector, later Sir, John Appleby, and also in retirement)

James, P. D. (Commander Adam Dalgliesh)

Jones, Elwyn (Detective Chief Superintendent Barlow)

Kenyon, Michael (Inspector Henry Peckover)

Lemarchand, Elizabeth (Detective Inspector Tom Pollard and Inspector Gregory Toye)

Lewis, Roy (Inspector Crow)

Lovesey, Peter (Sergeant Cribb and Constable Thackeray, nineteenth century)

MacKenzie, Donald (Detective Inspector Raven, retired)

Marric, J. J. (Commander George Gideon)

Marsh, Ngaio (Inspector Roderick Alleyn)

Martin, Ian Kennedy (Inspector Jack Regan)

Moyes, Patricia (Chief Superintendent Henry Tibbett and his wife Emmy)

Ormerod, Roger (Detective Harry Kyle)

Perry, Anne (Inspector Pitt, nineteenth century)

Selwyn, Francis (Sergeant Verity, nineteenth century)

Smith, D. W. (Harry Fathers)

Stubbs, Jean (Inspector Lintott, nineteenth century)

Symons, Julian (Inspector Bland)

Tey, Josephine (Inspector Alan Grant)

Todd, Charles (Inspector Ian Rutledge)

Wainwright, John (Chief Inspector Lennox)

Winslow, Pauline (Superintendent Merle Capricorn and Inspector Copper)

Parodies of Scotland Yard

Giles, Kenneth (Inspector Harry James and Sergeant Honeybody)

Porter, Joyce (Inspector Dover)

Great Britain: Other Than Scotland Yard

Aird, Catherine (Inspector Sloan)

Anderson, J. R. L. (Chief Constable Pier Deventer)

Ashford, Jeffrey (Detective Inspector Don Kerry)

Atkins, Meg Elizabeth (Chief Inspector Henry Beaumont)

Banister, Jo (Inspector Liz Graham and Sergeant Cal Donovan)

Barnard, Robert (Chief Inspector Meredith, Superintendent Ian Dundy)

Beaton, M. C. (Constable Hamish MacBeth, Scotland)

Burley, W. J. (Chief Superintendent Wycliffe)

Cork, Barry (Angus Straun)

Dexter, Colin (Chief Inspector Morse, Oxford)

Eccles, Marjorie (Inspector Mayo)

Evans, Geraldine (Detective Inspector Rafferty and Sergeant Llewellyn)

Fraser, Anthea (Chief Inspector David Webb)

Geddes, Paul (Ludovic Fender)

George, Elizabeth (Inspector Thomas Lynley, Sergeant Barbara Havers)

Gilbert, Michael (Chief Superintendent Charlie Knott, Luke Pagan, Patrick Petrella)

Graham, Caroline (Chief Inspector Tom Barnaby)

Granger, Ann (Chief Inspector Markby and former Foreign Service Officer Meredith Mitchell)

Hart, Roy (Inspector Roper)

Haymon, S. T. (Detective Inspector Benjamin Jurnet)

Hill, Reginald (Superintendent Dalziel and Sergeant Pascoe)

Hilton, John Buxton (Inspector Pickford, Detective Brunt, and Sergeant Nadin, Derbyshire, nineteenth century)

James, Bill (Chief Superintendent Colin Harpur)

Knox, Bill (Colin Thane and Phil Moss, Glasgow; Webb Carrick, Fishery Protection Service)

LaPlante, Lynda (Chief Inspector Jane Tennison)

McGowan, Jill (Detective Chief Inspector Lloyd and Inspector Judy Hall)

McIlvanney, William (Detective Inspector Laidlaw, Glasgow)

Melville, Jennie, pseudonym of Gwendoline Butler (Sergeant Charmian Daniels)

Murray, Stephen (Alec Stainton)

Penn, John (Detective Superintendent George Thorne and Sergeant Abbott, the Cotswolds)

Peters, Ellis (Detective Inspector George Felse)

Radley, Sheila (Chief Inspector Douglas Quantrill, Suffolk)

Rankin, Ian (Inspector John Rebus, Edinburgh)

Rendell, Ruth (Chief Inspector Wexford and Inspector Borden)

Robinson, Peter (Chief Inspector Alan Banks)

Ross, Jonathan (Detective Superintendent George Rogers)

Ruell, Patrick (Detective Inspector Dog Cicero)

Scott, Jack S. (Detective Sergeant Rosher, Detective Chief Inspector Peter Parsons, and Sergeant Wammo Wimbrush)

Simpson, Dorothy (Inspector Thanet, Kent)

Stacey, Susannah, pseudonym of Jill Staynes and Margaret Storey (Superintendent Bone)

Thomson, June (Detective Inspector Finch; in U.S. editions, Detective Inspector Rudd)

Turnbull, Peter (Police Constable Phil Hamilton, Detective Roy Sussock, Glasgow)

Watson, Colin (Inspector Purbright and Miss Teatime)

Webster, Noah (Jonathan Gaunt, Treasury agent; Andrew Laird)

Whitehead, Barbara (Police Inspectors Dave Smart and Bob Southwell, York)

Hong Kong

Marshall, William (Yellowthread Street Police Station, Chief Harry Feiffer)

India

Keating, H. R. F. (Inspector Ghote, Bombay)

Ireland

Brady, John (Inspector Matt Minogue)

Gill, Bartholomew (Chief Inspector Peter McGarr, Dublin)

Israel

Gur, Batya (Detective Michael Ohayon, Jerusalem)

Rosenberg, Robert (Avram Cohen, head of the Jerusalem District Criminal Investigations Department)

Italy

Dibdin, Michael (Aurelio Zen)

Holme, Timothy (Achille Peroni, Venice)

Leon, Donna (Commissario Guido Brunetti, Venice)

Nabb, Magdalen (Marshal Guarnaccia, Florence)

Pears, Iain (Flavia di Stefano, Rome, Art Squad)

Williams, Timothy (Commissario Trotti)

Japan

Melville, James (Superintendent Otani, Tokyo)

Luong (Fictional Southeast Asian Kingdom)

Alexander, Gary (Superintendent Bamsan Kiet)

Netherlands

Baantjer, Albert (Inspector Dekok)

Freeling, Nicolas (Inspector Van der Valk)

Van de Wetering, Janwillem (Detective Grijpstra and Detective Sergeant de Grier)

New Zealand

Mantell, Laurie (Chief Inspector Peacock and Detective Steven Arrow)

Russia

Hill, Reginald (Inspector Lev Chislenko, Moscow)

Kaminsky, Stuart (Inspector Rostnikov, Moscow)

Smith, Martin Cruz (Chief Homicide Investigator Arkady Renko)

White Robin A. (Gregori Nowek in *Siberian Light*)

South Africa

McClure, James (Lieutenant Tromp Kramer, Afrikaner; Detective Sergeant Zondi, Bantu)

Spain

Jeffries, Roderic (Inspector Enrique Alverez, Majorca)

Serafin, David (Superintendent Louis Bernal, Madrid)

Sweden

Blom, K. Arne

Hubert, Tord

Mankell, Henning (Inspector Kurt Wallander)

Sjöwall, Maj, and Per Wahlöö (Martin Beck)

United States

• Alabama

Cook, Thomas H. (Ben Wellman, *Streets of Fire*)

• Arizona

Garfield, Brian (Sam Watchman, Navajo, Arizona Highway Patrol)

Hillerman, Tony (Lieutenant Joe Leaphorn and Jim Chee, Navajo Tribal Police)

Jance, J. A. (Joanna Brady, Cochise County Sheriff)

• Arkansas

Hess, Joan (Chief Arly Hanks, woman)

- California
    - Ball, John (Virgil Tibbs, African-American, Pasadena)
    - Bass, Milton (Benjamin Friedman, San Diego)
    - Boucher, Anthony (Lieutenant Jackson, Los Angeles)
    - Campbell, Robert (Eddie Heath, Wilbur Monk, Los Angeles)
    - Connelly, Michael (Detective Harry Bosch, Los Angeles)
    - Crowe, John (Sheriff Beckett, Buena Costa)
    - Cunningham, E. V. (Masao Masuto, Nisei, Beverly Hills)
    - Davis, Robert (Harry Edwards, Los Angeles)
    - Dunlap, Susan (Detective Jill Smith, Berkeley)
    - Egan, Lesley (Detective Varallo, Glendale)
    - Ellroy, James (Sergeant Lloyd Hopkins, Los Angeles)
    - Gillis, Jackson (Jonas Duncan, Los Angeles, retired)
    - Harris, Alfred (Baroni, Southern California)
    - Kellerman, Faye (Peter and Rina Lazarus, Los Angeles)
    - Lantique, John (San Francisco)
    - Lewis, Lange (Detective Tucker, Los Angeles, *The Birthday Murder*)
    - Linington, Elizabeth (Sergeant Maddox, Hollywood)
    - Ludwig, Jerry (Detective Sergeant Edward Brenner, Los Angeles)
    - Montecino, Marcel (Los Angeles)
    - Oster, Jerry (Lieutenant Sam Branch and Jeff Derry)
    - Petievich, Gerald (Charles Carr and Jack Kelly, U.S. Treasury agents, Los Angeles)
    - Pike, Robert L. (Lieutenant Jim Reardon, San Francisco)
    - Pronzini, Bill (John Quincannon, Federal Secret Service, San Francisco, 1890s)
    - Ray, Robert (Newport Beach)
    - Shannon, Dell (Lieutenant Luis Mendoza and Delia Reardon, Los Angeles)
    - Wallace, Marilyn (Sergeant Carlo Cruz and Jay Goldstein, Oakland)
    - Wambaugh, Joseph (Los Angeles Police Department)
    - Westbrook, Robert (Nicky Rachmaninoff, Beverly Hills)
    - Weston, Carolyn (Detective Casey Kellog and Sergeant Al Krug, Santa Monica)
    - Wilcox, Collin (Lieutenant Hastings, San Francisco)
- Colorado
    - Burns, Rex (Gabriel Wager, Chicano, Denver)
    - Doss, James D. (Scott Parris and Charlie Moon, Southwest area and Ute Reservation)
    - Paulsen, Gary (Ed Tincker, Denver)

- Connecticut
    Forrest, Richard (Detective Tommy Lark)
    Skedgell, Marian (Lieutenant Dave Littlejohn, State Trooper)
    Waugh, Hillary (Police Chief Fred Fellows)

- District of Columbia
    Patterson, James (Alex Cross, police forensic psychologist)

- Florida
    King, Rufus (Stuff Driscoll)
    Willeford, Charles (Sergeant Hoke Moseley, Miami)

- Georgia
    Cook, Thomas H. (Clemons, Atlanta)

3

- Hawaii
    Biggers, Earl Derr (Inspector Charlie Chan, Honolulu)

- Illinois
    Bland, Eleanor Taylor (Marti MacAlister and Vik Jessenovik, Lincoln Prairie)
    Blank, Martin (John Lamp, Chicago)
    Campbell, Robert (Jimmy Flannery, sewer inspector)
    Cormay, Michael (Kruger, Chicago)
    Di Pego, Gerald (Chicago)
    Holton, Hugh (Chicago)
    Kaminsky, Stuart M. (Sergeant Abe Lieberman, Chicago)
    Pulver, Mary Monica (Sergeant Peter Brichter)

- Indiana
    Lewin, Michael Z. (Lieutenant Leroy Powder, Indianapolis)

- Kansas
    Weir, Charlene (Police Chief Susan Wren, Hampstead)

- Louisiana (all have New Orleans locales or connections)
    Burke, James Lee (Dave Robicheaux)
    Colbert, James (Skinny)
    Corrington, John William (Rat Trapp)
    Smith, Julie (Skip Langdon)

- Massachusetts
    Burke, Alan Dennis (Assistant District Attorney Jack Meehan, Boston)
    Dunham, Dick (Sergeant Joe Knight, Boston)
    Langton, Jane (Homer Kelly, retired detective)

McDonald, Gregory (Inspector Francis Xavier Flynn, Boston)

Rennert, Maggie (Detective Lieutenant Guy Silvestri, Buxford)

• Michigan

Jackson, Jon A. (Sergeant Mulheisen, Detroit)

• Minnesota

Hinkemeyer, Michael T. (Sheriff Emil Whippletree)

McInerny, Ralph (Sheriff Oscar Ewbank)

Sandford, John (Lucas Davenport)

• Montana

Bowen, Peter (Gabriel Du Pre, cattle brand inspector)

Guthrie, A. B. (Sheriff Chick Charleston and Jason Beard)

• Nevada

Kellerman, Faye (Detective Sergeant Romulus Poe, Steve Jensen, Patricia Deluca, and M. E. Rukmani Kalil)

• New Jersey

Kent, Bill (Louis Monroe, Atlantic City)

• New Mexico

Hackler, Micah S. (Sheriff Cliff Lansing)

Havill, Steven F. (Undersheriff Bill Gastner)

Hillerman, Tony (Lieutenant Joe Leaphorn and Jim Chee, Navajo Tribal Police)

Stern, Richard Martin (Lieutenant Johnny Ortiz, Apache)

• New York (New York City unless otherwise noted)

Arrighi, Mel (Detective Romano)

Bagby, George (Inspector Schmidt)

Baxt, George (Pharaoh Love, African-American; Detective Van Larsen)

Boyle, Thomas (De Sales)

Caunitz, William J. (Gallegher)

Charyn, Jerome (Isaac Sidel)

Chastain, Thomas (Deputy Chief Inspector Max Kauffman)

Cunningham, E. V. (Lieutenant Harry Golding and wife Fran)

Delman, David (Lieutenant Jacob Horowitz, Nassau County)

Early, Jack (Police Chief Waldo Halleck, Long Island)

Glass, Leslie (April Woo)

Heffernan, William (Stanislaus Polk)

Hentoff, Nat (Detective Noah Green)

Himes, Chester (Coffin Ed Johnson and Grave Digger Jones, Harlem)

Horansky, Ruby (Nikki Trakos, Brooklyn)

Jahn, Michael (Donovan)

Katz, William (Detective Leonard Anthony Karlov)

Lance, Peter (Fire Inspector Eddie Burke, Jr., *First Degree Burn*)

Leuci, Bob (Detective Alexander Simon)

Lieberman, Herbert (Lieutenant Frank Mooney)

Lockridge, Richard (Captain Heinrich, State Police; Lieutenant Nathan Shapiro)

McBain, Ed (Steve Carella, 87th Precinct)

Minahan, John ("Little John" Rawlings)

Newman, Christopher (Lieutenant Joe Dante) **3**

O'Connell, Carol (Sergeant Kathleen Mallory, sociopath)

O'Donnell, Lillian (Norah Mulcahany, Detective Ed Stiebeck, and Mici Anhalt)

Paul, Barbara (Detective Marian Larch and Lieutenant Murtaugh)

Reilly, Helen (Inspector McKee)

Rifkin, Shepard (Detective Damian McQuaid)

Robb, J. D. (Eve Dallas and Peabody, twenty-first century)

Sanders, Lawrence (Edward X. Delaney, retired chief of detectives)

Uhnak, Dorothy (Detective Christie Opara and Detective Miranda Torres)

Waugh, Hillary (Detective Fred Sessions)

- North Carolina
  Cornwell, Patricia (Chief Judy Hammer, Deputy Virginia West, Andy Brazil)

  Malone, Michael (Chief Cudbarth Mangum)

- Ohio
  Leeke, Jim

  Pyle, A. M. (Cesar Frank, Cincinnati)

- Oklahoma
  Cooper, Susan Rogers (Milt Novack)

  Hager, Jean (Chief Mitch Bushyhead)

- Pennsylvania
  Constantine, K. C. (Chief of Police Mario Balzic, Rocksburg)

- Tennessee
  McCrumb, Sharyn (Sheriff Spencer Arrowood)

- Texas

    Cooley, Marilyn, and James Edward Gunn (Tony McIver, Houston)

    Crider, Bill (Sheriff Don Rhodes)

    Herndon, Nancy (Elena Jarvis, Los Santos)

    Lindsey, David L. (Stuart Haydon, Houston)

    Martin, Lee (Policewoman Deb Ralston, Fort Worth)

    Wingate, Anne (Mark Shigata, Bayport)

- Utah

    Levitt, J. R. (Jason Coulter, Salt Lake City)

- Vermont

    Koenig, Joseph

    Mayor, Archer (Lieutenant Joe Gunther, Brattleboro)

- Washington

    Beck, K. K. (Seattle)

    Emerson, Earl (Mac Fontana, fire chief)

    Jance, J. A. (Jonas Piedmont Beaumont, Seattle)

    Pearson, Ridley (Detective Lou Boldt and police psychiatrist Daphne Matthews, Seattle)

- West Virginia

    Douglas, John (Detective Edward Harter, Shawnee)

- U.S. Military

    Deutermann, P. T. (*Official Privilege; Zero Option; Sweepers; The Edge of Honor*)

West Indies

    York, Andrew (Colonel James Munro Tallant, black police commissioner, Caribbean island)

Private Detectives

I'm talking private eyes here. Think gumshoe, shamus, peeper, private dick. He doesn't necessarily have to be licensed, he may consider himself a "salvage consultant" and a "guy that helps people out," he may be a bounty hunter or a troubleshooter or a freelance reporter, but he's generally a freelancer, a loner, an outsider, with an essence of toughness that has more to do with character than how many sailors he can toss out of a bar. And it goes without saying (or it should) that he might very well be a she.

—Kevin Burton Smith, The *Thrilling Detective* Web site, http://www.colba.net/~kvnsmith/thrillingdetective/intro.html (accessed 13 November 1999)

The Private Eye Writers of America, who make it their business to honor excellent work in the genre with their Shamus Awards, define a "private eye" as any mystery protagonist who is a professional investigator, "but not a police officer or government agent."

The official private detective started out as one of two types—the employee of a large agency or a lone operator—but now is often part of a small one- or two-investigator agency. Dashiell Hammett created two immortal prototypes: the Continental Op, simply identified for his agency and never named, and Sam Spade, a detective who strikes out on his own after his partner is killed in *The Maltese Falcon*. Sam Spade also became the prototype for the hard-boiled private eye, a character often short on morals but long on integrity.

Argentina

Borges, Jorge Luis (Don Isidro Parodi, *Six Problems of Don Isidro Parodi*)

Australia

Corris, Peter (Cliff Hardy)

Day, Marele (Claudia Valentine)

West, Charles (Paul Crook, Sydney)

Canada

Engel, Howard (Benny Cooperman)

Ritchie, Simon (J. K. G. Jantarro, one-armed)

France

Demouzon, Alain (Robert Flecheux)

Great Britain

Bush, Christopher (Ludovic Travers, insurance investigator)

Butler, Ragan (Captain Nash, eighteenth century)

Christie, Agatha (Tuppence and Tommy Beresford, Hercule Poirot)

Cody, Liza (Anna Lee, London)

Creasey, John (Emmanuel Cellini, psychiatrist)

Doyle, Arthur Conan, Sir (Sherlock Holmes)

Fredman, Mike (Willie Halliday, vegetarian and Buddhist)

Geddes, Paul (Ludovic Fender)

James, P. D. (Cordelia Gray, *An Unsuitable Job for a Woman, The Skull Beneath the Skin*)

Kavanagh, Dan (Duffy)

Kirk, Michael (Andrew Laird, insurance investigator)

Milne, John (Jimmy Jenner, London)

Tripp, Miles (John Sampson and Shandy)

Wentworth, Patricia (Miss Maude Silver)

Whalley, Peter (Harry Somers)

Yuill, P. B. (James Hazell)

Mexico

Alexander, Gary (Louis Balam, Mayan Indian)

Taibo, Paco Ignacio, II (Hector Belascoaran Shayne)

United States

• Alaska

Stabenow, Dana (Kate Shugak, former district attorney)

• California

Alverson, Charles (Joe Goodey, San Francisco)

Babula, William (Jeremiah St. John)

Boucher, Anthony (Fergus O'Breen, Los Angeles)

Byrd, Max (Mike Haller, San Francisco)

Campbell, Robert (Whistler)

Chandler, Raymond (Philip Marlowe, Los Angeles; classic)

Crais, Robert (Elvis Cole)

Cutler, Stan (Rayford Goodman)

Dawson, Janet (Jeri Howard, Oakland)

Dunlap, Susan (Kiernan O'Shaugnessy, Hollywood)

Gault, William (Brock Callahan, former guard, Los Angeles Rams)

Gores, Joe (Neal Fargo, Daniel Kearny Associates, skip-tracing agency)

Grafton, Sue (Kinsey Millhone)

Grant, Linda (Catherine Saylor, high-tech P.I., Berkeley)

Greenleaf, Stephen (John Marshall Tanner, San Francisco)

Hammett, Dashiell (the Continental Op, Sam Spade, Nick Charles; classics)

Hansen, Joseph (David Brandstetter, insurance investigator, gay)

Israel, Peter (B. F. Cage, Los Angeles)

Kaminsky, Stuart (Toby Peters, Los Angeles)

Kennealy, Jerry (Nick Polo)

Larson, Charles (Blixon, television executive, Los Angeles)

Lochte, Dick (Leo G. Bloodworth, Los Angeles)

Lupoff, Richard A. (insurance investigator Hobart Lindsey and Marvia Plum, police officer)

Lyons, Arthur (Jacob Asch, Los Angeles)

Macdonald, Ross (Lew Archer, Santa Barbara)

Maxwell, A. E. (Fiddler)

Mosley, Walter (Easy Rawlins, Los Angeles)

Muller, Marcia (Sharon McCone, San Francisco)

Pierce, David M. (Vic Daniel, San Fernando Valley)

Platt, Kin (Max Roper, Los Angeles)

Prather, Richard S. (Shell Scott, Los Angeles)

Pronzini, Bill (nameless detective, San Francisco)

Ray, Robert J. (Matt Murdock)

Roberts, Les (Saxon)

Sadler, Mark (Paul Shaw, Los Angeles)

Sangster, Jimmy (James Reed)

Simon, Roger L. (Moses Wine, Los Angeles)

3

Singer, Shelley (Jake Samson and Rosie)

Upton, Robert (Amos McGuffin, Los Angeles)

Wager, Walter (Alison Gordon, Los Angeles)

Walker, Walter (Hector Gronig, San Francisco)

Washburn, L. J. (Lucas Hallam)

- Colorado

Allegretto, Michael (Jake Lomax)

Burns, Rex (Devlin Kirk)

Downing, Warwick (Joe Reddman, Cheyenne, Denver)

- District of Columbia

Grady, James (John Rankin)

Law, Janice (Anna Peters)

Pelecanos, George P. (Nick Stefanos)

Schutz, Benjamin B. (Leo Haggerty)

Sucher, Dorothy (Victor Newman)

- Florida

Halleran, Tucker (Cam Maccardle)

Lutz, John (Fred Carver, physically handicapped)

MacDonald, John D. (Travis McGee)

- Illinois

Brown, Fredric (Ed and Am Hunter, Chicago)

Dewey, Thomas B. (Mac, Chicago)

McConnell, Frank (Harry Garnish)

Paretsky, Sara (V. I. Warshawski)

Raleigh, Michael (Paul Whelan, Chicago)

Spencer, Ross H. (Kirby, Willow, Luke Lassiter, Chance Purdue)

- Indiana

    Lewin, Michael Z. (Albert Samson, Indianapolis)

- Iowa

    Gorman, Ed (Sam McCain, Black River Falls, 1950s, in *The Day the Music Died*)

- Louisiana

    Donaldson, D. J. (Dr. Kit Franklin, criminal psychologist, and Chief Medical Examiner Andy Broussard)

    Shuman, M. K. (Micah Dunn, one-armed)

    Wiltz, Chris (Neal Rafferty)

- Massachusetts

    Barnes, Linda (Carlotta Carlyle; Michael Spraggue, Boston)

    Coxe, George Harmon (Jack Fenner, Boston; Ken Murdock, photographer)

    David, Daniel (Alex Rasmussen, Lowell)

    Doolittle, Jerome (Tom Bethany)

    Kiker, Douglas (Mac McFarland)

    Lehane, Dennis (Patrick Kenzie and Angie Gennaro)

    Parker, Robert B. (Spenser, Boston)

    Rosen, Richard (Blissberg)

    Ross, Philip (James Marley)

- Michigan

    Bunn, Thomas (Jack Bodine)

    Estleman, Loren D. (Ralph Poteet; Amos Walker, Detroit)

    Leonard, Elmore (Frank Ryan, process server, Detroit)

    Werry, Richard (J. D. Mulroy and Ahmad Dakar, African-American)

- Missouri

    Lutz, John (Alo Nudger, St. Louis)

- Montana

    Crumley, James (Sughrue and Milo Milodragovitch)

    Prowell, Sandra West (Phoebe Siegel)

- Nebraska

    Reynolds, William J. (Nebraska)

- New Jersey

    Gallison, Kate (Nick Magaracz, Trenton)

- New Mexico

    Anaya, Rudolfo (Sonny Baca)

    Brewer, Steve (Bubba Mabry)

    Zollinger, Norman (Jack Lautrec)

- New York
    Beinhart, Larry (Tony Cassella)
    Berger, Thomas (Russel Wren)
    Block, Lawrence (Matthew Scudder)
    Box, Edgar (Peter Cutler Sargent III, public relations man. Reprints of the Box novels reveal the author's real name, Gore Vidal.)
    Burke, J. F. (Sam Kelly, house detective, African-American)
    Chesbro, George C. (Dr. Robert "Mongo" Frederickson, Ph.D., little person)
    Coe, Tucker (Mitch Tobin, museum night guard)
    Coffey, Brian (Harris, clairvoyant) **3**
    Cohen, Stephen Paul (Eddie Margolis)
    Collins, Michael (Dan Fortune, one-armed)
    Cook, Thomas H. (Frank Clemons)
    Daly, Elizabeth (Henry Gamadge, rare book investigator)
    DeAndrea, William (Matt Cobb, television troubleshooter)
    Dobyns, Stephen (Charles Bradshaw, Saratoga)
    Friedman, Kinky (Kinky Friedman)
    Geller, Michael (Reznick)
    Hall, Parnell (Stanley Hastings)
    Jeffers, H. Paul (Harry MacNeil)
    Kaplan, Arthur (Charity Bay)
    Kaye, Marvin (Hilary Quayle, public relations woman)
    Livingston, Jack (Joe Binney, deaf)
    Lundy, Mike (Raven)
    Mason, Clifford (Joe Cinquez, African-American, Harlem)
    Pentecost, Hugh (Julian Quist, public relations man)
    Randisi, Robert J. (Miles Jacoby)
    Resnicow, Herbert (Norma and Alexander Gold)
    Rosten, Leo (Sidney "Silky" Pincus)
    Rozan, S. J. (Lydia Chin and Bill Smith)
    Schorr, Mark (Red Diamond)
    Scoppettone, Sandra (Lauren Laurano)
    Smith, J. C. S. (Quentin Jacoby)
    Solomita, Stephen (Stanley Moodrow)
    Spillane, Mickey (Mike Hammer)
    Stout, Rex (Nero Wolfe and Archie Goodwin)
    Tidyman, Ernest (John Shaft, African-American)
    Vachss, Andrew (Burke)

- Ohio
  - Roberts, Les (Milan Jacovich)
  - Valin, Jonathan (Harry Stoner, Cincinnati)

- Oklahoma
  - Knickmeyer, Steve (Steve Cranmer, Oklahoma City)

- Oregon
  - Wren, M. K. (Conan Flagg)

- South Dakota
  - Adams, Harold (Carl Wilcox, Depression era)

- Tennessee
  - Womack, Steven (Harry James Denton, Nashville)

- Texas
  - Abshire, Richard (Jack Kyle)
  - Mathis, Edward (Dan Roman, Dallas)

- Utah
  - Irvine, R. R. (Moroni Traveler)

- Virginia
  - Hornig, Doug (Loren Swift, Charlottesville)

- Washington (all Seattle)
  - Beck, K. K. (Jane da Silva)
  - Emerson, Earl W. (Thomas Black)
  - Ford, G. M. (Leo Waterman)
  - Hoyt, Richard (John Denson)

Ex-Cops

Former police officers now working as private investigators are featured in a subgenre that offers the best of both major types of sleuths. The investigator has an autonomy and independence that are not possible within the confines of an official law enforcement agency, while at the same time he or she can believably display a knowledge and use of police procedures. The sleuth often still has friends on the force who can give him or her inside information and test results. Some of the following sleuths are also listed in the "Police Detectives" section (see p. 71) because they played the role of police detectives in their earlier books.

Abshire, Richard (Jack Kyle)
Barnes, Linda (Carlotta Carlyle)
Bass, Milton (Vinnie Altob)
Block, Lawrence (Matthew Scudder)
Burke, James Lee (Dave Robicheaux)

Cook, Bruce (Chico Cervantes)

Craig, Philip R. (Jeff Jackson)

Daniel, David (Alex Rasmussen)

Dobyns, Stephen (Charlie Bradshaw)

Dunning, John (Cliff Janeway)

Geller, Michael (Slots Resnick)

Gillis, Jackson (Jonas Duncan)

Haddam, Jane (Gregor Demarkian)

Love, William F. (Davey Goldman)

Lutz, John (Fred Carver, physically handicapped)

Margolis, Seth Jacob (Joe Di Gregorio)

Pendleton, Don (Joe Copp)

Raleigh, Michael (Paul Whelan)

Solomita, Stephen (Stanley Moodrow)

Wambaugh, Joseph (Winnie Farlowe)

Wesley, Valerie Wilson (Tamara Hayle)

Whittingham, Richard (Joe Morrison)

Amateur Detectives

Amateur detectives appear in every walk of life. The amateur detective may simply be nosy, becoming inquisitively involved in mysteries natural to the amateur's ordinary life. Others are in somewhat unusual occupations. Most have their share of eccentricities. Unlike either the police or private investigators, they have no official responsibilities. Indeed, they are often an annoyance to the police. Their means of investigation are limited, although they often work cooperatively with the police. Women are often portrayed as amateur detectives and the curious spinster has been a stereotype from earlier years. Retirees with extra time on their hands are an emerging subgenre of the amateur detective. In the following list of amateur detectives, occupations are noted. The following lists include various groupings (for example, senior citizens, doctors, psychologists, lawyers, rogues, or thieves).

Allbert, Susan Wittig (China Bayles, herb shop proprietor)

Allen, Rene (Elizabeth Elliot, clerk of a Quaker meeting)

Asimov, Isaac (Henry, a waiter; Black Widowers series)

Barrett, Neal, Jr. (Wiley Moss, illustrator; wacky but grisly humor)

Barthelme, Peter (Beaumont, ad man)

Berry, Carole (Bonnie Indermill, office temp)

Borland, John C. (Donald McCarry, stockbroker)

Breen, Jon L. (Jack Brogan, racetrack announcer, California)

Brett, Simon (Charles Paris, actor)

Chittenden, Margaret. (Charlie Plato, co-owner of a country western dance club)

Cole, Jameson (*A Killing in Quail County*, teenager, 1957)

Delving, Michael (Dave Cannon and Bob Eddison, dealers in antiquities)

Dentinger, Jane (Jocelyn O'Roarke, actor)

Dominic, R. B. (Ben Stafford, member of Congress)

Fennelly, Tony (Matt Sinclair, antiques dealer)

Ferrars, E. X. (Andrew Basnett, retired professor)

Foley, Rae (Hiram Potter, New York society figure)

Gash, Jonathan (Lovejoy, antiques dealer)

Gollin, James (Alan French, musician)

Hadley, Joan (Theo Bloomer, botanist)

Hammond, Gerald (Keith Calder, gunsmith, Scotland)

Holt, Samuel (Sam Holt, actor)

Jacobs, Jonnie (Kate Ausern, mom, Marin County, California)

Jorgensen, Christine T. (Stella the Stargazer, astrological advice columnist, Denver)

Lacey, Sarah (Leah Hunter, tax inspector)

Lathen, Emma (John Putnam Thatcher, banker)

Leasor, James (Dr. Jason Love, insurance investigator)

Leather, Edwin (Rupert Conway, art dealer)

Lee, Barbara (Eve Elliot, real estate agent, rural Virginia)

Linscott, Gillian (Birdie Linnett)

Malcolm, John (Tim Simpson, art investment advisor)

McCormick, Clair (John Wirtz, "headhunter")

McCrumb, Sharyn (Elizabeth MacPherson, anthropologist)

Moore, Barbara (Gordon Christy, veterinarian, New Mexico)

Morison, B. J. (Elizabeth Lamb, child)

Murray, William ("Shifty" Lou Anderson, gambler-magician, Los Angeles racetrack)

Orenstein, Frank (Ev Franklin, advertising)

Pentecost, Hugh (Pierre Chambrun, hotel manager)

Pickard, Nancy (Jenny Cain, administrator)

Pulver, Mary Monica (Kori Brichter, heiress and cop's wife)

Rowe, Jennifer (Verity Birdwood, Australian TV researcher)

Sherwood, John (Celia Grant, botanist)

Sprinkle, Patricia (Sheila Travis)

Sublett, Jesse (Martin Fender, R & B bass player)

Taylor, Phoebe Atwood (Asey Mayo, New Englander)

Williams, David (Mark Treasure, banker)

Womack, Steven (Jack Lynch, troubleshooter, New Orleans)

Senior Citizen Sleuths

Active, inquisitive retired folks with time on their hands turn to solving crime. The prototype is of course Agatha Christie's Miss Jane Marple. Even though many of the sleuths are still working and not retired, they have the seasoning of age and those listed here have passed age 60.

Babson, Marian (Trixie Dolan and Evangaline Sinclair, aging movie stars)

Barth, Richard (Margaret Binton, retired)

 3

Burton, D. B. (Cat Caliban, 60-year-old widow)

Comfort, B. (Tish McWinny, septuagenarian, Vermont)

Dams, Jeanne M. (Dorothy Martin, widow, American living in England)

Ferrars, E. X. (Andrew Basnett, retired professor)

Gray, Gallagher (T. S. Hubbert, retired Wall Street executive and his octogenarian Aunt Lil)

Landrum, Graham (members of Borderville, Virginia, and Tennessee clubs)

Livingston, Nancy (G. D. H. Pringle, retired accountant, and Mavis Bignell, London)

Mancini, Anthony (Minnie Santangelo, elderly resident of New York's Little Italy)

Matteson, Stefanie (Charlotte Graham, 70-something movie star)

Ruryk, Jean (Cat Wilde, 60-something furniture restorer)

Sawyer, Corinne Holt (Angela Benbow and Caledonia Wingate, widowed residents of a San Diego retirement home)

Healthcare Professionals

The doctor is a natural amateur who is often involved with a suspicious or unnatural death. P. D. James has used the background effectively in her Commander Dalgliesh. Psychologists, psychiatrists, and pathologists are included. In the following list, the healthcare provider is the actual sleuth. Because this setting is closely linked to that of forensic science, readers may enjoy both.

Physicians and Nurses

Bell, Josephine (Dr. David Wintringham)

Boyer, Rick (Doc Adams, oral surgeon)

Eberhart, Mignon Good (Nurse Sarah Keate)

Kittredge, Mary (Edwina Crusoe, R.N.)

Rinehart, Mary Roberts (Nurse Adams, *Miss Pinkerton*)

Psychologists and Psychiatrists

Those that deal with the mind find more than their fair share of crimes that need solving. In many ways the psychological sleuth is like the doctor or nurse sleuth.

> Kellerman, Jonathan (Alex Delaware, psychologist)
>
> Kennett, Shirley (P. J. Gray, psychological profiler)
>
> Matthews, Alex (Cassidy McCabe, therapist)
>
> White, Stephen Walsh (Dr. Alan Gregory, psychologist, Colorado)
>
> Zimmerman, Bruce (Quinn Parker, phobia therapist)

Forensic Scientists

> Connor, Beverly (Lindsay Chamberlain, forensic anthropologist)
>
> Cornwell, Patricia D. (Kay Scarpetta, medical examiner series)
>
> Deaver, Jeffery. (Lincoln Rhyme, quadriplegic criminologist)
>
> Donaldson, D. J. (Dr. Kit Franklin, criminal psychologist, and Chief Medical Examiner Andy Broussard)
>
> Elkins, Aaron (Gideon Oliver, forensic anthropologist)
>
> Johansen, Iris: *The Face of Deception; The Killing Game* (Eve Duncan, forensic sculptor)
>
> McCloy, Helen (Dr. Basil Willing, forensic psychiatrist)
>
> Reichs, Kathy: *Deja Dead; Death du Jour* (Tempe Brennan, forensic anthropologist)

Lawyers

Lawyers might qualify more as private investigators than as amateurs because they seek to extricate clients from jeopardy. This type of detective story often features scenes of courtroom interrogation in which all is revealed, often dramatically. In some of the following books, the reader is treated to considerable analysis of the law, which can be confusing for U.S. readers when the focus is on British jurisprudence. Jon Breen's bibliography, *Novel Verdicts: A Guide to Courtroom Fiction,* supplies this background information.

The legal thriller achieved great prominence in the 1990s. Scott Turow, John Grisham, and Steve Martini all made it to the best-seller lists with their crime novels that feature lawyers. However, the legal thriller's emphasis is not necessarily on detection but rather on a crafty attorney's abilities to extricate himself, herself, or others from danger. The legal thriller is covered later in this chapter (see p. 131).

Canada

> Deverell, William (Carrington Barr, Toronto, *Street Legal: The Betrayal*)

Great Britain

Caudwell, Sarah (Professor Hilary Tamar, Oxford don, and his inimitable Lincoln's Inn lawyer friends, including two delightful women lawyers, Julia Larwood and Selena Jardine)

Cecil, Henry (The detection and mystery in this British author's novels are urban social comedy concerning both lawyers and judges. *Daughters in Law* features women lawyers.)

Giroux, E. X. (Robert Forsythe)

Meek, M. R. D. (Lennox Kemp)

Mortimer, John (Horace Rumpole of the Bailey)

Underwood, Michael (Rose Epton, London)

Woods, Sara (Anthony Maitland)

United States

Egan, Lesley (Jesse Falkenstein, Los Angeles)

Gardner, Erle Stanley (Over 80 novels, the first in 1933, celebrate Perry Mason with his aides, Paul Drake and Della Street. Gardner's total is about 103 volumes.)

Hailey, J. P. (Steve Winslow)

Hall, Parnell (Stanley Hastings, ambulance chaser)

Hensley, Joe L. (Don Robak)

Jacobs, Jonnie (Kali O'Brien, San Francisco)

Kruger, Paul (Phil Kramer, Colorado)

Lewis, Roy (Eric Ward)

Maron, Margaret (Deborah Knott, North Carolina)

McBain, Ed (Matthew Hope, Florida)

McInerny, Ralph (Andrew Broom, Indiana)

Murphy, Haughton (Reuben Frost)

Nielsen, Helen (Simon Drake, Los Angeles)

Pairo, Preston (Dallas Henry, Ocean City, Maryland)

Parker, Barbara (Gail Connor, Miami)

Phillips, Edward (Chadwick)

Smith, Julie (Rebecca Schwartz, San Francisco)

Stockley, Grif (Gideon Page, Arkansas)

Tapply, William G. (Brady Coyne, Boston)

Van Gieson, Judith. (Neil Hamel, Albuquerque)

Wilhelm, Kate. (Barbara Holloway, Oregon)

Yarbro, Chelsea Quinn (Charles Spotted Moon, Ojibwa, San Francisco)

Rogue or Thief

The tradition of rogue or thief as detective is so well established in detective novels that it nearly eclipses the status of amateur detectives. However, this is a convenient niche for listing the following books. Some private investigators skirt the fringes of roguery. The rogues in the following novels are all cheerfully amoral.

Block, Lawrence (Bernard Rhodenbarr is a burglar who runs a bookstore on the side. One of his adventures, *The Burglar Who Liked to Quote Kipling*, will intrigue those who like bibliography and rare books mixed with murder.)

Bonfiglioli, Kyril (Honorable Charles Mortdecai, rogue)

Charteris, Leslie (Simon Templar, "The Saint," Robin Hood type)

Creasey, John (the honorable Richard Rollison, "The Toff," gentleman burglar, "the poor man's Lord Peter Wimsey")

Hoch, Edward D. (Nick Velvet, thief)

Hornung, E. W. (The exploits of Raffles, gentleman cracksman, have been continued by Barry Perowne.)

Morton, Anthony (Reprints reveal authorship by John Creasey, who used this pseudonym for the cases of John Mannering, "The Baron," jewel thief turned detective.)

Parrish, Frank (Don Mallett, poacher, British)

Shaw, Simon (Philip Gletcher, actor and murderer)

Ecclesiastical

While those in the clergy usually watch out for the souls of the faithful and those in need, the following sleuths often find themselves investigating people wrongly accused and subsequently discovering the real culprits. Historical mysteries featuring the clergy are included in the historical mystery section later in this chapter.

Black, Veronica (Sister Joan, Catholic nun, Cornwall)

Chesterton, G. K. (Father Brown, Roman Catholic, British)

Coel, Margaret (Father John O'Malley, Arapaho Indian reservation, Wyoming)

Greeley, Andrew (Father Blackie Ryan)

Holmes, H. H. (Sister Mary Ursula, Order of the Sisters of Martha of Bethany, Los Angeles. Also reprinted under the better-known pseudonym Anthony Boucher.)

Kemelman, Harry (Rabbi David Small, New England)

Kienzle, William X. (Father Bob Koesler, Roman Catholic, Detroit)

Love, William F. (Bishop Ragan)

McInerny, Ralph (Father Dowling, Roman Catholic, Chicago area)

O'Marie, Sister Carol Anne (Sister Mary Helen)

Pérez-Reverte, Arturo (Father Lorenzo Quart, Holy Office's Institute for External Affairs, in *The Seville Communion*)

Quill, Monica (Sister Mary Teresa Dempster)

Smith, Charles (Reverend C. P. Randolph, Episcopal Church, Chicago)

Sullivan, Winona (Sister Cecile, licensed private investigator and nun)

English Aristocrat

That everyone loves a lord is a questionable truism, but many readers of detective stories are intrigued by the aristocrat as amateur detective. This detective is similar to the gentleman detective, whether as police or amateur: Ngaio Marsh's Inspector Roderick Alleyn, Michael Innes's Sir John Appleby, S. S. Van Dine's Philo Vance, and Frederic Dannay's Ellery Queen are a few examples. The following are notable upper-class detectives.

Allingham, Margery (Albert Campion)

Dickinson, Peter (King of England, *King and Joker*)

George, Elizabeth (Inspector Thomas Linley, Eighth Earl of Asherton)

Ross, Kate (Julian Kestrel)

Sayers, Dorothy L. (Lord Peter Wimsey)

Academic

The "College and University" section (see p. 108) lists novels that have academic backgrounds, but the professors therein are not necessarily the detectives. The professors in the following novels use their scholarly training for crime detection, and not always on the campus. Eccentricity—that obvious characteristic of academics—is present in most.

Arnold, Margot (Penny Spring and Sir Toby Glendower)

Bowen, Gail (Joanne Kilbourne, widowed professor, Saskatchewan, Canada)

Bruce, Leo (Carolus Deane, schoolteacher, London)

Clinton-Baddeley, V. C. (Dr. Davie, Cambridge don)

Cory, Desmond (Professor John Dobie)

Crispin, Edmund (Dr. Gervase Fen, Cambridge don)

Cross, Amanda (Dr. Kate Fansler, professor of English)

Dean, S. F. X. (Professor Neal Kelly)

Elkins, Aaron (Dr. Gideon Oliver, anthropologist)

Haynes, Conrad (Professor Bishop)

Kelly, Nora (Gillian Adams, professor of history)

Kemelman, Harry (Professor Nicky Welt)

Levi, Peter (Ben Johnson)

MacLeod, Charlotte (Professor Peter Shandy, New England)

Reeves, Robert (Professor Thomas Theron)

Smith, Joan (Loretta Lawson, London University lecturer)

Stinson, Jim (Stoney Wilson, film instructor)

Truman, Margaret (Mac Smith, law professor)

Journalists

The investigative reporter may also be considered a private detective (without license) and is often listed as a detective type in critical works on the genre. Books by the following authors illustrate this type of character.

Babson, Marian (Doug Perkins)

Beechcroft, William (Forrest)

Burke, Jan (Irene Kelly)

Dalheim, Mary (Emma Lord, Washington, owner-publisher of a small newspaper)

D'Amato, Barbara (Cat Marsala)

Gorman, Ed (Tobin)

Jaffe, Jody (Natalie Gold, North Carolina)

Kiker, Douglas (Mac McFarland)

Lupica, Mike (Peter Finley, television newsman)

Phillips, Mike (Sampson Dean, African-American)

Porter, Anna (Judith Hayes, reporter)

Rawlings, Ellen (Rachel Crowne)

Riggs, John R. (Garth Ryland, newspaper editor and owner)

Robinson, Kevin (Stick Foster, wheelchair-bound reporter)

Shuman, M. K. (Pete Brady, Louisiana)

Stout, David (Will Schafer, newspaper editor)

Walker, Mary Willis (magazine journalist, Texas)

Warmbold, Jean (Sarah Calloway)

Wilcox, Collin (Stephen Drake, crime reporter)

Wilcox, Stephen F. (T. S. W. Sheridan, freelance reporter)

Husband-and-Wife Teams

A combination of considerable charm is the married pair of sleuths. The increase in recent years of the importance of relationships in the lives of sleuths is evidenced by the increasing number of paired significant others appearing on the following list.

Allen, Steve (Steve Allen and Jayne Meadows, *The Murder Game*)

Browne, Gerald A. (Mitch and Maddie Laughton, *West 47th*)

Dank, Gloria (Bernard and Snooky Woodruff)

Ferrars, E. X. (Virginia and Felix Freer. He is an ex-husband, but still they are a *pair* of sleuths.)

Hammett, Dashiell (Nick and Nora Charles, *The Thin Man*)

Hammond, Gerald (Inspector Ian Fellows and wife Deborah)

Kellerman, Faye (Orthodox Jewish housewife Rina Lazarus and her husband, LAPD Detective Sergeant Peter Decker)

Lockridge, Frances, and Richard Lockridge (Pam and Jerry North)

MacGregor, T. J. (Quin St. James and Mike McCleary)

Sandstrom, Eve K. (Sheriff Sam and wife Nicky Titus, Oklahoma)

Sayers, Dorothy L. (Lord Peter and Harriet Vane, *Busman's Honeymoon, Thrones, Dominations*)

Truman, Margaret (Mac Smith and Annabel Reed)

Whitney, Polly (Abby Abbegnarro and Ike Tygart, divorced but still a pair)

Wilhelm, Kate (Charlie Meiklejohn and Constance Leidl)

 3

Human-and-Animal Teams

Americans have a great affection for and fascination with the pets in their lives. Several authors write about human sleuths or animal sleuths working together with the other species. The most famous team is probably that of Qwilleran and his cats KoKo and YumYum, in the series written by Lilian Jackson Braun.

Adamson, Lydia (Alice Nestleton cat mysteries: 13 titles as of 1998)

Benjamin, Carol Lea (Rachel Alexander, P.I., and her pit bull Dashiell)

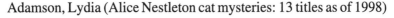

Berenson, Laurien (Melanie Travis dog fancier series: 5 titles as of 1998)

Braun, Lilian Jackson (The Cat Who series: 20 titles as of 1998, featuring Qwilleran, a human journalist, and KoKo and YumYum, of the Siamese persuasion)

Brown, Rita Mae (Mary Minor "Harry" Haristeen, postmistress, and feline Sneaky Pie, with occasional assistance from canine Tee Tucker)

Cleary, Melissa (Jackie Walsh and her shepherd, Jake)

Conant, Susan J. (The Dog Lover's series, featuring Holly Winter and Alaskan malamutes Rowdy and Kimi; 11 titles as of 1998)

Douglas, Carole Nelson (Midnight Louis series:(Las Vegas publicist Miss Temple Barr and Midnight Louie, a studly, big black cat)

Guiver, Patricia (Delilah Doolittle, British widow, and her Doberman, Watson, California)

Detective Backgrounds

Who a detective is—his or her gender, race, ethnicity, and sexual orientation—plays a major role in how that detective relates to the crime to be solved, as well as to the world in general. A variety of backgrounds bring a wealth of diversity to the detective novel, adding fascinating insights to the unfolding of the characters within.

Gay and Lesbian

Mysteries featuring lesbian characters are a staple of the lesbian publishing trade. Naiad Press and Cleis Press frequently publish lesbian mysteries. Often, the stories contain sex and romance along with the mystery. Many are published in trade paperback; however, mysteries featuring gay men are more often produced in hardcover by major publishers. Alyson does publish gay mysteries, but gay detectives are just as likely to be published by major houses. Joseph Hansen's Dave Brandstetter novels have been published by Viking and Mysterious Press, while Michael Nava's mysteries have been published by HarperCollins.

Nancy Clue and the Case of the Not-So-Nice Nurse, by Mabel Maney, is a delightful parody of both long-standing series read and loved by children (for example, Nancy Drew, Cherry Ames) and lesbian mystery novels.

> Allen, Kate (Alison Kane, *Tell Me What You Like*)
>
> Baker, Nikki (Virginia Kelly)
>
> Hansen, Joseph (David Brandstetter, insurance investigator)
>
> Hart, Ellen (Jane Lawless, restaurateur)
>
> Knight, Phyllis (Lil Ritchie, private investigator)
>
> Maiman, Jaye (Robin Miller)
>
> McNab, Claire (Detective Inspector Carol Ashton)
>
> Myers, John L. (David Harriman, *Holy Family*)
>
> Nava, Michael (Henry Rios, lawyer)
>
> Outland, Orland (Doan McCandler, drag queen, *Death Wore a Smart Little Outfit*)
>
> Phillips, Edward (Chadwick)
>
> Redman, J. M. (Micky Knight, lesbian P.I.)
>
> Scoppettone, Sandra (Lauren Laurano)
>
> Welch, Pat (Helen Black)
>
> Wings, Mary (Emma Victor, private investigator)

Black Sleuths

Frankie Y. Bailey takes a historical and scholarly look at black characters in his *Out of the Woodpile: Black Characters in Crime and Detective Fiction* (Greenwood, 1991). The author includes a directory of black characters in crime and detective fiction, film, and television. The book lists exotic settings and backgrounds and includes historical crime novels. There is an annotated sampling of detective cases and, most important (to readers of this guide), a list of black detectives in fiction. Paula L. Woods's award-winning anthology *Spooks, Spies and Private Eyes: Black Mystery, Crime, and Suspense Fiction of the 20th Century* (Doubleday, 1995) features original, long-lost, and recent examples of the diversity to be found in tales of crime written by blacks. The following list of books is just a small sampling of detective novels featuring black sleuths.

> Ball, John D. (Virgil Tibbs)
>
> Baxt, George (Pharaoh Love)
>
> Bland, Eleanor Taylor (Marti MacAlister, homicide detective)
>
> Burke, J. F. (Sam Kelly, house detective)
>
> Edwards, Grace F. (Mali Anderson, ex-cop)
>
> Grimes, Terris McMahan (Theresa Galloway, *Somebody Else's Child*)
>
> Haywood, Gar Anthony (Aaron Gunner, private investigator, Los Angeles)
>
> Hill, Reginald (Sixsmith, a lathe operator turned private detective)
>
> Holton, Hugh (Chicago Police Commander Larry Cole)
>
> Komo, Dolores (Clio Browne)
>
> Mason, Clifford (Joe Cinquez, Harlem)
>
> Mosley, Walter (Easy Rawlins, private investigator)
>
> Neely, Barbara (Blanche, a cleaning woman*)*
>
> Patterson, James (Alex Cross, police forensic psychologist)
>
> Smith-Levin, Judith (police lieutenant Starletta Duvall, Worcester, Massachusetts)
>
> Wesley, Valerie Wilson (Tamara Hayle, private investigator)
>
> Woods, Paula L. (Charlotte Justice, police officer)
>
> York, Andrew (Colonel James Munro Tallant, black police commissioner, Caribbean island)

Hispanic Sleuths

Unfortunately, there is not yet a book like Bailey's *Out of the Woodpile* for either Hispanic or Native American crime and detective fiction, but it is likely that publishing in these areas will continue to grow in the next years to meet increasing reader demand.

> Anaya, Rudolfo (Sonny Baca, P.I., Albuquerque)
>
> Burns, Rex (Gabe Wager, Denver)
>
> Cook, Bruce (Chico Cervantes, private investigator)
>
> Ramos, Manuel (Luis Montez, lawyer, Denver)
>
> Taibo, Paco Ignacio (Hector Belascoaran Shayne, Mexico City)

Native American Sleuths

Bowen, Peter (Gabriel Du Pre, Metis)

Doss, James D. (Charlie Moon, Ute Tribal Police)

Hager, Jean (Mitch Bushyhead, police chief; Molly Bearpaw, Native American League)

Hillerman, Tony (Jim Chee and Joe Leaphorn, Navajo Tribal Police)

Medawar, Mardi Oakley (Tay-bodal, a Kiowa healer in the 1860s)

Perry, Thomas (Jane Whitehead, Seneca)

Stabenow, Dana (Kate Shugak, Aleut)

Stern, Richard Martin (Lieutenant Johnny Ortiz, Apache)

Thurlo, Aimee, and David Thurlo (Agent Ella Clah, Navaho, FBI)

Yarbro, Chelsea Quinn (Charles Spotted Moon, Ojibwa, San Francisco)

Asian Sleuths

Cunningham, E. V. (Masao Masuto, Nisei, Beverly Hills)

Furutani, Dale (Ken Tanaka, Japanese-American; Matsuyama Kaze, seventeenth-century Japan)

Glass, Leslie (April Woo, Chinese-American)

Massey, Sujata (*The Salaryman's Wife; Zen Attitude;* Rei Shimura, Japanese-American English teacher living in Tokyo)

Rowland, Laura Joh (Samurai Sano Ichiro, seventeenth-century Japan)

Rozan, S. J. (Lydia Chin, Chinese-American)

Wingate, Anne (Mark Shigata, Japanese-American)

Women Detectives

The species deadlier than the male appears in all types of detective stories. In her nineteenth-century origins in the genre, the woman detective tended to lean heavily on intuition. In more modern examples, while often remaining womanly, she uses her wits as ably as does the male detective. Many fans still identify with the stereotyped, sometimes memorable, spinster sleuth, neatly described by the vicar in Agatha Christie's first Miss Marple case, *Murder at the Vicarage* (1930): "There is no detective in England equal to a spinster lady of uncertain age with plenty of time on her hands."

Women detectives have steadily been gaining ground since 1980. Since 1990 the growth has been explosive. V. I. Warshawski had her own eponymous film; Arly Hanks and Harry Haristeen have been seen on television. Much of the growth of women in the genre can be attributed to Sisters in Crime, an organization that promotes and provides support to women who write crime fiction. Several books dealing with women and mysteries have been published recently. *By a Woman's Hand*, second edition, by Jean Swanson and Dean James (Berkley, 1996), profiles over 200 women authors, their characters, book plots, and titles. Willetta L. Heising's *Detecting Women 3* (Purple Moon Press, 2000) lists more than 800 series detectives and over 3,700 mystery titles written by women, in order of mystery series.

It would be impossible to list all female sleuths appearing in crime fiction, but the following list serves to provide a sampling of the great variety of women solving crimes in novels. Several of the listings in this category are repeated from other sections.

Barnes, Linda (Carlotta Carlyle, private investigator)

Barth, Richard (Margaret Binton, retired)

Berry, Carole (Bonnie Underhill, amateur)

Bland, Eleanor Taylor (Marti MacAlister, black homicide detective)

Brett, Simon (Mrs. Melita Pargeter, amateur)

Brown, Rita Mae (Mary Minor "Harry" Haristeen, postmistress)

Burke, Jan (Irene Kelly, newspaper reporter)

Cannell, Dorothy (Ellie Haskell)

Carlson, P. M. (Maggie Ryan, statistician)

Carvic, Heron, continued by Hamilton Crane and Hampton Charles (Miss Seaton, British spinster)

Christie, Agatha (Miss Jane Marple, spinster)

Coker, Carolyn (Andrea Perkins, art restorer)

Cooper, Susan Rogers (E. J. Pugh, romance-writing suburban mom)

Cornwell, Patricia D. (Kay Scarpetta, medical examiner)

Cross, Amanda (Kate Fansler, professor, New York)

D'Amato, Barbara (Cat Marsala, freelance journalist)

Davis, Dorothy Salisbury (Julie Hayes, amateur)

Dunlap, Susan (Detective Jill Smith, police; Vejay Haskell, meter reader)

Evanovich, Janet (Stephanie Plum, bounty hunter and former discount lingerie buyer)

Fowler, Earlene (Benni Harper, curator of folk art museum, California)

Fraser, Antonia (Jemima Shore, television reporter)

Grace, C. L. (Kathryn Swinbrooke, medieval physician)

Grafton, Sue (Kinsey Millhone, private investigator)

Grant, Linda (Catherine Saylor, high-tech P.I.)

Hager, Jean (Molly Bearpaw, investigator for the Native American Advocacy League)

Hess, Joan (Arly Hanks, small-town chief of police; Claire Malloy, amateur)

Holt, Hazel (Sheila Malory, British widow)

Hornsby, Wendy (Maggie MacGowen, investigative filmmaker)

Jance, J. A. (Joanna Brady, widow of a sheriff's deputy)

Keating, H. R. F. (Mrs. Craggs, charlady, England)

Kelly, Susan (Liz Connors, writer)

Kijewski, Karen (Kat Colorado, private investigator)

Kittredge, Mary (Charlotte Kent, writer; Edwina Crusoe, R.N.)

Knight, Kathryn Lasky (Calista Jacobs, illustrator)

MacLeod, Charlotte (Sarah Kelling, amateur)

Martin, Lee (Deb Ralston, Fort Worth Police Department)

McCrumb, Sharyn (Elizabeth MacPherson, anthropologist)

McQuillan, Karin (Jazz Jasper, safari guide and animal activist)

Melville, Jennie (Detective Sergeant Charmian Daniels, British)

Mitchell, Gladys (Dame Beatrice Bradley, psychiatrist)

Morice, Anne (Tessa Chrichton, actress)

Muller, Marcia (Sharon McCone, private eye; Elena Oliverez, art curator)

O'Donnell, Lillian (Detective Norah Mulcahany, New York Police Department)

Osborn, David (Margaret Barlow, 50-something photojournalist)

Palmer, Stuart (Hildegarde Withers, spinster)

Papazoglou, Orania (Patience McKenna, writer)

Paretsky, Sara (V. I. Warshawski, private investigator)

Peters, Elizabeth (Amelia Peabody, archaeologist; Jacqueline Kirby, librarian)

Pickard, Nancy (Jenny Cain, administrator)

Quinn, Elizabeth (Lauren Maxwell, widowed mom and investigator for a nonprofit wildlife organization)

Roberts, Gillian (Amanda Pepper, English teacher)

Roosevelt, Elliott (First Lady Eleanor Roosevelt)

Shankman, Sarah (Samantha Adams, crime reporter)

Shannon, Dell (Delia Reardon, Los Angeles Police Department)

Sherwood, John (Celia Grant, botanist)

Slovo, Gillian (Kat Baeier, private investigator)

Smith, Joan (Loretta Lawson, London University lecturer)

Smith, Julie (Skip Langdon, New Orleans homicide detective)

Smith, Julie (Rebecca Schwartz, lawyer. Interestingly enough, there are two Julie Smiths. Their novels are quite different from each other, but both feature strong, engrossing women detectives.)

Stabenow, Dana (Kate Shugak, former district attorney)

Taylor, Elizabeth Atwood (Maggie Elliott, private investigator)

Trocheck, Kathy Hogan (Callahan Garrity, cleaning lady, formerly a cop)

Van Gieson, Judith (Neil Hamel, private investigator)

Warner, Mignon (Mrs. Edwina Charles, clairvoyant)

Watson, Clarissa (Persis Willum, art curator)

Weir, Charlene (Susan Wren, police chief)

White, Gloria (Ronnie Ventana, private investigator)

Wings, Mary (Emma Victor, private investigator)

Wolzien, Valerie (Susan Henshaw, suburban homemaker)

Detective Story Settings and Subjects

Just as many readers of detective fiction prefer a particular type of detective, others seek those stories with a particular background of country, social order, activity, organization, or profession. With the advent of automated catalogs and Library of Congress/OCLC GSAFD fiction subject headings and products like NoveList from Carl Corp., it is now fairly easy to locate mysteries with particular settings or subjects. There is also a guide for selecting titles by locale, Nina King's *Crimes of the Scene: A Mystery Novel Guide for the International Traveler* (St. Martin's Press, 1997).

Following are several of the available anthologies that deal with settings and subjects. A few examples of subject groupings are included after the list to show the readers' advisory potential of analysis by type.

Douglas, Carole Nelson. *Midnight Louie's Pet Detectives*. Forge, 1998.

Gorman, Ed, Martin H. Greenberg, and Larry Segriff, eds. *Cat Crimes Through Time*. Carroll & Graf, 1999.

Hillerman, Tony, ed. *The Mysterious West*. HarperCollins, 1994.

MacLeod, Charlotte, ed. *Christmas Stalkings: Tales of Yuletide Murder*. Warner, 1992.

Marks, Jeffrey, ed. *Canine Crimes*. Ballantine, 1998.

Mosiman, Billie Sue, and Martin Harry Greenberg, eds. *Blowout in Little Man Flats: And Other Spine-Tingling Stories of Murder in the West*. Rutledge Hill Press, 1998.

Pickard, Nancy, ed. *Mom, Apple Pie, and Murder*. Prime Crime, 1999.

Wheat, Carolyn, ed. *Murder on Route 66*. Prime Crime, 1999.

Locked Room

The locked room is a classic plot device used by many different authors over the years. John Dickson Carr wrote several of these. In *The Three Coffins* (British title: *The Hollow Man*), his detective, Dr. Gideon Fell, explains the problem of the locked room in a neat discourse. More recent examples can be found in *Death Cruise: Crime Stories on the Open Seas,* edited by Lawrence Block (Cumberland House, 1999), in which a cruise ship is the ultimate "locked room."

Sports

The players, owners, and commentators find the final score in settings involving both amateur and high-stakes professional sports.

> Coben, Harlan (Myron Bolitar, sports agent)
>
> Elkins, Charlotte, and Aaron Elkins (Lee Ofsted, women's professional golf)
>
> Enger, L. L. (Gun Pedersen, baseball)
>
> Francis, Dick (jockey, trainer, and others connected with British horse racing)
>
> Geller, Michael (Slots Resnick, baseball)
>
> Gordon, Alison (Kate Henry, baseball writer)
>
> Hammond, Gerald (John Cunningham, hunting)
>
> Llewellyn, Sam (boating)
>
> Miles, Keith (professional golf)
>
> Nighbert, David F. (Bull Cochran, baseball)
>
> Soos, Troy (Mickey Rawlings, baseball player in the second decade of the twentieth century)

Strip Joints

The environs of ecdysiasts have appeared with great frequency in crime stories in the last several years. Somehow the denizens of these dens of iniquity make interesting witnesses and victims of crime.

Block, Lawrence
The Topless Tulip Caper: A Chip Harrison Novel.

Douglas, Carole Nelson
Pussyfoot.

Fennelly, Tony
The Hippie in the Wall.

Gilpin, T. G.
The Death of a Fantasy Life.

Hamilton, Laurell K.
Guilty Pleasures. An eccentric variation of mystery combined with science fiction and horror, in which the murders take place in a vampire strip joint.

Hiaasen, Carl
Strip Tease.

Ritz, David
Take It Off, Take It All Off.

Cookery

Mm-mm-good … Dining plays a major role in the following selection of mysteries, in which food and cooking are very important. Some even include recipes!

Babson, Marian
Death Warmed Over.

Barnes, Linda
Cities of the Dead.

Bond, Michael
The character's dog is Pommes Frites.

3

> **Monsieur Pamplemousse.**
>
> **Monsieur Pamplemousse and the Secret Mission.**
>
> **Monsieur Pamplemousse Aloft.**

Davidson, Diane Mott

> **Catering to Nobody.**
>
> **Dying for Chocolate.**
>
> **The Cereal Murders.**
>
> **The Last Suppers.**
>
> **Killer Pancake.**
>
> **The Main Corpse.**
>
> **The Grilling Season.**
>
> **Prime Cut.**

Laurence, Janet
Featuring Darina Lisle, caterer/cookbook writer.

Lewis, Shelby
Delicious. A romantic mystery featuring Bailey Walker, an African-American caterer.

Lyons, Nan, and Ivan Lyons
> **Someone Is Killing the Great Chefs of Europe.**
>
> **Someone Is Killing the Great Chefs of America.**

Myers, Tamar
Pennsylvania Dutch Mystery series. Featuring Magdalena Yoder.

Page, Katherine Hall
Featuring Faith Fairchild, gourmet chef.

Pence, Joanne
Featuring Chef Angie Amalfi.

Pickard, Nancy
27-Ingredient Chili con Carne Murders. Continues the series originated by Virginia Rich.

Rich, Virginia
The series has been continued by Nancy Pickard.

> **The Cooking School Murders.**
>
> **The Baked Bean Supper Murders.**
>
> **The Nantucket Diet Murders.**

Richman, Phyllis
Featuring Chas Wheatley, restaurant critic.

Roudybush, Alexandra
A Gastronomic Murder.

Simmel, Johannes Mario
It Can't Always Be Caviar.

Stout, Rex
Too Many Cooks.

Temple, Lou Jane
Featuring Heaven Lee, restaurateur.

Bibliomysteries

In the following books the amateur sleuths are somehow involved in the world of books, whether as librarians, writers, illustrators, publishers, or booksellers.

Asimov, Isaac
Murder at the ABA.

Blackburn, John
Blue Octavo (alternate title: *Bound to Kill*).

Blackstock, Charity
Dewey Death.

Carter, Robert A.
Casual Slaughters.

Dunning, John
Featuring Cliff Janeway, book collector and expert.

Fiechter, Jean-Jacques
  Death by Publication.

Goodrum, Charles
  Featuring Edward George, Crighton Jones, and Steve Carson.

Hall, Parnell
  Suspense.

Hart, Carolyn G.
  Featuring Annie Laurance and Max Darling, bookstore owner.

Hess, Joan
  Featuring Claire Malloy, bookseller.

  3

James, P. D.
  Original Sin.

Jordan, Jennifer
  Featuring Mr. and Mrs. Barry Vaughan, writers.

Kaewert, Julie Wallin
  Unsolicited.

Knight, Kathryn Lasky
  Featuring Calista Jacobs, illustrator.

Lewis, Roy
  Featuring Matthew Coll, English book dealer.

McGaughey, Neil
  Featuring Stokes Moran, mystery reviewer.

Morley, Christopher
  The Haunted Bookshop.

Papazoglou, Orania
  Featuring Patience McKenna, writer.

Peters, Elizabeth
  Featuring Jacqueline Kirby, librarian/romance writer.

Philbrick, W. R.
  Featuring Jack Hawkins, wheelchair-bound mystery writer.

Rhode, John, and Carter Dickson
  Fatal Descent.

Richardson, Robert
Featuring Augustus Maltravers.

Shankman, Sarah
Featuring Samantha Adams, writer.

Stern, Richard Martin
Manuscript for Murder.

Symons, Julian
The Narrowing Circle.

Valin, Jonathan
Final Notice.

College and University

The college campus, often perceived as a protected environment, becomes a site of crime and intrigue in the following books.

Bernard, Robert
Deadly Meeting.

Blake, Nicholas
The Morning After Death.

Boucher, Anthony
The Case of the Seven of Calvary.

Bradberry, James
The Seventh Sacrament.

Clinton-Baddeley, V. C.
My Foe Outstretched Beneath the Tree.

Cole, G. D. H., and Margaret Cole
Off with Her Head.

Constantine, K. C.
The Blank Page.

Dillon, Ellis
Death in the Quadrangle.

Eustis, Helen
The Horizontal Man.

Fiske, Dorsey
Academic Murder.

Graham, John Alexander
The Involvement of Arnold Wechsler.

Hodgkin, M. R.
Student Body.

Innes, Michael
Death at the President's Lodging.

Old Hall, New Hall.

Johnson, W. Bolingbroke
The Widening Stain.

Levin, Ira
Juliet Dies Twice.

 3

MacKay, Amanda
Death Is Academic.

Masterman, J. C.
An Oxford Tragedy.

Mitchell, Gladys
Fault in the Structure.

Spotted Hemlock.

Rees, Dilwyn
The Cambridge Murders.

Rennert, Maggie
Circle of Death.

Robinson, Robert
Landscape with Dead Dons.

Sayers, Dorothy L.
Gaudy Night.

Vulliamy, C. E.
Don Among the Dead Men.

Genre Writers' Conventions

There is something fascinating about concentrating a number of genre authors and fans in a small space that leads to murder. The Papazoglou and Peters books in the following list take place at romance writers' conventions and contain some very witty criticism, along with delicious quotations, of the romance genre. The McCrumb title, available only in paperback, is about a science fiction convention and has become somewhat of a cult classic. Jessica Fletcher is a fictional author from television's *Murder She Wrote*.

Barnard, Robert
> **The Cherry Blossom Corpse (Death in Purple Prose).**

Fletcher, Jessica, and Donald Bain
> **Gin and Daggers.**

Jones, Diana Wynne
> **Deep Secret.**

McCrumb, Sharyn
> **Bimbos of the Death Sun.**

Papazoglou, Orania
> **Sweet, Savage Love.**

Peters, Elizabeth
> **Die for Love.**

Taylor, L. A.
> **A Murder Waiting to Happen.**

Art World

> Coker, Carolyn (Andrea Perkins, art restorer)
> Inchbald, Peter (Francis Corti, Art and Antiques Squad)
> Leather, Edwin (Rupert Conway, art dealer)
> Malcolm, John (Tim Simpson, art investment advisor)
> Muller, Marcia (Elena Oliverez, art curator)
> Pears, Iain (Art History Mystery series; Jonathan Argyll and Flavia di Stefano)
> Pérez-Reverte, Arturo (*The Flanders Panel*)
> Watson, Clarissa (Persis Willum, art curator)

Historical Mysteries

Mystery and detection novels are essentially timeless: Readers simply accept the period backgrounds. One of the fastest-growing subgenres in mystery is the historical, with the nineteenth century and the medieval period being particularly popular. Some readers seek out the nineteenth-century sources of the detective story in Edgar Allan Poe, Wilkie Collins, Sheridan LeFanu, and others who wrote before the creation of Sherlock Holmes. History fans might find the backgrounds as interesting as the plots. The first few books listed are anthologies indicating the scope of the subgenre.

Hutchings, Janet. *Once Upon a Crime: Historical Mysteries from Ellery Queen's Mystery Magazine*. St. Martin's Press, 1994.

Monfredo, Miriam Grace, and Sharan Newman, eds. *Crime Through Time*. Berkley, 1997. *Crime Through Time II*. Berkley, 1998.

Ackroyd, Peter

Hawksmoor. Some supernatural aspects as a twentieth-century Scotland Yard case is linked to the seventeenth century.

Alexander, Bruce

Featuring Sir John Fielding, eighteenth-century London.

Alexander, Lawrence

The Big Stick.

Speak Softly. Teddy Roosevelt as police commissioner.

Barron, Stephanie

Jane Austen Mystery series.

3

Baxt, George

The Dorothy Parker Murder Case.

The Alfred Hitchcock Murder Case.

Borowitz, Albert

The Jack the Ripper Walking Tour Murder.

Brown, Molly

Invitation to a Funeral. Restoration London.

Buckley, Fiona

Featuring Ursula Blanchard, lady-in-waiting to Queen Elizabeth I.

Burns, Ron

Enslaved.

The Mysterious Death of Meriwether Lewis. Featuring Harrison Hull.

Carr, Caleb

Featuring Dr. Laszlo Kreizler, a psychologist working for the New York Police Force under Teddy Roosevelt, 1896.

The Alienist.

The Angel of Darkness.

Clark, Robert

Mr. White's Confession. Minnesota, 1939.

Clynes, Michael

The White Rose Murders. Featuring Sir Richard Shattot, sixteenth-century Britain.

Collins, Max Allen

The Million-Dollar Wound. Featuring private eye Nate Heller in Chicago of the 1940s.

Cooney, Eleanor, and Daniel Altieri
Deception: A Novel of Murder and Madness in T'ang China.

Davis, Lindsey
Featuring Marcus Didius Falco, Ancient Rome.

Day, Dianne
Featuring Fremont Jones, an independent career woman in turn-of-the-century San Francisco.

The Strange Files of Fremont Jones.

Fire and Fog.

The Bohemian Murders.

Emperor Norton's Ghost.

De La Torre, Lillian
The Exploits of Dr. Sam Johnson, Detector.

Doherty, P. C.
Featuring Hugh Corbett, clerk and spy in the court of Edward II.

Doody, Margaret
Aristotle Detective.

Douglas, Carole Nelson
Featuring Irene Adler, antagonist of Sherlock Holmes, Victorian.

Dunn, Carola
Damsel in Distress. A Daisy Dalrymple Mystery series set in 1920s England.

Eco, Umberto
The Name of the Rose. Featuring Brother William of Baskerville, fourteenth century.

Farnol, Jeffery
Jasper Shrig, Bow Street Runner, appeared in 10 novels by this author of Regency romances; the best known is **The Amateur Gentleman.**

Furutani, Dale
Death at the Crossroads: A Samurai Mystery. Seventeenth-century Japan.

Goulart, Ron
Featuring Groucho Marx, 1930s Hollywood.

Grace, C. L.
Featuring Kathryn Swinbrooke, medieval physician.

Hambly, Barbara

A Free Man of Color.

Fever Season. Featuring Ben January, 1833 New Orleans.

Haney, Lauren

Featuring Lieutenant Bak, ancient Egypt.

Harper, Karen

The Poyson Garden: An Elizabethan Mystery. Sleuthing by the future queen.

Harrison, Ray

Featuring Sergeant Bragg and Constable Morton, 1890s London City Police.

Deathwatch.

Harvest of Death.

Heller, Keith

Featuring George Man, London parish watchman, eighteenth century.

Man's Illegal Life.

Man's Storm.

Hervey, Evelyn

The Governess. London, 1870s.

Hilton, John Buxton

Featuring Inspector Pickford, Detective Brunt, and Sergeant Nadin, Derbyshire, nineteenth century.

Jeffreys, J. G.

Featuring Jeremy Sturrock, Bow Street Runner.

Kaminsky, Stuart M.

Featuring Toby Peters, private eye, Hollywood, in the 1940s, in a series in which actual motion picture stars are characters (for example, John Wayne, Charlie Chaplin).

Lawrence, Margaret

Hannah Trevor, a midwife in eighteenth-century Maine, is drawn into solving mysteries.

Hearts and Bones. Hannah finds the body of a woman who had been tortured, raped, and murdered. A letter left by the deceased points a finger at three men, one of whom Hannah loves.

Blood Red Roses.

The Burning Bride.

Linscott, Gillian

Hanging on the Wire.

Sister Beneath the Sheet. Featuring Nell Bray, English suffragette.

Lovesey, Peter

Featuring Sergeant Cribb and Constable Thackeray, London, nineteenth century.

Bertie and the Seven Bodies.

Bertie and the Tinman. Featuring Prince Albert.

Maher, Mary

The Devil's Card. Nineteenth-century Chicago.

McConnor, Vincent

Featuring François Vidocq, founder of the Sûreté, Paris, nineteenth century.

McMillan, Ann

Dead March. Civil War, Virginia.

Meyers, Maan

The Dutchman. Featuring Sheriff Pieter Tonneman, New Amsterdam, 1664.

The Kingsbridge Plot. Plot to assassinate Washington.

The High Constable. New York, early nineteenth century.

Monfredo, Miriam Grace

Seneca Falls Inheritance. Librarian Glynis Tyron teams up with the sheriff to solve a murder at the First Women's Rights Convention.

Newman, Sharan

Featuring Catherine and Edgar, twelfth-century Europe. This couple travels!

Death Comes as Epiphany.

The Devil's Door.

The Wandering Arm.

Strong as Death.

Cursed in the Blood.

Oates, Joyce Carol

Mysteries of Winterthurn. Featuring Xavier Kilgarvan, detective, United States, late nineteenth and early twentieth centuries.

Paige, Robin

Featuring Sir Charles Sheridan and Kathryn Ardleigh, nineteenth-century England.

Palmer, William J.

The Detective and Mr. Dickens.

The Highwayman and Mr. Dickens. Featuring Inspector William Field with Charles Dickens and Wilkie Collins.

Pears, Iain

An Instance of the Fingerpost. Restoration England.

Penman, Sharon Kay
Medieval Mystery series. Featuring Justin de Quincy.

Pérez-Reverte, Arturo
The Fencing Master. Nineteenth-century Spain.

Perry, Anne
Featuring Inspector Thomas Pitt and wife Charlotte, London, nineteenth century; William Monk, amnesiac Victorian police detective then private investigator.

Peters, Elizabeth
Featuring Amelia Peabody, Victorian Egyptologist.

Peters, Ellis
Featuring Brother Cadfael, Benedictine monastery, Shrewsbury, twelfth century.

3

Pronzini, Bill
Featuring John Quincannon, Federal Secret Service agent, San Francisco, 1890s.

Pullman, Philip
The Ruby in the Smoke.
A Shadow in the North.
The Tiger in the Well. A young adult series enjoyed by adults.

Robb, Candace
Featuring Owen Archer, fourteenth-century England.

Robinson, Lynda S.
Featuring Lord Meren, ancient Egypt.

Ross, Kate
Featuring Julian Kestrel, Regency England.

Rowland, Laura Joh
Featuring Samurai Sano Ichiro, seventeenth-century Japan.

Satterthwait, Walter
Masquerade. 1920s Paris.

Saylor, Steven
Featuring Gordanius the finder, ancient Rome.

Sedley, Kate
Featuring Roger the Chapman, fifteenth-century peddler–cum–amateur detective.

Selwyn, Francis
Featuring Sergeant Verity, London, nineteenth century.

Smith, Martin Cruz

Rose. Lancashire, England, 1872.

Stubbs, Jean

Dear Laura. Inspector Lintott, Scotland Yard, nineteenth century.

Wolf, Joan

No Dark Place. Hugh Corbaille, Norman England.

Futuristic Mysteries

In direct counterpoint to historical mysteries are those set in the future. They often have the same appeal of an exotic setting in a place we cannot go now. Futuristic mysteries are listed in the science fiction chapter (Chapter 6). Readers may also want to consult the fantasy chapter (Chapter 7) for mysteries with a fantasy setting.

Suspense

This catchall term is applied by publishers to such a variety of books that it becomes difficult to determine exactly what does fit into the suspense category. In some novels of suspense the crime has not even been committed yet, but the reader knows that it is to come and fervently turns the pages to see what will happen. Even though detection is common in novels of suspense, the emphasis is not so much on "who done it" but on why it was done. The psychology of the perpetrator of the crime is of importance. Although in novels of detection the series sleuth has become the norm, in suspense the series is the exception rather than the rule. Often in novels of suspense, the reader knows the identity of the perpetrator early on but must keep reading to find out what happens next. The reader often feels a sense of impending doom. Many of the books listed under "Legal Thriller" are also novels of suspense.

Abrahams, Peter

Hard Rain.

A Perfect Crime.

The Fan.

Armstrong, Charlotte

A Dram of Poison.

Dream of Fair Women.

Lay On, Mac Duff!

Bayer, William

Switch.

Beck, Kathrine

Bad Neighbors. Comedic suspense.

Blackstock, Charity
The Foggy, Foggy Dew.

I Met Murder on the Way.

Blauner, Peter
The Intruder.

Man of the Hour.

Slow Motion Riot.

Clark, Mary Higgins
The Cradle Will Fall.

A Cry in the Night.

A Stranger Is Watching.

While My Pretty One Sleeps.

Pretend You Don't See Her.

You Belong to Me.

We'll Meet Again.

Clark, Mary Jane
Do You Want to Know a Secret?

Clarke, Anna
The Lady in Black.

Soon She Must Die.

The Case of the Paranoid Patient.

Collins, Wilkie
The Woman in White.

Cook, Thomas H.
Breakheart Hill.

The Chatham School Affair.

Instruments of Night.

Curtiss, Ursula
Dog in the Manger.

The Birthday Gift.

The Poisoned Orchard.

Deaver, Jeffery Wilds
A Maiden's Grave.

Praying for Sleep.

The Lesson of Her Death.

Eidson, Bill
> **Adrenaline.**

Ellin, Stanley
> **Very Old Money.**
> **House of Cards.**

Eustis, Helen
> **The Horizontal Man.**

Fielding, Joy
> **Kiss Mommy Goodbye.**
> **The Deep End.**
> **See Jane Run.**
> **Don't Cry Now.**
> **Missing Pieces.**

Fremlin, Celia
> **The Hours Before Dawn.**
> **The Jealous One.**
> **A Lovely Day to Die and Other Stories.**
> **Dangerous Thoughts.**

Fyfield, Frances
> **Blind Date.**

Gilbert, Anna
> **Miss Bede Is Staying.**
> **The Treachery of Time.**
> **The Wedding Guest.** Has the feeling of an old-fashioned gothic.

Gill, B. M.
> **Death Drop.**
> **Target Westminster.**

Graham, Winston
> **Marnie.**
> **The Walking Stick.**

Guest, Judith, and Rebecca Hill
> **Killing Time in St. Cloud.**

Highsmith, Patricia
> **Slowly, Slowly in the Wind.** Short stories.
> **Strangers on a Train.**

Japrisot, Sebastien
    The Lady in the Car with Glasses and a Gun.
    One Deadly Summer.
    Trap for Cinderella.

Kellerman, Jonathan
    Billy Straight.

King, Tabitha
    Survivor.

Maxim, John R.
    Haven.

 3

McGinley, Patrick
    Bogmail.

Millar, Margaret
    Beast in View.
    Beyond This Point Are Monsters.
    The Devil Loves Me.

Palmer, Michael
Medical suspense that verges on horror.

Rendell, Ruth
    The Crocodile Bird.
    A Judgment in Stone.
    The Killing Doll.
    Make Death Love Me.
    Master of the Moor.
    The New Girl Friend and Other Stories.
    The Tree of Hands.

Scholefield, Alan
    Night Child.

Vine, Barbara
These books are now being reissued under the name Ruth Rendell.

Walker, Mary Willis
    Under the Beetle's Cellar.
    The Red Scream.
    All the Dead Lie Down.
    Zero at the Bone.

Walters, Minette
The Breaker.

The Ice House.

The Scold's Bridal.

The Dark Room.

The Echo.

The Sculptress.

Wilhelm, Kate
The Good Children.

Serial Killers

A psychopathic killer pursuing (usually) a woman is as common a plot element in this subgenre as are serial killers. Madness and murder appear in other genres, and some examples are included in Chapter 8, "Horror" (for example, Robert Bloch's *Psycho*).

Bayer, William
Wallflower.

Cohen, Anthea
A curious aspect of this series is that it features a nurse murderer, and one critic has questioned the limited appeal of the murderer-as-heroine concept.

Angel Without Mercy.

Angel of Vengeance.

Angel of Death.

Connelly, Michael
Blood Work.

Cook, Thomas H.
Mortal Memory.

Crider, Bill
Blood Marks.

Fielding, Joy
The Deep End.

Kiss Mommy Goodbye.

Fremlin, Celia
The Parasite Person.

Hall, James W.
Body Language.

Heckler, Jonellen
    Circumstances Unknown.

Hunter, Jessie Prichard
    Blood Music.
    One Two Buckle My Shoe.

Kaminsky, Stuart
    Exercise in Terror.

King, Tabitha
    The Trap.

Lindsey, David L.
    Mercy.

3

    A Cold Mind.

Reichs, Kathy
    Deja Dead.

Sandford, John
Psychopathic killers appear frequently in his Prey series.

Wiltse, David
    The Edge of Sleep.
    Blown Away.

Romance/Suspense Writers

Romance writers who write suspenseful romances often include more suspense than romance. Many of the following authors are also included in the romance chapter (Chapter 5).

Brown, Sandra
    Unspeakable.

Cannell, Dorothy
    Down the Garden Path.

Coulter, Catherine
    The Cove.
    The Maze.
    The Target.
    The Edge.

Hoag, Tami
Guilty as Sin.

Night Sins.

Johansen, Iris
Face of Deception.

And Then You Die.

Ugly Duckling.

Lowell, Elizabeth
Amber Beach.

Jade Island.

Pearl Cove.

Michaels, Barbara
Someone in the House.

The Wizard's Daughter.

Paul, Barbara
The Renewable Virgin.

Peters, Elizabeth
The Camelot Caper.

Robards, Karen
The Midnight Hour.

Walking After Midnight.

Roberts, Nora
Oxymoron series.

Genuine Lies.

Carnal Innocence.

Brazen Virtue.

Stewart, Mary
My Brother Michael.

Whitney, Phyllis
Hunter's Green.

Crime/Caper

The following books focus on the crime and the perpetrators rather than on finding who did it or why it was done. Some of the protagonists are career criminals, while others may be ordinary folks pushed by circumstances into committing crimes. The one trait the diverse rogues all possess is cunning, regardless of social standing, education, economic level, gender, or race.

Many of the following authors write other types of books involving crime. The titles noted are examples of their novels that distinctly involve a caper.

Underworld

A few authors write with harsh realism about the underworld of crime (Burnett, Greene, and Higgins are in the following list, but one might include Dashiell Hammett). Other authors treat the underworld and its criminals with realism but combine the features of criminals and amoral rogues to create characters with whom the reader can sympathize.

Bayer, William
Blind Side.

Browne, Gerald A.

Hot Siberian.

19 Purchase Street.

11 Harrowhouse.

Green Ice.

Stone 588.

Burnett, W. R.
Little Caesar.

The Asphalt Jungle.

Chafets, Zev
Inherit the Mob.

The Bookmakers.

Chase, James Hadley
While no longer popular in the United States, Hadley has a loyal international following.

No Orchids for Miss Blandish.

Condon, Richard
Prizzi's Honor.

Prizzi's Family.

Prizzi's Glory.

Prizzi's Money.

DeMille, Nelson
The Gold Coast.

Diehl, William
Thai Horse.

Doctorow, E. L.
Billy Bathgate.

Dunet, Sarah
Snowstorms in a Hot Climate.

Estleman, Loren D.
Kill Zone.

Roses Are Dead.

Freemantle, Brian
The Choice of Eddie Franks.

Giancana, Sam, and Bettina Giancana
30 Seconds.

Greene, Graham
Brighton Rock.

This Gun for Hire.

Higgins, George V.
The Friends of Eddie Coyle.

Izzi, Eugene
Izzi's own death was more bizarre than anything in his books.

Invasions.

Prime Roll.

King of the Hustlers.

The Booster.

Kakonis, Tom
Michigan Roll.

Katzenbach, John
Day of Reckoning.

Leonard, Elmore
Stick.

Cat Chase.

Split Images.

Glitz.

Swag.

The Switch.

Lindsey, David L.
Requiem for a Glass Heart.

Puzo, Mario
>**The Godfather.**
>
>**The Sicilian.**

Reardon, James
>**Hard Time Tommy Sloane.**

Stevens, Shane
>**Dead City.**

Thomas, Ross
>**Chinaman's Chance.**

Vachss, Andrew
>**Strega.**

Woods, Stuart
>**L. A. Times.**

Rogues

The cheerfully amoral rogue is, with a few exceptions, a likable character who, although in contravention of the law, doesn't seem *too bad* to the reader. Many rogues appear in series. The following list includes indifferent thieves, con men, and shady rogues who pull off their deals with a blithe disregard of law and, usually, morality. The first list covers a miscellany of capers; it is followed by several groupings of patterned types of capers.

Archer, Jeffrey
>**Not a Penny More, Not a Penny Less.** A classic tale of the biter bit.

Butterworth, Michael
>**X Marks the Spot.**
>
>**Stealing Marx's Bones.**

Cain, James M.
>**The Postman Always Rings Twice.** Somber insurance swindle.

Cannell, Stephen J.
>**King Con.**

Canning, Victor
>**Fall from Grace.**

Cecil, Henry
Many of his law court comedies are also comic capers.
>**Much in Evidence.**
>
>**The Painswick Line.**

Crichton, Michael
The Great Train Robbery.

Drummond, Ivor
Series about a trio of roguish crime-busters: Lady Jennifer, Colley, and Count Sandro.

Gilbert, Michael
End-Game.

The Long Voyage Home. International business scams.

Godey, John
The Taking of Pelham One Two Three. Hijacking of a New York subway train.

Hallahan, William H.
The Ross Forgery.

Hill, Reginald
A Very Good Hater: A Tale of Revenge.

Hull, Richard
The Murder of My Aunt. A classic.

Lehman, Ernest
The French Atlantic Affair.

Leonard, Elmore
Get Shorty.

Be Cool. Gangster Chili Palmer tackles the movie industry and then the music business.

MacKenzie, Donald
John Raven series. An ex–Scotland Yard detective is involved in all types of capers.

Petievich, Gerald
To Die in Beverly Hills.

Roudybush, Alexandra.
A Gastronomic Murder. Jewel theft *and* food.

Taylor, Andrew
Caroline Minuscule. Jewel theft.

Wainwright, John
Clouds of Guilt.

Burglars

Block, Lawrence

These stories feature Bernard Rhodenbarr.

> **Burglars Can't Be Choosers.**
> **The Burglar in the Closet.**
> **The Burglar Who Liked to Quote Kipling.**
> **The Burglar Who Painted Like Mondrian.**
> **The Burglar Who Studied Spinoza.**

Dodge, David

> **To Catch a Thief.**

Gores, Joe

> **Come Morning.**

Hoch, Edward D.

> **The Thefts of Nick Velvet.**

Hornung, E. W.

> **The Complete Short Stories of Raffles—The Amateur Cracksman.** Series continued by Perowne (see below).

Leblanc, Maurice

> **The Extraordinary Adventures of Arséne Lupin, Gentleman-Burglar.**

Perowne, Barry

> **Raffles Revisited: Some New Adventures of a Famous Gentleman Crook.**
> **Raffles of the Albany.**

Royce, Kenneth

These books feature Spider Scott, reformed cat burglar.

> **The Crypto Man.**
> **Spider Underground.**
> **The Masterpiece Affair.**

Stark, Richard (pseudonym of Donald E. Westlake)

The *Parker series* had a long run as original paperbacks before appearing in hardcover.

> **Butcher's Moon.**
> **Deadly Edge.**

Art Crimes

Many art-scam titles appear in mystery/detection.

Bonfiglioli, Kyril
> **Don't Point That Thing at Me** (U.S. edition, *Mortdecai's Endgame*).
> **After You with the Pistol.** Features the Honorable Charlie Mortdecai.

Butterworth, Michael
> **A Virgin on the Rocks.**

Canning, Victor
> **Vanishing Point.**

Delahaye, Michael
> **The Sale of Lot 236.**

Follett, Ken
> **The Modigliani Scandal.**

Goldman, James
> **The Man from Greek and Roman.**

Harris, MacDonald
> **The Treasure of Sainte Foy.**

Page, Martin
> **The Man Who Stole the Mona Lisa** (British edition, *Set a Thief*).

Westheimer, David
> **The Olmec Head.**

Smuggling

Ellin, Stanley
> **The Luxembourg Run.**

Fish, Robert L.
> All of these are about Kek Huuygens.
>> **Kek Huuygens, Smuggler.**
>> **The Wager.**
>> **Whirligig.**
>> **The Tricks of the Trade.**

Hallahan, William H.
> **Foxcatcher.**

Amoral Rogue and Hit Man

Blincoe, Nicholas

Acid Casuals. Transsexual assassin Estela Santos has returned to Manchester, England, in an explosive mix of gangs, car chases, flying bullets, and lots of drugs.

Block, Lawrence

Hit Man.

Highsmith, Patricia

The Talented Mr. Ripley.

Ripley Under Ground.

Ripley's Game.

The Boy Who Followed Ripley.

Perry, Thomas

The Butcher's Boy.

Metzger's Dog.

Big Fish.

Smith, Evelyn

Miss Melville Rides a Tiger.

Miss Melville Returns.

Miss Melville Regrets.

Miss Melville's Revenge.

Van de Wetering, Janwillem

The Butterfly Hunter.

Elderly Rogues

Carson, Robert

The Golden Years Caper. Band of elderly people in Long Beach, California, find "the wages of sin are bankable."

Fish, Robert L.

These books feature three retired writers of mystery novels.

The Murder League.

Rub-A-Dub-Dub.

A Gross Carriage of Justice.

Women

Their capers are various.

Andress, Lesley
Caper.

Bailey, Hilary
Hannie Richards, or The Intrepid Adventures of a Restless Wife.

Cornelisen, Ann
Any Four Women Could Rob the Bank of Italy.

Garfield, Brian
Necessity.

Sheldon, Sidney
If Tomorrow Comes.

Comic Capers

Among the authors previously listed are several who use humor either broadly or sardonically. A determinedly comic treatment is used by the following authors, creating a felicitous union of comedy and crime without the defects of farce. (See Frank Norman's private detective novels for his lovely depiction of Cockney crooks.)

Barrett, Neal, Jr.
Pink Vodka Blues.
Dead Dog Blues.

Butterworth, Michael
The Man in the Sopwith Camel.
The Man Who Broke the Bank at Monte Carlo.

Cannell, Stephen J.
King Con.

Childress, Mark
Crazy in Alabama.

Fennelly, Tony
The Glory Hole Murders.

Follett, Ken
Paper Money.

Hiaasen, Carl
Double Whammy.
Tourist Season.
Skin Tight.
Native Tongue.
Strip Tease.
Stormy Weather.
Lucky You.
Sick Puppy.

Hunter, Evan
Every Little Crook and Nanny.

Leonard, Elmore
Get Shorty.

Lyons, Nan, and Ivan Lyons
Someone Is Killing the Great Chefs of Europe.
Champagne Blues.

Westlake, Donald E.
There are many, many more than those listed here, several featuring John Dortmunder, burglar, and all greeted with cheers by his many fans.
Good Behavior.
God Save the Mark.
High Adventure.
Why Me.

Legal Thriller

The legal thriller is currently playing big to movie houses and on bestseller lists. This type features as the hero a lawyer who has gotten into a fix and needs to extricate himself or herself through clever use of a superior intellect. There actually is variety within this subgenre, from the earnest young attorney who finds out that he is unwittingly representing organized crime to the attorney wrongly accused of murder who is duped by those close to her. The hero can be a young legal student who, as an intellectual exercise, tries to solve murders but then, because of her theories, ends up as the target of the killers, or an earnest judge who is manipulated into an explosive situation. In this type of story, the focus is not on the solving of a mystery but rather on the thrill of the chase, usually from the point of view of the one being chased!

The number one *Publishers Weekly* best seller for 1998 was John Grisham's *The Street Lawyer,* evidence that this subgenre remains popular.

Baldacci, David
> **The Simple Truth.**

Brandon, Jay
> **Angel of Death.**
>
> **Defiance County.**
>
> **Rules of Evidence.**
>
> **Local Rules.**

Diehl, William
> **Primal Fear.**
>
> **Show of Evil.**

Finder, Joseph
> **High Crimes.**

Freedman, J. F.
> **Disappearing Act.**

Grisham, John
> **A Time to Kill.**
>
> **The Firm.**
>
> **The Pelican Brief.**
>
> **The Client.**
>
> **The Chamber.**
>
> **The Rainmaker.**
>
> **The Partner.**
>
> **The Runaway Jury.**
>
> **The Street Lawyer.**
>
> **The Testament.**

Irving, Clifford
> **Final Argument.**

Lescroart, John T.
> **The 13th Juror.**
>
> **Hard Evidence.** Features Dismas Hardy, defense attorney.

Margolin, Phillip
> **The Undertaker's Widow.**
>
> **After Dark.**
>
> **The Last Innocent Man.**
>
> **The Burning Man.**

Martini, Steve
Compelling Evidence.

Prime Witness.

Undue Influence.

Patterson, Richard North
Degree of Guilt.

Silent Witness.

Rosenberg, Nancy Taylor
First Offense.

Mitigating Circumstances.

Interest of Justice.

Stern, Mark
Inadmissible.

Tanenbaum, Robert K.
No Lesser Plea.

Depraved Indifference.

Immoral Certainty.

Reversible Error.

Material Witness.

Turow, Scott
Presumed Innocent.

Burden of Proof.

Pleading Guilty.

Warfield, Gallatin
Silent Son.

State v. Justice.

Wheat, Carolyn
Sworn to Defend.

Topics

Immortal Investigators

Some sleuths achieve lives of their own, becoming so real that pastiches are done of them, biographies are written about them, and they appear in the works of other authors. Among the immortals are Dashiell Hammett's detectives and Chandler's Philip Marlowe, both noted in the "Private Detectives" section. Following are detectives who have become beings in their own right through the devotion of readers.

Christie, Agatha (Hercule Poirot, Miss Jane Marple)

"The first lady of crime" published 83 titles, including original collections of short stories. Many have been made into movies and television programs and more have been released as audio recordings and in large type. Her dapper detective Hercule Poirot, who said that one must "employ the little grey cells," appeared in her first novel (*The Mysterious Affair at Styles*, 1920) and in 34 other novels, as well as in some short stories. In 1998 one of her Hercule Poirot plays was adapted into novel form by Charles Osborne. Another Christie character, Miss Jane Marple, the inquisitive village spinster who insisted that "human nature is much the same in a village as anywhere else, only one has opportunities and leisure for seeing it at closer quarters," appeared in Christie's 11th novel (*Murder at the Vicarage*, 1930), in 11 other novels, and in 20 short stories (collected as *Miss Marple: The Complete Short Stories* [Dodd, 1985]). An amusing and loving biography of Miss Marple has been constructed by Anne Hart from Christie's novels and short stories: *The Life and Times of Miss Jane Marple* (Dodd, 1985). A comedy detective couple, Tommy and Tuppence, appeared in Christie's second novel (*The Secret Adversary*, 1922) and in three other novels, as well as in short stories, but they never rivaled the popularity of Poirot and Marple. In 1926, Christie successfully broke a sacred detective story law by having her narrator be murdered in *The Murder of Roger Ackroyd*. Her *Autobiography* (London: Collins, 1977; reissued in paperback in 1996 by Boulevard) reveals both the woman and the writer. The following are a few books from a growing bibliography of books related to Christie's work.

Jacquemard, Yves, and Jean-Michel Sénécal. *The Eleventh Little Indian.*
    This detective novel, featuring Superintendent Hector Parescot, Sûreté, is a spoof tribute to Christie and her *Ten Little Indians*. Published in English in 1979, it still remains available in public libraries.

Kaska, Kathleen. *What's Your Agatha Christie I.Q.?: 1,001 Puzzling Questions About the World's Most Beloved Mystery Writer*. Citadel Press, 1996.

Riley, Dick, Pam McAllister, and Julian Symons. *The New Bedside, Bathtub, Armchair Companion to Agatha Christie*. Continuum, 1994. A synopsis of all her novels, short stories, and plays. Includes articles about the poisons used and clothing worn by characters.

Sova, Dawn B. *Agatha Christie A to Z: The Essential Reference to Her Life and Writings*. Facts on File, 1997. A brief biography of Agatha Christie, followed by a complete descriptive bibliography of her oeuvre.

Several Web pages are devoted to Dame Agatha; following are merely a few of them:

http://www.dalton.org/students/bkyaffe/wwwac/achome.html (accessed 20 January 2000)

http://web.pinknet.cz/AgathaChristie/e-menu.html (accessed 20 January 2000)

http://www.zinezone.com/zines/arts/literature/mysteries/agatha/index.html (accessed 20 January 2000)

Doyle, Arthur Conan, Sir (Sherlock Holmes and Dr. John Watson)

Four novels (*The Hound of the Baskervilles*, 1902; *The Sign of Four*, 1890; *A Study in Scarlet*, 1887; and *The Valley of Fear*, 1915) and 56 short stories, some of novella length, make up the canon of "sacred" writings presented with elaborate notes and period illustrations in the two-volume *The Annotated Sherlock Holmes*, edited by William S. Baring-Gould (Crown, 1967). A host of devout followers have continued the canon in novels and short stories.

Derleth, August. *The Solar Pons Omnibus*. Arkham House, 1982. 2 vols. Contains the eight titles of Solar Pons's adventures.

Douglas, Carole Nelson
Irene Adler series.

> Good Night, Mr. Holmes.
> Good Morning, Irene.
> Irene at Large.
> Irene's Last Waltz.

Fish, Robert L.

> The Incredible Sherlock Holmes.
> The Memoirs of Sherlock Holmes (A Bagel Street Dozen).

Gardner, John.
> The Return of Moriarty.

Hanna, Edward B.
> The Whitechapel Horrors.

Irvine, R. R.
Short stories about Niles Brundage, actor of Sherlock Holmes roles.

King, Laurie R.
The Beekeeper's Apprentice, or, On the Segregation of the Queen.

A Monstrous Regiment of Women.

A Letter of Mary.

Siciliano, Sam
The Angel of the Opera.

Symons, Julian
The Three-Pipe Problem. Novel about an actor of Holmes roles.

Watson, John H.
The Seven-Per-Cent Solution, Being a Reprint from the Reminiscences of John H. Watson, M.D., as edited by Nicholas Meyer. With this 1974 pastiche, Nicholas Meyer (who did two more) incited a flood of imitators. These novels portray Sherlock Holmes either in his own period or (as, of course, he still lives!) in modern times. Many of these are of indifferent quality.

Writings about Sherlock Holmes are more voluminous than the canon of Conan Doyle's works. An association of admirers, the Baker Street Irregulars, publishes the *Baker Street Journal* and hosts events honoring Holmes. A novel by Anthony Boucher, *The Case of the Baker Street Irregulars*, has several of the Irregulars involved in and trying to solve a murder in Los Angeles.

A recent biography is *Teller of Tales: The Life of Arthur Conan Doyle,* by Daniel Stashower (Henry Holt, 1999).

Web sites devoted to Sherlock Holmes abound; the following offer information and links to other related sites and groups.

http://www.zinezone.com/zines/arts/literature/mysteries/sherlock/index.html (accessed 20 January 2000)

http://members.tripod.com/~msherman/holmes.html (accessed 20 January 2000)

Sayers, Dorothy L. (Lord Peter Wimsey, Montague Egg)

Twelve novels (all but one featuring Lord Peter; the first published in 1923) and 45 short stories (22 featuring Lord Peter) ensure Lord Peter's immortality. In 1998 *Thrones, Dominations,* an unfinished manuscript about Lord Peter and Harriet Vane upon starting their married life together that was finished by Jill Paton Walsh, was published. The short stories can be found in *Lord Peter*, compiled by James Sandoe. Dorothy L. Sayers is so beloved of mystery fans that the online mystery discussion group named Dorothyl. Sayers has been a popular topic for scholarly dissertations. Her spiritual writings, rather than her wonderful mysteries, have been the emphasis of many of the most recent books about her.

Brabazon, James. *Dorothy L. Sayers: The Life of a Courageous Woman*. With
a preface by Anthony Fleming and a foreword by P. D. James. Gollancz,
1981. The "authorized" (by her son) biography, published early (Sayers
stipulated that no biography be published until 50 years after her death),
while now close to 20 years old, has not been superseded and can be found
on library shelves although it is out of print. Brabazon knew Sayers, had
access to all her papers, and was given complete editorial freedom. In style,
wit, intelligence, and spirit, he matches his subject to perfection.

Brunsdale, Mitzi. *Dorothy L. Sayers: Solving the Mystery of Wickedness*. St.
Martin's Press, 1990.

Kenney, Catherine McGehee. *The Remarkable Case of Dorothy L. Sayers*.
Kent State University Press, 1991.

Reynolds, Barbara. *Dorothy L. Sayers: Her Life and Soul*. St. Martin's Press,
1993.

Stout, Rex (Nero Wolfe and Archie Goodwin)

Nero Wolfe's bulk is unmatched by the number of published books about
his detective genius: 46 titles (the first in 1934; of these, 12 are collections of
novellas). He never leaves his house willingly; legmen and witnesses bring
him the information and *he* thinks. He loves food, orchids, language, and his
privacy. Archie, his assistant, is of the hard-boiled detective mold. In *Gambit*,
Archie informs a prospective client, who has been told that Wolfe is indig-
nantly burning a copy of *Webster's Third*: "Once he burned up a cookbook because it said to remove the hide from a ham end before putting it in the pot with
lima beans. Which he loves most, food or words, is a tossup." Nero Wolfe has
an enthusiastic following: The Wolfe Pack has held annual Black Orchid Ban-
quets since 1977, using the recipes from *The Nero Wolfe Cookbook*. They also
bestow the Nero Wolfe Award for Mystery Fiction. The series was continued
by Robert Goldsborough.

Baring-Gould, William Stuart. *Nero Wolfe of West Thirty-Fifth Street: The
Life and Times of America's Largest Private Detective*. Penguin, 1982.

Stout, Rex, and the editors of Viking Press. *The Nero Wolfe Cookbook*. Reprinted by Cumberland House, 1996.

Biography of Fictional Detectives

The detective as a fictional character is given a biographical write-up in
some studies on the detective story with a blandly literal tone, as though the
detectives were actual living beings. Some books with biographical listings
are noted later, but following are three works on, simply, the detectives
themselves.

Kaufman, Kay, Natalie Hevener, and Carol McGinnis. *'G' Is for Grafton: The World of Kinsey Millhone*. Henry Holt, 1997. Everything you could ever want to know about Kinsey, including photos!

Penzler, Otto. *The Private Lives of Private Eyes, Spies, Crimefighters, & Other Good Guys*. Grosset, 1977. Twenty-six lives are illustrated from books and motion pictures, with bibliography and filmography for each: Lew Archer, Modesty Blaise, James Bond, Father Brown, Nick Carter, Charlie Chan, Nick and Nora Charles, Bulldog Drummond, C. Auguste Dupin, Mike Hammer, Sherlock Holmes, Jules Maigret, Philip Marlowe, Miss Jane Marple, Perry Mason, Mr. Moto, Hercule Poirot, Ellery Queen, The Shadow, John Shaft, Sam Spade, Dr. Thorndyke, Philo Vance, Lord Peter Wimsey, Nero Wolfe.

Penzler, Otto, ed. *The Great Detectives*. Little, Brown, 1978. Although this is quite old, it remains in many library collections and is of interest to fans of the genre, the detectives for the most part being timeless. Twenty-six detectives are described by their creators: Roderick Alleyn (Ngaio Marsh); John Appleby (Michael Innes); Lew Archer (Ross Macdonald); Father Bredder (Leonard Holton); Flash Casey (George Harmon Coxe); Pierre Chambrun (Hugh Pentecost); Inspector Cockrill (Christianna Brand); Captain José Da Silva (Robert L. Fish); Nancy Drew (Carolyn Keene); the 87th Precinct (Ed McBain); Fred Fellows (Hillary Waugh); Inspector Ghote (H. R. F. Keating); Matt Helm (Donald Hamilton); Duncan Maclain (Baynard H. Kendrick); Mark McPherson (Vera Caspary); Lieutenant Luis Mendoza (Dell Shannon); Mr. and Mrs. North (Richard Lockridge); Patrick Petrella (Michael Gilbert); Superintendent Pibble (Peter Dickinson); Quiller (Adam Hall); Inspector Schmidt (George Bagby); The Shadow (Maxwell Grant); Michael Shayne (Brett Halliday); Virgil Tibbs (John Ball); Dick Tracy (Chester Gould); and Inspector Van der Valk (Nicholas Freeling).

Best-Selling Authors

In 1998 the best-selling crime authors, selling over 100,000 copies for the year, were John Grisham (*The Street Lawyer*), Mary Higgins Clark (*All Through the Night, You Belong to Me*), Sidney Sheldon (*Tell Me Your Dreams*), David Baldacci (*The Simple Truth*), Sue Grafton (*N Is for Noose*), John Sandford (*Secret Prey*), Steve Martini (*Critical Mass*), Catherine Coulter (*The Target*), Jonathan Kellerman (*Billy Straight*), Sandra Brown (*Unspeakable*), Tony Hillerman (*The First Eagle*), W. E. B. Griffin (*The Investigators*), Dick Francis (*Field of Thirteen*), Faye Kellerman (*Moon Music*), Lilian Jackson Braun (*The Cat Who Sang for the Birds*), Lawrence Sanders (*Guilty Pleasures*), Michael Connelly (*Blood Work*), Iain Pears (*An Instance of the Fingerpost*), James Lee Burke (*Sunset Limited*), and Elizabeth Lowell (*Jade Island*). This list illustrates the diversity of the genre, with legal thrillers, historical mysteries, private investigators, human-and-cat teams, and romance writers writing suspense all present. It is quite a different list from that of 1990, a year in which only four authors of crime fiction had books with sales in excess of 100,000 copies: Joseph Wambaugh (*The Golden Orange*), Tony Hillerman (*Coyote Waits*), P. D. James (*Devices and Desires*), and Robert B. Parker (*Stardust*). In 1975, the leading crime fiction authors, in order of most sales (to that date), were Mickey Spillane, Erle Stanley Gardner, Robert Traver, Joseph Wambaugh, and John D. MacDonald. Ten years earlier, Joseph Wambaugh did not appear and MacDonald was 11th. Following Spillane, Gardner, and Traver were Ellery Queen, Agatha Christie, Richard S. Prather, A. A. Fair (Erle Stanley Gardner's pseudonym), Dashiell Hammett, Raymond Chandler, Earl Derr Biggers, Leslie Charteris, and Marco Page. One of the most amazing facts about looking at nearly 40 years of best-selling crime is that of all the authors mentioned in this section, all but two, Richard S. Prather and Marco Page, remain in print.

What type of detective has the greatest appeal? Grafton's female sleuth is tough and smart. Wambaugh's Los Angeles policemen are realistic. Hillerman's detectives are Native Americans in a setting unfamiliar to most readers. Spillane's private eye is notorious for sex and sadism. Ellery Queen, the investigator, is a sophisticated gentleman. Christie's Poirot and Miss Marple are genteel figures suitable to social comedy. Bigger's Charlie Chan is unique. Charteris's Saint is a rogue and a gentleman. The readers, then, take their choice.

3

For sheer number of titles (which collectively have large sales), John Creasey's books belong among the best sellers. Creasey used some 28 pseudonyms to produce about 650 titles, largely mystery, detective, and spy stories, and some Westerns (under three pseudonyms). He averaged about 12 titles per year. Reprints now appear with the pseudonymous works showing Creasey's authorship. The Toff series was written under Creasey. His best-known pseudonyms are Kyle Hunt (psychiatrist Emmanuel Cellini series), Anthony Morton (The Baron John Mannering series), J. J. Marric (Commander Gideon of Scotland Yard series), Gordon Ashe (Pat Dawlish of Scotland Yard series), and Jeremy York (Superintendent Folly of Scotland Yard series).

Anthologies

Almost all of the early and current writers of detective stories have written short stories, and the following anthologies provide a satisfactory introduction for choosing those authors whose style in the subgenre is pleasing to individual readers' tastes. Many of the anthologies also include other types of thrillers: spy, psychological suspense, crime, and the like. The following listing is selective. Included are several annual series.

Anthology Series

Best American Mystery Stories. Edited by a different prominent author each year; in 1998 it was Sue Grafton, in 1997 it was Robert B. Parker.

Best Detective Stories of the Year. 1945–1981. Includes list of award winners and bibliography of nonfiction for the year. Title change: See *The Year's Best Mystery and Suspense Stories.*

Crime Writers Association Annual. Sampling of titles: *Butcher's Dozen, A Pride of Felons, Crime Writers' Choice, Choice of Weapons, Some Like Them Dead, Planned Departures, John Creasey's Crime Collection, 1st Culprit, 2nd Culprit, 3rd Culprit.* This is no longer being published.

Malice Domestic. Cozy mysteries; the eighth appeared in 1999.

The Year's Best Mystery and Suspense Stories. 1982–1995. Superseded *Best Detective Stories of the Year.* Continued the section "The Yearbook of the Mystery and Suspense Story" and added a list of the best novels of the year.

The Year's 25 Finest Crime and Mystery Stories. Edited by the staff of *Mystery Scene.* Carroll & Graf, 1993, annual. The overview of the previous year's highlights and mystery news is great fun.

Anthologies

Bernhardt, William, ed. *Legal Briefs: Stories by Today's Best Thriller Writers.* Doubleday, 1998.

Cox, Michael, ed. *Twelve English Detective Stories.* Oxford University Press, 1998.

Deadly Allies: Private Eye Writers of America/Sisters in Crime Collaborative Anthology. Doubleday, 1992.

Deadly Allies II. Doubleday, 1994.

Dibdin, Michael, ed. *The Vintage Book of Classic Crime.* Vintage Crime, 1997.

Haycraft, Howard, and John Beecroft, eds. *A Treasury of Great Mysteries.* Simon & Schuster, 1957. 2 vols. Includes four novels—Agatha Christie, *Murder in the Calais Coach*; Eric Ambler, *Journey into Fear*; Raymond Chandler, *The Big Sleep*; Daphne Du Maurier, *Rebecca*—and stories by Erle Stanley Gardner, Edgar Wallace, Georges Simenon, Patrick Quentin, Mary Roberts Rinehart, John Dickson Carr, Ellery Queen, Margery Allingham, William Irish, Dorothy L. Sayers, Leslie Charteris, Ngaio Marsh, Rex Stout, Stuart Palmer and Craig Rice, and Carter Dickson.

Manson, Cynthia, ed. *Death on the Verandah: Mystery Stories of the South from Ellery Queen's Mystery Magazine and Alfred Hitchcock's Mystery Magazine.* Carroll & Graf, 1994.

Mystery Writers of America Anthologies. Sampling of titles: *Guilty as Charged; Crime Across the Sea; Sleuths and Consequences; With Malice Toward All; Crime Without Murder; Murder Most Foul; Dear Dead Days; Mirror Mirror, Fatal Mirror; Every Crime in the Book; When Last Seen.*

Penzler, Otto. *The 50 Greatest Mysteries of All Time.* Newstar Press, 1999.

Queen, Ellery, ed. *Ellery Queen's.* Too many different titles to list here, but a great source of crime anthologies. The stories in earlier collections were all reprinted from *Ellery Queen's Mystery Magazine*, but now they also feature stories from *Alfred Hitchcock's Mystery Magazine.*

Westlake, Donald E., ed. *Murderous Schemes: An Anthology of Classic Detective Stories.* Oxford University Press, 1998.

Hard-Boiled Detectives

The hard-boiled detective first achieved glory in pulp magazines in the United States in the 1920s. Many of the authors of note in the history of the detective story in the United States first appeared in pulp magazines. They wrote largely of the underworld of crime in which their tough detectives held their own.

Gorman, Ed, Bill Pronzini, and Martin H. Greenberg, eds. *American Pulp.* Carroll & Graf, 1997. Thirty-five stories of hard-boiled and noir fiction from the pulp magazines of the 1950s and 1960s.

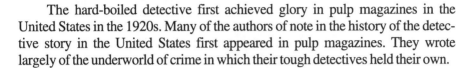

Gorman, Ed, Lee Server, and Martin H. Greenberg, eds. *The Big Book of Noir.* Carroll & Graf, 1998. Fiction, graphic novels, film, and audio formats featuring hard-boiled detectives are explored in articles and interviews.

Haut, Woody. *Neon Noir: Contemporary American Crime Fiction.* Serpent's Tail, 1999. A look at American culture as portrayed by authors such as James Ellroy, Elmore Leonard, Walter Mosley, James Lee Burke, Lawrence Block, James Sallis, George P. Pelecanos, Charles Willeford, Jerome Charyn, Sara Paretsky, Vicki Hendricks, KC Constantine, George V. Higgins, and James Crumley.

Jakubowski, Maxim, ed. *London Noir.* Serpent's Tail, 1994.

————. *The Mammoth Book of Pulp Fiction.* Carroll & Graf, 1996.

Pronzini, Bill, and Jack Adrian, eds. *Hard-Boiled: An Anthology of American Crime Stories.* Oxford University Press, 1995.

Women Detectives

Women appeared as fictional detectives as early as 1861. The following anthologies show the varieties of women detectives and how their modern role has changed dramatically.

Greenberg, Martin H., and Beth Foxwell, eds. *Murder They Wrote.* Boulevard, 1998.

Greenberg, Martin H., and Bill Pronzini, eds. *Women Sleuths.* Academy Chicago, 1985. (Academy Mystery Novellas, vol. 1)

Manley, Seon, and Gogo Lewis, comps. *Grande Dames of Detection: Two Centuries of Sleuthing Stories by the Gentle Sex.* Lothrop, 1973. Among the authors covered are Baroness Orczy, Carolyn Wells, Agatha Christie, Dorothy L. Sayers, and Margery Allingham.

Manson, Cynthia, ed. *Women of Mystery*. Berkley Books, 1993. Includes stories by the big names of the 1990s: Mary Higgins Clark, Ruth Rendell, Antonia Fraser, Joan Hess, and many more.

Queen, Ellery, ed. *The Female of the Species*. Little, Brown, 1943. This early short story anthology includes women as both detectives and criminals.

Slung, Michele B., ed. *Crime on Her Mind: Fifteen Stories of Female Sleuths from the Victorian Era to the Forties*. Pantheon, 1975. The introduction presents a critical history, and an appendix lists the lady detectives in chronological order from 1861 to 1973, with annotations.

Wallace, Marilyn, ed. *Sisters in Crime*. This annual anthology started in 1989 and continued for five years. The best of the stories are included in *The Best of Sisters in Crime* (Berkley, 1997).

Detectives and Science Fiction

In Chapter 6, "Science Fiction," there is a section on the detective in science fiction, an intriguing combination of genres. The following anthologies offer brief examples of this combination.

Asimov, Isaac, Martin H. Greenberg, and Charles G. Waugh, eds. *The 13 Crimes of Science Fiction*. Doubleday, 1979.

Resnick, Mike, and Martin H. Greenberg, eds. *Sherlock Holmes in Orbit*. DAW, 1995.

Waugh, Charles G., and Martin H. Greenberg, eds. *Sci-Fi Private Eye*. New American Library, 1997.

Bibliographies

The following bibliographies vary in coverage. Some cover the authors in the genre, some include material on allied genres, some are of secondary works, and several embrace a number of aspects.

Barzun, Jacques, and Wendell Hertig Taylor. *A Catalogue of Crime*. Revised and enlarged ed. Harper & Row, 1989. Selective, idiosyncratic, and delightful for the personal annotations by two devoted academic fans who sometimes disagree, this is a bibliography to read for its critical flavor and bite. The vast scope encompasses novels, short stories, plays, magazines, studies and histories of the genre, true crime, and much more, annotating 5,045 works. It is an essential reference.

Breen, Jon L. *What About Murder? A Guide to Books About Mystery and Detective Fiction*. Scarecrow Press, 1981. Supplemented in 1993 with *What About Murder? 1981—1991*. There are 239 books listed and critically annotated in seven sections: "General Histories," "Reference Books," "Special Subjects," "Collected Essays and Reviews," "Technical Manuals," "Coffee-Table Books," and "Works on Individual Authors." The annotations are extensive and reveal Breen's wide reading and obvious enjoyment of the genre. Indispensable for serious fans.

The Crown Crime Companion: The Top 100 Mystery Novels of All Time. Selected by the Mystery Writers of America, annotated by Otto Penzler, and compiled by Mickey Friedman. Crown, 1995. This compact volume, in addition to listing the top 100, has lists of favorite writers, sleuths, cities for murder, murder weapons, places for hiding the bodies, animals, and mystery movies. The second section features essays by luminaries in the field: "Classics," by H. R. F. Keating; "Suspense," by Mary Higgins Clark; "Hard-Boiled/Private Eye," by Sue Grafton; "Police Procedural," by Joseph Wambaugh; "Espionage/Thriller," by John Gardner; "Criminal," by Richard Condon; "Cozy/Traditional," by Margaret Maron; "Historical," by Peter Lovesey; "Humorous," by Gregory Mcdonald; and "Legal/Courtroom," by Scott Turow. It also lists all Edgar Award winners through 1994.

 3

Heising, Willetta L. *Detecting Women 3: A Reader's Guide and Checklist for Mystery Series Written by Women.* Purple Moon Press, 1998. Lists women authors who have written mystery series that have had at least two titles published. They are included with a list of titles and a short biographical note. It includes a glossary, a great list of resources, convention and award information, pseudonyms, geographical settings, types, series characters, and a chronology.

Hubin, Allen J. *Crime Fiction: A Comprehensive Bibliography, 1749–1990.* Garland, 1994. *The* most comprehensive bibliography of crime fiction, in its expanded third edition. Noted are series detectives and pseudonyms. There are two indexes, title and series characters. In this edition are several new features: For each author are code-noted citations to eight reference books; a series character chronology; and an extensive "Settings Index" (50 pages), largely geographical but including academic, church, future, hospital, ships, theater, and trains.

Keating, H. R. F. *Crime & Mystery: The 100 Best Books,* 2d ed. Carroll & Graf, 1996. Contains critical essays on each of the titles selected, ranging from Edgar Allan Poe, *Tales of Mystery and Imagination* (1845), to P. D. James, *A Taste for Death* (1986).

Olderr, Steven. *Mystery Index: Subjects, Settings and Sleuths of 10,000 Titles.* American Library Association, 1987. Books that have a good possibility of being in a public library collection are indexed by title, subject and setting, and characters.

Oleksiw, Susan. *A Reader's Guide to the Classic British Mystery.* G. K. Hall, 1988. This covers more than 1,440 mystery novels and 121 authors; access is provided by indexes to characters' occupations, time periods, and settings.

Pederson, Jay P. *St. James Guide to Crime & Mystery Writers,* 4th ed. St. James Press, 1996. Formerly titled *Twentieth-Century Crime & Mystery Writers.* Some 600 writers are given bibliographical and critical coverage. The signed critical essays vary greatly in length and quality.

Swanson, Jean, and Dean James. *By a Woman's Hand: A Guide to Mystery Fiction by Women,* 2d ed. Berkley, 1996. Contemporary women mystery writers are listed in alphabetical order. The listings talk about the authors' style, series characters, and other important points. The indexes of character names, geographic settings, and type of detective are invaluable.

History

There is now a voluminous body of history and criticism on the detective sub-genre. Many titles include material on mystery, crime, spy, and horror stories as well. Although *Genreflecting* makes a distinction between history and criticism, this categorization reflects each book's formal organization: Both provide history *with* criticism. Despite the many works of history and criticism on the detective story, the definitive history has yet to be written. The following works, excepting Haycraft's, are too specialized and idiosyncratic to be definitive.

Haining, Peter. *Mystery! An Illustrated History of Crime and Detective Fiction.* Souvenir Press, 1977. Reprinted by Stein and Day, 1981. The history is sketchy but the illustrations are voluminous and imaginative.

Haycraft, Howard. *Murder for Pleasure: The Life and Times of the Detective Story.* Appleton, 1941. Still the basic history despite its date. It includes a list of "Cornerstones" (1841–1938) and a guide to characters, "Who's Who in Detection."

Siegel, Jeff. *The American Detective: An Illustrated History.* Taylor, 1993.

Symons, Julian. *Bloody Murder: From the Detective Story to the Crime Novel: A History.* Viking, 1985. First published in 1972 (the U.S. edition is titled *Mortal Consequences*). In this edition the author brings the history up-to-date and assesses as still valid his conclusion that the classic detective story is played out and the more realistic, psychological, sociological crime novel is in ascendance.

Thomson, H. Douglas. *Masters of Mystery: A Study of the Detective Story.* With a New Introduction by E. F. Bleiler. Dover, 1978. First published by Collins of London in 1931. Still cited often for its criticism of the early authors.

Criticism

The "Bibliographies" section (see p. 142) provides a guide to the voluminous critical material on the detection and mystery subgenres, including works on individual authors. The following selection from this voluminous literature is indicative of the many types of criticism available.

Gorman, Ed, and Martin H. Greenberg. *Speaking of Murder: Interviews with Masters of Mystery and Suspense.* Berkley Prime Crime, 1998. *Speaking of Murder, Vol. 2.* Berkley Prime Crime, 1999. Between the two volumes, 42 of today's most popular authors are interviewed.

Haycraft, Howard, ed. *The Art of the Mystery Story: A Collection of Critical Essays*. Simon & Schuster, 1946. Re-released by Carroll & Graf in 1983. The best all-around anthology of classic essays by both authors and fans of the genre. Includes "The Detection Club Oath"; "Who Cares Who Killed Roger Ackroyd?," by Edmund Wilson; "The Locked-Room Lecture," by John Dickson Carr; "Watson Was a Woman," by Rex Stout; and a host of others.

Jakubowski, Maxim, ed. *100 Great Detectives, or, The Detective Directory*. Carroll & Graf, 1991. Includes 100 essays on fictional detectives, written by the authors who selected them as favorites, each handily including listings of works featuring the detectives. In addition to the essays, Jakubowski has included (in a very condensed format) listings of the contributors' sleuths as well as a list of several beloved detectives who weren't included. This is a delightful book for browsing as well as a useful reference.

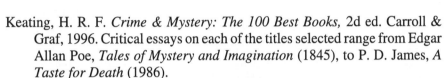

Keating, H. R. F. *Crime & Mystery: The 100 Best Books,* 2d ed. Carroll & Graf, 1996. Critical essays on each of the titles selected range from Edgar Allan Poe, *Tales of Mystery and Imagination* (1845), to P. D. James, *A Taste for Death* (1986).

Landrum, Larry N. *American Mystery and Detective Novels*. Greenwood, 1999. An academic approach to looking at the relationship between mysteries and popular culture.

Magill, Frank N., ed. *Critical Survey of Mystery and Detective Fiction*. Salem Press, 1988. This four-volume set provides critical surveys of several thriller subgenres, including espionage and romantic suspense. Covered are 270 authors.

Pronzini, Bill. *Gun in Cheek: A Study of "Alternative" Crime Fiction*. Coward, McCann & Geoghegan, 1982. A charmingly amusing survey of "bad," in every literary sense, but popular mystery fiction. The liberal use of quotations relieves one of the need to read the books! It can still be found in libraries.

Sayers, Dorothy L. "Introduction," in *Great Short Stories of Detection, Mystery and Horror*. Gollancz, 1928. This classic critical history on the origins and development of the detective story is often reprinted. There is also an excellent shorter introduction to the second series and one to her other anthology, *Great Tales of Detection* (J. M. Dent/Charles E. Tuttle, 1991.

Symons, Julian. *Bloody Murder: From the Detective Story to the Crime Novel*. Mysterious Press, 1992. The third edition of a classic reviews every type of crime fiction.

Winks, Robin W., ed. *Mystery and Suspense Writers: The Literature of Crime, Detection, and Espionage*. Charles Scribner's Sons, 1998. Essays on major writers and subgenres.

Parody

So formalized a genre as detection is readily parodied. To enjoy parody, the reader must be familiar with the authors being parodied.

Bruce, Leo. *Case for Three Detectives*. Bles, 1936. Reissued by Academy in 1996. Sergeant Beef solves the murder handily while Lord Simon Plimsoll (Peter Wimsey), Monsieur Amer Picon (Hercule Poirot), and Monsignor Smith (Father Brown) conjecture deviously and vainly.

Carper, Steve, ed. *The Defective Detective: Mystery Parodies by the Great Humorists.* Citadel Press, 1992.

Christie, Agatha. *Partners in Crime*. Collins, 1929. Tommy and Tuppence, Christie's husband-and-wife detective team, solve a series of cases and, in each, approach the problem as would one of the classic detectives. They mock the detectives' eccentricities of manner and speech. All the detectives were popular before 1929, when *Partners in Crime* was first published. (It is still available in paperback reprint.) Among the detectives parodied are Dr. Thorndyke, Bull Dog Drummond, Sherlock Holmes, Father Brown, The Old Man in the Corner, Hanaud, Inspector French, Roger Sheringham, Dr. Fortune, and Hercule Poirot.

The Floating Admiral [by] Certain Members of the Detection Club. Jove, 1993. First published in 1932. Thirteen authors successively wrote a chapter of this book, none knowing the final solution of the crime (although in the appendix each of them provides one, not revealed to the other authors). Among the familiar creators of this pseudo-parody are G. K. Chesterton, G. D. H. and M. Cole, Henry Wade, Agatha Christie, Dorothy L. Sayers, Ronald A. Knox, Freeman Wills Crofts, Edgar Jepson, and Anthony Berkeley ("Clearing up the Mess").

Kaye, Marvin. *The Game Is Afoot: Parodies, Pastiches and Ponderings of Sherlock Holmes*. St. Martin's Press, 1995. A collection of parodies and pastiches, both old and new, by authors such as Bret Harte, O. Henry, Manly Wade Wellman, and many more. Several essays by various writers are also included.

Mainwaring, Marion. *Murder in Pastiche; Or, Nine Detectives All at Sea*. Macmillan, 1954. Reprinted in 1989 by Rowan Press. Seeking to solve the murder on the luxury liner are passengers Atlas Poireau, Sir Jon Nappleby, Jerry Pason, Broderick Tourneur, Trajan Beare, Miss Fan Silver, Spike Bludgeon, Mallory King, and Lord Simon Quinsey.

Melling, John Kennedy. *Murder Done to Death: Parody and Pastiche in Detective Fiction.* Scarecrow Press, 1996. Analysis of novel and short story
parodies and pastiches.

Naked Came the Manatee. Putnam, 1997. Carl Hiaasen, Elmore Leonard,
Edna Buchanan, Dave Barry, James W. Hall, Lee Standiford, Paul
Levine, Brian Antoni, Vicki Henricks, Tananarive Due, John Dufresne,
Carolina Hospital, and Evelyn Mayerson all contributed a chapter in this
riotous tale featuring a manatee named Booger, three severed heads, four
murders, and several Castro impersonators.

Encyclopedias

DeAndrea, William L. *Encyclopedia Mysteriosa: A Comprehensive Guide to
the Art of Detection in Print, Film, Radio, and Television.* Macmillan,
1994. Entries for authors, major characters, titles for all media, and genre
performers. Essays include "The Batman," "Comic Art Detectives,"
"Dime Novels," "Fandom," "The Hard-Boiled Detective," "Juvenile Mysteries," "Mystery Magazines," "Pulps," "Science Fiction Mysteries,"
"Sherlockiana," and "Dick Tracy." Also included are a glossary and listings of bookstores, organizations and awards, and magazines and journals.
Winner of the 1994 Edgar Award for Best Critical or Biographical Work.

Steinbrunner, Chris, and Otto Penzler. *Encyclopedia of Mystery and Detection.* McGraw-Hill, 1976. Entries are largely under authors and fictional
detectives or other important characters. There are a few encyclopedia articles: "Black Mask"; "Collecting Detective Fiction"; "Comic Art Detectives"; "Dime Novels"; "Had-I-But-Known School"; "Locked Room
Mysteries"; "Organizations"; "Orientals, Sinister"; "Pulp Magazines";
"Radio Detectives"; "Scientific Detectives"; "TV Detectives." Author
bibliographies include full stage, screen, radio, and television versions.
The author essays are usually critical. Illustrations are from books and
films; there are also many portraits.

Who's Who: Pseudonyms and Characters

Many of the reference works provide pseudonyms and lists of characters,
particularly the detective. Hubin lists all pseudonyms, provides cross-
references, and indexes the series characters. The book by Penzler and others
(see entry in this list) provides little that is not in Steinbrunner (above), but the
organization of the material is appealing, as is the tone.

Penzler, Otto, Chris Steinbrunner, Charles Shibuk, Marvin Lachman, and
Francis M. Nevins, Jr., comps. *Detectionary: A Bibliographical Diction-
ary of Leading Characters in Detective and Mystery Fiction, Including
Famous and Little Known Sleuths, Their Helps, Rogues Both Heroic and
Sinister, and Some of Their Memorable Adventures, as Recounted in
Novels, Short Stories, and Films.* Overlook Press, 1977. There are four

sections. "Detectives" lists the fictional detective with a biographical sketch. "Rogues & Helpers" gives a biographical sketch for criminals and villains as well as for all types of Dr. Watsons, including police detectives secondary to the major private or amateur detective. "Cases" provides a summary of selected mystery novels. "Movies" annotates under detective or movie title a selection of movies, particularly those in series. An author index includes detectives and titles of novels. Illustrations are from motion pictures. While this is no longer in print, there is no other work that replaces it. It can still be found in many library collections.

Writers' Manuals

Although meant for the writer of mysteries, the following manuals are informative, critical, and interesting reading for the detective/mystery fan.

Blythe, Hal, Charlie Sweet, and John Landreth. *Private Eyes: A Writer's Guide to Private Investigating*. Writer's Digest Books, 1993.

Mystery Writers of America. *Writing Mysteries: A Handbook.* Edited by Sue Grafton. Writer's Digest Books, 1992.

Roth, Martin. *The Writer's Complete Crime Reference Book*. Writer's Digest Books, 1993.

Magazines and Fanzines

The pulp magazines that made the fame of many detective story writers are long gone. Two magazines remain important to the detective short story: the venerable *Ellery Queen's Mystery Magazine* (since 1941) and *Alfred Hitchcock's Mystery Magazine* (started in 1956). Beginning in 1985 in trade paperback format, *The New Black Mask Quarterly* has provided excellent selections of new fiction. *Mysterious Intent* began publishing in 1995. It includes short stories by new and established mystery writers as well as interviews and mini-synopses of new books. Wide review coverage is available in *Mystery News* (bimonthly, 1981) and in *I Love a Mystery* (monthly, 1984). *The Drood Review* (bimonthly, 1986), *Mystery Review* (quarterly, 1991), and *Mystery Scene Magazine* (bimonthly, 1984) review hardcover and paperback editions. Unfortunately for those looking for reviews, but luckily for those who just read voraciously, it is estimated that the annual output of crime novels is now between 1,500 and 1,800, meaning, of course, that not all new novels can (or will) be reviewed. *The Armchair Detective,* formerly a good resource for hardcover reviews, ceased publication in 1997.

Associations and Conventions

Associations of mystery and crime writers serve to further the status and publishing of the subgenre as well as the economic welfare of writers. The U.S. and British associations present annual prizes. The prestige of these associations is recognized by publishers, who note an author's prize-winning status in advertisements and on book jackets.

Associations

Crime Writers' Association. This British group was founded in 1953. The "Gold Daggers" are the annual awards. There is a memorial John Creasey First Novel award.

Crime Writers of Canada. Founded in 1982, this group presents Arthur Ellis Awards (named after the traditional pseudonym for Canada's official hangman) in the categories of best novel, best first novel, best true crime book, best short story, and best work of criticism or reference.

Detection Club. This British honorary association was founded in 1928. It has a delightful oath to which new members subscribe. The association has published several anthologies to benefit the club. Several novels in which members of the Club wrote successive chapters (all unknowing of the final solution to the mystery) were published in the 1930s and have been reprinted in the 1970s: *Ask a Policeman, Crime on the Coast, No Flowers by Request, Double Death, The Floating Admiral, The Scoop,* and *Behind the Screen.*

International Association of Crime Writers. Founded in 1986, its national chapters present Hammett Awards.

Mystery Writers of America. This U.S. organization was founded in 1945. "Edgars" (Edgar Allan Poe Awards) are presented in several categories at the annual dinner. An annual anthology (the first one published in 1946) is published for the benefit of the association. The 33d annual anthology, *The Edgar Winners* (Dial, 1980), has an appendix listing "Edgar and Special Awards, 1945–1978" for Grand Master, Best Novel, Best First Novel, Best Short Story, Best Paperback Original, Best Juvenile, Best Fact-Crime, Best Critical/Biographical Study, Outstanding Mystery Criticism, Best Motion Picture, and Special Awards.

Private Eye Writers of America. This U.S. group was established in 1982. The Shamus award is for outstanding paperback and hardcover novels. The Eye award is for career achievement.

Sisters in Crime. Formed in 1985 to work for gender equality in crime publishing, this is an international organization, with over 3,000 members in 2000.

Conventions

BoucherCon. This is the annual Anthony Boucher memorial convention. The first was held in 1969 and 29th in 1998. Anthony Boucher, a pseudonym, of William Anthony Parker White, wrote detective and science fiction stories and was notable as a critic and reviewer. In *Rocket to the Morgue* (1942), published under the pseudonym H. H. Holmes and reprinted in paperback under the name Anthony Boucher, is found a neat combination of this author's detection and science fiction interests: The suspects are science fiction writers, amusingly articulate about the genre, and a science fiction character seemingly come to life.

International Congress of Crime Writers. The first congress was held in London in 1975, the second in New York in 1978, and the third in Stockholm in 1981. (The last brought forth the statement that crime really pays in Sweden: Both Swedish and translated authors sell extremely well.)

Left-Coast Crime. Awards the Lefty Award for the funniest novel of the previous year. The 10th annual convention is scheduled for March 2000 in Tucson, Arizona.

Malice Domestic. An annual convention celebrating "cozy mysteries." It's held annually in the Washington, D.C. area. The twelfth convention is in May of 2000.

Book Clubs

The Detective Book Club reprints current titles by three authors together in one volume. All are good buys for public libraries.

Mystery Guild (Doubleday) distributes book club editions of selected current thrillers. Mystery Guild also stocks for distribution some older titles and omnibus volumes (usually three titles in one volume, by a single author).

Publishers

Almost all major U.S. and British houses publish some crime novels, and a few have large lines or named series. New mystery novels are often reprinted within the year of publication, either by the house that issued the original hardcover or by a mass market paperback publisher. The following are houses that published crime novels in 1998 and 1999.

Arrow (UK)
Avon
Ballantine
Bantam
Berkley
Black Lizard (Vintage)
Carroll & Graf
Century (UK)
Corgi (UK)
Crime Line
Crown
Delacorte
Dell
Dutton
Faber and Faber (UK)
Fawcett Books
Forge
Harcourt Brace

HarperCollins

Heinemann (UK)

Henry Holt & Co.

Hodder & Stoughton (UK)

Hyperion

Intrigue Press

Ivy

Kensington

Knopf

Little, Brown

Macmillan (UK) **3**

Minotaur (imprint of St. Martin's Press)

Mysterious Press (imprint of Warner): http://www.twbookmark.com/
   mystery (accessed 20 January 2000)

Newstar

Norton

Orion (UK)

Penguin Books (UK)

Pocket Books

Poisoned Pen Press (reprints of classic mysteries): http://www.
   poisonedpenpress.com (accessed 20 January 2000)

Prime Crime (imprint of Berkley)

Putnam

Random House

Rue Morgue Press (reprints of classic mysteries)

Scribner

Signet

Simon & Schuster

Soho Press

St. Martin's Press

Twilight (imprint of Avon): http://www.avonbooks.com/twilight
   (accessed 20 January 2000)

Villard

Vintage Crime/Black Lizard

Walker

Warner Books

Weidenfeld & Nicolson (UK)

William Morrow

Write Way Publishing: http://www.writewaypub.com/mystery/ (Accessed 20 January 2000)

Online Resources

The plethora of resources on the World Wide Web is overwhelming. The following sites are of particular interest and use to librarians and booksellers. Additional online resources and updates to the links listed here are regularly published on the Genreflecting Web site at http://www.mancon.com/genre.

African-American Mystery Page, http://www.aamystery.com (accessed 20 January 2000).

ClueLass, http://www.cluelass.com (accessed 20 January 2000). Links to many sites of interest to mystery fans. Lists forthcoming titles.

The Gumshoe Site, http://www.nsknet.or.jp/~jkimura (accessed 20 January 2000).

The MacGuffin Guide to Detective Fiction, http://www.macguffin.net (accessed 20 January 2000).

Miss Lemon, http://www.iwillfollow.com/dorothyl/introduction.html (accessed 20 January 2000). Subscription information for DorothyL.

Mysterious Home Page, http://www.webfic.com/mysthome (accessed 20 January 2000). Links to reviews, information on mystery organizations, conferences, magazines, awards, and much more.

MysteryNet.Com, http://www.MysteryNet.com (accessed 20 January 2000).

Overbooked, http://freenet.vcu.edu/education/literature/mystpage.html (accessed 20 January 2000). A volunteer project by the Chesterfield County (Virginia) Public Library collection management staff, it features information about awards, bookstores, authors, charcters, magazines, organizations, publishers, reviews, reading lists, and new mysteries.

The Thrilling Detective, http://www.colba.net/~kvnsmith/thrillingdetective (accessed 20 January 2000).

D's Crime Picks

Cannell, Stephen J. *King Con.*

Evanovich, Janet. *One for the Money.*

Grant, Linda. *Vampire Bytes.*

Hiaasen, Carl. *Lucky You.*

Johansen, Iris. *The Face of Deception.*

Lawrence, Margaret. *Hearts and Bones.*

Margolin, Phillip. *The Undertaker's Widow.*

Newman, Sharan. *The Wandering Arm.*

Chapter 4

Adventure

"The thirst for adventure is the vent which Destiny offers; a war, a crusade, a gold mine, a new country, speak to the imagination and offer swing and play to the confined powers."

—Ralph Waldo Emerson, *Natural History of Intellect* (1893)

"There are two kinds of adventurers: those who go truly hoping to find adventure and those who go secretly hoping they won't."

—William Least Heat-Moon, *Blue Highways: A Journey into America* (1983)

"I am not an adventurer by choice but by fate."

—Vincent Van Gogh, *The Complete Letters of Vincent Van Gogh*, Vol. 2 (1958)

"The test of an adventure is that when you're in the middle of it, you say to yourself, 'Oh, now I've got myself into an awful mess; I wish I were sitting quietly at home.' And the sign that something's wrong with you is when you sit quietly at home wishing you were out having lots of adventure."

—Thornton Wilder, *The Matchmaker* (1955)

"If we didn't live venturously, plucking the wild goat by the beard, and tumbling over precipices, we should never be depressed, I've no doubt; but already should be faded, fatalistic and aged."

—Virginia Woolf, *A Writer's Diary* (1924)

Themes and Types

The novel of adventure can take many different directions—it can be a story of survival, exploration, intrigue, or battle. For several decades, the leading adventure subgenre was that of spy or espionage, but the end of the Cold War in the 1980s contributed to a decline in its popularity. (Although the wacky *Austin Powers* movies may be contributing to a resurgence.) In the 1990s, the technothriller is the leading adventure genre. Writers in this genre are making big money. An item in *Publishers Weekly* reported that, in 1994, Clive Cussler was paid a $14 million advance for his next two Dirk Pitt novels. Tom Clancy's 1998 best seller *Rainbow Six* reportedly sold over 2 million copies. The adventure and its subgenres are alive and well!

Adventure can be described as the pure essence of why people read genre fiction. The heroic exploits of larger-than-life protagonists and the ultimate triumph of the good guys over the bad are the driving forces in this type. Strong plots, heavy with action, are powerful lures to readers. Adventure readers often also thrive on Westerns, science fiction, and fantasy.

Sometimes it is difficult to place titles or authors into subgenres. For example, Clive Cussler's novels typify adventure, with a little bit of just about every thriller subgenre thrown in somewhere: In the various adventures of Dirk Pitt, one finds struggles for survival, exploration of the sea and exotic locales, intrigue, daring rescues, treasure hunting, exploits of a soldier-for-hire, and male romance.

Spy/Espionage

The spy or secret agent has never been a fully respectable figure. He or she seldom appeared in literature before the twentieth century as a major figure; by the 1990s the spy character had all but disappeared. Throughout the middle part of the century, however, spies in all their various permutations were the epitome of adventure. The pattern for this subgenre was set in the following early classics, which were still in print in 1999.

Buchan, John

The Thirty-Nine Steps (1915). This book introduces Richard Hannay, spy-catcher and spy, who appears in several novels. *The Thirty-Nine Steps* has one of the greatest, long chase scenes in the genre. It became a classic motion picture, directed by Alfred Hitchcock.

Chesterton, G. K.

The Man Who Was Thursday: A Nightmare (1908). The surreal world of anarchists and double agents.

Childers, Erskine

The Riddle of the Sands (1903). Introduces the theme of the German plot to invade England, complete with a British traitor and an amateur hero.

Conrad, Joseph

The Secret Agent (1907). *The Secret Agent* brings in the world of revolutionaries and anarchists.

Under Western Eyes (1911). *Under Western Eyes* introduces the double agent.

Kipling, Rudyard

Kim. (1901). "The Great Game," as Kim calls his spying for British intelligence in India, introduces the exotic background, an aspect that adds greatly to the appeal of the genre. How Kim, as a boy, is trained for his work is described marvelously.

Maugham, W. Somerset

Ashenden: Or, The British Agent (1928). Maugham was an agent during World War I, probably the first of the agents to turn his experience into a novel. He introduces the antihero as agent. His tone is realistic and sardonic, and the outrageous or sensational is toned down to the ordinary.

Oppenheim, E. Phillips

The Great Impersonation (1920). This is the only one of Oppenheim's many spy novels to survive. His first published novel of international intrigue was issued in 1898 and several more appeared during World War I. He introduced the spy world of elegant high society and exotic European cities; Monte Carlo with its gambling setting was often used.

Orczy, Baroness

The Scarlet Pimpernel (1905). The aristocratic fop as a disguise for the highly intelligent agent is here at its most romantic. The theme is introduced of daring rescues from enemy countries, in this case aristocrats saved from the guillotine during the French Revolution.

The early classic authors have successors in a small group of writers who have set the tone for the spy/espionage novel. They have been imitated, but rarely surpassed. Among the successors that continue to be available in libraries and in print are the following.

Ambler, Eric

The Middle East and the Balkans are the settings for Ambler's tales of antiheroes and amateurs unwittingly caught up in a spy network run by unromanticized spymasters directing sardonic agents.

Fleming, Ian

James Bond, 007, the British Secret Service agent, is of course among the immortals. Fleming had experience in naval intelligence during World War I. The first Bond adventure, *Casino Royale* (1953), established his flamboyant characteristics. Sex and sadism in an international setting were ingredients for some outrageous adventures with Cold War spies. Linked to Bond is the tag "Licensed to Kill." The Bond legend has continued beyond the death of its creator. The most recent 007 title is *The Facts of Death* (1998), written by Raymond Benson, who has taken over from John E. Gardner.

Greene, Graham

Greene is not considered a genre fiction author, but has written three spy novels important to the genre, his first being *The Confidential Agent* (1939). During World War II he was in intelligence and undoubtedly drew from his experience for *the* classic parody of the genre, *Our Man in Havana*, which reduces everything to the ridiculous.

The Quiet American (1955). A somber spy novel.

Our Man in Havana (1958).

Household, Geoffrey

Rogue Male (1938). This is the prototype story of the private individual who undertakes his own spy mission, encountering extreme danger and exciting chases.

Innes, Michael

Best known for his detective stories, Innes wrote several spy novels notable for sometimes outrageously fantastical plots and characters:

The Secret Vanguard (1940).

Appleby on Ararat (1941).

The Journeying Boy (1949).

Operation Pax (1951).

The Man from the Sea (1955).

Le Carré, John

Le Carré's experience was in the British Foreign Office. In *Tinker, Tailor, Soldier, Spy* (1975) and *Smiley's People* (1979), the main character is George Smiley, the antithesis of James Bond.

The Spy Who Came in from the Cold (1963). This set the classic pattern for the unheroic spy, the pattern of double agents, and the anatomization of the bureaucracy of intelligence headquarters operations.

Tailor of Panama (1996). Inspired by Greene's classic *Our Man in Havana*.

The international scene and exotic locales set the backdrop for competent professionals, who often are sandbagged by corrupt intelligence departments. Often there is a generous dollop of sex and sadism.

There are also several spy/espionage series that trace the exploits of particular spies. Many of these authors write in other subgenres of the thriller as well. The authors are grouped by the spy's country of allegiance (although, occasionally, any spy's allegiance may seem confused).

The greatest number of spies belong to the United States and Great Britain; spies of both nationalities are usually in conflict, using their wits *and* physical force, with Russia's spies. The protagonist is usually an intelligence agency employee but may be a freelance.

The end of the Cold War seemingly sounded the death knell for the spy thriller. A few titles have been added recently, mostly by long-established authors, but by and large the following lists of spy books feature the tried and true that still have followings in public libraries.

United States

Archer, Jeffrey
The Eleventh Commandment.

Block, Lawrence
Tanner on Ice. Evan Michael Tanner, last seen in the early 1970s, has been thawed from cryogenic sleep and heads to Burma. The earlier books in the series have been reissued.

The Canceled Czech.

The Thief Who Couldn't Sleep.

Breton, Thierry, and Denis Beneich
Softwar. Computer espionage.

Buckley, William F., Jr. Featuring Blackford Oates.
Saving the Queen.

Stained Glass.

Who's on First.

Marco Polo, If You Can.

The Story of Henri Tod.

See You Later, Alligator.

High Jinx.

Mongoose R.I.P.

Tucker's Last Stand.

A Very Private Plot.

Chacko, David
The Black Chamber: A Novel.

Condon, Richard
The Manchurian Candidate.

Crosby, John
Men in Arms. Featuring Horatio Cassidy.

DeAndrea, William L. Featuring Jeffrey Bellman. Also known as Clifford Driscoll and Allan Trotter.
Cronus.

Snark.

Azrael.

Atropos.

Finder, Joseph
Extraordinary Powers.

Granger, Bill. Featuring Deveraux, code name November Man.

The November Man.

League of Terror.

Henry McGee Is Not Dead.

The Man Who Heard Too Much.

The Infant of Prague.

The British Cross.

The Shattered Eye.

The Zurich Numbers.

The Last Good German.

Burning the Apostle.

Griffin, W. E. B.

The Last Heroes. Originally published under the pseudonym Alex Baldwin.

Hamilton, Donald

Featuring Matt Helm in paperback series.

Hood, William

Spy Wednesday.

Cry Spy.

The Sunday Spy.

Hoyt, Richard

James Burlane series.

Hughes, Dorothy B.

The Davidian Report.

Hyde, Anthony

The Red Fox.

China Lake.

Formosa Straits.

Hynd, Noel. Featuring Bill Mason.

Flowers from Berlin.

The Sandler Inquiry.

False Flags.

Ignatius, David

Agents of Innocence.

Lambert, Derek

The Man Who Was Saturday.

The Red Dove.

Lindsey, David L.
The Color of Night.

Littell, Robert

The Amateur.

The October Circle.

The Debriefing.

The Defection of A. J. Lewinter.

Walking Back the Cat.

Agent in Place.

Ludlum, Robert

"Ludlum deals in male fantasies, and there are few two-fisted scribes with seven-figure advances who do it better."—*Time*, March 10, 1986

Featuring Jason Bourne.

The Bourne Identity.

The Bourne Supremacy.

The Bourne Ultimatum.

Featuring Brian Scofield.

Matarese Circle.

Matarese Countdown.

Lustbader, Eric Van
Jian.

Mason, F. Van Wyck. Featuring Hugh North.

Pollock, J. C.
Payback.

Shelby, Philip

Gatekeeper.

Thomas, Ross. Featuring Mac McCorkle and Mike Padillo.
Missionary Stew.

The Eighth Dwarf.

The Cold War Swap.

Twilight at Mac's Place.

Trevanian
The Eiger Sanction.

Loo Sanction.

Warga, Wayne
Hardcover.

Woods, Stuart
Deep Lie.

Great Britain

Allbeury, Ted
Moscow Quadrille.

The Judas Factor.

Armstrong, Campbell
White Light.

Bagley, Desmond
Running Blind.

The Enemy.

Canning, Victor
Birds of a Feather.

Memory Boy.

Coles, Manning
Drink to Yesterday.

Creasey, John
A number of series characters appear under his several pseudonyms: Peter Ross, Gordon Craigie, Bruce Murdoch, Mary Dell, Dr. Palfrey, Patrick Dawlish.

Deighton, Len
The Ipcress File.

Funeral in Berlin.

Spy Story.

Catch a Falling Spy. (Twinkle, Twinkle, Little Spy.)

Bernard Samson is the spy in the following three trilogies.

Trilogy:
Berlin Game.

Mexico Set.

London Match.

Trilogy:
Spy Hook.

Spy Line.

Spy Sinker.

Trilogy:

    Faith.

    Hope.

    Charity.

Denham, Bertie

    Two Thyrdes.

    The Man Who Lost His Shadow.

Dickinson, Peter

    Walking Dead.

Eagleton, Clive

    Skirmish.

    Missing from the Record.

Follett, Ken

    Lie Down with Lions.

    Eye of the Needle.

    The Man from St. Petersburg.

    Key to Rebecca.

Forbes, Bryan

    The Endless Game.

    The Spy at Twilight.

Forrest, Anthony

    A Balance of Dangers. Featuring Captain John Justice, Napoleonic Wars.

Forsyth, Frederick

    The Fourth Protocol.

    The Devil's Alternative.

    The Day of the Jackal.

    The Odessa File.

    The Dogs of War.

    The Deceiver.

    The Fist of God.

    Icon.

Freemantle, Brian. Featuring Charlie Muffin.

    Charlie Muffin.

    Goodbye to an Old Friend.

    Betrayals.

Gardner, John E.

The Nostradamus Traitor.

The Garden of Weapons. Featuring Herbie Kruger.

The Secret Generations. Featuring the Railton family.

Continuation of Ian Fleming's James Bond series:

License Renewed.

For Special Services.

Icebreaker.

Role of Honor.

Win, Lose, or Die.

Brokenclaw.

Garner, William

A Big Enough Wreath. Featuring Michael Jagger.

Gethin, David

Point of Honor. Featuring Halloran.

Gilbert, Michael

Mr. Calder and Mr. Behrens.

The Empty House.

Haggard, William

Hard Sell.

The Money Man. Featuring Charles Russell.

Hale, John

The Whistle Blower.

Hall, Adam. Featuring Quiller.

Quiller.

The Quiller Memorandum.

The Sinkiang Executive.

Quiller Meridian.

Harcourt, Palma

A Matter of Conscience.

Shadows of Doubt.

Climate for Conspiracy.

Cover for a Traitor.

Higgins, Jack.

Featuring Liam Devlin.

The Eagle Has Landed.

Touch the Devil.

Confessional.

Featuring Sean Dillon.

Thunder Point.

On Dangerous Ground.

Angel of Death.

Drink with the Devil.

Eye of the Storm.

Hill, Reginald

The Spy's Wife.

Traitor's Blood.

Hone, Joseph

The Oxford Gambit. Featuring Peter Marlow.

Hunter, Stephen

The Spanish Gambit.

Luard, Nicholas

The Robespierre Serial.

The Shadow Spy.

Lyall, Gavin. Featuring Major Harry Maxim.

The Secret Servant.

The Conduct of Major Maxim.

The Crocus List.

Masters, John

The Himalayan Concerto.

Mather, Berkely

With Extreme Prejudice.

Mitchell, James

Smear Job. Featuring Callan.

Moss, Robert

Carnival of Spies.

Perry, Ritchie
Fools' Mate. Featuring Phillis.

Price, Anthony
Our Man in Camelot.

The Labyrinth Makers.

Gunner Kelly.

Sion Crossing. Featuring Dr. David Audley.

Ross, Angus. Featuring Marcus Farrow and Charlie McGowan.

Royce, Kenneth
The Mosley Receipt.

The XYZ Man. Featuring Spider Scott.

Russell, Charles
The Spy Is Dead.

Savarin, Julian Jay
The Hammerhead.

Seaman, Donald
The Wilderness of Mirrors.

Sela, Owen
The Kiriov Tapes.

Thomas, Craig
Foxfire.

Wolfsbane.

Wild Cat.

Wheatley, Dennis. Featuring Gregory Sallus.

U.S.S.R.

Burke, Martyn
The Commissar's Report.

Demille, Nelson
The Charm School.

Eagleton, Clive
Troika.

Furst, Alan
    Night Soldiers.

Giovannetti, Alberto
    Requiem for a Spy.

Pape, Gordon, and Tony Aspler
    The Music Wars.

Sela, Owen
    The Kremlin Control.

Trenhaile, John
    A View from the Square.
    The Man Called Kyril.
    Nocturne for a General.
    The Gates of Exquisite View.
    The Mahjongg Spies.

France

Furst, Alan
    The World at Night.
    Red Gold.

Lescroart, John T.
    Son of Holmes. Combined spy and detection with August Lupin and a very young Nero Wolfe.

Bulgaria

Furst, Alan
    Night Soldiers.

Pearson, Ridley
    Never Look Back.

West Germany

Herlin, Hans
    Solo Run.

Comic

Spy stories tend to be quite grim. There are, however, a few inept and comic spies.

Butterworth, Michael
Remains to Be Seen.

Dowling, Gregory
Double-Take.

Gardner, John
Air Apparent. Featuring Boysie Oakes.

Greene, Graham
Our Man in Havana.

Women

Women as spies appear frequently as secondary characters. In each of the following books, a woman is the main character; four of the women are series characters.

Aaron, David
Crossing by Night. Featuring Elizabeth Pack.

Aline, Countess of Romanones
The Well-Mannered Assassin.

Anthony, Evelyn. Featuring Davina Graham.
The Defector.

The Avenue of the Dead.

Albatross.

The Company of Saints.

Deverell, Diana
12 Drummers Drumming.

Night on Fire. Kathryn "Casey" Collins works for a terrorist-fighting State Department agency.

Duffy, Margaret
Ingrid Langley is married to fellow agent Patrick Gillard in this comedic British series.

Brass Eagle.

Death of a Raven.

Who Killed Cock Robin?

Rook Shoot.

Gilman, Dorothy. Featuring Mrs. Pollifax.
The Unexpected Mrs. Pollifax.

Mrs. Pollifax and the Hong Kong Buddha.

Mrs. Pollifax and the China Station.

Mrs. Pollifax and the Second Thief.

Mrs. Pollifax Pursued.

Mrs. Pollifax and the Lion Killer.

Mrs. Pollifax, Innocent Tourist.

The first book in the series appeared in 1966 and the 13th in 1997, all with exotic locales.

Ludlum, Robert

The Scorpio Illusion.

Lynds, Gayle

Masquerade.

MacInnes, Helen

Above Suspicion (1941). With this book MacInnes began a best-selling line of novels of romantic international intrigue. Her female spy is usually an amateur and often paired romantically with another amateur, all in the most exotic spots in Europe.

Ride a Pale Horse (1985). Her 21st, and last, novel.

O'Donnell, Peter

Featuring Modesty Blaise, a character who began in the comic strips in 1962 and appeared first in book form in 1965. She is the female equivalent of James Bond.

Truman, Margaret

Murder in the CIA. Featuring Colette Cahill.

Williams, Amanda Kyle

A Singular Spy.

Club Twelve.

The Providence File. Featuring CIA agent Madison McGuire, lesbian.

The following two spy novels defy simple categorization.

Batchelor, John Calvin

American Falls. A historical novel of the U.S. Civil War, about the origin of the Union Secret Service and the Confederate Secret Service.

Gollin, James

The Philomel Foundation. A group of young American musicians, The Antiqua Players, get involved with a spy from East Germany. Later titles about the group belong in the amateur detective category. Originally published in 1980, it was reissued in 1997.

Nasty Nazis

Somehow Nazis keep right on popping up in adventure fiction. Often they are not of the neo kind but rather remnants of old Hitlerian plots. Titles about Nazis can usually be identified by a swastika or the lightning bolt symbol of the SS on the cover.

Diehl, William
27. On the eve of World War II an ex-bootlegger takes on agent 27, the Third Reich's perfect spy.

Folsom, Allan
The Day After Tomorrow. Hitler makes a guest appearance.

Gifford, Thomas
The Wind Chill Factor. Nazi survivors plan to resurrect the Reich.

Heywood, Joseph
Berkut.

Johnson, Haynes
The Landing.

Levin, Ira
Boys from Brazil.

Llewellyn, Sam
Maelstrom. Modern-day Norwegian Nazis.

Ludlum, Robert
The Apocalypse Watch. An American Agent disappears after infiltrating the neo-Nazi Brotherhood of the Watch.

Pollock, J. C.
Goering's List. Nazi plunder leads to recent assassinations.

Technothrillers

Technothrillers emerged in the 1980s as one of the most popular types of adventure tale. Tom Clancy's *The Hunt for Red October* generated an interest in books that used technology to the extreme that the gadget became as important as a character. Until the enormous changes in Eastern Europe late in the 1980s, the enemy was usually the Soviets, and a common theme was that of the "good Russian" who in some way conveyed superior Soviet technology to the United States. More recent technothrillers use the Middle East and South America for settings. The war on drugs is also finding an important place in the plots of technothrillers.

Anderson, Kevin J., and Doug Beason
Ignition.

Ballard, Robert, and Tony Chiu
Bright Shark.

Berent, Mark

Rolling Thunder.

Steel Tiger.

Phantom Eagle.

Eagle Station.

Storm Flight.

Bond, Larry
Red Phoenix.

Vortex.

Cauldron.

Brown, Dale
Silver Tower.

Flight of the Old Dog.

Hammerheads.

Chains of Command.

Day of the Cheetah.

Night of the Hawk.

Storming Heaven.

Shadows of Steel.

Fatal Terrain.

The Tin Man.

Butler, Jimmie
The Iskra Incident.

Carpenter, Scott

The Steel Albatross.

Deep Flight.

Clancy, Tom. Featuring Jack Ryan.

Hunt for Red October.

Red Storm Rising.

Cardinal of the Kremlin.

Sum of All Fears.

Clear and Present Danger.

Patriot Games.

Without Remorse.

Debt of Honor.

       Executive Order.

       Rainbow Six.

Clancy, Tom, and Steve R. Pieczenik

       Tom Clancy's Op Center series.

Cobb, James H. Featuring Naval Commander Amanda Lee Garrett.

       Choosers of the Slain.

       Sea Strike.

       Sea Fighter.

Cook, Nick

       Aggressor.

Coonts, Stephen. Featuring Jake Grafton.

       Under Siege.

       Final Flight.

       Flight of the Intruder.

       Minotaur.

       Fortunes of War.

Coyle, Harold

       Sword Point.

       Team Yankee.

       Bright Star.

Crichton, Michael

       Airframe.

Deutermann, P. T.

       Scorpion in the Sea.

DiMercurio, Michael

       Voyage of the Devilfish.

       Attack of the Seawolf.

       Phoenix Sub Zero.

       Barracuda Final Bearing.

Durham, Guy

       Stealth.

Friedman, Gary

       Gun Men.

Garn, Jake, and Stephen Paul Cohen

       Night Launch.

Grace, Tom
>Spyder Web.

Harrison, Payne
>Storming Intrepid.
>
>Black Cipher.
>
>Thunder of Erebus.
>
>Forbidden Summit.

Herman, Richard, Jr.
>The Warbirds.
>
>Dark Wing.
>
>Iron Gate.
>
>Power Curve.
>
>Against All Enemies.

Houston, James W.
>Balance of Power.

Ing, Dean
>The Ransom of Black Stealth One.
>
>Butcher Bird.

Joseph, Mark
>To Kill the Potemkin.

Kunetka, James W.
>Parting Shot.

Leib, Franklin Allen
>Fire Arrow.
>
>Fire Dream.

Mason, Robert
>Weapon.
>
>Solo.

Massucci, Joseph
>The Millennium Project.
>
>Code: Alpha.

Mayer, Bob. Featuring Dave Riley.
>Eyes of the Hammer.
>
>Synbat.
>
>Dragon Sim 13.
>
>Cut-Out.

Eternity Base.

Z.

Merek, Jack
Target Stealth.

Blackbird.

Mezrich, Ben
Reaper.

Moore, Robert Payton
Silent Doomsday.

Peters, Ralph
Red Army.

Pineiro, R. J.
01-01-00: A Novel of the Millennium.

Pollock, J. C.
Payback.

Goering's List.

Poyer, David. Featuring Dan Lenson.
The Med.

The Gulf.

The Circle.

The Passage.

Tomahawk.

Robinson, Patrick
Nimitz Class.

Kilo Class.

Stewart, Chris
Shattered Bone.

The Kill Box.

Weber, Joe
Shadow Flight.

DEFCON One.

White, Robin A.
The Flight from Winter's Shadow.

Afterburn.

Sword of Orion.

The Last High Ground.

Biothrillers

With the advances in genetic engineering and the rise of terrorist activities in the 1990s, an emerging subgenre that combines the two arose: biothrillers. News of new and gruesomely horrible diseases has fueled the fire. As in technothrillers, the agent of change, in this case biological rather than technological, plays a major role, on a par with and sometimes ahead of characterization and plot. Cataclysmic disaster, narrowly averted, is a frequent theme. Terrorists who have genetically engineered a disease or stolen biological weapons often appear. Occasionally the culprit is merely science gone awry to disastrous ends.

Readers of biothrillers often enjoy technothrillers, disaster novels, science fiction, and horror novels that deal with medicine or science gone bad.

Anderson, Kevin J., and Doug Beason
Ill Wind.

Case, John F.
The First Horseman.

The Genesis Code.

Gerritsen, Tess
Gravity.

Bloodstream.

Harvest.

Life Support.

Hogan, Chuck
The Blood Artists.

Johansen, Iris
And Then You Die.

Koontz, Dean
Fear Nothing.

Land, Jon
Fires of Midnight.

Lynch, Patrick
Omega.

Carriers.

Marr, John S., and John Baldwin
The Eleventh Plague.

Massucci, Joseph
Code: Alpha.

Mayer, Bob
Z.

Mezrich, Ben
Reaper. Yikes! Shades of *Snow Crash.*

Nance, John J.
Pandora's Clock.
Scorpion Strike.

Patterson, James
When the Wind Blows.

Preston, Douglas, and Lincoln Child
Mount Dragon.

Preston, Richard
Cobra Event.

Financial Intrigue/Espionage

Paul Erdman started this subgenre in 1973 with *The Billion Dollar Sure Thing,* and authors have gleefully taken on the world of international banking, oil cartels, and multinational corporations as well as lesser businesses. Political chicanery is often involved, along with crooked doings among the rich and powerful. The following novels show wide variation in their plots, but money is always the prime factor.

Aaron, David
Agent of Influence.

Ambler, Eric
Send No More Roses.

Black, Gavin
The Golden Cockatrice. Featuring Paul Harris.

Blankenship, William
The Programmed Man.

Brady, James
Paris One.

Browne, Gerald A.
Hot Siberian.

Chafets, Zev
The Project.
Hang Time.

Cudlip, David
>Comprador.

Davies, Linda
>Nest of Vipers.
>Wilderness of Mirrors.

Deutermann, P. T.
>Zero Option.

Duncan, Robert L.
>Temple Dogs.

Durand, Loup
>Daddy.

Erdman, Paul E.
>The Billion Dollar Sure Thing.
>The Palace.

Finder, Joseph
>The Zero Hour.

Fowlkes, Frank
>The Peruvian Contracts.

Frey, Stephen W.
>The Vulture Fund.
>The Take Over.

Haig, Alec
>Sign on for Tokyo.

Keagan, William
>A Real Killing.

Lehman, Ernest
>The French Atlantic Affair.

Lindsey, David L.
>An Absence of Light.

Lustbader, Eric Van
>The Miko.

Maling, Arthur
>Schroeder's Game.

Patterson, James
Black Market.

Reich, Christopher
Numbered Account.

Rhodes, Russell L.
The Styx Complex.

Sanders, Lawrence
The Tangent Objective.

Stewart, Edward
Launch.

Sulitzer, Paul-Loup
Money.
Fortune.

Thomas, Ross
The Money Harvest.

Political Intrigue and Terrorism

Common to this subgenre are many of the characteristics of the spy/espionage subgenre and the disaster subgenre, with frequent overtones of science fiction. Agencies such as the CIA are often featured. The threat of terrorism is pervasive. The following books show how involved the plots of these stories are with current political problems and situations.

Abercrombie, Neil, and Richard Hoyt
Blood of Patriots.

Aellen, Richard
The Cain Conversion.

Alexander, Patrick
Show Me a Hero.

Allbeury, Ted
The Twentieth Day of January.

Archer, Jeffrey
Shall We Tell the President?
The Eleventh Commandment.

Armstrong, Campbell
Jig.

Bagley, Desmond
Juggernaut.

Bond, Larry
Day of Wrath.
The Enemy Within.

Brierley, David
Skorpion's Death.

Brown, Dale
The Tin Man.

Buchanan, William J.
Present Danger.

Cohen, William S., and Gary Hart
The Double Man.

Cole, Burt
Blood Note.

Collins, Larry, and Dominique Lapierre
The Fifth Horseman.

Coonts, Stephen
The Red Horseman.

Coppel, Alfred
The Hastings Conspiracy.

Crosby, John
An Affair of Strangers.

Cussler, Clive
Deep Six.

de Borchgrave, Arnaud
The Spike.

Drury, Allen
Pentagon.

Duncan, Robert L.
In the Enemy Camp.

Easterman, Daniel
    The Last Assassin.

Finder, Joseph
    The Zero Hour.

Fitzgerald, Gregory, and John Dillon
    The Druze Document.

Folsom, Allan
    Day After Tomorrow.
    Day of Confession.

Forsyth, Frederick
    The Devil's Conspiracy.
    The Negotiator.

Garve, Andrew
    Counterstroke.

Griffin, W. E. B.
    The New Breed.

Henissart, Paul
    Margin of Error.

Higgins, Jack
    The President's Daughter.

Hoyt, Richard
    Head of State.

Hunter, Stephen
    Point of Impact.

Lehmann-Haupt, Christopher
    A Crooked Man.

Leib, Franklin Allen
    Fire Arrow.

Littell, Robert
    The Amateur.

Ludlum, Robert
    The Bourne Identity.
    The Bourne Supremacy.
    The Bourne Ultimatum.
    The Icarus Agenda.

Malashenko, Alexei
  The Last Red August.

Mills, Kyle
  Rising Phoenix.

Morrell, David
  The League of Night and Fog.

Moss, Robert
  Moscow Rules.

Moss, Robert, and Arnaud de Borchgrave
  Monimbo.

Nance, John J.
  Medusa's Child.
  The Last Hostage.

Order, Lewis, and Bill Michaels
  The Night They Stole Manhattan.

Patterson, Richard North
  No Safe Place.

Paul, Barbara
  Liars and Tyrants and People Who Turn Blue.

Peters, Ralph
  The Devil's Garden.
  The Perfect Soldier.

Quinell, A. J.
  In the Name of the Father.

Salinger, Pierre, and Leonard Gross
  The Dossier.

Seymour, Gerald
  The Harrison Affair.

Sharp, Marilyn
  Falseface.

Shelby, Philip
  Gatekeeper.
  Days of Drums.
  Last Rights.

Stone, Robert
>Damascus Gate.

Thayer, James Stuart
>Pursuit.
>
>Ringer.

Thomas, Craig
>The Last Raven.

Thomas, Ross
>The Mordida Man.
>
>Out on the Rim.

Wager, Walter H.
>The Spirit Team.

Washburn, Mark
>The Armageddon Game.

West, Morris
>Proteus.

Wiltse, David
>Prayer for the Dead.
>
>Close to the Bone.
>
>Bone Deep.
>
>Into the Fire.
>
>The Edge of Sleep.
>
>Prayer for the Dead.

Survival

Survival is a strong motive for adventure thrillers. The survival can involve escape from a burning high-rise or from the steppes of Mongolia. The main theme that the following books have in common is this: Through wit and dogged determination, the heroes of the tale survive.

The Lone Survivor

One or a few individuals, for some reason cut off from civilization (as we know it!), resourcefully make their way out of danger.

Garber, Joseph R.
>**Vertical Run.** Dave Elliott has only himself to depend on as he tries to stay alive while being stalked in a 50-story office building.

L'Amour, Louis

The Last of the Breed. A Native American pilot crashes over Siberia.

Wood, Stuart

White Cargo. An entrepreneur goes after the drug cartel that had his yacht pirated.

Disaster

Reviewers have labeled several types of novels as "disaster" thrillers. The catastrophe may be natural (that is, nature's fury or an act of God) or man-made. Natural disasters include earthquakes, volcanic eruptions, tidal waves, meteor strikes, a new ice age, floods, plagues, aberrant behavior of bird or animal life—the only limit is the author's imagination. (However, not within that imaginative limit is the matter of the supernatural. Disasters of supernatural origin reside in horror.) Man-made disasters include nuclear explosions, accidents caused by experimenting with bacteria or with humanity's biological heritage, accidents involving aircraft or ocean vessels, or accidents caused by tampering with nature's equilibrium (for example, destroying the ozone layer); again, the range is determined by the author's imagination. Frequently, the disaster has a political link, relating this type of book to the spy/espionage subgenre. There is also a science fiction aspect in the themes of apocalypse, doomsday, and colliding worlds.

The trend in the 1990s seems to be toward narrowly averted disaster and is paralleled in movies such as *Deep Impact* and *Armageddon,* but the complete disaster with some survivors, as occurred in *Titanic,* is also popular.

Anderson, Kevin J., and Doug Beason

Ill Wind.

Bagley, Michael

The Plutonium Factor.

Bell, Madison Smartt

Waiting for the End of the World.

Block, Thomas

Mayday.

Airship.

Nine.

Orbit.

Buchanan, William J.

Present Danger.

Byrne, Robert

The Dam.

Skyscraper.

The Tunnel.

Canning, Victor
    The Doomsday Carrier.

Corley, Edwin
    The Genesis Rock.

Cravens, Gwyneth
    The Black Death.

Crichton, Michael
    The Andromeda Strain.
    Jurassic Park.

Cussler, Clive
    Raise the Titanic.

De Lillo, Don
    White Noise.

Demille, Nelson, and Thomas Block
    Mayday.

Godey, John
    The Snake.

Hailey, Arthur
    Airport.

Herbert, James
    The Rats.

Hernon, Peter
    8.4.

Herzog, Arthur
    IQ 83.
    The Swarm.
    Earthsound.
    Heat.

Hoyt, Richard
    Cool Runnings.

Hyde, Christopher
    The Wave.

Johnson, Stanley
    The Doomsday Deposit.

MacLean, Alistair
    Goodbye California.

McCullough, Colleen
    A Creed for the Third Millennium.

Moan, Terrance
    The Deadly Frost.

Moran, Richard
    Cold Sea Rising.
    Empire of Ice.

Nance, John J.
    Final Approach.

    Pandora's Clock.
    Medusa's Child.

    Scorpion Strike.

North, Edmund H., and Franklin Coen
    Meteor.

Orgill, Douglas, and John Gribbin
    The Sixth Winter.

Page, Thomas
    Sigmet Active.

Pearson, Ridley
    The Seizing of Yankee Green Mall.

Pruess, Paul
    Core.

Racine, Thomas
    The Great Los Angeles Blizzard.

Robinson, Logan
    Evil Star.

Rubens, Howard, and Jack Wasserman
    Hambro's Itch.

Scortia, Thomas N., and Frank M. Robinson
    The Nightmare Factor.
    The Prometheus Crisis.
    The Glass Inferno.
    Blowout.

Slater, Ian
> **Firespell.**

Slattery, Jesse
> **The Juliet Effect.**

Smith, Martin Cruz
> **Nightwing.**

Stern, Richard Martin
> **Flood.**
>
> **Snowbound.**
>
> **The Tower.**
>
> **Wildfire.**

Stone, George
> **Blizzard.**

Strieber, Whitley, and James W. Kunetka
> **War Day.**

Warner, Douglas
> **Death on a Warm Wind.**

Wiltse, David
> **The Fifth Angel.**
>
> **Six Days in November.**
>
> **Blown Away.**

Male Romance

In this specific subgenre, the adventurer is one who seeks adventure on land, sea, or in the air, following the old tradition of the hero who matches his strength against the powers of natural elements and enjoys the danger. While the following description of male romance is specific to the subgenre, it also applies to many of the other subgenres within adventure.

Many of these books are set in wild and primitive areas of the world. Often they feature treasure hunts or lost mines; some involve piracy; most are full of combat with villains of all sorts. The adventure is considered the subgenre of male interest just as the romance is identified for women (the sweet-and-savage romance provides women with their adventure element).

There is a political angle to adventures because many involve revolutionary action in non-European countries, gun-running, or mercenary activities. The story may concern the search for a friend or relative lost in strange circumstances, a ship or plane wreck, hijacking, hunting wild animals, pioneering treks, exploration expeditions, the overcoming of natural disasters, or an escape and the ensuing chase—the possibilities are limitless.

A few classic authors, both those described as genre writers and those considered to be writers of "literature," are listed first. The adventure story has been popular since earliest times and is not always simple to label. The subsequent groupings of adventure authors note the more popular types of backgrounds and characters.

Classic Authors

Buchan, John
> John McNab.

Burroughs, Edgar Rice
> *Tarzan series.*

Conrad, Joseph
> The Arrow of Gold.
>
> Heart of Darkness.

Curwood, James Oliver
> Nomads of the North.

Falkner, J. M.
> Moonfleet.

Haggard, H. Rider
> She.
>
> The Return of She.
>
> King Solomon's Mines.

Hughes, Richard
> A High Wind in Jamaica.

Kipling, Rudyard
> Kim.

London, Jack
> The Sea Wolf.

Macauley, Rose
> **The Towers of Trebizond.** A young Englishwoman traveling through Turkey and other parts of the Middle East on a white camel.

Sabatini, Rafael
> Captain Blood.
>
> The Sea Hawk.

Verne, Jules

Around the World in Eighty Days.

Journey to the Center of the Earth.

20,000 Leagues Under the Sea.

The Mysterious Island.

White, Stewart Edward

The Mystery.

The Rifle.

Wren, P. C.

Beau Geste.

Wild Frontiers and Exotic Lands

> We shall not cease from exploration
> And the end of all our exploring
> Will be to arrive where we started
> And know the place for the first time.

> —T. S. Eliot, from "Little Gidding" (1942)

Exotic lands and unexplored frontiers are the perfect backdrop for action-filled adventure. The following grouping lists titles with plots that take place in Asia and Africa. Many of these authors, of course, also write adventure of other types.

Bagley, Desmond

Flyaway.

Becker, Stephen

The Chinese Bandit.

The Last Mandarin.

The Blue-Eyed Shan.

Bosse, Malcolm

The War Lord.

Clavell, James

Whirlwind.

Cleary, Jon

High Road to China.

Crichton, Michael

Congo.

Davidson, Lionel

The Rose of Tibet.

Easterman, Daniel
    The Ninth Buddha.

Forester, C. S.
    The African Queen.

Grant, Maxwell
    Blood Red Rose.

Haggard, H. Rider
    King Solomon's Mines.
  The She series.
  The Alan Quartermain series.

Halkin, John
    Kenya.

Hoyt, Richard
    Tyger! Tyger!

4

Innes, Hammond
    The Big Footprints.

Lustbader, Eric Van
    French Kiss.

Mather, Berkely
  Stafford trilogy.
      Pagoda Tree.
      The Midnight Gun.
      Hour of the Dog.

Moore, William
    Bush War!

Smith, Wilbur
    The Leopard Hunts in Darkness.
    The Eye of the Tiger.
    The Burning Shore.
    The Sunbird.
  Ballantyne family saga.
      A Falcon Flies.
      Men of Men.
      The Angels Weep.

Soldier-of-Fortune

The adventure hero as picaresque soldier-of-fortune appears in many adventure novels. He is frequently an antihero. The following titles exemplify the type.

Aylward, Marcus

Harper's Folly.

Harper's Luck.

Marcinko, Richard

Rogue Warrior series.

Pollock, J. C.

Mission M.I.A.

Centrifuge.

Scott, Douglas

Eagle's Blood.

Sela, Owen

The Portuguese Fragment.

Women

Although women usually appear in adventure novels as a secondary love interest, an object of sexual desire, or an enemy/challenge, they are beginning to play the role of the adventurer. The following titles are about women as adventurers.

Haggard, H. Rider

She series. See "Classic Authors" (**p. 185**).

Llywelyn, Morgan

Grania: She-King of the Irish Seas.

O'Donnell, Peter

Modesty Blaise series. Noted among the spy/espionage titles, but Modesty Blaise is a true adventurer.

Robertson, E. A.

Four Frightened People.

Stevenson, Janet

Departure. A nineteenth-century sea adventure.

Parody

The adventure subgenre is very susceptible to parody because it takes very little exaggeration in action or character to make the heroic seem ridiculous. The popular *Austin Powers* movies are evidence of this fact. The following novels are examples of parodies.

Bonfiglioli, Kyril
All the Tea in China.

Fraser, George MacDonald
The Flashman series. The ninth in the series about this rogue antihero appeared in 1990.

> **The Pyrates.** A bawdy reworking of the romantic adventure tradition of Rafael Sabatini and Jeffery Farnol.

Gundy, Elizabeth
The Disappearance of Gregory Pluckrose.

Military and Naval Adventure

The following books belong in the adventure genre rather than with serious portrayals of warfare, although many have excellent scenes of battle. The literary (or mainstream) war novel is not included here.

Twentieth Century

Beach, Edward L.
Cold Is the Sea.

Run Silent, Run Deep. Submarines, United States, post–World War II.

Clancy, Tom
The Hunt for Red October. Submarines, U.S.-Russian political adventure that started the popular technothriller subgenre.

Cleary, Jon
A Very Private War. Australia, World War II.

Collerette, Eric J.
Ninety Feet to the Sun. Submarines, Great Britain, World War II.

Fullerton, Alexander
Featuring Nick Everard, World War II.

Gray, Edwyn
Featuring Nicholas Hamilton, submarines.

Griffin, W. E. B.
The Brotherhood of War series.

The Corps series.

Heath, Layne
CW2.

Hennessey, Max
Commander Kelly Maguire trilogy. British navy.

> **The Lion at Sea.**
>
> **The Dangerous Years.**
>
> **Back to Battle.**

Higgins, Jack
> **Luciano's Luck.**
>
> **The Eagle Has Landed.**
>
> **The Eagle Has Flown.**
>
> **Storm Warning.** World War II, U.S. forces.

Homewood, Harry
Submarines, United States, World War II.

> **Final Harbor.**
>
> **Torpedo!**
>
> **Silent Sea.**

Hough, Richard
Buller trilogy. British navy, World War I.

> **Buller's Guns.**
>
> **Buller's Dreadnought.**
>
> **Buller's Victory.**

Jackson, Robert. Featuring Wing Commander George Yoeman.

MacLean, Alistair
British army and navy, World War II. The first title is the author's first, the second is his 27th.

> **H.M.S. Ulysses.**
>
> **San Andreas.**
>
> **The Guns of Navarone.**
>
> **South by Java Head.**
>
> **Force Ten from Navarone.**
>
> **Where Eagles Dare.**

Masters, John
India, World Wars I and II.

Nightrunners of Bengal.

Bhowani Junction.

Monsarrat, Nicholas
The Cruel Sea. British navy, World War II.

Reeman, Douglas
British navy, World War II. The last title is about submarines.

Torpedo Run.

Rendezvous–South Atlantic.

A Ship Must Die.

Strike from the Sea.

The Deep Silence.

Rosenbaum, Ray
Falcons.

Hawks.

Scott, Leonard B.
The Iron Men.

The Last Run.

The Hill.

Charlie Mike.

Stanley, William
British air force, World War I.

Bomber Patrol.

Cloud Nineteenth.

Thomas, Craig
Aircraft espionage, United States–Russia.

Foxfire.

Foxfire Down.

Westheimer, David
U.S. Army and Army Air Force, World War II.

Rider in the Wind.

Von Ryan's Express.

Von Ryan's Return.

Wingate, John

Frigate.

Carrier.

Submarine.

Red Mutiny.

Go Deep. Submarines, World War II.

Wouk, Herman

The Caine Mutiny. U.S. Navy, World War II.

Historical Naval and Military Adventure

Most of the following books are in series. Many of the naval warfare series concern the Napoleonic Wars. The imitated prototype is C. S. Forester's Hornblower series, which follows Hornblower's career from midshipman to admiral. The life of Hornblower is the subject of a "biography" by C. Northcote Parkinson, *The Life and Times of Horatio Hornblower*, which is so authentic as to persuade the unwary that he really existed. Parkinson so regretted the end of the series that he started a series of his own (see entry in the following list).

This is currently one of the "hot" subgenres. To feed this hunger, publishers are even reissuing titles that originally appeared more than 150 years ago! One series that does this is The Heart of the Oak Sea Classics. The trend is also evident in science fiction, where David Feintuch's character, Nick Seafort, has been called "Horatio Hornblower in space."

Cornwell, Bernard

Featuring Richard Sharpe.

Sharpe's Eagle.

Sharpe's Gold.

Sharpe's Company.

Sharpe's Sword.

Sharpe's Enemy.

Sharpe's Honor.

Sharpe's Regiment.

Sharpe's Siege.

Sharpe's Rifles.

Sharpe's Revenge.

Sharpe's Waterloo.

Sharpe's Devil.

Sharpe's Battle.

Sharpe's Tiger.

Featuring Nathanial Starbuck, U.S. Civil War.

Forester, C. S. Featuring Horatio Hornblower.

Mister Midshipman Hornblower.

Lieutenant Hornblower.

Hornblower and the Hotspur.

Hornblower and the Atropes.

Ship of the Line.

Flying Colours.

Commodore Hornblower.

Admiral Hornblower in the West Indies.

Hall, James Norman

Doctor Dogbody's Leg. Collection of rollicking, jolly sea tales.

Heyer, Georgette

By the author of Regency romances.

An Infamous Army. An excellent story of the Battle of Waterloo.

The Spanish Bride. The Peninsular Campaign in the Napoleonic Wars.

4

Kent, Alexander

Featuring Richard Bolitho.

Lambdin, Dewey

Featuring Alan Lewrie, Royal Navy.

Logan, Mark Nicholas Minette

French navy.

MacNeill, Duncan

Captain James Ogilvie series. Frontier of India.

Marryat, Frederick. Featuring Peter Simple.

Frank Mildmay or the Naval Officer.

Mr. Midshipman Easy.

Newton Forster or the Merchant Service.

Maynard, Kenneth. Featuring Matthew Lamb.

McCutchan, Philip

Featuring Donald Cameron and St. Vincent Halfhyde, both Royal Navy and merchant marine, and Commodore Kemp.

O'Brian, Patrick

Featuring Captain Jack Aubrey and Stephen Maturin, physician. In the second title in the series, there is a meeting with Hornblower.

Parkinson, C. Northcote. Featuring Richard Delancey.

Pope, Dudley

Featuring Captain Lord Nicholas Ramage, the Yorke family.

Reeman, Douglas

Royal Marines series. Featuring the Blackwood family.

Suthren, Victor H.

Featuring Edward Mainwaring, eighteenth century.

Featuring Captain Paul Gallant, eighteenth-century French navy.

Woodman, Richard

Featuring Nathaniel Drinkwater.

Pirates

Powers, Tim

On Stranger Tides. Pirate adventure combined with dark fantasy.

Sabatini, Rafael

Captain Blood.

Smith, Wilbur

Birds of Prey. Sir Francis Courteney and his son, Hal, privateers in the seventeenth century for the British Crown, swashbuckle up and down the African coast.

Male-Action/Adventure Series

The Western has always been considered an action/adventure genre, as have many of the examples of detective and spy/espionage stories, all of which often appear with a series hero. The following series are all original titles issued by paperback publishers and noted in trade parlance as action/adventure. They are specifically aimed at a male audience. The prototypes for plots and characters may be found in the pulp magazines that flourished before the paperbacks took over as purveyors of action/adventure in the 1940s. In these series are found men (and sometimes women) who function as vengeance squads, martial arts experts, mercenaries, soldiers-of-fortune, detectives, and adventurers of almost any type. Such series, when successful, are highly lucrative, and publishers continually experiment with them. It would be futile to list all the evanescent series, of which perhaps only two dozen may be current at any time. The following, however, are a few of the enduring ones.

Johnstone, William W.
Ashes series.

Maloney, Mack
Wingman series.

Murphy, Warren, and Richard Sapir
Destroyer series. The 92d title was published in 1995 by Signet.

Pendleton, Don
Mack Bolan, The Executioner series. The 145th title was published in 1991 by Gold Eagle Books.

Robeson, Kenneth
Doc Savage series. Currently being released by Bantam in omnibus editions containing up to five previously published titles.

A Miscellany

The types within the adventure novel are diverse and frequently share characteristics with other genres. The following sampling suggests the difficulty in labeling as adventure novels those novels of suspense (which often involve a chase theme) that do not fall into a simple genre pattern. Most of these authors specialize in adventure.

Adler, Warren
    Trans-Siberian Express.

Benchley, Peter
    Jaws.
    The Deep.
    The Island.

Cannell, Stephen J.
    Riding the Snake.

Cleary, Jon
    The Golden Sabre.
    The Sundowners. A Western set in Australia.

Cussler, Clive
The adventures of underwater recovery mariner Dirk Pitt often have elements of the disaster subgenre and also political overtones.

    Raise the Titanic.
    Deep Six.
    Iceberg.

       Cyclops.

       Vixen 03.

       Night Probe.

       Pacific Vortex.

       The Mediterranean Caper.

       Flood Tide.

Gann, Ernest K.

Aviation adventure.

       The Aviator.

       The High and the Mighty.

       Blaze of Noon.

       Fate Is the Hunter.

Garfield, Brian

       Recoil.

Hagberg, David

       Critical Mass.

Hayden, Sterling

       The Voyage.

Herley, Richard

The Pagans trilogy. Stone Age England.

       The Stone Arrow.

       The Flint Lord.

       The Earth Goddess.

Household, Geoffrey

       Rogue Male.

       Rough Justice.

Ing, Dean

       Blood of Eagles.

       Flying to Pieces.

       Spooker.

Innes, Hammond

       The Black Tide.

       The Wreck of the Mary Deare.

       Medusa.

Jennings, Gary

       The Journeyer. Marco Polo's adventures.

Langley, Bob
    Falklands Gambit.

Lustbader, Eric
    Dark Homecoming.

    Floating City.

Mundy, Talbot
    King of the Khyber Rifles.

Nance, John J.
    The Last Hostage.

Nordhoff, Charles B., and James Norman Hall
    Mutiny on the Bounty.

Peters, Ralph
    Twilight of Heroes.

Poyer, D. C.
    Hatteras Blue.

Seymour, Gerald
    In Honor Bound.

Trevanian
    Shibumi.

Trew, Anthony
    Sea Fever.

    Death of a Supertanker.

Wales, Robert
    Harry. Cattle drive in Australia, 1882.

Woodhouse, Martin, and Robert Ross
    Leonardo da Vinci trilogy. Leonardo as adventure hero.

        The Medici Guns.

        The Medicine Emerald.

        The Medici Hawks.

Yates, Dornford
    Curious period pieces from the 1920s (being reprinted) about the thriller adventures of a group of wealthy friends.

        Berry and Co.

        Adele and Co.

        Blind Corner.

        Perishable Goods.

Topics

Bibliographies

Because many of the authors of spy/espionage novels also wrote mystery and detective novels, material on spy/espionage authors can also be found in some of the bibliographies (see p. 142) listed in Chapter 3, "Crime."

Drew, Bernard A. *Action Series & Sequels: A Bibliography of Espionage, Vigilante, and Soldier of Fortune Novels.* Garland, 1988.

McCormick, Donald, and Katy Fletcher. *Spy Fiction.* Facts on File, 1990. The biocritical annotations list the works. The introduction is historical and critical. In the appendix, "List of Abbreviations, Titles and Jargon Used in Espionage in Fact and Fiction," the definitions are often amusing.

Bio-Bibliographies

Benson, Raymond. *James Bond Bedside Companion.* Dodd, Mead, 1988.

Cussler, Clive, and Craig Dirgo. *Dirk Pitt Revealed.* Pocket Books, 1998.

Greenberg, Martin Harry. *The Tom Clancy Companion.* Berkley, 1992. Interview, essays, and details on the technological objects of Clancy's books.

Greenberg, Martin H., ed. *The Robert Ludlum Companion.* Bantam Books, 1993.

Macdonald, Gina. *Robert Ludlum: A Critical Companion.* Greenwood, 1997.

History and Criticism

Additional material on the spy/espionage novel can be found under "History" (see p. 144) and "Criticism" (see p. 144) of the crime story.

Smith, Myron J., Jr., and Terry White. *Cloak and Dagger Fiction: An Annotated Guide to Spy Thrillers,* 3d ed. Greenwood, 1995.

Journals and Associations

Journals

The Dossier: The Official Journal of the International Spy Society. 1981– . Quarterly. Contains both fact and fiction, also reviews.

Associations

International Spy Society. Fellowships are awarded by invitation. In 1984 the Society presented its first awards, the Oppy Awards, named for E. Phillips Oppenheim.

Writers' Guides

Newton, Michael. *Armed and Dangerous: A Writer's Guide to Weapons.* Writer's Digest Books, 1990.

————. *How to Write Action/Adventure Novels.* Writer's Digest Books, 1989.

Publishers

All the major trade publishers publish some adventure books, although they usually call them novels or sometimes thrillers. NTC/Contemporary Publishing is issuing reprints. A recent one was *Greenmantle,* by John Buchan. Buccaneer and Dover are also issuing reprints of classic spy thrillers. Penguin, Ameron, Oxford University Press, Regnery, and Carroll & Graf all publish adventure novels.

D's Adventure Picks

 4

Anderson, Kevin J., and Doug Beason. *Ill Wind.*

L'Amour, Louis. *The Last of the Breed.*

Nance, John J. *Medusa's Child.*

Preston, Richard. *Cobra Event.*

Chapter 5

Romance

> *"Romance novels comprise 55% of all mass market paperback fiction published in the U.S. and generate $1 billion in annual sales. More than 45 million people in North America alone read them."*
> —Romance Writers of America Web page

> *"I still choose to enjoy the fact that, somewhere, a warrior is being tamed by an angel."*
> —Kelly Kimbrough, a romance reader

> *"It is a truth universally acknowledged, that a single man in possession of a good fortune must be in want of a wife."*
> —Jane Austen, *Pride and Prejudice* (1813)

The Appeal of Romance

Romance is primarily a women's genre. This is not to say that men don't read romances; some do, but often covertly. Many women, sensitive to what others may think, cannot comfortably read a romance while riding on public transportation. The world as a whole has a distorted view of what romance is and who reads it. Everyone knows the stereotype of a pink-negligée-clad housewife lounging on a settee devouring bonbons along with romances, but that view couldn't be farther from the truth. Cathie Linz profiles romance readers in *Dangerous Men and Adventurous Women* (Jayne Ann Krentz, ed., University of Pennsylvania Press, 1992), using data from Harlequin Enterprises market research: "Approximately 70 percent of the readers are women under 49 years of age; 45 percent of them have attended college."

In essence, women read romance because these novels are an avenue of escapist fantasy in which a heroine gentles a warrior (his battleground can be anywhere from the boardroom to the bedroom to the sites of historic wars) and the two live happily ever after. Romance appeals to the heart and celebrates the power of love. It is a literature of optimism in which the woman (almost) always wins. Why women love the romance genre is endlessly discussed in online forums. It even has been the topic of television news shows and magazine articles.

Whatever the reason, romance seems to have a global appeal. Cathie Linz writes: "Harlequin Enterprises has reported annual sales of over 190 million books worldwide. These books are translated into over twenty languages, including Japanese, Greek, and Swedish. They are published in over 100 international markets: from North and South America, to the Far East, to Western Europe and ... Eastern Europe as well."

The appeal of romance is addressed by 19 popular romance authors in the delightful *Dangerous Men and Adventurous Women*. Demonstrating the intellectual curiosity and avid interest of romance readers, this scholarly work, due to popular demand, was reissued as a mass market paperback by Harper in 1996. Unlike most paperbacks that are pulled after mere weeks on the shelves, *Dangerous Men and Adventurous Women* can still be found in the romance sections of chain bookstores. These writers, who obviously read and love the genre in which they write, display great respect for their readers. Some of the essays discuss the coded language that is used in the novels, which to outsiders appears as purple prose but to those in the know conveys in a few words a wealth of information about the characters and situations. Jayne Ann Krentz writes that "they celebrate female power, intuition, and a female worldview that affirms life and expresses hope for the future."

That Was Then

It is about time this most personal of genres is given its due. Times were very different in library land when Betty Rosenberg wrote in the second edition of *Genreflecting*:

> Critics of Literature, suitably capitalized, avert their eyes disdainfully from the popular romance novels or dismiss their authors and readers with witty contempt. Yet their devoted readers, blissfully unaware that their taste is lamentable, have ensured by their demand the steady supply of romantic fiction since Henry Richardson's Pamela staunchly defended her virtue and attained her heart's desire. Pamela and novels by authors including Jane Austen, Charlotte and Emily Brontë, and Anthony Trollope are scorned by critics of Literature. —*Genreflecting: A Guide to Reading Interests in Genre Fiction*, 2d edition, Libraries Unlimited, 1986.

Libraries and Romance

Romance may be the least comfortable of genres for librarians. Even though it makes up a majority of all the mass market paperbacks sold in the United States, it is a genre that has traditionally not been well accepted in libraries. Many libraries don't buy paperback romances and many of the ones that buy them don't catalog them. All one needs to know that they are not ephemeral is to view the postings on one of the Internet newsgroups or e-mailing lists. Slowly and gradually acceptance is coming. *Library Journal* now publishes a quarterly romance column written by Kristin Ramsdell, winner of the Romance Writers of America Librarian of the Year Award and author of *Romance Fiction: A Guide to the Genre* (Libraries Unlimited, 1999). The September 15, 1998, cover of *Booklist* featured romance and kicked off a new era in romance reviewing: "Call us unromantic or call us elitist, but like many reviewers, we've never much bothered to review genre romance, at least until one of the genre's stars, Janet Dailey, say, made the jump into the hardcover mainstream. The continuing popularity of the genre among library patrons has finally snapped us to our senses, and beginning with this issue, romance fiction will be reviewed regularly alongside all the other genres." Because of the lack of acceptance over the years, many romance readers don't even expect to use the library for their reading needs, instead exchanging books with friends and buying them new and used. As libraries begin to provide more of what romance readers want, more romance readers will become library users.

There is no way that one can be conversant with the entire genre (approximately 2,700 romance novels were published in 1997 alone), but it behooves librarians to try samplings from different authors and dip into the online resources from time to time to try to stay current with trends.

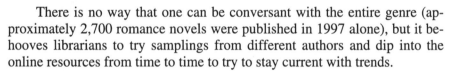

Things are getting better. It seems that librarians and reviewers are beginning to take romance seriously. Romance Writers of America (RWA) awards an annual librarian of the year award. Romance writers (and readers) have been a presence at the last four American Library Association conferences and the last two Public Library Association conferences. Romance was such a hot topic at the 1998 PLA conference that the programs on the topic were standing room only.

A Readers' Advisory Caution

Romance is a very personal kind of reading. Advising readers requires a great deal of tact and diplomacy. It is important to discern what a reader means when asking for a romance as well as determining the era, setting, degree of sexiness, and overall tone that reader is looking for.

One might classify romance readers into two types. The first is the avid reader, who knows the coded language referred to by Krentz and understands that a real romance has to end "happily ever after." The other type of romance reader is looking for the romantic story but does not require the "happily ever after" ending. This type of reader, much to the horror of the first type, considers romantic tragedy such as seen in the movie *Sommersby* or portrayed in *Romeo and Juliet* to be romance. Often this reader is looking for Danielle Steel–type books. It is important to keep in mind that each reader's definition is valid to that person even if one does not agree with it.

Readers' advisors can become more familiar with the genre by using resources such as Ramsdell's *Romance Fiction: A Guide to the Genre* (Libraries Unlimited, 1999) and by perusing the online forums such as RRA-L. Of course the best way to become conversant with the genre is to read a variety of types. With the prevalence of genre blending it is also helpful to keep in mind the romantic aspects that appear in other genres and bring those books to the attention of romance readers who may enjoy them. Elizabeth Peters's Amelia Peabody series in mystery, Lois McMaster Bujold's Vorkosigan saga in science fiction, and Patricia C. Wrede's regency-era fantasy novels are just some examples of genre crossovers.

Themes and Types

When trying to categorize romance, the first dividing line usually falls between contemporary and historical. Because romance has been a popular genre for so long (the earliest novels could be considered romances), many of the contemporaries of bygone times read as historicals now. An example that most readers are familiar with is the works of Jane Austen. A recent trend has been toward the paranormal, futuristic, or fantasy romance, which is often a romance out of time. Although some of those fall into the historical or contemporary time frame, they are treated separately here.

Within the romance genre are several quite distinctive subgenres, differentiated for appeal to disparate audiences by setting, types of characters, and handling of sexual relations, which can range from a chaste kiss to explicit and extreme. At one time publishers identified the subgenres on paperback spines or on hardcover dust jackets (for example, gothic, career, romantic suspense) but now the trend seems to be moving away from that. On paperbacks one is likely to find only the designations "romance," "historical romance," and "regency romance." Increasingly, romance novels are being published with merely the designation "novel" or "fiction."

Contemporary

Keep in mind that yesterday's contemporary is tomorrow's historical. The section that follows, written by Betty Rosenberg for the second edition of *Genreflecting,* remains pertinent for readers' advisory for that segment of readers who began reading romance in an earlier time and prefer to stay within that framework. It is also of historical interest for those who follow trends in romance.

Womanly Romance

Rosenberg's Historical Overview of Womanly Romances

The classic encompassing type of romance is the womanly romance (dominant, for example, in the Harlequin romances), contemporary in setting, with home and marriage the goals for living happily ever after. (The period romance—notably Barbara Cartland—may be essentially a womanly romance, but the historical setting adds a glamour appealing to a readership different from those who want the everyday present romantically rendered.) The earlier contemporary womanly romance was essentially "boy meets girl," in either a small town or metropolis, often in a business office (the woman marries the boss or his son), and equally often in a plot of relationships among a group of friends or family. (Much quoted is the anecdote about William Faulkner's scriptwriting days at Warner Brothers: When he left, in his office were found an empty bottle and a sheet of yellow foolscap on which he had written, five hundred times, "Boy Meets Girl.") An exotic setting was sometimes used, as in Ethel Dell's Indian romances.

After World War II, and with the change in woman's position in the world (feminism and women's liberation movements), there were definite changes in the womanly romance: more use of foreign settings, heroines were increasingly independent women (though still desirous of love and marriage), and a relaxing of social mores (i.e., permissible sexual behavior).

However, the tried-and-true romance patterns, providing a story in which happy endings are obligatory, are pursued faithfully by a large number of women authors. (The Harlequin/Mills and Boon series consist of authors who turn them out regularly; a total of 50 or more titles by each author is not unusual.) The authors continuing the traditions of womanly romances are myriad.

The following authors wrote the prototype womanly romance.

Ayres, Ruby M.

British author: over 140 novels, the first published in 1917.

Baldwin, Faith

"The First Lady of the Love Story": currently about 100 novels in hardcover and paperback.

Bloom, Ursula British

"The Queen of the romantic novel": over 500 titles.

Dell, Ethel

British author. Her first work was published in 1912, and on the best-seller list in 1916. Several have been reprinted and condensed in Barbara Cartland's Library of Love series. A sample: " 'Yes, I am mad,' he said, and the words came quick and passionate, the lips that uttered them close to her own. 'I am mad for you, Anne, I worship you. And swear that while I live no other man shall ever hold you in his arms again. Anne—goddess—queen woman—you are mine—you are mine-you are mine.' "

Norris, Kathleen

The American woman's dream in best-selling novelists, her first was published in 1911 and on the best-seller lists in 1916.

Among the prototype authors are the following, who write inspirational romance.

Hill, Grace Livingston

Over 50 novels (20 million copies) reprinted by Bantam Books and written from 1882 to 1947. The second edition of *Genreflecting* said: "Mrs. Hill's novels of romance are about wholesome people whose profound faith and generous hearts let them cope with the problems of the modern world."

Loring, Emilie

Over 50 novels, more properly belonging with the inspirational type.

Montgomery, Lucy Maude

The Anne of Green Gables series. First published in 1908.

The Emily series. Now considered for the young adult audience.

Porter, Gene Stratton

A best seller in the early twentieth century, she created a world of homely innocence and sentimental purity.

Freckles.

A Girl of the Limberlost.

Webster, Jean

Daddy-Long-Legs (1912). Now considered to be for a young adult audience.

The following authors continued the tradition of the womanly romance.

Cadell, Elizabeth

British author: about 50 novels. Light comedy and suspenseful romance. The second edition of *Genreflecting* said: "Presents a love story bound to warm the coldest heart."

The Waiting Game.

Caldwell, Taylor

Wrote 38 novels before her death in 1985. Twenty-five paperback titles, 25 million copies. Often the novels have a religious aspect and, according to the second edition of *Genreflecting,* are "liberally peopled by villains and schemers, and often ... deal with family dynasties." " 'But you can't marry me. You are—Jeremy Porter—and a rich man and a lawyer, and I am only a servant girl.' "—*Ceremony of Innocence.*

Answer as a Man.

Eden, Dorothy

Wrote over 40 novels (including gothic and historical romances). "If you put Dorothy Eden's name on a seed catalogue it would sell."—Ace Books editor.

Stevenson, D. E.

British author: over 50 novels. "Funny, entertaining and clean."

Mrs. Tim series. The second edition of *Genreflecting* said: "With her usual charm and friendly understanding, Mrs. Tim makes friends, influences people and straightens out a lot of problems, including her own."

Several titles available in large print from G. K. Hall.

Van Slyke, Helen

Her nine novels sold 6 million copies. "It's all soap opera and it's all grand."—*The Best Place to Be.* "When did you last feel you really knew the people in a book ... that you shared their pain and pleasure, in some form, in your own life? When did you find yourself smiling at something on one page and staining the next one with nice therapeutic tears? ... Millions of readers want the kind of reality they can interpret in terms of their own experience, or within the scope of their own imagination. They don't scoff at sentiment; it never goes out of style. They believe in good and evil, in love and loyalty, and in bitterness and betrayal. This is the stuff real life is made of." —*The Writer,* November 1975. " 'Old-fashioned' and 'Up to the Minute' by Helen Van Slyke."—*The Writer,* November 1975.

Soap Opera

Within the definition of womanly romance must be included a type with gloomy overtones: the "soap opera" romance. Sin, suffering, and retribution permeate its pages, with an occasional relief of joy or spiritual uplift. The pattern was set in the nineteenth century with *East Lynne.* ("Next week East Lynne."—The touring stock company's placard, for the stage version, was seldom missing in small towns in both England and the United States in the first quarter of this century.) Notably, the pattern continued with *Stella Dallas* (as book, radio serial, and motion picture), the story of a wife who strayed, the unforgiving husband who kept the child, and so forth. Included also in this type are romances with excessive attention to anguish. Some of the older prototypes are:

Finley, Martha
Elsie Dinsmore series. First title published in 1868.

Porter, Gene Stratton
Freckles (1904).

Prouty, Olive Higgens
Stella Dallas (1923).

Wood, Ellen Price
East Lynne (1861).

Examples of more recent prototypes are:

Metalious, Grace
Peyton Place (1956).

Segal, Erich
Love Story (1970).

The sob-sister kin of this type of romance are the pulp magazine and radio and television soap opera series. All are heavy on problems and afflictions, divorces and love triangles, illness and suffering, with "mixed-up" and "messed-up" being fixed attributes of emotions. For those who missed the pulps, the following anthology comes complete with the original advertisements and illustrations.

Moriarty, Florence, ed. *True Confessions: Sixty Years of Sin, Suffering and Sorrow, 1919–1979, from the Pages of True Confessions, True Story, True Experience, True Romance, True Love, Secrets, Modern Romance.* Simon and Schuster, 1979.

Fantasies of Passion

Firmly in the womanly romance subgenre are fantasies of passion, which are erotic and purple but do not wallow in the sexual adventures filling the sweet-and-savage romance. The following two prototypes have influenced many writers and have been imitated but never surpassed.

Glyn, Elinor
Three Weeks. Her only erotic romance, published in 1907, treats illicit love with a high moral tone. ("And so, as ever, the woman paid the price.") The young hero is initiated into the rites of love by a mature woman (and this on a tiger-skin rug!).

> "Would you like to sin
> With Elinor Glyn
> On a tiger skin
> Or would you prefer
> To err with her
> On some other fur?"

Elinor Glyn coined the sex term "It" and also taught Rudolph Valentino how to kiss the palm, not the back, of a woman's hand.

Hull, Ethel M.

The Sheik (1919). "The first romantic heroine to be sexually assaulted, to learn during three hundred pages of it to enjoy it, and to marry the man who did it."—Rachel Anderson, *The Purple Heart Throbs.* From *The Sheik:*

> Diana's eyes passed over him slowly till they rested on his brown, clean-shaven face, surmounted by crisp, close-cut brown hair. It was the handsomest and the cruelest face that she had ever seen.... He was looking at her with fierce burning eyes that swept her until she felt that the boyish clothes that covered her slender limbs were stripped from her, leaving the beautiful white body under his passionate stare.

> She shrank back, quivering, dragging the lapels of her riding jacket together over her breast with clutching hands, obeying an impulse that she hardly understood.

> "Who are you?" she gasped hoarsely.

> "I am the Sheik Ahmed Ben Hassan."

The "sand-and-tit" epics inspired by *The Sheik* usually descend into "sweet-and-savage romance."

Contemporary Soap Opera

Even though it is declining in popularity as a written subgenre, soap opera romance continues to have readers. Most are part romance and part family saga, and they often attempt to include suspense. Many of the following have been reissued by reprint houses in regular or large print.

Cowie, Vera

The Rich and the Mighty.

Games.

Designing Woman.

Freeman, Cynthia

Illusions of Love.

Seasons of the Heart.

The Last Princess.

Portraits.

Gouge, Eileen

Garden of Lies.

Thorns of Truth.

Trail of Secrets.

Jaffe, Rona
Class Reunion.

After the Reunion.

The Cousins.

Five Women.

Plain, Belva
Legacy of Silence.

Thayer, Nancy
Bodies and Souls.

Family Secrets.

An Act of Love.

Traditional Womanly Romance

The traditional womanly romance focuses on a woman's relationships with her spouse or lover, family, and friends. These books do not always have a happy ending.

Binchy, Maeve
Echoes.

Circle of Friends.

Copper Beech.

Glass Lake.

Silver Wedding.

Pilcher, Rosamunde
The Carousel.

Shell Seekers.

September.

Sleeping Tiger.

Under Gemini.

Another View.

Snow in April.

Wild Mountain Thyme.

Voices in Summer.

Siddons, Anne Rivers
Hill Towns.

Outer Banks.

Downtown.

Homeplace.

Up Island.

Low Country.

Trollope, Joanna

    The Best of Friends.

    The Choir.

    The Men and the Girls.

    A Spanish Lover.

    A Village Affair.

Contemporary Mainstream Womanly Romances

The following romances may not satisfy the avid reader of the "happily ever after school" but may appeal to the other type of reader. They are usually marketed as novels rather than as romance.

Coscarelli, Kate

    Perfect Order.

    Fame & Fortune.

    Living Color.

Dailey, Janet

    Glory Game.

    Heiress.

    Aspen Gold.

Delinsky, Barbara

    Lake News.

    Coast Road.

    Three Wishes.

    A Woman's Place.

Laker, Rosalind

    This Shining Land.

Lipman, Elinor

    Isabel's Bed.

McCaffrey, Anne

    The Lady.

Steel, Danielle

    Accident.

    Five Days in Paris.

    The Ghost.

    The Gift.

    Changes.

    Daddy.

Family Album.

Full Circle.

Remembrance.

The Ring.

Secrets.

Stone, Katherine

Home at Last.

Promises.

Thomas, Rosie

Strangers.

Bad Girls, Good Women.

Other People's Marriages.

Trollope, Joanna

The Best of Friends.

Glitz and Glamour

There appears to be a trend toward absorption of the contemporary womanly romance into the mainstream novel tradition. The following have as settings the international jet set of the rich, famous, international business tycoons (both sexes), Hollywood, polo-playing, and holiday resorts. The sex is usually steamy. Amazingly, these novels do fall into the pattern of the womanly romance at an exaggerated extreme. Both Danielle Steel and Janet Dailey (in *Glory Game*) would fit the pattern.

Beauman, Sally

Destiny.

Booth, Pat

American Icon.

Miami.

Malibu.

Beverly Hills.

Palm Beach.

Marry Me.

Bradford, Barbara Taylor

A Woman of Substance.

Hold the Dream.

To Be the Best.

Dangerous to Know.

The Voice of the Heart.

Everything to Gain.

Power of a Woman.

Brayfield, Celia
    Pearls.

Briskin, Jacqueline
    The Naked Heart.

    Too Much Too Soon.

    Everything and More.

    Paloverde.

Brown, Sandra
    Where There's Smoke.

    French Silk.

Collins, Jackie
    Lady Boss.

    Chances.

    Lucky.

    Lucky's Revenge.

    Vendetta.

    Dangerous Kiss.

    American Star.

    Hollywood Husbands.

    Hollywood Wives.

    Thrill.

Conran, Shirley
    Savages.

    Lace.

    Lace II.

    Crimson.

Harvey, Kathryn
    Butterfly.

    Stars.

Korda, Michael
    The Fortune.

Krantz, Judith
    Dazzle.

    I'll Take Manhattan.

    Lovers.

    Scruples.

    Scruples II.

    The Jewels of Tessa Kent.

McNaught, Judith
    Perfect.

Michael, Judith
    Inheritance.
    Private Affairs.
    Acts of Love.
    Pot of Gold.

Mortman, Doris
    Rightfully Mine.
    First Born.

Plain, Belva
    Blessings.

Sheldon, Sidney
    Windmills of the Gods.
    If Tomorrow Comes.

Steel, Danielle
    Bittersweet.
    Passion's Promise.
    Secrets.
    Daddy.

Stone, Katherine
    Bed of Roses.
    Bel Air.
    Happy Endings.

Vincenzi, Penny
    Old Sins.

Wilde, Jennifer
    The Slipper.

Wilkins, Barbara
    Elements of Chance.

Contemporary Romance

The contemporary romance is more of a "purist's" romance than the contemporary mainstream romance, focusing on the relationship between one man and one woman with a happily-ever-after ending. Some readers will enjoy both categories. Most of the following authors write prolifically. Individual titles are not mentioned because while it is easy to locate books by a specific author, it is extremely difficult to locate specific titles. Peggy J.

Jaegly, in *Romantic Hearts: A Personal Reference for Romance Readers* (Scarecrow, 1997), lists titles, but there is no way to keep up with them all. As more libraries begin cataloging paperback original romances, this should improve. As the large print houses and reprint publishers such as Severn House have started reprinting in hardcover, more and more are showing up in library catalogs.

Crusie, Jennifer.

Delinsky, Barbara.

Eagle, Kathleen.

Freethy, Barbara. Rita award winner.

Greene, Jennifer. Multiple Rita award winner.

Hannah, Kristin.

Kimberlin, Annie.

Korbel, Kathleen. Multiple Rita award winner.

Krentz, Jayne Ann.

Linz, Cathie.

Macomber, Debbie.

Neggers, Carla.

Paige, Laurie.

Phillips, Susan Elizabeth.

Robards, Karen.

Roberts, Nora. More than 100 titles. Multiple Rita award winner.

Seidel, Kathleen Gilles.

Spencer, LaVyrle.

Standard, Patti.

Weir, Theresa.

Sensuous Contemporaries

Andersen, Susan.

Blake, Jennifer.

Crusie, Jennifer.

Davis, Justine.

Greene, Debbie.

Hoag, Tami.

Howard, Linda.

Phillips, Susan Elizabeth.

Reavis, Cheryl.

Richards, Emilie.

Sanders, Glenda.

Young, Karen.

Sweet Contemporaries

Sweet is the romance code word for innocent romances. Harlequin Romance and Silhouette Romance series are both this type. Avalon romances, frequently found as standing-order plans in libraries, also fall into this category.

Campbell, Bethany.

Chandler, Lauryn.

Early, Margot.

Ferrarella, Maria.

Macomber, Debbie.

Sites, Elizabeth.

Standard, Patti.

Romantic-Suspense

The romantic-suspense subgenre frequently eludes easy labeling. Novels in this category may blend into the mystery-suspense thriller subgenre (in which the mystery dominates the romance, making the novel of equal interest to both types of readers) or into the spy/espionage thriller subgenre in the hands of authors such as Helen MacInnes (whose novels have equal amounts of romance and espionage). Most clearly defined is the gothic novel, but its publishers often label it a suspense novel rather than a gothic, seeking to evade the negative attitude toward the gothic and the ridicule directed at its stereotyped plots.

Romantic-suspense novels are women's novels: while full of adventure and suspense, neither is allowed to diminish the heroine's romantic involvement. Many other types of romance have elements of suspense and mystery, and authors of romantic-suspense novels usually write in several other subgenres of romance as well. (Some of the following authors are also listed for other types of romance.) The background may be basically domestic (girl marries, goes to family estate, and husband dies or disappears; family secret leads to murder, scandal, and so forth), be exotic/foreign (an archaeological dig), or have the trappings of the period romance. Mary Stewart, the queen of this subgenre, rates so high in romantic appeal and so strong in suspenseful foreign adventure involving both romantic leads as to be the one author in this category of interest to men as well as women readers. Many of the following authors appear in hardcover editions as well as in paperback.

Contemporary Romantic Suspense

Brown, Sandra.

Cameron, Stella.

Clark, Mary Higgins. *Still Watch.*

Dreyer, Eileen.

Foley, Rae. *Fear of a Stranger.*

Forster, Suzanne.

Gerritsen, Tess.

Hoag, Tami.

Hooper, Kay.

Howard, Linda. *Kill and Tell.*

Johansen, Iris.

Krentz, Jayne Ann.

Lowell, Elizabeth.

Mortman, Doris. *Out of Nowhere.*

Pozzessere, Heather Graham.

Historical Romantic Suspense

Aiken, Joan

The Smile of the Stranger.
The Five-Minute Marriage.

Black, Laura
Falls of Gard.

Brent, Madeleine
Moonraker's Bride.
Stormswift.
A Heritage of Shadows.

Butler, Gwendoline
Sarsen Place.

Carr, Philippa
Midsummer's Eve.

Eberhart, Mignon Good
Fifty-nine mysteries, the first published in 1929, equally romantic and mysterious.

Gaskin, Catherine
The Charmed Circle.

Gilbert, Anna
The Wedding Guest.

Hodge, Jane Aiken
Windover.
Polonaise.
Savannah.
Purchase.
Here Comes a Candle.

Johnston, Velda
Masquerade in Venice.

Kaye, M. M.
      Death in Berlin.
      Death in Cyprus.
      Death in Kashmir.
      Death in Kenya.
      Death in the Andamans.
      Death in Zanzibar.

Lofts, Norah

Peters, Elizabeth
Amelia Peabody series.
      Crocodile on the Sandbank.
      Curse of the Pharoahs.
      The Snake, the Crocodile & the Dog.
      The Mummy Case.
      The Last Camel Died at Noon.
      Lion in the Valley.
      The Hippopotamus Pool.
      Seeing a Large Cat.
      The Ape Who Guards the Balance.
      Falcon at the Portal.

Fantasy/Science Fiction Romantic-Suspense

Castle, Jayne
St. Helen's trilogy.
      Amaryllis.
      Zinnia.
      Orchid.

Conway, Laura
      Take Heed of Loving Me.

Coulter, Catherine
      Hellion Bride.
      The Sherbrooke Bride.
      The Rebel Bride.

Hannah, Kristin
      Waiting for the Moon. Telepathy.

Howard, Linda
      Now You See Her. Psychic.

Pozzessere, Heather Graham
  If Looks Could Kill. Psychic.

Robb, J. D.
  Near-future.

Stuart, Anne
  Paranormal, vampires.

Gothic

Once the most enduring of romance subgenres, the gothic has been eclipsed by other types. See earlier editions of *Genreflecting* for discussions of the gothic and lists of authors who (though no longer writing—the majority are no longer living) are still quite popular with readers.

The following three prototypes have never lost their magic and popularity, remaining ever in print in hardcover and paperback editions. All became classic motion pictures.

Brontë, Charlotte
  Jane Eyre (1847).

Brontë, Emily
  Wuthering Heights (1847).

Du Maurier, Daphne
  Rebecca (1938).

While gothics have declined in popularity and are now very rarely published, the following authors continue to have devoted readers and to garner new ones.

    Michaels, Barbara.

    Holt, Victoria.

    Stewart, Mary.

    Whitney, Phyllis A.

Historical Romance

Historical settings are often romantic to begin with, and when a tale of love is set against the backdrop of another time, lush romance ensues. Historical romance varies as much in sensuality levels and authentic detail as in all the different time periods used as settings. While some historical romances take a serious look at past people and events, using the love story to provide a reason for relating authentic historical detail, others merely use the costumes of the past to add interest to their tales of passion. Readers who enjoy the authentic details of historical romance may also enjoy historical fiction. Readers who revel in the exotic attire and settings may also enjoy futuristic or fantasy romances.

Adler, Elizabeth
Leonie. Turn-of-the-century France.

Aiken, Joan
Many of her novels use period backgrounds.

Alexander, Kate
Fields of Battle.

Friends and Enemies.

The House of Hope. Victorian era.

Arlen, Leslie
Borodin family series. Early twentieth-century Russia.

Ashfield, Helen
Emerald.

Pearl.

Ruby.

Sapphire.

The Michaelmas Tree. Victorian era.

Beverley, Jo
Regency and Georgian settings.

My Lady Notorious.

Black, Laura
Albany. Georgian era.

Blake, Jennifer
Arrow to the Heart. Nineteenth-century Louisiana.

Borchardt, Alice
Devoted.

Beguiled. Medieval with fantasy elements.

Bristol, Leigh
Legacy. Post-Reconstruction Charleston.

Brooks, Betty
Viking Mistress. Thirteenth-century North America.

Jade. Carolinas, eighteenth century.

Burns, Patricia
Stacey's Flyer. Victorian era.

Kezzy. Nineteenth century.

Carr, Robyn

The Braeswood Tapestry. Seventeenth century.

By Right of Arms. Fourteenth century.

The Troubadour's Romance. Twelfth century.

Cartland, Barbara

"The world's all-time best-selling romantic novelist." *Genreflecting*, 2d ed., 1986. Over 300 novels to date.

A biography has been written by Henry Cloud: *Barbara Cartland: Crusader in Pink* (London: Weidenfeld, 1979).

"The Cartland formula is costume romance, fairy tales with passive heroines, men who are never less than perfection, and love that is spiritual. Although Cartland always finds a way to titillate her readers by maneuvering the lovers into bed, sex is never consummated without marriage." *Genreflecting*, 2d ed., 1986.

There are always happy endings in her books.

Chadwick, Elizabeth

The Wild Hunt.

The Running Vixen.

The Leopard Unleashed. Twelfth-century Wales.

Cleeve, Brian

Judith.

Kate.

Coleman, Bob

The Later Adventures of Tom Jones. Georgian era.

Cookson, Catherine

Victorian settings.

The Bannaman Legacy.

The Black Velvet Gown.

The Whip.

Tilly Trotter.

Tilly Trotter Wed.

Tilly Trotter Widowed.

Costain, Thomas

The Black Rose. Medieval.

The Silver Chalice.

Coulter, Catherine

Lord of Raven's Peak. Middle Ages.

Night Shadows. Nineteenth century.

Rosehaven. Middle Ages.

Secret Song. Middle Ages.

Dailey, Janet

The Pride of Hannah Wade. U.S. West, nineteenth century.

De Blasis, Celeste

The Proud Breed.

The Tiger's Woman. U.S. West.

Wild Swan.

Swan's Chance. U.S. Civil War period.

A Season of Swans.

Drummond, Emma

Beyond the Frontier.

Forget the Glory. Victorian era.

Eulo, Elena Yates

A Southern Woman. Civil War, Tennessee.

Faulkner, Colleen

To Love a Dark Stranger. Restoration London.

O'Brian's Bride. Colonial America.

Once More.

Fitzgerald, Valerie

Zeminda. India, nineteenth century.

Garlock, Dorothy

With Hope. Depression-era Oklahoma.

Gear, Kathleen O'Neal

Thin Moon and Cold Mist. Civil War.

Gellis, Roberta

Roselynde chronicles. Medieval. Original paperback series, reprinted in hardcover by Gregg Press, 1984.

Roselynde.

Alinor.

Joanna.

Gilliane.

Rhiannon.

Sybelle.

Gibbs, Mary Ann
Author of many Victorian-era romances.

Gilbert, Anna

The Look of Innocence. England of the 1880s; winner of Britain's Romantic Novel of the Year Award.

Gluyas, Constance

Born to Be King.

Golon, Sergeanne
Angelique series.

Gower, Iris

Black Gold.

Copper Kingdom.

Destiny's Child. War of the Roses.

Sea Witch.

Spinner's Wharf.

Grant, Maxwell
Blood Red Rose. China, 1920s.

Guhrke, Laura Lee
Breathless. Small town, early twentieth century.

Hardwick, Mollie

The Crystal Dove. Victorian era.

The Merry Maid. Elizabethan era.

Heaven, Constance

Castle of Doves. Spain, 1830s.

The House of Kuragin.

Heir to Kuragin. Tsarist Russia.

The Queen and the Gypsy. Elizabethan era.

The Wind from the Sea. England, 1793–1803.

Heyer, Georgette

While most books by this queen of Regency romance fall into that subgenre, a few are set in other time periods.

My Lord John.

Beauvallet.

Hinger, Charlotte
Come Spring. Kansas, 1881.

Hodge, Jane Aiken
Red Sky at Night.

Lovers' Delight.

Holland, Cecelia
Belt of Gold. Ninth century.

Pillar of the Sky. England, prehistoric.

Holt, Victoria
Demon Lover.

My Enemy the Queen.

The Devil on Horseback.

Ibbotson, Eva
Magic Flutes. England, France, nineteenth century.

A Company of Swans. Early twentieth century.

A Song for Summer. Pre–World War II Austria.

Irwin, Margaret
The Bride.

Royal Flush. England, France, seventeenth century.

The Stranger Prince. Prince Rupert, seventeenth century.

Jagger, Brenda
A Song Twice Over. Victorian era.

Jarman, Rosemary Hawley
Crown in Candlelight.

The King's Grey Mare.

Jekel, Pamela
Natchez. Louisiana, eighteenth and nineteenth centuries.

Johansen, Iris
The Beloved Scoundrel. England, nineteenth century.

The Magnificent Rogue. Scotland, sixteenth century.

Kaye, M. M.
The Far Pavilions. Described as an Indian *Gone with the Wind*.

Kells, Susannah
A Crowning Mercy. Seventeenth century.

The Fallen Angels. Eighteenth century.

Kelly, Carla
Daughter of Fortune. American West, seventeenth century.

Kent, Katherine
Tawney Rose. Georgian era.

Knight, Alanna
The Black Duchess. Elizabethan era.

Koen, Karleen
Through a Glass Darkly.

Now Face to Face. Eighteenth century.

Laker, Rosalind
Jewelled Path.

What the Heart Keeps. Edwardian era.

To Dance with Kings. Five generations of women and kings.

The Silver Touch. Eighteenth century.

Llywelyn, Morgan
Grania. Elizabethan era.

Lofts, Norah
Day of the Butterfly. Victorian era.

The Pargeters. England, seventeenth century.

A Wayside Tavern. England, from sixteenth-century on.

Knight's Acre.

The Maud Reed Table.

MacCoun, Catherine
The Age of Miracles. Medieval.

Macdonald, Malcolm
Dancing on Snowflakes. Nineteenth-century Sweden.

Goldeneye.

To the End of Her Days.

Tomorrow's Tide.

A Woman Scorned.

Marshall, Edison
Benjamin Blake.

Yankee Pasha.

Martin, Kat
Gypsy Lord.

Midnight Rider.

Martin, Rhona
Gallows Wedding. Fifteenth century.

Michaels, Barbara
Wait for What Will Come.

Wings of the Falcon.

Miller, Linda Lael
Orphan Train trilogy. United States, nineteenth century.

Mitchell, Margaret
Gone with the Wind.

Montague, Jeanne
Midnight Moon. Georgian era.

Montupet, Janine
The Lacemaker. Seventeenth-century France.

Murray, Frances
The Belchamber Scandal. Victorian era.

Ogilvie, Elisabeth
Scotland/Maine, early nineteenth century.

> **Jennie About to Be.**

> **The World of Jennie G.**

Pearson, Diane
Czardas.

The Summer of the Barshinskeys.

Plaidy, Jean
"Queen of popular historical novels."

Georgian saga (10 titles).

Victorian saga (6 titles).

Norman trilogy.

> **The Bastard King.**

> **The Lion of Justice.**

> **The Passionate Enemies.**

Plantagenet saga (14 titles).

Also a trilogy on Lucrezia Borgia and quartets on each of the following: Catherine de Medici, Charles II, Isabella and Ferdinand, Catherine of Aragon, and the Stuarts.

Plain, Belva
Crescent City. U.S. South, nineteenth century.

Potter, Patricia

Starfinder. Colonial America.

Price, Eugenia

Titles are listed in the historical chapter (Chapter 1), but the stories contain much romance and emphasis on relationships.

Quick, Amanda

Regency settings.

Ripley, Alexandra

Charleston.

On Leaving Charleston. Antebellum South.

The Time Returns. Lorenzo de' Medici, Florence.

From Fields of Gold. Early twentieth century.

Scarlett: The Sequel to Margaret Mitchell's *Gone with the Wind.*

Roberts, Ann Victoria

Louisa Elliott. Victorian era.

Morning's Gate. Early twentieth century.

Robinson, Margaret A.

Courting Emma Howe. Early twentieth-century rural Washington.

Rofheart, Martha

The Alexandrian. Cleopatra.

Fortune Made His Sword.

Sabatini, Rafael

Scaramouche.

Seton, Anya

My Theodosia. Theodosia Burr.

Katherine. Wife of John of Gaunt.

The Winthrop Woman. Niece of first governor of Massachusetts.

Shannon, Dell

The Dispossessed. Seventeenth century.

The Scalpel and the Sword. Napoleonic era.

Shannon, Doris

Family Money. United States, early twentieth century.

Shellabarger, Samuel

Captain from Castille.

Prince of Foxes.

The King's Cavalier.

Spencer, LaVyrle
Morning Glory. United States, 1940s.

November of the Heart. Victorian era.

Stirling, Jessica
The Good Provider. Nineteenth-century Scotland.

Suyin, Han
The Enchantress. China, eighteenth century.

Thornton, Elizabeth
Dangerous to Hold.

Tremaine, Jennie (Marion Chesney)
She has 11 other single-name titles in the Edwardian era.

Maggie.

Veryan, Patricia
The Golden Chronicles Series. Set in the Georgian era.

Practice to Deceive.

Journey to Enchantment. Georgian era.

Loves Alters All.

Dedicated Villain.

Tales of the Jewelled Men Series.

Time's Fool.

Had We Never Loved.

Ask Me No Questions.

Villars, Elizabeth
One Night in Newport.

The Normandy Affair.

Winsor, Kathleen
Forever Amber. England, seventeenth century.

Wolf, Joan
Born of the Sun. Saxons.

Woodhouse, Sarah
A Season of Mists. Georgian era.

Enchanted Ground.

Woodiwiss, Kathleen E.
The beginning of the trend toward sensual romance is attributed to Woodiwiss's *The Flame and the Flower* (1972).

The Flame and the Flower.

The Elusive Flame.

Shanna.

Yerby, Frank
The Saracen Blade.
Devil's Laughter. French Revolution.

Zaroulis, Nancy
The Last Waltz. Boston, nineteenth century.

Frontier and Western Romance

For a few years a newsletter called *Rawhide and Lace* was published. It contained information for writers and readers of frontier and Western romances. When it met its demise a new quarterly research magazine called *Calico Trails* appeared, emphasizing a woman's point of view, for American readers and writers of historicals. Unfortunately, there currently are no specific Web sites or bibliographies for this subgenre.

Busbee, Shirlee.

Donati, Sara. *Into the Wilderness.*

Gaffney, Patricia.

Garlock, Dorothy. *Sins of Summer* (Idaho, nineteenth century).

Hatcher, Robin Lee.

Landis, Jill Marie.

Miller, Linda Lael. The Orphan Train trilogy: *Lily and the Major; Emma and the Outlaw; Caroline and the Raider. Two Brothers: The Lawman and the Gunslinger.*

Morsi, Pamela.

Osborne, Maggie. *The Promise of Jenny Jones; The Best Man.*

Spencer, LaVyrle. *The Gamble; Years.*

Williamson, Penelope.

Wulf, Jessica.

Native American

At one time many of the romances featuring Native American heroes were of the sweet-and-savage type, featuring abductions and rapes, but times change and so have the books (for the most part). However, romance is not a politically correct genre and many readers still love the earlier type of Native American romance, where the hero is a noble savage. The following list fits in the sweet-and-savage category.

Baker, Madeline
Apache Runaway.

Bittner, Rosanne.

Forty-nine titles in 1999, all with a western setting and most with Native American characters.

Mystic Indian series.

Savage Destiny series.

Edwards, Cassie

Savage Heat.

Savage Wonder.

Flaming Arrow.

Faulkner, Colleen

Fire Dancer.

Scott, Theresa

Apache Conquest.

Wulf, Jessica

Grey Eagle's Bride.

Medieval

Becnel, Rexanne

A Dove at Midnight.

Beverley, Jo

The Shattered Rose.

Lord of Midnight.

Dark Champion.

Cody, Denée

The Golden Rose.

The Court of Love.

Queen of the May.

The Conquered Heart.

Deveraux, Jude

Montgomery family saga.

Velvet Song.

Velvet Angel.

Highland Velvet.

Velvet Promise.

The Conquest.

Garwood, Julie

Saving Grace.

The Bride.

Gellis, Roberta
  Roselynde chronicles.

Graham, Heather
  The Lord of the Wolves.
  Viking Surrender.

Henley, Virginia
  The Hawk and the Dove.

Kaufman, Pamela
  Shield of Three Lions.
  Banners of Gold.

Lamb, Arnette
  Border Lord.

Lindsey, Johanna
  Prisoner of My Desire.

Lowell, Elizabeth
  Forbidden.
  Untamed.

Woodiwiss, Kathleen E.
  The Wolf and the Dove.

Scotland

The fierce Scottish warrior has much the same appeal as the fierce Native American warrior. Movies such as *Rob Roy* and *Braveheart* have increased interest in this subgenre.

Deveraux, Jude
  Highland Velvet.

Gabaldon, Diana
  The Outlander series. Eighteenth century, time travel.

Garwood, Julie
  The Bride.

Lamb, Arnette
  Highland Rogue.
  Beguiled.
  Betrayed.

Langan, Ruth Ryan

Highland Barbarian.

Highland Heather.

Highland Fire.

McNaught, Judith

A Kingdom of Dreams.

Roberson, Jennifer

Lady of the Glen. Seventeenth century, Battle of Glencoe.

Regency (England)

The most distinctive period romances feature the Regency period (England in the first third of the nineteenth century) and are epitomized by the novels of Georgette Heyer. She, in the diction of the Regency, was "The Nonpareil," and all other authors using the period are "poor drab" imitators. (For example, publishers' notes on jackets or paperback covers often say things like "In the grand tradition of Georgette Heyer" or "The best since Georgette Heyer.) Unfortunately the Regency has fallen on hard times in the late 1990s, with some publishers discontinuing their Regency lines. Fighting for their genre, fans have started an e-mail group called Regency@onelistcom, which can be accessed on the World Wide Web at http://www.onelist.com (accessed 14 November 1999).

The wildly successful adventure tales of Patrick O'Brian are set during this time period, and fans of the era may well enjoy them. The Friends of the English Regency, a California association of devotees of Georgette Heyer and the Regency romance, holds an annual assemblée (at which there is period dancing in costume). They have a Web site at http://www.geocities.com/~foter/ (accessed 14 November 1999). Regency dancing has quite mysteriously become an event at some science fiction conventions.

The Beau Monde chapter of Romance Writers of America publishes a monthly newsletter for their members and a quarterly listing of regency titles, the *Regency Reader,* that is free to libraries. The address is:

The Beau Monde
c/o Susan Lantz
550 Gardendale
Terre Haute, IN 47803

http://simegen.com/out-t/romance/1005/beaumonde-3.html
(accessed 14 November 1999)

The Regency world is one of high society: the London Season of the wealthy and titled enjoying the assemblies at Almack's, the dandies in their fashionable garb. The country estate is also featured, as are the fashionable doings at Bath. Frequently, the heroine is impoverished, the daughter of a poor country parson or an orphan, but always she is a lady. Manner and dress are of utmost importance.

Kristin Ramsdell's *Romance Fiction: A Guide to the Genre,* Libraries Unlimited, 1999, features extensive information on regencies and lists many more authors and titles.

The following prototypes differ in style, but all reflect a mode of life immediately recognizable as characterizing the Regency. Fanny Burney's *Evelina,* published prior to the Regency period, foreshadows the Regency tone.

Several authors have written novels about Jane Austen's characters, of more interest to Janeites than to the usual Regency fan, with the exception of the one by John Coates (listed below).

Aiken, Joan

Mansfield Revisited.

Bulwer-Lytton, Edward

Pelham; or, The Adventures of a Gentleman. First published in 1828 but revised in 1840 because the libertine Regency tone offended Victorian taste.

Burney, Fanny

Evelina; or, The History of a Young Lady's Entrance into the World (1778).

Coates, John

The Watsons. Continuation of an unfinished novel by Jane Austen.

Farnol, Jeffery

"He took the standard ingredients [of the Regency]—bucks, duelists, pugilists, smugglers and haughty ladies—and fitted them into variations of the standard nineteenth-century plot based on usurped or disputed birthrights. . . . [A novelist] wearing his heart on his sleeve but writing with his tongue in his cheek." —*Genreflecting*, 2d ed., 1986.

Many of his books feature Jasper Shrig, the Bow Street Runner, as a solver of mysteries. His first novel was published in 1910.

Gillespie, Jane

Ladysmead.

Teverton Hall.

Karr, Phyllis Ann

Lady Susan. Reworking of an unfinished novel.

Royde-Smith, Naomi

Jane Fairfax.

White, T. H.

Darkness at Pemberly. A detective story about the present-day Darcys, with a nice romance as well.

Wilson, Barbara Ker

Antipodes Jane. Jane Austen in Australia. An 1803 fictional trip to Australia, not really Regency in tone.

The following authors capitalize on the surefire plot in which a spirited heroine captures a rakish hero in an aristocratic setting. While traditional Regencies tend to be short, with witty repartee, a recent trend has been longer sensuous tales in Regency or Georgian settings. Both types appear in the following list.

Aiken, Joan

The Smile of the Stranger.

Angers, Helen

A Lady of Independence.

Ashfield, Helen

The Marquis & Miss Jones.

Balogh, Mary

A Masked Deception.

The Notorious.

Daring Masquerade.

Christmas Belle.

Courting Julia.

Dancing with Clara.

The Famous Heroine.

The Incurable Matchmaker.

Lord Carew's Bride.

The Obedient Bride.

Bell, Anthea

A London Season.

Bennett, Janice

The Matchmaking Ghost.

Logical Lady.

A Dangerous Intrigue.

Beverley, Jo

Forbidden Magic.

Deidre and Don Juan.

Emily and the Dark Angel.

The Fortune Hunter.

Lord Wraybourne's Betrothed.

Brown, Diana

Come Be My Love.

Cartland, Barbara

Perhaps the most prolific of authors with over 600 books to her credit, she is the "self-styled queen of romantic fiction."—Kate Watson-Smyth, "Women Join the Ranks of Britain's Highest Earners," *Independent,* January 12, 1998, p. 5.

Loves, Lords, and Lady-Birds.

Chase, Loretta

English Witch.

Isabella.

The Last Hellion.

Chesney, Marion

The Six Sisters series.

A House for the Season series.

The Traveling Matchmaker series.

Clark, Gail

The Baroness of Bow Street.

Dulcie Bligh.

Both novels involve detection and Bow Street Runners.

Coffman, Elaine

Emerald Flame.

Courtney, Caroline

Libertine in Love.

Cummings, Monette

The Beauty's Daughter.

Lady Sheila's Groom.

See No Evil.

Darcy, Clare

Her 14 Regencies all have a name as title and have been called "the best since Georgette Heyer."

Elyza.

Gwendolyn.

Delmore, Diana

Leonie.

Diamond, Jacqueline
Forgetful Lady.

A Lady of Letters.

Drummond, June
The Bluestocking.

The Unsuitable Miss Pelham.

The Imposter.

Dunn, Carola
Lavender Lady.

Lord Iverbrook's Heir.

Crossed Quills.

The Improper Governess.

Mayhem and Miranda.

Once Upon a Time.

The Frog Earl.

Ellingson, Marnie
Dolly Blanchard's Fortune.

The Wicked Marquis.

Fairchild, Elisabeth
Lord Endicott's Appetite.

Lord Ramsay's Return.

Marriage à la Mode.

Miss Dorton's Hero.

The Silent Suitor.

Freeman, Joy
The Last Frost Fair.

A Suitable Match.

Harbaugh, Karen
Cupid's Darts.

The Devil's Bargain.

The Reluctant Cavalier.

The Vampire Viscount.

Cupid's Mistake.

Hern, Candice
An Affair of Honor.

A Change of Heart.

A Garden Folly.

Heyer, Georgette

To her 29 Regency romances should be added *These Old Shades, Devil's Cub,* and *The Talisman Ring.* Not only do they have the tone of the Regency, but the characters in the first two titles are found, along with various descendants, in *An Infamous Army,* as are those from *Regency Buck.* The Talisman Ring is one of the great examples of Heyer's inimitable dialogue: One rereads the novels for the sheer amusement in the dialogue and delight in the use of period language. Her gift, or talent, in this respect has been imitated but never equaled. The biography of Heyer by Jane Aiken Hodge, *The Private World of Georgette Heyer* (London: Bodley Head, 1984), is lavishly illustrated and of particular interest for the details about Heyer's collection of information on historical background.

Hill, Fiona

The Autumn Rose.

The Stanbroke Girls.

Kelly, Carla

Miss Milton Speaks Her Mind.

Mrs. Drew Plays Her Hand.

Mrs. McVinnie's London Season.

Kerstan, Lynn

Celia's Grand Passion.

Francesca's Rake.

Lucy in Disguise.

Marry in Haste.

Kidd, Elizabeth

A Hero for Antonia.

Lane, Allison

Devall's Angel.

The Impoverished Viscount.

Lord Avery's Legacy.

The Second Lady Emily.

Too Many Matchmakers.

Lee, Elsie

The Nabob's Widow.

A Prior Betrothal.

Ley, Alice Chetwynd

A Reputation Dies.

Lovelace, Jane
> Eccentric Lady.

Mack, Dorothy
> The Awakening Heart.
> The Counterfeit Widow.
> The Gamester's Daughter.
> A Prior Attachment.
> A Temporary Betrothal.
> The Last Waltz.

Mansfield, Elizabeth
> The Counterfeit Husband.
> Duel of Hearts.
> The Fifth Kiss.
> Her Heart's Captain.
> My Lord Murderer.
> A Regency Charade.
> A Regency Match.
> Regency Sting.

Maxwell, Cathy
> Falling in Love Again.

Metzger, Barbara
> My Lady Innkeeper.

Putney, Mary Jo
> The Rake.
> Dancing on the Wind.
> Dearly Beloved. Spicier than most Regencies.

Randolph, Ellen
> The Rusden Legacy.

Simonson, Sheila
> Bar Sinister.
> A Cousinly Connection.
> Lady Elizabeth's Comet.

Smith, Joan
> Imprudent Lady.
> Lover's Vows.

Thornton, Elizabeth

Dangerous to Kiss.

You Only Love Twice.

Veryan, Patricia

Feathered Castle.

Married Past Redemption.

The Noblest Frailty.

Sanguinet's Crown.

Some Brief Folly.

The Riddle of the Alabaster Royal.

The Riddle of the Lost Lover.

Vivian, Daisy

Fair Game.

The Forrester Inheritance.

Rose White, Rose Red.

A Lady of Quality.

A Marriage of Convenience.

Return to Cheyne Spa.

Walsh, Sheila

A Highly Respectable Marriage.

Westhaven, Margaret

The Willful Wife.

Inspirational Historical Romance

The inspirational historical romance is being issued by several denominational publishers, including Bethany House, Harvest House, Nelson, Tyndale, and Zondervan. Bantam Doubleday Dell has even stepped into the picture, with its Waterbrook imprint. Although in the past these books have not received wide distribution, some of the trade paperback series are now frequently found on chain bookstore shelves, on supermarket racks, and in prebound editions. The settings differ from series to series; the North American frontier is popular, but other settings abound, including Eastern Europe during World War II and Ireland during the "troubles."

Bacher, June Masters

Love Follows the Heart.

Love's Enduring Hope.

Gunn, Robin Jones
Clouds.

Echoes.

Secrets.

Sunsets.

Waterfalls.

Hill, Grace Livingston
Tyndale is reprinting her titles.

Morris, Alan, and Gilbert Morris
Katy Steele Adventures series.

Oke, Janette
Canadian West series.

Seasons of the Heart series.

Love Comes Softly series.

Orcutt, Jane
The Hidden Heart.

The Fugitive Heart.

Peart, Jane
Brides of Montclair series.

American Quilt series.

Orphan Train West trilogy.

Edgecliff Manor Mystery series.

Phillips, Michael R.
Stonewyke trilogy.

Phillips, Michael R., and Judith Pella
The Highland Collection.

Rivers, Francine
Mark of the Lion series.

The Scarlet Thread.

Snelling, Lauraine
Red River of the North series.

Thoene, Bodie, and Brock Thoene

Galway Chronicles.

Zion Chronicles.

Zion Legacy.

Shiloh Legacy.

Wick, Lori

The Californians series.

Saga

The family saga romance has ties to both the historical and period romances, although there are popular examples with contemporary settings. Most of these romances span several volumes. The saga, or generational history, covers the interrelations of succeeding generations within a family, usually with emphasis on a patriarchal or matriarchal figure. Those series in which the family relationships provide the basic plot elements are firmly in the romance tradition. Those with an embracing historical sweep (notably the series devised by Engel, such as The Kent Family Chronicles and Wagons West) have men as the pivotal characters. Women are not ignored in these historical series, but they provide romantic background rather than the dominant romantic story line.

Because the genre proved so popular in the 1970s, the saga label appears in publishers' advertising and on paperback covers for single-volume novels that barely fit the definition. Some novels, such as the Poldark series, achieve the saga label through sheer number of volumes and an extensive cast of characters. Others among historical and period romances have a sequel, or sequels, without real similarity to the saga pattern.

Several patterns are dominant in current sagas. In the United States, the pattern might be an immigrant family rising to wealth and power over several generations; plantation life in the Deep South, with an emphasis on master-slave relations; history from colonial times; or the movement westward. In Britain, the pattern might be landed family history and relations between aristocrats and their servants or a family of any class or period or periods, changing through the generations.

Several of the series current in the United States are designed and "produced" by Book Creations, Inc., the brainchild of the late Lyle Kenyon Engel. Engel's successor originates the series idea, makes contracts with the authors, does the editorial work, and arranges for publication with major paperback publishers.

The following prototype books show that one or two dominant characters may ensure an enduring readership for a saga.

De La Roche, Mazo

Jalna series (16 novels). The first novel of the series was published in 1927.

Galsworthy, John

The Forsyte Saga (3 volumes). The first volume was published in 1906. Followed by:

A Modern Comedy (3 volumes).

End of the Chapter (3 volumes).

Walpole, Hugh

The Herries chronicle (4 volumes). The first volume was published in 1930.

Many generational series or sagas are now appearing. The matriarchy-dominated saga seems to be gaining in importance, as does the saga centered on a business empire, sometimes run by a woman. Only time will tell which of the following generational sagas will survive for continued readership. The historical adventure series tends to intermingle with the saga. In some of the following instances, the number of volumes is noted (although the series may be ongoing). Readers of romance sagas may also enjoy the titles listed in the "Saga" section of Chapter 2.

Anand, Valerie

The Proud Villeins.

The Ruthless Yeomen. Thirteenth century.

Argo, Ellen

Projected to be a trilogy:

The Crystal Star.

The Yankee Girl.

Birmingham, Stephen

The Auerbach Will.

The LeBaron Secret.

Bissell, Elaine

Women Who Wait.

As Time Goes By.

Family Fortunes.

Bosse, Malcolm

Chinese background.

The Warlord.

Fire in Heaven.

Bradford, Barbara Taylor

Woman of Substance.

Hold the Dream.

To Be the Best.

Act of Will.

Briskin, Jacqueline
    Paloverde.

Carr, Philippa
    Knave of Hearts.

    Voices in a Haunted Room.

    The Return of the Gypsy.

Cleary, Jon
    The Beauford Sisters. Australian background.

Coffman, Virginia
    The Gaynor Women.

    Dinah Faire.

    Veronique.

    Marsanne.

Coleman, Lonnie
    Beulah Land series (3 volumes).

      Plantation South. United States.

Cookson, Catherine
    Tilly (British title: *Tilly Trotter*).

    Tilly Wed (British title: *Tilly Trotter Wed*).

    Tilly Alone (British title: *Tilly Trotter Widowed*).

Cradock, Fanny
    Lorme family (5 volumes). Britain.

Dailey, Janet
    Calder saga.

      This Calder Sky.

      This Calder Range.

      Stands a Calder Man.

      Calder Born, Calder Bred.

Danielson, Peter
    Children of the Lion.

Delderfield, R. F.
    Set in Britain.

    Swann family (3 volumes).

    Craddock family (2 volumes).

Dennis, Adair, and Janet Rosenstock
    The Story of Canada.

Doig, Ivan
Dancing at the Rascal Fair.
English Creek.
Ride with Me, Mariah Montana.

Drummond, Emma
Knightshill saga.

Elegant, Robert
Dynasty.
Mandarin.

Ellis, Julie
The South:

The Hampton Heritage.
The Hampton Women.

Fast, Howard
Lavette family (5 volumes). United States.

Gaan, Margaret
Chinese background:

Red Barbarian.
White Poppy.
Blue Mountain.

Gaskin, Catherine
The Ambassador's Women.

Gavin, Catherine
The Sunset Dream.

Gellis, Roberta
Roselynde chronicles. Medieval England.

Heiress series. The French Revolution.

Royal Dynasty series. Engel creation. History of England.

Gilchrist, Rupert
Dragonard series (5 volumes). Caribbean plantation.

Giles, Janice Holt
Cooper and Fowler families (4 volumes). U.S. West.

Goldreich, Gloria
Leah's Journey.
Leah's Children.

Graham, Winston
Poldark series (10 volumes). Britain.

Haines, Pamela
The Diamond Waterfall.

Harris, Marilyn
Eden family (7 volumes). Eden series follows the Eden family from England to the American South.

The Other Eden.

The Prince of Eden.

The Eden Passion.

The Women of Eden.

Eden Rising.

American Eden.

Eden and Honor.

Harrison, Sara
Tennent family.

The Flowers of the Field.

A Flower That's Free.

Highland, Monica
Lotus Land.

Hill, Deborah
Merrick family (2 volumes). New England.

Hill, Pamela
The House of Cary.

Howatch, Susan
The Rich Are Different.

Sins of the Fathers.

The Wheel of Fortune.

The Church of England series.

Glittering Images.

Glamorous Powers.

Ultimate Prizes.

Scandalous Risks.

Mystical Paths.

Jakes, John
North and South.

Love and War.

Heaven and Hell.

Kent Family chronicles. Engel creation. United States.

The Bastard.

The Rebels.

The Seekers.

The Furies.

The Titans.

The Warriors.

The Lawless.

The Americans.

Jekel, Pamela
Bayou.

Johnson, Walter Reed
Oakhurst saga (4 volumes). United States. Engel creation; sweet-and-savage.

Jourlet, Marie de
Windhaven series (14 volumes). Bouchard family, U.S. South and West; sweet-and-savage.

Laker, Rosalind
Easthampton trilogy. England.

Lavender, William
Hargrave Journal trilogy. United States.

Long, William Stewart
The Australians series. Engel creation.

Longstreet, Stephen
All or Nothing.

Our Father's House.

Lord, Shirley
Golden Hill.

Macdonald, Malcolm
The Carringtons of Helston.

Stevenson family.

The World from Rough Stones.

The Rich Are with You Always.

Abigail.

Mackey, Mary
    McCarthy's List.
    A Grand Passion.

Masters, John
    Rowlands family.

McCullough, Colleen
    The Thorn Birds. Australia.

Melville, Ann
    The Lorimer Line.
    Alexa.

Nicolayson, Bruce
    de Kuyper family. Colonial United States. Projected to be 5 volumes.

Nicole, Christopher
    Caribbean saga (5 volumes).
    Haggard family. England. Projected to be 5 volumes.

Ogilvie, Elisabeth
    Bennett's Island series.

Park, Ruth
    The Harp in the South.
    Missus.
    Poor Man's Orange.

Porter, Donald Clayton
    Colonization of America series. Engel creation.

Price, Eugenia
    Savannah.
    To See Your Face Again.
    Stranger in Savannah.

Rayner, Claire
    Performers series (10 volumes). England.

Rofheart, Martha
    The Savage Brood.

Ross, Dana Fuller
Wagons West series. Engel creation.

Scott, Michael William
Rakehell Dynasty (3 volumes). United States. Engel creation.

Skelton, C. L.
The Regiment quartet.

Smith, George
The American Freedom series (2 volumes). Glencannon family.

Smith, Wilbur
Ballantyne family. Africa.

Spellman, Cathy Cash
So Many Partings.
An Excess of Love.

Stine, Whitney
The Oklahomans series.

Stirling, Jessica
Beckman trilogy.

Stubbs, Jean
Brief Chronicles saga/Howarths of Garth. Victorian era.
Kit's Hill. (By Our Beginnings)
The Ironmaster. (Imperfect Joy)
The Vivian Inheritance.
The Northern Correspondent.

Thane, Elswyth
Williamsburg series (7 volumes). United States.

Wall, Robert E.
The Canadians series.

Winston, Daoma
The Fall River Line.

Hot Historicals

Kathleen E. Woodiwiss is credited with starting the trend to sensuous historical romances with *Flame and the Flower* (1972). Now scenes of explicitly depicted lovemaking seem requisite for some publishers.

Sweet-and-Savage

Famous for clinch covers, featuring a torridly embracing, scantily clad couple, this subgenre sometimes derogatorily called the "bodice ripper" changed the face of romance forever in the 1970s. Rosemary Rogers launched the subgenre called "sweet-and-savage" in 1974 with *Sweet, Savage Love.* A reviewer succinctly epitomized the subgenre's plot in *Sweet, Savage Love* in one sentence: "The heroine is seduced, raped, prostituted, married, mistressed." Another reviewer just as tersely summed up the subgenre's characteristics: "The prose is purple, the plot thin, and the characters thinner" (referring to *The Wolf and the Dove,* by Kathleen E. Woodiwiss). —*Genreflecting*, 2d ed., 1986. Exotic historical settings were used lavishly, particularly those allowing for pirates, sultans, and harems. A variation of the sweet-and-savage romance was the plantation romance, with basic ingredients of miscegenation, incest, Cain versus Abel, slave uprisings, insanity, and murder. Usually they were set in the post–Civil War South but some were set in the West Indies or in any locale in which the basic plot ingredients could seethe. Both types were loaded with sex scenes, explicit to the extent of justifying the label "soft porn."

These sultry romances had their heyday in the 1970s, mainly as paperback originals. They have become part of the standard historical romance pattern, usually in a more subdued form. There has also been a trend in paperback series toward much more sensuous and erotically explicit plots. Sweet-and-savage characteristics are being subsumed within the saga or historical romance rather than becoming dominating aspects.

Authors who specialized in this subgenre were Jennifer Blake, Shirlee Busbee, Anthony Esler, Gimone Hall, Susanna Leigh, Fern Michaels, Marilyn Ross, Jennifer Wilde, and Donna Comeaux Zide. Others who wrote in the genre (many not exclusively) were Susannah Kells, Patricia Matthews, Laurie McBain, Natasha Peters, Janette Radcliffe (a.k.a. Janet Louise Roberts), Rosemary Rogers, Beatrice Small, Kathleen Winsor, and last, but not least, Kathleen E. Woodiwiss, who has said, "I'm insulted when my books are called erotic. I believe I write love stories with a little spice."

Spicy

The spicy romance has grown out of the sweet-and-savage type. It features erotic scenes but without the kidnappings and rapes so often found in its predecessor. Generally, the characters are monogamous or serially monogamous. Marriage plays an important role.

Jude Deveraux's many novels involving different, far-flung members of the Montgomery family throughout history have evolved from sweet-and-savage to spicy romance. Even though her early works in the Velvet series and James River trilogy featured rapes and kidnappings, the characters were not promiscuous. The women are proactive rather than reactive, as in the sweet-and-savage type.

Other popular authors writing in this vein are:

> Bretton, Barbara.
>
> Busbee, Shirlee.
>
> Devine, Thea.
>
> Graham, Heather.
>
> Henley, Virginia.
>
> Johnson, Susan.
>
> Ryan, Nan.
>
> Taylor, Janelle.
>
> Woodiwiss, Kathleen E.

Fantasy and Science Fiction Romance

All sorts of different settings and characters have been popping up in romances. Vampires, ghosts, angels, and werewolves may be a love interest or just a being to facilitate the lovers coming together. The time for a romance can be in the future or in a shadowing place out of time, a parallel universe, or a magical land. The characters may be human but may have the powers of telepathy, precognition, or others found under psionics in science fiction. Magic may work in the world instead of just in the heart.

This type is so popular that it has its own award, the Sapphire Award, a bibliography, *Enchanted Journeys Beyond the Imagination* by Susan W. Bontly and Carol J. Sheridan (Blue Diamond Publications, 1996), and even a monthly print newsletter, *The Alternative Reality Romance Connection*, and a monthly online newsletter, *Science Fiction Romance* at http://members.aol.com/sfreditor/index.htm (accessed 14 November 1999).

Fantasy

A major trend in the romance genre in the 1990s was the combination of fantasy with romance. Time travel, supernatural beings, faerie, and other fantasy tropes have been showing up frequently in romance novels. The combination of the genres is a delight to those who love both.

Ashe, Rebecca

Masque of the Swan. An interesting combination of Greek mythology and *The Phantom of the Opera.*

Carroll, Susan

The Bride Finder. Anatole St. Leger, the scion of a family gifted with strange powers, sends the "Bride Finder" to bring him back a sturdy, plain, horse-loving wife. The "Bride Finder" has always found the right spouse for the St. Legers, and those who marry one not so chosen are doomed. Reverend Fitzleger, the current "Bride Finder," brings back sensible, tiny, book-loving, red-haired Madeline, who grows to love this lord who frightens all others.

The Night Drifter.

Jones, Jill

Circle of the Lily.

Essence of My Desire. Occult magic.

Krinard, Susan, Maggie Shayne, Lisa Higdon, and Amye Liz Saunders

Bewitched. Four novellas featuring magic from a cat who transforms into a woman, witchcraft, and love spells.

McReynolds, Glenna

The Chalice and the Blade.

Dream Stone. Alternate world, magic.

Resnick, Laura.

In Legend Born. A group of five comes together forging an alliance against the hedonistic Valdani who have forced the Sileria mountain clans into slavery.

Roberts, Nora, Jill Gregory, Ruth Ryan Langan, and Marianne Willman

Once Upon a Castle. An anthology of fairy tale romances.

Shayne, Maggie

Annie's Hero. In a heroic but deadly act, a young father loses his life and memory of the present when he becomes a knight fighting the evil Dark Knights.

Fairytale. Is the power of Faerie needed for Adam to find his own true love?

Forever Enchanted. Bridin takes up life on our world after Tristan steals her throne, but then he follows her here.

Wrede, Patricia C.

The Magician's Ward. Magic in a Regency setting.

Wrede, Patricia C., and Caroline Stevermer

Sorcery and Cecelia. Epistolary novel set in Regency London, featuring two girls beset by magic.

Time Travel

The books that fall into this category use time travel as a backdrop for the romance. The obstacle facing the lovers is not merely one of having different backgrounds or one of living in different time zones, but of living in different centuries. This is a very popular type in paperback but is also published in hardcover. Unlike most romances, male authors are found frequently in this subgenre.

Alexander, Karl

Time After Time. H. G. Wells in late twentieth-century San Francisco.

Bonds, Parris Afton

For All Time. Stacie suddenly finds herself in 1872 and falls for her own grandfather.

Bretton, Barbara

Tomorrow and Always.

Somewhere in Time.

Craig, Emma

Enchanted Christmas.

A Gentle Magic. Magic just seems to happen near McMurdo's Wagon Yard in nineteenth-century New Mexico.

Deveraux, Jude

Knight in Shining Armor. Tears at a crypt bring a medieval knight into the present.

Frank, Suzanne

In these books Dallas artist Chloe Kingsley finds herself first in ancient Egypt, then in the body of an oracle in Atlantis, and eventually as a slave helping David take Jerusalem.

Reflections in the Nile.

Shadows on the Aegean.

Sunrise on the Mediterranean.

Gabaldon, Diana

Outlander.

Dragonfly in Amber.

Voyager.

Drums of Autumn.

Outlander is the standard against which all time travel romances are judged. Following World War II, a former army nurse vacationing in Scotland is cast back into the eighteenth century. The series is so popular that the author has come out with a guide to it, *The Outlandish Companion: In Which Much Is Revealed Regarding Claire and Jamie Fraser, Their Lives and Times, Antecedents, Adventures, Companions and Progeny with Learned Commentary (and Many Footnotes) by their Humble Creator* (Delacorte Press, 1999).

Howard, Linda

Son of the Morning.

Krinard, Susan

Twice a Hero.

Kurland, Lynn

The Very Thought of You.

Matheson, Richard

Somewhere in Time (originally titled *Bid Time Return*). Using self-hypnosis, a playwright goes back in time to find a woman he fell in love with from an old portrait.

What Dreams May Come. Reissued in 1998, 20 years after its first publication, to coincide with the movie version.

Millhiser, Marlys

The Mirror. Looking into a hideously ornate mirror on the eve of her wedding, a young woman is snapped back in time and into the body of her grandmother on the eve of *her* wedding.

Moon, Modean

Evermore. Civil War–era lovers are reunited through reincarnation.

Paranormal Beings

Ashley, Amanda

Deeper Than the Night. Vampire.

Embrace the Night.

A Darker Dream.

Shades of Gray. Vampire.

Baker, Madeline

The Angel & the Outlaw. Angel.

Cresswell, Jasmine

Prince of the Night. Vampire.

Hamilton, Laurell K. Featuring Anita Blake, vampire killer.

Guilty Pleasures.

The Laughing Corpse.

Circus of the Damned.

The Lunatic Café.

Bloody Bones.

The Killing Dance.

Blue Moon.

Harbaugh, Karen

The Vampire Viscount.

Huff, Tanya

Vampire stories.

  Blood Price.

  Blood Trail.

  Blood Lines.

  Blood Pact.

  Blood Debt.

Klause, Annette Curtis

Silver Kiss. Vampire.

Blood and Chocolate. Werewolf.

Both titles are published as young adult books, but adults who find them fall in love.

Krinard, Susan

Body & Soul. Ghost.

Prince of Shadows. Werewolf.

Prince of Wolves. Werewolf.

Prince of Dreams. Vampire.

Touch of the Wolf. Werewolf.

Macomber, Debbie

Angel stories.

A Season of Angels.

Mrs. Miracle.

The Trouble with Angels.

Touched by Angels.

Miller, Linda Lael

Vampire stories.

Tonight and Always.

Forever and the Night.

Shayne, Maggie

Born in Twilight. Angelica's dreams of being a nun are shattered when she is turned into a vampire, who then becomes pregnant by Jameson, who himself did not want to become a vampire.

Stuart, Anne

Prince of Magic.

Falling Angel.

Stuart, Anne, Chelsea Quinn Yarbro, and Maggie Shayne

Strangers in the Night. Three vampiric romance novellas:

"Dark Journey."

"Catching Dreams."

"Beyond Twilight."

Thacker, Shelly

Timeless. Immortals.

Futuristic/Science Fiction

Asaro, Catherine
Catch the Lightning.

Primary Inversion.

The Radiant Seas.

The Last Hawk.

Bujold, Lois McMaster
Shards of Honor. Written by the award-winning science fiction author, it does not have the sex or sensuality levels found in so many romances.

Castle, Jayne (Jayne Ann Krentz)
Amaryllis.

Zinnia. Orchid brings a psychic and a private investigator together on a distant space colony.

Joy, Dara
Matrix of Destiny series.

Knight of a Trillion Stars.

Rejar.

Mine to Take.

Robb, J. D. (Nora Roberts)
Futuristic romantic detective tales.

Immortal in Death.

Naked in Death.

Glory in Death.

Ethnic Romance

In recent years African-American romances have done extremely well. The Pinnacle Arabesque line publishes four each month by successful authors such as Eboni Snoe, Roberta Gayle, Angela Benson, Francis Ray, Shirley Hailstock, Brenda Jackson, and Bette Ford. Beverly Jenkins writes romances with African-American characters for Avon.

It is to be hoped that more ethnic heroes and heroines will be appearing in the future.

Topics

"Best" Authors

The following list of "best" romance authors was compiled from polls taken by All About Romance (http://www.likesbooks.com/stars.html, accessed 20 January 2000), The Romance Reader (http://www.theromancereader.com/top100.html, accessed 20 January 2000), Bookbug's Top One-Hundred (http://www.geocities.com/Athens/Forum/8078/readers-favorites.html, accessed 20 January 2000), Rita Award winners, and best-seller lists from *USA Today, Publishers Weekly,* and *The New York Times Book Review.* The names are arranged in alphabetical order.

Anderson, Catherine
Annie's Song.

Austen, Jane
Pride and Prejudice.

Barnett, Jill
Bewitching.

Beverley, Jo
Emily and The Dark Angel.

My Lady Notorious.

Forbidden Magic.

Blake, Jennifer
Prolific writer who was an early winner of the Romance Writers of America Lifetime Achievement Award.

Brontë, Charlotte
Jane Eyre.

Brown, Sandra
French Silk.

Chase, Loretta
Lord of Scoundrels.

Coulter, Catherine
Midsummer Magic.

Calypso Magic.

Moonspun Magic.

The Sherbrooke Bride.

Curtis, Sharon, and Tom Curtis
Sunshine and Shadow.

Deveraux, Jude
A Knight in Shining Armor.
Twin of Fire.
Twin of Ice.
Sweet Liar.
Highland Velvet.

Gabaldon, Diana
The Outlander series.

Outlander.
Dragonfly in Amber.
Voyager.
Drums of Autumn.

Garwood, Julie
The Bride.
Castles.
The Gift.
Guardian Angel.
Honor's Splendour.
The Lion's Lady.
Saving Grace.
The Secret.

Gellis, Roberta
Roselynde Chronicles.

Graham, Heather (also writes as Heather Graham Pozzessere and Shannon Drake)
The Viking's Woman.
Every Time I Love You.

Heath, Lorraine
Always to Remember.
Parting Gifts.
Texas Destiny.

Henley, Virginia
The Hawk and the Dove.

Hibbert, Eleanor Burford (wrote under the names Victoria Holt, Philippa Carr, and Jean Plaidy)

Hoag, Tami
Cry Wolf.
Night Sins.
Guilty of Sin.

Howard, Linda
    After the Night.
    Dream Man.
    Heart of Fire.
    MacKenzie's Mountain.
    Sarah's Child.
    Son of the Morning.

Johansen, Iris
    Golden Barbarian.
    Lion's Bride.
    And Then You Die.

Kinsale, Laura
    Flowers from the Storm.
    Prince of Midnight.
    The Shadow and the Star.

Kleypas, Lisa
    Dreaming of You.
    Then Came You.

Krentz, Jayne Ann
    Family Man.
    Trust Me.
    Wildest Hearts.

Kurland, Lynn
    Stardust of Yesterday.
    This Is All I Ask.

Landis, Jill Marie
    Come Spring.

Lowell, Elizabeth
    Only His.
    Only Mine.
    Only You.

Macomber, Debbie
    This Matter of Marriage.
    The Trouble with Angels.

McNaught, Judith
    Whitney, My Love.
    Something Wonderful.
    Kingdom of Dreams.
    Almost Heaven.
    Once and Always.
    Paradise, Perfect.

Mertz, Barbara (writes as Barbara Michaels and Elizabeth Peters)

Michaels, Kasey
The Lurid Lady Lockport.

Miller, Linda Lael
The Orphan Train trilogy.

Mitchell, Margaret
Gone with the Wind.

Morsi, Pamela
Courting Miss Hattie.
Simple Jess.

Orczy, Baroness Emmuska
The Scarlet Pimpernel.

Osborne, Maggie
The Promise of Jenny Jones.

Phillips, Susan Elizabeth
Dream a Little Dream.
Honey Moon.
Fancy Pants.
Heaven.
Texas.
It Had to Be You.
Kiss an Angel.
Nobody's Baby but Mine.

Putney, Mary Jo
Silk and Shadows.
Angel Rogue.
The Rake and the Reformer (revised edition: *The Rake*).

Quick, Amanda
Mistress.
Ravished.
Scandal.

Robards, Karen
One Summer.

Roberts, Nora (also writes as J. D. Robb)
>   Public Secrets.
>   Born in Fire.
>   Born in Ice.
>   Born in Shame.
>   Finding the Dream.
>   Hidden Riches.
>   Honest Illusions.
>   Montana Sky.

Seidel, Kathleen Gilles
>   Till the Stars Fall.

Seton, Anya
>   Katherine.

Spencer, LaVyrle
>   Bitter Sweet.
>   The Fulfillment.
>   The Hellion Hummingbird.
>   Morning Glory.
>   Separate Beds.
>   Twice Loved.
>   Years.

Stewart, Mary
>   Nine Coaches Waiting.

Taylor, Janelle
>   The Ecstasy series.

Whitney, Phyllis A.

Williamson, Penelope
>   Keeper of the Dream.
>   Once in a Blue Moon.

Woodiwiss, Kathleen E.
>   Shanna.
>   The Flame and the Flower.
>   A Rose in Winter.
>   Ashes in the Wind.
>   The Wolf and the Dove.

Bibliographies and Biographies

Biographical sketches of the authors currently writing romantic novels for both hardcover and paperback publishers appear in the journals listed under "Review Journals" (see p. 263). Recognizing the great popularity of the romance, many women's magazines have in recent years featured articles on best-selling authors of romantic novels.

Bontly, Susan W., and Carol J. Sheridan. *Enchanted Journeys Beyond the Imagination: An Annotated Bibliography of Fantasy, Futuristic, Supernatural, and Time Travel Romances.* Blue Diamond, 1996. The title says it all. Bontly and Sheridan have identified romance books that fall into the science fiction, fantasy, and supernatural areas. They have managed to categorize this diverse and unusual but wildly popular area with panache, listing time travel romances written by over 90 authors, identifying times and destinations, and grouping the books by American West, American Revolution/Frontier, America, Contemporary, Europe, Old South/Civil War, Regency England, and an area for the time travel romances that don't fit elsewhere. Other classifications include fantasy-myth and legend; futuristic, Earth-related; other worlds and UFOs; supernatural romance with angels, ghosts, vampires, magic; and more. This unique bibliography is a boon to readers' advisors, both in libraries and bookstores, offering access to some of the most popular subgenres of romance fiction. Readers of these genres will be delighted to find old favorites and discover new ones. The book includes listings of pseudonyms and listings by category and series. Author/title index.

Jaegly, Peggy J. *Romantic Hearts: A Personal Reference for Romance Readers,* 3d ed. Scarecrow Press, 1997. Includes 75 publicist-type biographies, many with photos of currently active romance writers. Lists series romance titles and author pseudonyms. Not quite as comprehensive as it would appear, but nonetheless a good attempt at documenting a large number of the overwhelming abundance of romance novels.

North American Romance Writers. Mussell, Kay, and Johanna Tunon, eds. Scarecrow Press, 1999. Essays by Judith Arnold, Mary Balogh, Jo Beverley, Loretta Chekani (Chase), Sue Civil-Brown (Rachel Lee), Judy Cuevas (Judith Ivory), Sharon and Tom Curtis (Laura London), Justine Davis, Eileen Dreyer (Kathleen Korbel), Kathleen Eagle, Patricia Gaffney, Alison Hart (Jennifer Greene), Lorraine Heath, Tami Hoag, Susan Johnson, Dara Joy, Lynn Kerstan, Sandra Kitt, Susan Krinard, Jill Marie Landis, Pamela Morsi, Maggie Osborne, Mary Jo Putney, Alicia Rasley, Emilie Richards, Paula Detmer Riggs, Nora Roberts, Barbara Samuel (Ruth Wind), Kathleen Gilles Seidel, and Jennifer Crusie. It also has an extensive bibliography of resources in the romance genre.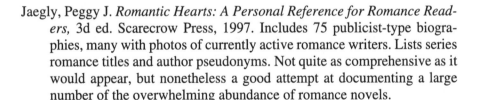

Ramsdell, Kristin. *Romance Fiction: A Guide to the Genre*. Libraries Unlimited, 1999. The definitive guide to the romance genre, Ramsdell's book offers users a thorough treatment of the genre with thousands of titles described and organized in romance subgenres of contemporary, mystery, historical, regency, alternative reality, saga, gay and lesbian, inspirational, and ethnic/multicultural. Ramsdell also provides history and background notes along with thorough guidelines for readers' advisors for the genre as a whole and each of its subgenres. Information on awards, publishers, research aids, a list of young adult romance titles, and guidelines for the core collection are some of the other features of the book. Author/title and subject indexes complete the work. An updated and expanded edition of *Happily Ever After: A Guide to Reading Interests in Romance Fiction* (Libraries Unlimited, 1987).

————. *What Romance Do I Read Next: A Reader's Guide to Recent Romance Fiction*. Gale, 1997.

Twentieth-Century Romance and Gothic Writers, 3d ed. Edited by Aruna Vasudevan and Lesley Henderson. Preface by Alison Light. St. James Press, 1994. Hundreds of authors and their pseudonyms are listed. There are brief biographical data, a list of all published works, a statement by the author (if supplied), and a critical summation. *Twentieth-Century Romance and Historical Writers*, 2d edition. Edited by Lesley Henderson and D. L. Kirkpatrick with a preface by Kay Mussell. St. James Press, 1990. The first edition was titled *Twentieth-Century Romance and Gothic Writers*. Edited by James Vinson and D. L. Kirkpatrick. Preface by Kay Mussell. London: Macmillan, 1982.

History and Criticism

Romance has not received the critical or scholarly interest given to many of the other genres. It is rarely the subject of academic study. It seems that the heyday for study of the genre was the early part of the 1980s, when several books were published that are now out of print. Several resources are listed in Ramsdell's *Romance Fiction: A Guide to the Genre* (Libraries Unlimited, 1999), but they are not widely available. The notable exception is:

Krentz, Jayne Ann, ed. *Dangerous Men & Adventurous Women: Romance Writers on the Appeal of the Romance*. University of Pennsylvania Press, 1992. Reissued in mass market paperback by Harper Monogram in 1996. Nineteen authors, beloved of romance readers, contributed essays on the appeal of their genre, the aspects of fantasy and character in the books they write, and descriptions of their readers. Many of the essays rebut feminist criticism of the genre.

Writers' Manuals

The market for paperback romances took off in the 1970s, and there was a need for authors to produce a seemingly unlimited number of titles, many issued monthly in the several serials. It has been estimated that in certain years upwards of 200 new authors have appeared. Now available for such authors are several manuals providing instruction in the very formalized patterns demanded by the different types of romances. Readers of romance should find the manuals illuminating and amusing.

The organization of each of the following manuals differs, but basically each provides information on the types of romance, plots, characters (particularly hero and heroine), publishers and their requirements, and tips on how to write effectively (dialogue, descriptions, etc.).

Borcherding, David H., ed. *Romance Writer's Sourcebook: Where to Sell Your Manuscripts.* Writer's Digest Books, 1996.

Gallagher, Rita, and Rita Clay Estrada, eds. *Writing Romances: A Handbook by the Romance Writers of America.* Writer's Digest Books, 1997.

Grant, Vanessa. *Writing Romance.* Self Counsel Press, 1997. "A how-to-do-it romance writer's workshop under one cover."

MacManus, Yvonne. *You Can Write a Romance! And Get It Published,* rev. ed. Pocket Books, 1997. An inspirational and concise manual, with a good deal of advice on selling the manuscript, including publisher guidelines.

Pianka, Phyllis Taylor. *How to Write Romances.* Writer's Digest Books, 1998.

Not a manual, but definitely a help for those writing romance, is the following:

Kent, Jean Salter, and Candace Shelton. *The Romance Writers' Phrase Book.* Even for those who don't plan to write a romance, this slender but packed guide to the coded language of love will be a delight.

Review Journals

The following journals are for the devoted readership of the genre and are much more than review journals, as the annotations indicate. Their emergence parallels the genre's recent and amazing publishing activity and growth in reading audience.

Affaire de Coeur: For the Romantic at Heart. 1981– . Monthly, published by Barbara N. Keenan, Fremont, California. Provides star-rated reviews, news, and brief articles. Sponsors the annual Rom-Con conference.

The Gothic Journal. A bimonthly magazine that reviews romantic suspense, romantic mystery, gothic romance, supernatural romance, and woman-in-jeopardy romance. It also offers author profiles and articles for both readers and writers of suspenseful romance. Web site at http://gothicjournal.com/romance (accessed 20 January 2000). From 1991–1998, this was a print magazine. In 1999, it ceased publishing a hard copy and is now available only on the World Wide Web.

The Literary Times. Starting as a newsletter in 1988, it became a quarterly magazine in 1992, featuring book reviews, author profiles, and information for romance writers.

Romantic Times. 1981– . This publication contains reviews, annotations, excerpts from new romances, publishing and author news, biographies of romance authors, interviews, and advertisements. The romance reader who is as enthralled as the publisher with every tidbit about romance will have a feast. The publisher and editor, Kathryn Falk, is an active apologist and publicist for romance. *Romantic Times* and Long Island University's Institute for Continuing Education, with Kathryn Falk as a conference director, announced the first Romantic Book Lovers Conference in New York City for April 17, 1982. In 1986 this publication became a monthly. The reviewers seem to rate the books more on the quality of lovemaking than on the quality of plot and characterization. Web site at http://www.romantictimes. com (accessed 20 January 2000).

Authors' Associations

Romance writers often do not feel comfortable within the standard authors' associations, so they have formed their own groups. Although the association in the United States is some 20 years behind its British counterpart, it has been very successful, with more than 8,200 members in 1998.

Romantic Novelists Association. This British group was founded in 1960. It presents an annual award for the best romance, often having runner-up awards and a historical romance award. Its members are highly articulate apologists for the genre. They have a Web site at http://freespace.virgin.net/marina.oliver/rna.htm (accessed 14 November 1999).

Romance Writers of America. The founding convention was held in Houston, Texas, in June 1981 and drew an unexpectedly large attendance of writers and fans. An award, the Rita, was established as the association's official prize for published work. The 18th annual convention was held in Chicago in July 1999. The organization also has local chapters in many communities and chapters devoted to different types of romance writing.

Awards

The most prestigious and well-known romance awards are the "Ritas," awarded by the Romance Writers of America in several different categories.

Publishers

Along with the continuing predominant publication of romance in the paperback lines, there has been an increase in the amount of hardcover romance publication. Three publishers issue the greatest number: Doubleday, St. Martin's Press, and Walker. Also, almost all hardcover publishers now have their own paperback lines. There has been an increase in the number of trade paperback genre titles.

The library market benefits from the increase in hardcover and trade paperback romances available. Whether the pattern of reprinting paperback series in library editions will continue is not clear. Gregg Press (Chivers Press, London) has reprinted Silhouette titles in hardcover, and some Harlequin titles have been reprinted in large-print format by Thorndike Press. Brandywyne Books is issuing Heirloom editions in hardcover, but they are priced out of the library market at $35 to $50 for authors such as Jennifer Wilde, Janet Dailey, and Jude Devereaux. Five Star and Severn House are issuing reasonably priced reprints in hardcover, some of authors who did not receive the recognition due them in paperback, others of early works by popular authors that were originally issued in paperback only. That romances are appearing regularly on the best-seller lists in both hardcover and paperback editions should make for a steady publishing program in the genre.

It is notable that in hardcover the following types of romance are the most prominent: historical and period romances, with a great many Regencies; gothic and romantic suspense; and sagas, both period historical and contemporary. The following British publishers have strong hardcover lines: Bodley Head, Century, Collins, Gollancz, Robert Hale, Hodder, Michael Joseph, and Macdonald. Many of their titles are released in the United States, with the strongest romance programs coming from Doubleday (with a labeled line, Starlight Romances), St. Martin's Press, and Walker (heavy importation of British titles). Other publishers in the United States that regularly publish romance are Arbor House, Delacorte, Dodd, Dutton, Five Star, Harper, Macmillan, Morrow, Putnam, and Simon and Schuster.

Several large-print houses actively bring older titles back into print; a few are Dales, Magna, and Thorndike.

Paperback Publishers

While great numbers of romances still appear regularly, the number of issuing publishers has recently decreased drastically. Several publishers have series lines, noted in the following list, in addition to issuing both original titles and reprints. There has been an increase in the number of trade paperback romances, despite some price resistance, and these are in a satisfactory format for libraries. (Avon, Ballantine/Fawcett, and Jove have issued many; this may relate to the fact that several paperback publishers are now also publishing in hardcover, such as Ballantine, Bantam, and Pocket Books/Poseidon.)

The following U.S. paperback publishers issue romances regularly: Ace/Charter, Avon Ballantine/Fawcett, Bantam, Berkley, Dell, Harlequin/Worldwide, Jove, Leisure, NAL/Signet, Sonnet/Pocket Books, Popular Library/Warner, and Zebra. Strong lines for all these houses are the historical and Regency romances. Romance in the American West appears in many of the period romances. There has been a trend toward "futuristic" romance (romance combined with the genres of fantasy and science fiction). The Timeswept imprint from Love Spell features time-travel fantasy-romances.

For years, Harlequin led sales in category romances. Silhouette was started up as competition, but now both houses are owned by the Canadian company Torstar. They have numerous imprints.

The "inspirational" romance is being issued by several denominational publishers (and also in the Silhouette Inspiration series). Guideposts started up a book club in 1993 called "Forever" Romances. They are reprints of paperbacks that are sold only through mail order. Zondervan, now an imprint of HarperCollins, and Waterbrook Press both issue inspirational romances.

Tip sheets (guidelines) are available for most of the series romance lines. These guidelines spell out the characters (and age limits) of the hero and heroine, their economic situation, clothes, setting, and the type of love story permissible. Tip sheets require constant revision as the limits of sensuality are steadily extended. Whereas once a series might have been labeled "sweet," meaning no explicit sex, it may now be labeled "spicy," "sensual," or "steamy" (stopping just short of soft-core pornography). The tip sheets are available on request from the publishers, and both libraries and readers of romance might find them useful. Several of the writers' manuals for the romance novel reprint tip sheets.

D's Romance Picks

Beverley, Jo. *Forbidden Magic.*

Cody, Denée. *The Golden Rose.*

Donati, Sara. *Into the Wilderness.*

Frank, Suzanne. *Sunrise on the Mediterranean.*

Kimberlin, Annie. *Stray Hearts.*

Chapter 6

Science Fiction

"The last man on Earth sat in a room. There was a knock on the door."

—Anonymous

"I love you sons of bitches. You're the only ones with guts enough to really care about the future, who really notice what machines do to us, what wars do to us, what cities do to us, what tremendous misunderstandings, mistakes, accidents and catastrophes do to us. You're the only ones zany enough to agonize over time and distances without limit, over mysteries that will never die, over the fact that we are right now determining whether the space voyage for the next billion years or so is going to be Heaven or Hell."

—Kurt Vonnegut, *God Bless You, Mr. Rosewater* (1965)

"S[cience] f[iction] allows us to understand and experience our past, present, and future in terms of an imagined future."

—Kathryn Cramer, *The Ascent of Wonder* (1994)

Mary Wollstonecraft Shelley has been called "the mother of science fiction" for her creation of *Frankenstein*, written when she was still in her teens and published in 1818. Pioneering works were written by Edgar Allan Poe, Jules Verne, and H. G. Wells in the nineteenth century. In the early part of the twentieth century, magazines featuring serialized novels and short stories were popular and science fiction became a mainstay, but it was not called "science fiction" until 1929, the term becoming commonly accepted in the 1930s. John Clute's *Science Fiction: The Illustrated Encyclopedia* (DK Publishing, 1995) does a wonderful job of presenting the history of science fiction in relation to the surrounding world situation. The decade-by-decade charts relate important events in science fiction, film, radio, television, magazines, and world events. Early science fiction, during "the golden age," focused on the mechanical, on how machines would change the world. The technology was the essence, with characterization and plot taking a backseat. In the 1950s an interest in alien contact developed, as society began to wonder who was out there, giving rise to the now mostly forgotten BEM (bug-eyed monster) stories. In the 1960s science fiction began to recognize non-mechanical sciences, and many of the novels written dealt with psychology, sociology, and how humans relate to their world and to change, heralding a "new wave" of science fiction. Cyberpunk, in which technology was portrayed as being perhaps not all that it had been cracked up to be, began to appear in the 1980s. In the 1990s, scientific advances in nanotechnology, artificial intelligence, and bioengineering became a visible force in the field.

There are a number of works focusing on the history and evolution of science fiction. Some are listed at the end of this chapter.

Themes and Types

The reader trying to understand science fiction is faced with a lack of an encompassing definition for all aspects and types of science fiction. Science fiction, fantasy, and horror are all very closely linked, sharing the common thread of imagination. It is not at all uncommon for writers to cross the lines between these genres from book to book, and, indeed, sometimes even within the same book.

Science fiction could be described as the literature of "what if?" What if there were life on other planets? What if someone were to travel faster than light? What if there were people who lived inside a world rather than on its surface? What if all the men on a planet were to die off? What if one could go into a world created by a computer program? What if … ? The possibilities of science fiction are as endless as the human imagination. The areas covered in science fiction are as diverse as the readers of the genre. Some stories are set in a near future, with scenarios that are probable. Others are set so far in the future, or in the past, that they seem nigh on impossible. A science fiction reader needs both a willing suspension of disbelief and a questioning mind.

Many science fiction readers like to communicate with other readers. Fans are responsible for a multitude of fanzines as well as frequent conventions. (For a look at science fiction fandom from a mystery point of view, try Sharyn McCrumb's *Bimbos of the Death Sun* [TSR, 1988] and *Zombies of the Gene Pool* [Simon and Schuster, 1992].) Science fiction readers, editors, and writers "talk" over the Internet on several different newsgroups. To keep up with what fans are reading, one can subscribe to rec.arts.sf.written and read reviews and criticism firsthand.

How to differentiate between fantasy and science fiction is a frequently debated question. Because the readers, writers, and publishers of science fiction (SF) and fantasy tend to have strong opinions about where a particular work fits into the genre categories, there is never going to be any one good way of making distinctions. Even questioning the authors themselves sometimes elicits surprising opinions. One might think that dragons, being mythical creatures, fall into the fantasy realm. Anne McCaffrey, best-selling author of the Pern series, emphatically claims that her dragons, and the unique characteristics of the planet Pern, have a scientific basis, so her works dealing with the dragons of Pern are science fiction rather than fantasy. Many of her fans disagree. Orson Scott Card, Nebula and Hugo award–winning author, claims that his knowledge of science is not extensive, that his stories come entirely from his imagination, so they are fantasy. Also, Card has stated (rather tongue-in-cheek but true nonetheless) that one can tell the genre by the cover illustration: Rivets denote science fiction, while foliage denotes fantasy. Some consider science fiction to be a subgenre of fantasy and others consider fantasy to be a subgenre of science fiction.

For this guide, the author's personal opinion was used as the criterion when deciding where each book fits. Because no two people ever seem to have agreed on exactly where the demarcation is, this seemed to be the most expedient means of categorizing the books. Science fiction readers should check Chapter 7, "Fantasy" (just as fantasy readers should check this chapter). IMHO (Internetese for "in my humble opinion"), science fiction novels are those that deal with scientific topics, space travel, aliens, and recognizably Earth-variant worlds or life-forms that have not been touched by magic. Time travel, not occasioned by magic, is here, as are stories of distant civilizations (whether present-day or set many years in the future or in the past) that show some relationship to Earth or its life-forms.

However, the late Betty Rosenberg wrote in 1986 in the second edition of *Genreflecting*:

> Science fiction is speculative—speculative about the potential uses of science and speculative about the potential future of mankind on this world and within the universe. The two themes may combine within the same novel, usually with one being subordinate. Although authors in the field tend to specialize in an aspect or aspects of science fiction, most do wander through the universe of science fiction themes. Unlike other genres, the best examples of the work and ideas of science fiction authors are often found in the short story.

That it is short on characterization and long on gimmicks and ideas is a frequent criticism of science fiction. (Space opera is said to have only adventure and neither characterization nor ideas.) Much science fiction is thesis fiction, bearing a statement about science fact, human nature, man in relation to nature or the universe, man in conflict with the universe, man speculating on his future in the universe. Greater emphasis, therefore, is often placed on situations or solutions than on the creatures (not necessarily human) who are the protagonists.

The critical works pose science fiction as the most philosophical, poetical, intellectual, and religious of the genre fictions. It is concerned with the mystery of the universe, man's place in it, and man's ultimate destiny: the continuation of humankind in its basic nature and humanity. Science fiction expresses faith in human ingenuity, human intelligence, and the human spirit. Technology is considered in terms of service to mankind and the natural world. The biological sciences are considered as they might heighten or increase the capacity and quality of the human mind. Religion is viewed as a means of salvation. The end is to augment the quality of life.

Mention must be made of the great variations in length of published science fiction. Short stories are vitally alive and well, as are short shorts, novelettes, novellas, novels, and multivolume tomes. More so than in any other genre, readers are willing to read science fiction of any length.

The titles in this chapter are grouped by themes because science fiction is not a patterned genre. Some titles involve many themes, so a listing in one category does not mean that title could not also fit into others, and some may be listed under more than one theme.

Hard Science

"At the core of hard sf lies the experience of science."

—Gregory Benford

The term *scientific extrapolation* is often used in reference to stories of hard science—not necessarily predictions of what will come with scientific experimentation and increased knowledge, but imaginative projections of possibility, if not probability. (The folklore of science fiction abounds in tales of scientific discoveries first predicted in a science fiction story.) The pride of authors in this field is that their scientific information is authentic, although what they do with it may not, as yet, be known to science.

Some of the hard sciences played with in science fiction are:

Mathematics (the fourth dimension, spatial or in time)

Nanotechnology (engineering on a molecular level)

Cybernetics (the mind of the machine, artificial intelligence)

Meteorology (characters do something about or to affect the weather)

Archaeology (carbon-14 dating)

Exobiology ("The study of life-forms beyond the earth has been defined as a science without a subject. Despite this, its nonexistent material has fascinated mankind for at least 2000 years."—*Time Probe: The Sciences in Science Fiction,* edited by Arthur C. Clarke)

Physics (gravity, relativity, faster-than-light travel, atoms and neutrons, antimatter)

Medicine (extraterrestrial medicine, brain surgery, plague)

Astronomy (space flight, black holes)

Physiology (effects of change of atmosphere on the human body in space travel)

Chemistry (drugs)

Biology (mutations, genetic future, immortality)

Other topics are computers, cosmology, cryonics, cyborgs, rockets, technology, and inventions.

Many examples of the use of hard science will be found in the short story as well as in the novel. *The Ascent of Wonder: The Evolution of Hard SF,* edited by David G. Hartwell and Kathryn Cramer (Tor, 1994), is a terrific collection of the best of hard SF short stories. It includes works by all authors prominent in the subgenre.

The following list is only a brief sampling of authors, many of whom have real scientific credentials.

Anderson, Poul

Tau Zero.

Brain Wave (1953). When Earth finally escapes a forcefield that has inhibited "certain electromagnetic and electrochemical processes," humans are transfigured by a huge increase in intelligence.

Asimov, Isaac

Asimov created the "Three Laws of Robotics" that have become conventional wisdom in much of the genre.

I, Robot.

The Rest of the Robots.

Bear, Greg

Moving Mars. Brilliant physicist Charles Franklin makes discoveries relating to matter and energy that lead Mars and Earth into conflict.

Benford, Gregory

Artifact. Originally published in 1985 and revised in 1997, it deals with an archaeological find in the form of a small cube that contains the heat of a sun.

Carver, Jeffrey A.

Chaos chronicles. Chaos theory and alien life-forms.

Neptune Crossing.

Strange Attractors.

Clarke, Arthur C.

The Fountains of Paradise.

Rendezvous with Rama.

Clement, Hal

Mission of Gravity (1953). Set on a world with high gravity.

Forward, Robert L.

Dragon's Egg.

Starquake!

Camelot 30K. The remote-controlled exploration of an inhabited world where the temperature is only 30 degrees above absolute zero.

McCarthy, Wil

Bloom. Space travel and biotechnology.

Nagata, Linda

Vast.

Niven, Larry

Neutron Star.

Pohl, Frederik

Heechee Saga.

Gateway.

Beyond the Blue Event Horizon.

Heechee Rendezvous.

Annals of the Heechee.

The Gateway Trip.

Robinson, Kim Stanley

Red Mars.

Green Mars.

Blue Mars. Terraforming Mars to make it habitable by humans.

Sagan, Carl

Contact.

Sheffield, Charles

Several titles, including the *YA Jupiter series*.

Simak, Clifford D.

    Way Station. A Hugo award winner by a Grand Master.

Slonczewski, Joan

    The Children Star. Bioengineering.

Sullivan, Tricia

    Lethe.

    Dreaming in Smoke.

Wells, H. G.

    The War of the Worlds.

    The First Men in the Moon.

White, James

Sector General series. Eleven novels set at a medical center that caters to the needs of all types of intergalactic species.

Williamson, Jack

    Beachhead.

    Exploration of Mars.

New Wave

In these novels deriving from the soft sciences (psychology, sociology, religion, and the like), human nature realistically treated, however exotic the context, takes precedence over hard science and gadgetry (although still liberally used). Sex, drugs, Eastern religions, art, morality, ecology, overpopulation, politics—the topics encompassed within the subgenre seemingly have no limit. The lack of clear definition of "new wave" as a distinctive type of science fiction simply indicates that new wave aspects were always present in the works of some science fiction writers. There has been, however, a movement toward liberalizing the scope of themes acceptable for science fiction and expanding the imaginative vision of writers and readers. So much current science fiction, apart from the strictly adventure types, is imbued with new wave aspects that the new wave label is now used to define a historical movement in the genre, roughly from the mid-1960s to the early 1980s. The following authors are those who were influential in making new wave ideas standard in science fiction.

Aldiss, Brian

    Barefoot in the Head.

Ballard, J. G.

    The Crystal World.

    Love and Napalm.

Brunner, John
  The Sheep Look Up.
  Stand on Zanzibar.

Budrys, Algis
  Rogue Moon.

Burgess, Anthony
  A Clockwork Orange.

Delany, Samuel R.
  Driftglass.

Dick, Philip K.
  Martian Time-Slip.
  The Three Stigmata of Palmer Eldritch.

Disch, Thomas M.
  334.
  Camp Concentration.

Ellison, Harlan
  Alone Against Tomorrow.
  Dangerous Visions.

Farmer, Philip José
  Riverworld series.
    To Your Scattered Bodies Go.
    The Fabulous Riverboat.
    The Dark Design.
    The Magic Labyrinth.
    Gods of Riverworld.

Harrison, Harry
  Make Room! Make Room!

Malzberg, Barry N.
  Beyond Apollo.

Moorcock, Michael
  The Final Programme.

Russ, Joanna
  The Female Man.

Sheckley, Robert
  Journey Beyond Tomorrow.

Sladek, John
>**The Muller-Fokker Effect.**
>**Roderick at Random.**

Spinrad, Norman
>**Bug Jack Barron.**
>**Agent of Chaos.**

Sturgeon, Theodore
>**More Than Human.**

Tiptree, James, Jr.
>**Brightness Falls from the Air.**

Watson, Ian
>**The Embedding.**

Wolfe, Gene
>**The Fifth Head of Cerberus.**

Zelazny, Roger
>**Lord of Light.** Hugo and Nebula award winner.

Ecology

Three themes emerge in novels about humanity and its natural environment: manipulation and control of the environment; corruption of the environment by humans and the destruction of some or all forms of life on Earth; and alien environments with distinctive characteristics, flora, and fauna. Catastrophe is often linked to overpopulation and pollution as well as to planned changes in environmental patterns. The following authors use themes suggested by the discouraging kinds of ecological problems facing the world.

Aldiss, Brian
>**Helliconia Spring.**
>**Helliconia Summer.**
>**Helliconia Winter.**

Anthony, Piers
>**Omnivore.**

Ballard, J. G.
>**The Wind from Nowhere.**
>**The Crystal World.**

Blish, James, and Norman L. Night
>**A Torrent of Faces.**

Brunner, John
Stand on Zanzibar.
The Sheep Look Up.

Clement, Hal
Cycle of Fire.
Close to Critical.

Harrison, Harry
Make Room! Make Room!

Herbert, Frank
Dune.

Niven, Larry, and Jerry Pournelle
The Mote in God's Eye.

Ore, Rebecca
Gaia's Toys.

Robinson, Kim Stanley
Antarctica.

Silverberg, Robert
The World Inside.

Simmons, Dan
Hyperion.
The Fall of Hyperion.
Endymion.
The Rise of Endymion.

Thomas, Theodore L., and Kate Wilhelm
The Year of the Cloud.

Wilhelm, Kate
Where Late the Sweet Birds Sang. A 1970s classic reissued in 1998.

Yarbro, Chelsea Quinn
Time of the Fourth Horseman.

Messianic/Religious

In a science fiction world created for this theme, disillusionment has sullied the euphoric promise for the future offered by science and technology. Human needs and emotions somehow remain unsated in the millennium of technology. A savior, messiah, or superman brings redemption and salvation. Questions of theology and metaphysics regarding the expanding universe imagined by science fiction have uneasily juxtaposed science and faith and introduced speculation on future religions. The following authors base their books on religions currently in practice, or else they invent their own theologies.

Blish, James
> A Case of Conscience.

Butler, Octavia E.
> **The Parable of the Sower.** Hyperempathic Lauren Olamina diaries her journey as civilization collapses and wins converts to her "Earthseed" philosophy.
>
> **The Parable of the Talents.** Takes place several years after *Sower*.

Clarke, Arthur C.
> Rendezvous with Rama.
>
> Childhood's End.

Dick, Philip K.
> Galactic Pot-Healer.
>
> Divine Invasion.

Farmer, Philip José
> The Lovers.

Gunn, James
> This Fortress World.

Heinlein, Robert A.
> Stranger in a Strange Land.

Henderson, Zenna
> The People: No Different Flesh.
>
> Pilgrimage.

Herbert, Frank
> Dune.
>
> Dune Messiah.
>
> Children of Dune.
>
> The God Makers.
>
> Heretics of Dune.
>
> Chapterhouse: Dune.

Kleier, Glenn
> The Last Day.

La Plante, Richard
> Tegné.

Lewis, C. S.
Out of the Silent Planet.

Perelandra.

That Hideous Strength.

Miller, Walter M., Jr.
A Canticle for Leibowitz.

Saint Leibowitz and the Wild Horse Woman.

Moorcock, Michael
Behold the Man!

Russell, Mary Doria
The Sparrow.

The Children of God. Jesuits make first contact with an alien civilization.

Simak, Clifford D.
Time and Again.

Simmons, Dan
Hyperion.

The Fall of Hyperion.

Endymion.

The Rise of Endymion.

Smith, Cordwainer
Norstrilia.

Tepper, Sheri S.
Raising the Stone.

The Awakeners.

Northshore.

Southshore.

Vidal, Gore
Messiah.

Kalki.

Vonnegut, Kurt
The Sirens of Titan.

Cat's Cradle.

Zelazny, Roger
Lord of Light.

Isle of the Dead.

Dystopia/Utopia

Opposed to the ideal society, utopia, is the dystopia, a horrid society, frequently the subject of science fiction. Dystopia comes into existence through many causes. Frequently it derives from the failure or corruption of rule by a scientific elite. Technology and human nature prove incompatible; psychology is used to manipulate, not improve, human nature; biological tinkering evolves monsters; and so on. The pessimism of dystopian science fiction is political and sociological as well as antiscience and antitechnology. As this theme has a long literary history, it has been the topic of novels not usually considered science fiction. Among the following authors are several whose writings are outside the realm of this genre (Bellamy, Huxley, Orwell, and Skinner).

Asimov, Isaac
> **Pebble in the Sky.**

Foundation trilogy.

Bellamy, Edward
> **Looking Backward: 2000–1887.**

Bradbury, Ray
> **Fahrenheit 451.**

Brin, David
> **Glory Season.**

Brunner, John
> **Shockwave Rider.**

Burroughs, William S.
> **Nova Express.**

Gunn, James
> **The Joy Makers.**

Harrison, Harry
> **Make Room! Make Room!**

Heinlein, Robert A.
> **To Sail Beyond the Sunset.**

Hendrix, Howard V.
> **Lightpaths.**
> **Standing Wave.**

Hoyle, Fred
> **Ossian's Ride.**

Huxley, Aldous
Brave New World.
Island.

Le Guin, Ursula K.
Always Coming Home.

Leiber, Fritz
Gather, Darkness!

Lowry, Lois
The Giver. Destined to become a classic, this award-winning children's title is also popular with adults who have discovered it.

Orwell, George
1984.

Pohl, Frederik, and Cyril Kornbluth
The Space Merchants.

Reynolds, Mack
Looking Backward, from the Year 2000.

Robinson, Kim Stanley.
Pacific Edge.
Wild Shore.
The Gold Coast.

Skinner, B. F.
Walden Two.

Tepper, Sheri S.
The Gate to Women's Country.

Vonnegut, Kurt
Player Piano.

Post-Apocalypse

Survival after the almost total destruction of Earth as we know it—the nature of the disaster, its effect on the nature of man, and the shape of society thereafter—is a common SF theme. The disaster may be natural (e.g., plague, a planet colliding with Earth) or human-caused (e.g., nuclear war). This theme pervades the works of many science fiction writers besides those in the following list. It has been a popular theme for movies, from *A Boy and His Dog* to the Mad Max series and into the 1990s, with the Kevin Costner movies *Waterworld* and *The Postman* (read the book). *Tank Girl,* a comic book series and movie, is also set in this kind of world.

Ballard, J. G.
    The Drowned World.
    The Burning World.
    The Crystal World.

Brin, David
    The Postman.

Brunner, John
    The Sheep Look Up.

Burton, Levar
    Aftermath: A Novel About the Future.

Card, Orson Scott
    Folk of the Fringe.

Christopher, John
    The Death of Grass.

Crowley, John
    Engine Summer.

Dick, Philip K.
    Dr. Bloodmoney.

Dickson, Gordon R.
    Wolf & Iron. A lone traveler in a world following financial collapse.

Frank, Pat
    Alas, Babylon.

Hoban, Russell
    Riddley Walker.

Hoyle, Fred, and Geoffrey Hoyle
    The Inferno.

Lethem, Jonathan
    Amnesia Moon.

Lewitt, Shariann
    Memento Mori.

Miller, Walter M., Jr.
    A Canticle for Leibowitz. A monastery in Utah is the site of a miraculous discovery in an age of darkness following nuclear annihilation.

Murphy, Pat
The City, Not Long After.

Pangborn, Edgar
Davy.

Roessner, Michaela
Vanishing Point.

Sheffield, Charles
Aftermath.

Stewart, George R.
Earth Abides.

Tepper, Sheri S.
The Gate to Women's Country. Women live within walled cities, keeping science and medical knowledge alive, while most men live in garrisons outside the cities.

Tucker, Wilson
The Long Loud Silence.

Turner, George
Drowning Towers.

Vonnegut, Kurt
Cat's Cradle.

Whitmore, Charles
Winter's Daughter.

Wilhelm, Kate
Juniper Time.

Wylie, Philip, and Edwin Balmer
When Worlds Collide.

Wyndham, John
The Day of the Triffids.

Yarbro, Chelsea Quinn
Time of the Fourth Horseman.

Alternate and Parallel Worlds

History as it might have been: What if there had been a significant change in an historical event? What, then, would have been the pattern of history? What would the present be like, and why? This theoretical analysis of historical cause and effect is often conjoined to the parallel world theme: Parallel Earths and parallel universes exist simultaneously with our Earth, conceived, perhaps, along a spatial fourth dimension. (In some worlds of fantasy, characters can be transported out of one parallel universe and into another.) This theme has been used by many science fiction authors in addition to those in the following list, as well as by authors of the mainstream novel (e.g., Vladimir Nabokov). In the early 1990s, some of the cyberpunk authors started writing in the alternative history vein; these books were promptly christened "steam punk."

Anthony, Piers
Out of Phaze.

Robot Adept.

Phaze Doubt.

Asimov, Isaac
The End of Eternity.

Baxter, Stephen
Voyage.

Blaylock, James P.
Lord Kelvin's Machine.

The Paper Grail.

Bova, Ben
Triumph.

de Camp, L. Sprague
Lest Darkness Fall.

Dick, Philip K.
The Man in the High Castle.

Now Wait for Last Year.

Flow My Tears, the Policeman Said.

Eye in the Sky.

Farmer, Philip José
The Gate of Time.

Sail on, Sail On.

Gibson, William, and Bruce Sterling
The Difference Engine.

Gould, Steven
Wildside. A pristine, untouched world exists on the other side of a hidden door in a barn.

Harrison, Harry
Tunnel Through the Deeps.

West of Eden.

Winter in Eden.

Return to Eden.

Heinlein, Robert A.
Tunnel in the Sky.

Farnham's Freehold.

Hogan, James P.
The Proteus Operation.

Laumer, Keith
Worlds of the Imperium.

Leiber, Fritz
Destiny Times Three.

Lupoff, Richard A.
Countersolar!

Circumpolar!

Moorcock, Michael
The Wrecks of Time.

O'Leary, Patrick
Door Number Three.

Roberts, Keith
Pavane.

Rucker, Rudy
The Hollow Earth.

Sawyer, Robert J.
The Quintaglio trilogy.

Shaw, Bob
The Two-Timers.

Sheckley, Robert
Mindswap.

Simak, Clifford D.
Ring Around the Sun.

Somtow, S. P.
    The Aquiliad: Aquila in the New World.

Turtledove, Harry
World War series.

    In the Balance.
    Tilting the Balance.
    Upsetting the Balance.
    Striking the Balance.

Vance, Jack
    Alastor.

Williamson, Jack
    Legion of Time.

Wilson, Robert Charles
    Gypsies.
    Mysterium.
    Darwinia.

Wingrove, David
Chung Kuo series.

Time Travel, Time Warp

Travel into either the past or the future is a dream in all literature and not restricted to science fiction. Whether limited to the body or mind, the experience is both desirable and frightening. Science fiction writers use great ingenuity in the methods of travel and equal imagination in depicting the experiences of the travelers. This is a favorite ploy in space opera and fantasy. Playing with time has intrigued many science fiction and fantasy writers, and the following list merely suggests the number of books on the theme. Those who like science fiction time travel may also enjoy the examples found in the fantasy and romance chapters (Chapters 7 and 5). Many examples can be found in children's books as well.

Aldiss, Brian
    Cryptozoic!
    Frankenstein Unbound.

Anderson, Poul
    Tau Zero.
    The Corridors of Time.

Appel, Allen
>   Twice upon a Time.
>   Till the End of Time.
>   Time After Time.

Asimov, Isaac
>   Pebble in the Sky.
>   The End of Eternity.

Ballard, J. G.
>   The Crystal World.

Barnes, John
>   Kaleidoscope Century.

Benford, Gregory
>   Timescape.

Bester, Alfred
>   The Stars My Destination.

Bishop, Michael
>   No Enemy but Time.

Blish, James
>   Midsummer Century.

Brunner, John
>   The Productions of Time.
>   Quicksand.

Dalton, Sean
>   Turncoat.

David, James F.
>   Footprints of Thunder.

Dick, Philip K.
>   Counter-Clock World.

Dickson, Gordon R.
>   Time Storm.

Dunn, J. R.
>   **Days of Cain.** A time monitor goes renegade to try to stop the Nazi death camps.

Fenn, Lionel
>   Time: The Semi-Final Frontier.

Garcia y Robertson, R.
Atlantis Found.

Haldeman, Joe

The Forever War. Space travel collapses time so a soldier gone from home for 27 years has experienced and aged only the one year, leading draftee William Mandella to reenlist and spend centuries fighting an interstellar war.

Harness, Charles L.

The Paradox Men.

Harrison, Harry

The Technicolor Time Machine.

Heinlein, Robert A.
The Door into Summer.

Farnham's Freehold.

Hoyle, Fred

October the First Is Too Late.

Laumer, Keith
The Great Time Machine Hoax.
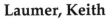

Back to the Time Warp.

MacDonald, John D.
The Girl, the Gold Watch and Everything.

Mason, Lisa

Summer of Love.

The Golden Nineties. Zhu Wong, a 25th-century Chinese woman imprisoned for possible murder, gets a ticket out of jail to work on the Golden Nineties project. Equipped with a neckjack and an archive of information from an artificial intelligence called Muse, she sets out into the wild and woolly world of 1895 San Francisco to find a golden brooch and ensure that it will be put into the hands of a green-eyed Chinese woman not yet born.

May, Julian

The Saga of Pliocene Exile.

The Many-Colored Land.

The Golden Torc.

The Nonborn King.

The Adversary.

Moorcock, Michael
The Dancers at the End of Time series.
> **An Alien Heat.**
> **The Hollow Lands.**
> **The End of All Songs.**

Morse, David E.
> **The Iron Bridge.**

Niven, Larry
> **A World out of Time.**
> **World of Ptavvs.**

O'Leary, Patrick
> **Door Number Three.**

Pohl, Frederik
> **The Age of the Pussyfoot.**

Powers, Tim
> **The Anubis Gates.**

Saberhagen, Fred
> **Pilgrim.**

Silverberg, Robert
> **The Masks of Time.**
> **The Time Hoppers.**

Stapledon, Olaf
> **Last and First Men** (1930).

Stirling, S. M.
> **Island in the Sea of Time.**

Varley, John
> **Millennium.** Agents from a dying future pop into contemporary accidents to snatch healthy people seconds before death, to repopulate the future.

Vinge, Vernor
> **Marooned in Real Time.**

Wells, H. G.
> **The Time Machine.**
> **When the Sleeper Wakes.**

Willis, Connie
> **The Doomsday Book.** A history student from the future travels back to 1348 and the Black Plague.

To Say Nothing of the Dog. Willis's delightfully wry humor takes us to a future where Lady Schrapnell, a filthy-rich American, is funding time travel so that she can rebuild Coventry Cathedral to the way it was when her great grandmother experienced an epiphany there in front of the Bishop's Bird Stump. When a time-lagged historian from the future is sent to the Victorian era to escape Lady Schrapnell, he finds love and a problem that could rend the fabric of time.

Wright, S. Fowler

The World Below.

Lost Worlds

Lost worlds are the matter of romantic science fiction, now largely displaced as a subject by the interplanetary universe. There are large elements of fantasy and adventure in the many examples that are still popular: prehistoric animals, strange races of people, and background in archaeology and anthropology. The prehistoric epic in Chapter 1, "Historical" (see p. 27) is very closely related, with substantial overlap. Some are serious novels about primitive humans and vanished types. The following books are some of the prototypes.

Aldiss, Brian

Helliconia trilogy. On a distant planet with two suns, the seasons in the generations-long year lead to the rise and fall of civilizations.

Bishop, Michael

Ancient of Days.

Burroughs, Edgar Rice

At the Earth's Core.

Doyle, Arthur Conan, Sir

The Lost World.

Golding, William

The Inheritors.

Haggard, H. Rider

She.

King Solomon's Mines.

Verne, Jules

Journey to the Centre of the Earth.

More recent books in this vein include Robert T. Bakker's *Raptor Red* and Edward Myers's Mountain Made of Light series.

Lost Colony

Far in the future, when other worlds have been colonized by humans, some of those worlds lose contact with Earth or are unable to maintain it in the first place. The worlds of these descendants of ours lead to many variations on the future of an isolated pocket of humanity.

Card, Orson Scott
Homecoming Saga series.

Gould, Steven
The Helm. Leland follows a rocky path to greatness after he ascends a forbidden peak during a festival and places a sacred helmet upon his head, even though the privilege of donning the mysterious artifact of the "founders" by right belongs to his oldest brother, who had been groomed to govern. After the event his father seemingly turns on Leland, charging his brothers with the task of beating him with a bamboo pole at random and unexpected times. After the intercession of a young woman of high station, Leland is invited to dine in company again, then sent off to a distant village where he studies martial arts, discovering that on an unconscious level he knows much that he has no rational explanation for knowing. As a war begins, Leland finds himself pressed into a position of leadership.

Niven, Larry
Destiny's Road.

Van Vogt, A. E.
The Beast.

Zettel, Sarah
Reclamation.

Immortality

Whether science can ultimately confer immortality upon humans is considered in science fiction, but whether such immortality would be a blessing or a curse is the real question. There are many immortal beings to be found in science fiction stories. (One such immortal in *Venus on the Half-Shell,* by Kilgore Trout, says bluntly, "Immortality is a pain in the ass." For more on this book, see "Parody and Comedy," p. 326.) The following books treat this theme seriously.

Aldiss, Brian
Moment of Eclipse.

Banks, Iain
Feersum Endjinn.

Barnes, John
Kaleidoscope Century.

Grimwood, Ken
    Replay.

Gunn, James
    The Immortals.

Haldeman, Joe
    Buying Time.

Heinlein, Robert A.
    Time Enough for Love.

Shaw, Bob
    One Million Tomorrows.

Silverberg, Robert
    Born with the Dead.

Simak, Clifford D.
    Way Station.

Spinrad, Norman
    The Iron Dream.
    No Direction Home.

Stableford, Brian
    Inherit the Earth.

Tucker, Wilson
    The Time Masters.
    Time Bomb.

Vance, Jack
    To Live Forever.

van Vogt, A. E.
    The Weapon Makers.

Zelazny, Roger
    This Immortal.

Psionic Powers

The powers of precognition, telepathy, clairvoyance, telekinesis, and tele-portation displayed by characters in science fiction make current research in parapsychology seem crude. Science fiction invented the term *psionics* (psychic electronics) to describe these powers of the mind. Such powers are often inherent in the superman theme and are often manifest among alien beings. The variations on this theme have fascinated many science fiction authors, not just those in the following list.

Asaro, Catherine
Primary Inversion.

Catch the Lightning.

The Last Hawk.

The Radiant Seas.

Ashwell, Pauline
Project Farcry.

Bester, Alfred
The Stars My Destination.

The Demolished Man.

Blish, James
Jack of Eagles.

Bradley, Marion Zimmer
Darkover series.

Brunner, John
The Whole Man.

Clement, Hal
Needle.

Dickson, Gordon R.
Dorsai!

Foster, Alan Dean
For Love of Mother Not.

Flinx of the Commonwealth.

Flinx in Flux.

Mid-Flinx.

Gould, Steven C.
Jumper.

Harrison, Harry
Death Word.

Henderson, Zenna
Pilgrimage.

Herbert, Frank
    Dune.

Ingrid, Charles
    The Patterns of Chaos series.

King, Stephen
    Firestarter.

Le Guin, Ursula K.
    The Lathe of Heaven.

McCaffrey, Anne
    To Ride Pegasus.
    Pegasus in Flight.
    Pegasus in Space.
    The Rowan.
    Damia.
    Damia's Children.
    Lyon's Pride.

Murphy, Pat
    Falling Woman.

Pohl, Frederik
    Drunkard's Walk.

Roberts, Keith
    The Inner Wheel.

Russ, Joanna
    And Chaos Died.

Schmitz, James H.
    The Witches of Karres. Often found in young adult or juvenile collections.

Silverberg, Robert
    Dying Inside.

Simak, Clifford D.
    Time Is the Simplest Thing.

Stewart, Sean
    Resurrection Man.

Sturgeon, Theodore
    The Dreaming Jewels.

van Vogt, A. E.
Slan.

Vinge, Joan D.
Catspaw.

Psion.

Dreamfall.

Wilson, Robert Charles
Gypsies.

Zelazny, Roger
The Dream Master.

Space Opera and Galactic Empires

Although much maligned, space operas are, in truth, a great deal of fun. They feature almost everything one could want in a story: action, adventure, intrigue, and romance. The *Star Wars* movies from George Lucas are prime examples of space opera. There is excellent writing turning up in space opera and, although many space operas are formulaic dreck, there are also well-written novels in this subgenre that have received (most deservedly) respected awards. The following titles deal adventurously with galactic empires and views of communities and worlds of humans and aliens in a variety of political and sociological relationships. Many of the shared worlds of science fiction fall into this category, so fans may also want to check the "Shared Worlds" section.

Pioneers in this subgenre were:

Smith, Edward E.
"Doc."

The Skylark of Space.

Lensman series.

Williamson, Jack
The Legion of Space.

The tradition has grown and flourished, as evidenced by the following in no way comprehensive listing.

Anderson, Poul
Mirkheim.

Trader to the Stars.

Harvest of Stars.

Harvest the Fire.

The Stars Are Also Fire.

Anthony, Piers
Total Recall.

Asimov, Isaac

Foundation series. A second Foundation series has been written by Greg Bear, Gregory Benford, and David Brin, continuing the saga of the world built by Asimov.

Bova, Ben
Privateers.

The Exiles trilogy.

Bradley, Marion Zimmer

Darkover series.

Brin, David

Uplift series.

Uplift trilogy.

Sundiver.

Startide Rising.

The Uplift War.

Uplift Storm trilogy.

Brightness Reef.

Infinity's Shore.

Heaven's Reach.

Brunner, John
Endless Shadow.

Bujold, Lois McMaster

The continuing saga of the militaristic Vorkosigan family.

Shards of Honor.

Barrayar.

Warrior's Apprentice.

The Vor Game.

Cetaganda.

Borders of Infinity.

Brothers in Arms.

Mirror Dance.

Memory.

Komarr.

A Civil Campaign.

Card, Orson Scott
The Memory of Earth.

The Call of Earth.

The Ships of Earth.

Earthfall. Earthborn.

Cherryh, C. J.
Downbelow Station. Award-winning science fiction set on a politically warring space station.

Cyteen.

Clark, Jan
Prodigy.

Delany, Samuel R.
Nova.

Heinlein, Robert A.
A Citizen of the Galaxy.

Starship Troopers.

Starman Jones.

Farmer in the Sky.

Have Spacesuit, Will Travel.

Podkayne of Mars.

Jablokov, Alexander
Deepdrive.

King, Stephen
The Dark Tower series.

The Gunfighter.

The Drawing of the Three.

The Wastelands.

Wizard and Glass. A very dark space opera from the king of horror fiction.

Laumer, Keith
Galactic Odyssey.

McCaffrey, Anne
Planet Pirates series.

Sassinak. Written with Elizabeth Moon.

The Death of Sleep. Written with Jody Lynn Nye.

Generation Warriors. Written with Elizabeth Moon.

Pern series.

    Dragonsdawn.

    Moreta: Dragonlady of Pern.

    Nerilka's Story.

    Dragonflight.

    Dragonquest.

    The White Dragon.

    The Renegades of Pern.

    All the Weyrs of Pern.

    The Chronicles of Pern.

    The Dolphins of Pern.

    Dragonseye.

    The Masterharper of Pern.

Harper Hall trilogy. Also set on Pern; written for young adults but read by adults.

    Dragonsong.

    Dragonsinger.

    Dragondrums.

McCaffrey, Anne, and Ann Scarborough

Petaybee trilogy.

    Powers That Be.

    Power Lines.

    Power Play.

Modesitt, L. E., Jr.

    The Ecolitan Enigma.

Moon, Elizabeth

Herris Serrano series.

    Hunting Party.

    Sporting Chance.

    Winning Colors.

Niven, Larry, and Jerry Pournelle

    The Mote in God's Eye.

Norton, Andre

The Solar Queen series. Started in 1955 with *Sargasso of Space,* the series took a hiatus of more than a quarter of a century before returning in the 1990s with *Redline the Stars,* cowritten with P. M. Griffin; *A Mind for Trade;* and *Derelict for Trade,* cowritten with Sherwood Smith.

Time Traders series.
> Firehand.
> Key out of Time.

Forerunner series.
> Forerunner.
> Forerunner: The Second Venture.

Sawyer, Robert J.
Starplex.

Segriff, Larry
Alien Dreams.

Shaw, Bob
Orbitsville.
The Palace of Eternity.

Simak, Clifford D.
Way Station.

Simmons, Dan
Hyperion.
The Fall of Hyperion.
Endymion.
The Rise of Endymion.

Sterling, Bruce
Schmismatrix.

Vance, Jack
The Five Gold Bands.
Ports of Call.

van Vogt, A. E.
The Voyage of the Space Beagle.
The Weapon Shops of Isher.
The Weapon Makers.

Weber, David
Honor Harrington series.
> On Basilisk Station.
> The Honor of the Queen.
> The Short Victorious War.
> Field of Dishonor.
> Flag in Exile.

Honor Among Enemies.
In Enemy Hands.
Echoes of Honor.

Weis, Margaret
The Star of the Guardians series.

Williams, Walter Jon
Rock of Ages.

Williamson, Jack
The Legion of Space.

Williamson, Jack, and James E. Gunn
Star Bridge.

Wolfe, Gene
Long Sun series.

Nightside the Long Sun.
Lake of the Long Sun.
Calde of the Long Sun.
Exodus from the Long Sun.

Zettel, Sarah
Fool's War.

Militaristic

Themes portraying all varieties of military connection are present in science fiction, from mercenaries and war to antimilitary and parody. Adventure plays a strong role. Often, a militaristic theme is present in space opera. In recent years women have been just as likely as men to be featured characters.

Bujold, Lois McMaster
Vorkosigan saga.

Cherryh, C. J.
Rimrunners.

Daley, Brian
Gammalaw series.

Dickson, Gordon R.
Dorsai series.

Drake, David
Many titles, all militaristic science fiction.

Feintuch, David
Hope series. Also called the Seafort saga. Featuring Nick Seafort, who has been called Horatio Hornblower in space.

Midshipman's Hope.

Patriarch's Hope.

Forstchen, William R.
Star Voyager Academy series.

Article 23.

Haldeman, Joe
The Forever War.

Harrison, Harry
Bill, the Galactic Hero. Parody.

Heinlein, Robert A.
Starship Troopers.

Hubbard, L. Ron
Mission Earth series (10 volumes).

Moon, Elizabeth
Once a Hero.

Heris Serrano series.

Hunting Party.

Sporting Party.

Winning Colors.

Pournelle, Jerry
Janissaries series.

Rosenberg, Joel
Not for Glory.

Hero.

Steakley, John
Armor.

Weber, David
Honor Harrington series.

Willis, Connie, and Cynthia Felice
Light Raid.

Space Travel

Although spaceflight has actually been achieved, its reality only adds to science fiction's obsession with spaceships, starships, interstellar travel, and galactic empires. This theme, as used by the following authors, ranges from space travel as science to space travel as fantasy.

Aldiss, Brian W.
Non-Stop.

Anderson, Poul
Tau Zero.

Barnes, John
Orbital Resonance.

Bear, Greg
Anvil of Stars.

Benford, Gregory, and David Brin
Heart of the Comet.

Brin, David
Startide Rising.

Cherryh, C. J.
Downbelow Station.

Clarke, Arthur C.
2001: A Space Odyssey.
Prelude to Space.
Rendezvous with Rama.
2061: Odyssey Three.

Forward, Robert L.
Rocheworld.
Return to Rocheworld.

Heinlein, Robert A.
Citizen of the Galaxy.
Have Space Suit, Will Travel.

McCarthy, Wil
Bloom.

Pohl, Frederik

The Heechee saga.

    Gateway.

    Beyond the Blue Event Horizon.

    Heechee Rendezvous.

    The Annals of the Heechee.

    The Gateway Trip: Tales and Vignettes of the Heechee.

Sheffield, Charles

    The Ganymede Club.

Simak, Clifford D.

    Shakespeare's Planet.

Stableford, Brian

    Man in a Cage.

van Vogt, A. E.

    Rogue Ship.

Verne, Jules

    From the Earth to the Moon.

Williamson, Jack

    The Black Sun.

Alien Beings

The possible and ingenious forms taken by alien beings are seemingly limitless, and authors' imaginations truly run wild. Throughout the history of science fiction they have appeared as everything from monsters (perhaps plantlike or reptilian), humanoid (a freak of Darwinian evolution, perhaps), godlike, or even disembodied intelligences (as in Fred Hoyle's *The Black Cloud*). They may be invaders of Earth or encountered on other planets. The relationships of human and alien, friendly or antagonistic, offer writers ingenious possibilities. Color paintings of the aliens found in the works of several novelists (e.g., Larry Niven's "Thrints," van Vogt's "Ixtl," Jack Chalker's "Czill," James Blish's "Lithians") are found in Wayne Douglas Barlowe and Ian Summer Barlowe's, *Guide to Extra-Terrestrials.* The following list is only a brief sampling.

Aldiss, Brian

    The Dark Light Years.

Arneson, Eleanor

    Ring of Swords.

Asimov, Isaac
  The Gods Themselves.

Bear, Greg
  The Forge of God.

  Anvil of Stars.

Bisson, Terry
  Pirates of the Universe.

Bova, Ben
  Voyagers.

  Voyagers II.

Brin, David
  The Uplift War.

Broderick, Damien
  The Dreaming Dragons.

Brown, Fredric
  Martians Go Home.

Brunner, John
  The Atlantic Abomination.

  The Crucible of Time.

Burkett, William R., Jr.
  Bloodsport.

Butler, Octavia E.
  Xenogenesis series.

      Dawn.

      Adulthood Rights.

      Imago.

Card, Orson Scott
  Ender saga.

      Ender's Game.

      Speaker for the Dead.

      Xenocide.

      Children of the Mind.

      Ender's Shadow.

Cherryh, C. J.
  Cuckoo's Egg.

  Foreigner.

  Invaders.

Clarke, Arthur C.
Imperial Earth.

Clement, Hal
Mission of Gravity.
Needle.

de Camp, L. Sprague
Rogue Queen.

Dick, Philip K.
The Game-Players of Titan.
Galactic Pot-Healer.
Our Friends from Folix-B.

Disch, Thomas M.
The Genocides.
Mankind Under the Leash.

Douglas, Carole Nelson
Probe.
Counterprobe.

Forward, Robert L.
The Dragon's Egg.
Starquake.

Foster, Alan Dean
A Call to Arms.
The False Mirror.
The Spoils of War.

Gentle, Mary
Ancient Light.
Golden Witchbreed.

Griffith, Nicola
Slow River.

Gunn, James
The Listeners.

Haldeman, Joe
The Forever War.

Heinlein, Robert A.
    The Puppet Masters.
    The Star Beast.

Hoyle, Fred
    The Black Cloud.

Le Guin, Ursula K.
    The Left Hand of Darkness.

Leiber, Fritz
    The Wanderer.

Lem, Stanislaw
    Solaris.

Lindholm, Megan
    Alien Earth.

McAuley, Paul J.
    Of the Fall.

Niven, Larry
    The Smoke Ring.
    The Integral Trees.

Niven, Larry, and Jerry Pournelle
    Footfall.
    The Mote in God's Eye.
    Ringworld.
    Ringworld Engineers.

Niven, Larry, Jerry Pournelle, and Steven Barnes
    The Legacy of Heorot.
    Beowulf's Children.

Park, Paul
    Celestis.

Pohl, Frederik
    The Day the Martians Came.
    The Other End of Time.

Reeves-Stevens, Garfield
    Nighteyes.

Robinson, Spider, and Jeanne Robinson
      Stardance.

Saberhagen, Fred
      The Berserker Throne.

Silverberg, Robert
      The Alien Years.
      Downward to the Earth.
      Invaders from Earth.

Stapledon, Olaf
      Star Maker.

Tepper, Sheri S.
      Grass.
      Raising the Stones.

Turtledove, Harry
      A World of Difference.

van Vogt, A. E.
      Voyage of the Space Beagle.

Wells, H. G.
      The War of the Worlds.

Computers, Automation, Artificial Intelligence

The computer is capable of an amazing number of ingenious functions under human programming, but in the hands of some science fiction authors it achieves sentience. So well does it think and plan and even reproduce itself in some stories that it makes humanity unnecessary and precipitates a future in which the machines hum contentedly and people are obsolete. Whether humans and computers will live in cooperative harmony or in a master-slave relationship provides a controversial theme for science fiction authors. The worry that the machine—computer or robot—may end up running human society is a recurrent theme in science fiction: Is science, in all its aspects, a blessing or a curse for humanity? The idea of a completely automated society is often analyzed in a similar manner. The following books present some aspects, both intriguing and disturbing, of our coexistence with the computer.

Anderson, Poul
      Boat of a Million Years.
      Harvest of Stars.
      The Stars Are Also Fire.
      Harvest the Fire.
      Fleet of Stars.

Blish, James
    Midsummer Century.

Brunner, John
    The Shockwave Rider.

Budrys, Algis
    Michaelmas.

Compton, D. G.
    The Steel Crocodile.

Dick, Philip K.
    Vulcan's Hammer.

Dunn, J. R.
    This Side of Judgement.
    Full Tide of Night.

Harrison, Harry, and Marvin Minsky
    The Turing Option.

Heinlein, Robert A.
    The Moon Is a Harsh Mistress.

Herbert, Frank
    Destination: Void.

Johannesson, Olaf
    The Tale of the Big Computer.

Lafferty, R. A.
    Arrive at Easterwine.

Ouellette, Pierre
    The Deus Machine.

Pohl, Frederik
    Man Plus.

Stableford, Brian
    The Walking Shadow.

Cyberpunk

All-pervasive technology and the perversion of it by a rebellious underground subculture are a major element of this subgenre. *Do Androids Dream of Electric Sheep?*, a 1968 title by Philip K. Dick from which the film *Blade Runner* was adapted, is a forerunner of modern cyberpunk. This subgenre came into its own in the 1980s with award-winning novels such as *Neuromancer*. Its demise was heralded shortly before *Snow Crash* was published, indicating that it really had not died. Cyberpunk is no longer the enfant terrible of the science fiction world; it now blends into genre and has become merely another theme, albeit an important one.

For a quick introduction to cyberpunk, try some of the stories in *Mirrorshades*, edited by Bruce Sterling. It has been called "the definitive collection of cyberpunk short fiction."

Baird, Wilhelmina
Carshcourse.

Clipjoint.

Besher, Alexander
Rim: A Novel of Virtual Reality.

Mir: A Novel of Virtual Reality.

Cadigan, Pat
Fools.

Gibson, William
Neuromancer.

Count Zero.

Mona Lisa Overdrive.

Idoru.

Burning Chrome.

Kadrey, Richard
Metrophage.

Kosko, Bart
Nanotime.

Mason, Lisa
Arachne.

Noon, Jeff
Vurt.

Pollen.

Rucker, Rudy
Wetware.

Scott, Melissa
    Burning Bright.

Stanwick, Michael
    Vacuum Flowers.

Stephenson, Neal
    Snow Crash.

Sterling, Bruce
    Islands in the Net.

Williams, Walter Jon
    Voice of the Whirlwind.
    Hardwired.

Virtual Reality

A popular theme that showed up more frequently in the 1990s is that of virtual reality, a computer-generated world within which people interact with each other and with computer-created constructs. It has elements of both cyberpunk and alternate worlds and often features game-playing.

Bova, Ben
    Death Dream.

Chalker, Jack L.
    The Wonderland Gambit series.

Friesner, Esther
    The Sherwood Game.

Hogan, James P.
    Bug Park.

McCarthy, Wil
    Murder in the Solid State.

Stephenson, Neal
    The Diamond Age, or, Young Lady's Illustrated Primer.

Williams, Tad
    Otherworld series.

Williams, Walter Jon
    Aristoi.

Robots, Androids, Cyborgs

The robot is a machine, usually with a somewhat human form, but purely mechanical. An android is an artificial human, organic in composition. A cyborg is a human altered with artificial parts to perform certain functions or modified to exist in conditions inimical to human life. The computer is essential to all three forms. Pervading all stories of robots, androids, and cyborgs is the often tricky problem of the interrelationship of human and machine. One bit of science fiction folklore exists for the robot: Asimov's three laws of robotics.

1. A robot may not injure a human being or, through inaction, allow a human being to come to harm.

2. A robot must obey the orders given by human beings, except where such orders would conflict with the first law.

3. A robot must protect its own existence as long as such protection does not conflict with the first or second law.

The robots in the following works are more sophisticated than those now available and give intriguing hints of possible futures.

Mary Shelley's *Frankenstein,* with its monster put together from various and sundry parts and reanimated by science, is a precursor of this subgenre.

Allen, Roger MacBride
> **Caliban.**

Asimov, Isaac
> **I, Robot.**
> **Caves of Steel.**

Barnes, John
> **Mother of Storms.**

Bayley, Barrington J.
> **The Garments of Caean.**

Benford, Gregory
> **Great Sky River.**

Bester, Alfred
> **Golem 100.**

Dick, Philip K.
> **Do Androids Dream of Electric Sheep?**
> **We Can Build You.**

Harrison, Harry
> **War with the Robots.**

Laumer, Keith
>A Plague of Demons.

Leiber, Fritz
>The Silver Eggheads.

Lem, Stanislaw
>The Cyberiad.

McCaffrey, Anne
>The Ship Who Sang.
>
>Partnership. Written with Margaret Ball.
>
>The Ship Who Searched. Written with Mercedes Lackey.
>
>The City Who Fought. Written with S. M. Stirling.
>
>The Ship Who Won. Written with Jody Lynn Nye.

Pohl, Frederik
>Man Plus.

Saberhagen, Fred
>*The Berserker series.* Constructed to annihilate all forms of life, these interstellar killing machines do NOT follow Asimov's laws of robotics.

Sawyer, Robert J.
>The Terminal Experiment.

Shelley, Mary
>Frankenstein, or, The Modern Prometheus. Not mechanical, but who can resist the first artificial man?

6

Silverberg, Robert
>Tower of Glass.

Simak, Clifford D.
>City.
>
>Time and Again.
>
>A Choice of Gods.

Sladek, John
>Roderick.
>
>Roderick at Random.
>
>Tik Tok.

Stirling, S. M.
>The Ship Avenged. Set, with permission, in Anne McCaffrey's Brain-Brawn Universe.

van Vogt, A. E.
>   Mission to the Stars.

Watson, Ian
>   The Cyborg and the Sorcerer.
>   The Wizard and the War Machine.

Zindell, David
>   Neverness.

Social Criticism

The sociological bases of human society are an insistent theme in science fiction, notably in the projection of utopias and dystopias (see p. 279). Science fiction authors also study the phenomena of social change to anticipate direction and project consequences. The following authors forecast possibilities, however strange the new societies may seem.

Aldiss, Brian W.
>   The Dark Light Years.

Asimov, Isaac
>   The Gods Themselves.

Ballard, J. G.
>   High-Rise.

Bear, Greg
>   Moving Mars.

Brackett, Leigh
>   The Long Tomorrow.

Brunner, John
>   Stand on Zanzibar.

Clarke, Arthur C.
>   The City and the Stars.

de Camp, L. Sprague
>   Rogue Queen.

Delany, Samuel R.
>   Triton.

Dick, Philip K.
>   Time out of Joint.
>   Radio Free Albemuth.

Disch, Thomas M.
On Wings of Song.

Farmer, Philip José
The Lovers.

Godwin, Parke
The Snake Oil Wars.
Waiting for the Galactic Bus.

Gunn, James
The Joy Makers.

Keyes, Daniel
Flowers for Algernon.

Kingsbury, Donald
Courtship Rite.

Le Guin, Ursula K.
The Left Hand of Darkness.

Lem, Stanislaw
One Human Minute.
A Perfect Vacuum.

McDevitt, Jack
Ancient Shores.

McDonald, Ian
Demolition Road.

Modesitt, L. E., Jr.
Adiamante.

Niven, Larry, and Jerry Pournelle
Oath of Fealty.

Panshin, Alexei
Rite of Passage.

Pohl, Frederik, and Cyril M. Kornbluth
The Space Merchants.

Roberts, Keith
Pavane.

Robinson, Spider
Mind Killer.

Simak, Clifford D.
> City.

Tepper, Sheri S.
> Grass.

Varley, John
> The Ophiuchi Hotline.

Wells, H. G.
> The First Men in the Moon.

Wylie, Philip
> The Disappearance.

The Superman

The superman in science fiction is not the comic-strip figure. Whether an evolutionary projection of man, an alien, or an immortal god, the superman is endowed with capacities of extraordinary, supersensory, or supernatural mental power and may also possess superhuman physical powers. The relationship between humanity and the superman is uneasy, and many stories show mutual antagonism or a humanity that fears (sometimes for good reason!) supermen. The superman as messiah is also used. As in the following books, this theme is usually accompanied by disturbing philosophical insights.

Anderson, Poul
> Brain Wave.

Bester, Alfred
> The Computer Connection.

Bova, Ben
> Orion.
> Orion Among the Stars.

Clarke, Arthur C.
> Childhood's End.

Henderson, Zenna
> Pilgrimage.
> The People: No Different Flesh.

Kleier, Glenn
> The Last Day.

Kress, Nancy
>**Beggars in Spain.**
>
>**Beggars and Choosers.**

La Plante, Richard
>**Tegné.**

Stapledon, Olaf
>**Odd John.**

Sturgeon, Theodore
>**More Than Human.**

van Vogt, A. E.
>**Slan.**

Watson, Ian
>**Alien Embassy.**
>
>**Converts.**

Williamson, Jack
>**Darker Than You Think.**

Women in Science Fiction

The independent woman has long been a science fiction tradition. Young adult novels were an early arena for strong, independent female characters. Examples of those are *Podkayne of Mars,* by Robert A. Heinlein (1963), and the Telzey series, by James H. Schmitz (started in 1964). Along the same lines is *Unwillingly to Earth,* by Pauline Ashwell. Strong women assuming the responsibility for rebuilding civilization after an apocalypse have been a common theme in science fiction, as evidenced in the Sargent, Tepper, and Wren titles.

Bradley, Marion Zimmer
Darkover series.

Butler, Octavia E.
>**The Parable of the Sower.**
>
>**The Parable of the Talents.**

Elgin, Suzette Harden
Native Tongue series.

McIntyre, Vonda N.
>**Dreamsnake.**

Moon, Elizabeth
Heris Serrano series.

Russ, Joanna
> **The Female Man.** An early classic.

Sargent, Pamela
> **The Shore of Women.**

Tepper, Sheri S.
> **Gate to Women's Country.**

Weber, David
> *Honor Harrington series.*

Wren, M. K.
> **A Gift upon the Shore.**

Bioengineering

One of the hottest topics in the news and in science fiction has been the incredible changes in the biological sciences when teamed with technology. Genetic screening has led to genetic manipulation. Cloning of mammals has been done. With each leap in science the "what ifs" in science fiction grow.

Bujold, Lois McMaster
> **Falling Free.** Bioengineered humans are rendered obsolete by changes in technology.

Freireich, Valerie J.
> **Becoming Human.**
>
> **Testament.**
>
> **Imposter.**

Goonan, Kathleen Ann
> **The Bones of Time.** Cen, a young runaway in Honolulu of 2007, is bewitched by visits from Kaiulani, the last princess of Hawaii. A romantic obsession develops, leading him to a mathematical trail to achieve time travel. In 2034, Lynn, a scientist, estranged from her prominent family, meets another young man, 13-year-old Akamu, the spitting image of the long-dead King Kamehameha. She saves him from being murdered and flees with him to China and then to Tibet and Thailand as he tries to reconstruct Cen's mathematical proofs.

Harris, Anne L.
> **Accidental Creatures.**

Kress, Nancy
> **Maximum Light.** Told from the viewpoints of a rebellious young woman, a dying doctor, and a gay young dancer, this story takes readers into a world where humanity is on the brink of extinction due to mutations and an alarming decline in the birthrate. Unable to nurture children, many people turn to surrogates, leading to a criminal underground experimenting with illegal genetic manipulations.
>
> **Beggars in Spain.**
>
> **Beggars and Choosers.** Genetic manipulation has created a race of people who need no sleep and are extra-intelligent and beautiful.

McAuley, Paul J.
Fairyland. Extinct pets are replaced with deadly artificial constructs.

Ore, Rebecca
Gaia's Toys.

Ransom, Bill
Viravax.

Burn.

Young, Jim
Armed Memory. Body modifications lead to a criminal race of human sharks who dominate the crime scene.

Love and Sex

The two themes of love and sex were late bloomers for science fiction and are often still of secondary or minor interest. They assumed importance and awoke the concern of many science fiction authors with the emergence of the new wave, or the soft sciences, particularly psychology and sociology. A shift in emphasis from a scientific thesis toward human relations, however bizarre the context, increased the scope for the love story and sexual relationships and, incidentally, often gave some much-needed depth to characterizations. (Sex often introduces some welcome humor: "On Saturn the sexes are three" begins a limerick by B. T. Xerxes, found in Tom Boardman's anthology *An ABC of Science Fiction*.) The following works are quite specific on the topics of love and sex.

Single-sex societies can bring up a number of issues and interesting situations for science fiction. In Lois McMaster Bujold's *Ethan of Athos,* an obstetrician from an all-male planet is sent out into what he perceives as the perverted heterosexual world to secure new ova needed for survival of the species on his planet. In David Brin's *Glory Season,* the featured planet was settled by women who did not want to live with men and thus created clone clans. In both books, some of the conflict derives from the necessity for heterosexual contact of some sort.

Anderson, Poul
Virgin Planet.

Atwood, Margaret
The Handmaid's Tale. Written by a mainstream author, it won an Arthur C. Clarke Award.

Barton, William, and Michael Capobianco
Alpha Centauri.

Charnas, Suzy McKee
Motherlines.
Furies.

Constantine, Storm
Wraethu series.

Delany, Samuel R.
Dhalgren.
Stars in My Pocket Like Grains of Sand.

Gilman, Carolyn Ives
Halfway Human.

Griffith, Nicola
Slow River.
Ammonite. Winner of both Lambda and James Tiptree awards.

Heinlein, Robert A.
Time Enough for Love.

Le Guin, Ursula K.
The Left Hand of Darkness.
The Dispossessed.

Piercy, Marge
Woman on the Edge of Time.

Pohl, Frederik, and Cyril Kornbluth
Search the Sky.

Russ, Joanna
The Female Man.
We Who Are About To ...

Scott, Melissa
Shadow Man.

Slonczewski, Joan
A Door into Ocean.

Sturgeon, Theodore
Venus Plus X.

Tepper, Sheri S.
Six Moon Dance.

Vinge, Joan D.
The Snow Queen.

The Summer Queen.

World's End.

Detectives in Science Fiction

An intriguing combination of detective and science fiction produces galactic policemen and PIs, human, alien, and mechanical. For a good historical survey, see the chapter "Crime: From Sherlock to Spaceships," in Sam Moskowitz's *Strange Horizons*. Anthologies collect some of the short stories, and readers may be interested in the following.

Asimov, Isaac, Martin H. Greenberg, and Charles G. Waugh, eds. *Sherlock Holmes Through Time and Space.* Bluejay, 1985.

———. *The 13 Crimes of Science Fiction.* Doubleday, 1979. Each of the stories is labeled: Hard-Boiled Detective, Psychic Detective, Spy Story, Analytical Detective, Whodunit, Why-Done-It, Inverted, Locked Room, Cipher, Police Procedural, Trial, Punishment.

Dozois, Gardner, and Sheila Williams. *Isaac Asimov's Detectives.* Ace, 1998.

Waugh, Charles G., and Martin H Greenberg, eds. *Sci-Fi Private Eye.* Roc, 1997.

As in the standard detective story, a series detective appears in several of the following examples.

Adams, Douglas
Dirk Gently's Holistic Detective Agency.

The Long Dark Tea-Time of the Soul.

Anderson, Kevin J.
Blindfold.

Asimov, Isaac
The Caves of Steel.

The Naked Sun.

Robots and Empire.

The Robots of Dawn. Features Detective Lije Baley and robot R. Daneel Olivaw.

Banks, Iain
Feersum Endjinn.

Bear, David
Keeping Time. "Last of the private eyes" in the twenty-first century.

Bear, Greg

Queen of Angels.

Slant.

Bester, Alfred

The Demolished Man. Features Lincoln Powell, telepathic cop, 2301 A.D.

Biggle, Lloyd J., Jr.

Watchers of the Dark. Features Jan Darzek, PI.

Blake, William Dorsey

My Time Is Yours. Features Reggie Moon, PI.

Carroll, Jerry Jay

Inhuman Beings. Features Goodwin Armstrong, PI, ex-cop.

Chandler, A. Bertram

Bring Back Yesterday. Features John Peterson, PI.

Clement, Hal

Needle.

Dick, Philip K.

Do Androids Dream of Electric Sheep? Features Rick Deckard, Blade Runner (PI).

Dietz, William C.

Features McCade, bounty hunter, in a pulpish, action-packed series.

Dozois, Gardner, and George Effinger

Nightmare Blue. Features Karl Jaeger, last PI on Earth.

Foster, Alan Dean

Cyber Way. Features a Navajo tribal police officer in the next century.

Montezuma Strip.

Goulart, Ron

Features Jake and Hildy Pace, PIs, twenty-first century, and Zack Tourney, Federal Police Agency.

Dr. Scofflaw.

Hail Hibbler.

The Big Bang.

Upside, Downside.

Green, Terence M.

Blue Limbo. Recently fired from the Toronto police department, Mitch Helwig bullies the hospital into giving his best friend and former supervisor, who has just been gunned down and killed, the "Blue Limbo" treatment, which brings the dead immediately back to life for a few weeks in a process that leaves the subject in blue void but able to communicate with the living. Armed with the name of the corrupt cop who murdered his friend, Mitch sets out on a rampage for justice and an attempt to rescue his kidnapped dad.

Haiblum, Isidore
Nightmare Express.

Outerworld.

Hamilton, Peter F.
Greg Mandel series. Psychic detective. Set in England.

Mindstar Rising.

A Quantum Murder.

The Nano Flower.

Hightower, Lynn S.
Alien series. Featuring Detective David Silver and his Elaki partner, String.

Jones, Gwyneth
Flower Dust.

Killough, Lee. Featuring Janna Brill and Mama Maxwell.
Deadly Silents.

The Doppelgänger Gambit.

Spider Play.

Dragon's Teeth.

Lem, Stanislaw
Tales of Pirx the Pilot. "Technological detective stories."

Lieberman, Herbert
Sandman.

MacLean, Katherine
Missing Man. Featuring George Sanford, telepathic PI.

McQuay, Mike
Mathew Swain series. Private investigator, twenty-first century.

Niven, Larry
Gil "The Arm" Hamilton.

The Patchwork Girl.

Flatlander: The Collected Tales of Gil "The Arm" Hamilton.

Nolan, William F.
Space for Hire. Featuring Sam Space, PI.

Panshin, Alexei
Star Well.

Reaves, J. Michael
Darkworld Detective. Featuring Kamus of Kadizar, PI.

Robb, J. D.
Lieutenant Eve Dallas series. Twenty-first century.

Shatner, William
Tek series.

> **Tekwar.**
>
> **Teklords.**
>
> **Teklab.**
>
> **Tek Secret.**
>
> **Tek Power.**
>
> **Tek Money.**
>
> **Tek Kill.**
>
> **Tek Net.**

Spruill, Steven G.
The Psychopath Plague.

The Imperator Plot. Featuring a detective team of a human and an alien.

Stableford, Brian
Inherit the Earth.

Tucker, Wilson
Novellas:

> **"To the Tombaugh Station."**
>
> **"Time Exposure."**

Vance, Jack
Miro Hetzel.

Wallace, Ian
The Purloined Prince.

Deathstar Voyage.

The Sign of the Mute Medusa. Featuring Claudine St. Eyre, detective.

Williams, Walter Jon
Rock of Ages. Featuring Jake Maijstral, burglar.

Zahn, Timothy
A Coming of Age.

Shared Worlds

While much more common in fantasy than in science fiction, the shared world, a collaboration of authors either working together or building on the work of another author, does appear. Often shared worlds are based on characters and worlds created for film or video games.

Alien Nation series. Based on the television series. Barry Longyear, Peter David, and K. W. Jeter are among the authors who have written books for the series.

Alien series. Based on the motion picture series.

Babylon 5. Based on the television series.

Battlestar Galactica. Based on the 1970s television series.

Battletech.

Bolos.

Dr. Who. Based on the British television series.

Foster, Alan Dean. *The Dig.* Based on a computer game from LucasArts.

Man-Kzin Wars. Based on a world created by Larry Niven.

Star Trek. Multiple series inspired by the multiple television series.

Star Wars. Inspired by the world created in the motion picture series but going far beyond it. Authors include Timothy Zahn, Michael A. Stackpole, Vonda N. McIntyre, Kevin J. Anderson, Barbara Hambly, Brian Daley, A. C. Crispin, Roger MacBride Allen, and others.

Science Fantasy

This term is not easy to define. While science fiction basically subscribes to the laws of nature as we know them, science fantasy invents new laws, new nature, a new cosmology. There was a close relationship between science fiction and fantasy in the early development of the genre (magazine titles such as *The Magazine of Fantasy and Science Fiction, Fantastic Science Fiction,* and *Science Fantasy* indicate the merging), and the current writers of science fiction may intermingle science fiction and fantasy. Some authors write both. (There is an arbitrary separation of some types of works into the later chapters on fantasy, Chapter 7, and horror, Chapter 8, while alternate and parallel worlds, time travel, and other fantasy themes are included in this chapter.) The following few authors illustrate an approach to science fiction now used by many authors.

Bradbury, Ray
Martian Chronicles.

Bradley, Marion Zimmer
Darkover series. A fully imagined world that has telepathic residents.

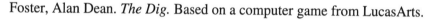

Brown, Fredric
   Martians Go Home.

Butler, Octavia E.
   Wild Seed.

Delany, Samuel R.
   Neverÿona: Or, The Tale of Signs and Cities.

Gentle, Mary
   Golden Witchbreed.
   Ancient Light.

Jones, Diana Wynne
   A Sudden Wild Magic.
   Hexwood.

McCaffrey, Anne
   Crystal Singer.
   Killashandra.
   Dragonriders of Pern series.

Silverberg, Robert
   Lord Valentine's Castle.
   Majipoor Chronicles.
   Valentine Pontifex.

Smith, Cordwainer
   Norstrilia.

Spinrad, Norman
   Child of Fortune.
   The Void Captain's Tale.

Williams, Walter Jon.
   Metropolitan.
   City on Fire.

Wolfe, Gene
   The Book of the New Sun.
   The Shadow of the Torturer.
   The Claw of the Conciliator.
   The Sword of the Lictor.
   The Citadel of the Autarch.

Parody and Comedy

Despite the serious tenor of most science fiction, there is a persistent stream of comedy and parody. Parody is the delight of the sophisticated reader, who will come across instances naturally.

Adams, Douglas
The Hitchhiker's Guide to the Galaxy.

The Restaurant at the End of the Universe.

Life, the Universe and Everything.

So Long, and Thanks for All the Fish.

Mostly Harmless.

Aldiss, Brian
The Eighty-Minute Hour: A Space Opera.

Brown, Fredric
Martians Go Home.

Harrison, Harry
Planet Story. Illustrated by Jim Burns.

Bill, the Galactic Hero.

Stainless Steel Rat series.

Jurasik, Peter, and William H. Keith, Jr.
Diplomatic Act.

Like, Russel C.
After the Blue.

Pratchett, Terry
Discworld series. Some call it science fiction but it is described in this book in "Fantasy" Chapter 7.

Pronzini, Bill, and Barry N.
Malzberg.

Prose Bowl.

Robinson, Spider
Callahan's Saloon series.

Sladek, John
The Lunatics of Terra.

Trout, Kilgore

Venus on the Half-Shell. The author is actually Philip José Farmer. Kilgore Trout is a character invented by Kurt Vonnegut. Trout is a writer of science fiction and his works are discussed, with much delightful quotation, in Vonnegut's *God Bless You, Mr. Rosewater.* (Among the many organizations and fan groups involved in science fiction is the "Friends of Kilgore Trout.")

Weiner, Ellis

National Lampoon's Doon.

Willis, Connie

Bellwether.

Topics

"Best" Authors and Their Best

A list of "best" authors and their best works is impossible to compile except on a subjective basis. Included here are most of the winners of Hugo and Nebula awards and their award-winning titles. Many of these authors are listed as examples earlier in this chapter. Most of the following authors are currently writing or appear regularly on lists of the "best." Many more titles could be listed for most of these authors. The ones listed are those most often cited. A few authors are listed without titles, indicating that critics consider important the influence of the author's work as a whole. James Wallace Harris maintains a wonderful Web site called Science Fiction Classics at http://www.scifan.com/classics (accessed 14 November 1999), where he has compiled a ranked list from seven critical works, six fan polls, and five award lists.

Aldiss, Brian

The Long Afternoon of Earth.

Anderson, Poul

Tau Zero.

Asimov, Isaac

The Gods Themselves.

The Foundation trilogy.

Barnes, John

Mother of Storms.

Bester, Alfred

The Demolished Man.

The Stars My Destination.

Bishop, Michael
    No Enemy but Time.

Blish, James
    Cities in Flight.
    A Case of Conscience.

Boucher, Anthony
    The Compleat Werewolf.

Bradbury, Ray
    The Martian Chronicles.
    Fahrenheit 451.

Brin, David
    Startide Rising.

Brunner, John
    Squares of the City.
    Stand on Zanzibar.

Budrys, Algis
    Rogue Moon.
    Who?

Bujold, Lois McMaster
    The Vor Game.
    Barrayar.
    Mirror Dance.

Burgess, Anthony
    A Clockwork Orange.

Card, Orson Scott
    Ender's Game.

Cherryh, C. J.
    Downbelow Station.
    Cyteen.

Clarke, Arthur C.
    Rendezvous with Rama.
    Childhood's End.
    The City and the Stars.

Clement, Hal
    Mission of Gravity.

Davidson, Avram
Or All the Seas with Oysters.

Delany, Samuel R.
Nova.

Babel 17.

Dhalgren.

Dick, Philip K.
Do Androids Dream of Electric Sheep?

Ubik.

The Man in the High Castle.

Dickson, Gordon R.
Soldier Ask Not.

Dorsai!

Disch, Thomas M.
334.

Ellison, Harlan
Short stories:

"I Have No Mouth and I Must Scream."

"The Beast Who Shouted Love at the Heart of the World."

Farmer, Philip José
To Your Scattered Bodies Go.

Gibson, William
Neuromancer.

Haldeman, Joe
The Forever War.

Forever Peace.

Harrison, Harry
Bill, the Galactic Hero.

Make Room! Make Room!

Heinlein, Robert A.
Time for the Stars.

Double Star.

Glory Road.

Starship Troopers.

Stranger in a Strange Land.

The Moon Is a Harsh Mistress.

Herbert, Frank
Dune.

Huxley, Aldous
Brave New World.

Keyes, Daniel
Flowers for Algernon.

Knight, Damon
Hell's Pavement.

Kornbluth, Cyril
The Syndic.

Kuttner, Henry
Mutant.

The Dark World.

Earth's Last Citadel.

Fury.

Lafferty, R. A.
The Reefs of Earth.

Past Master.

Le Guin, Ursula K.
The Left Hand of Darkness.

The Dispossessed.

Leiber, Fritz
The Wanderer.

A Spectre Is Haunting Texas.

Malzberg, Barry N.
Beyond Apollo.

Matheson, Richard
I Am Legend.

The Shrinking Man.

May, Julian
The Many-Colored Land.

McCaffrey, Anne
Dragonflight.

Restoree.

The Ship Who Sang.

McIntyre, Vonda N.
Dreamsnake.

Miller, Walter M., Jr.
A Canticle for Leibowitz.

Niven, Larry
Neutron Star.

Ringworld.

The Integral Trees.

Orwell, George
1984.

Pangborn, Edgar
A Mirror for Observers.

Davy.

Panshin, Alexei
Rite of Passage.

Pohl, Frederik
Man Plus.

Gateway.

Pohl, Frederik, and Cyril Kornbluth
The Space Merchants.

Roberts, Keith
Pavane.

Robinson, Kim Stanley
Red Mars.

Green Mars.

Blue Mars.

Russ, Joanna
And Chaos Died.

Shute, Nevil
On the Beach.

Silverberg, Robert
Dying Inside.

Simak, Clifford D.
Way Station.
City.
Here Gather the Stars.

Simmons, Dan
Hyperion.
The Rise of Endymion.

Smith, Cordwainer
Norstrilia.

Spinrad, Norman
The Iron Dream.

Stapledon, Olaf
Last and First Men.

Stephenson, Neal
Snow Crash.
The Diamond Age.

Strugatsky, Arkady, and Boris Strugatsky
Roadside Picnic.

Sturgeon, Theodore
More Than Human.
The Dreaming Jewels.

Tiptree, James, Jr.

Vance, Jack
The Dying Earth.
Eyes of the Overworld.

van Vogt, A. E.
The World of Null-A.
Slan.

Verne, Jules
20,000 Leagues Under the Sea.

Vonnegut, Kurt
Sirens of Titan.
Slaughterhouse Five.
Cat's Cradle.

Wells, H. G.
> **The Time Machine.**
> **War of the Worlds.**

Wilhelm, Kate
> **Let the Fire Fall.**
> **Where Late the Sweet Birds Sang.**

Williamson, Jack
> **The Humanoids.**

Willis, Connie
> **The Doomsday Book.**

Wolfe, Gene
> **The Claw of the Conciliator.**
> **The Citadel of the Autarch.**

Wyndham, John
> **The Midwich Cuckoos.**
> **Day of the Triffids.**
> **Rebirth.**

Zelazny, Roger
> **Lord of Light.**
> **Isle of the Dead.**
> **The Dream Master.**
> **The Doors of His Face, the Lamps of His Mouth.**

Anthologies

The best way to become acquainted with the characteristics of authors in the science fiction genre, and particularly with the work of new authors, is through anthologies. Both the theme anthologies and the critical and historical collections may have stories from all periods and often suffer from repetition of much-anthologized pieces. The short story is a very popular form in both science fiction and fantasy. Although the following listing of anthologies is long, it is by no means exhaustive.

The essential reference tool for contending with the massive number of short stories is William Contento's *Index to Science Fiction Anthologies and Collections,* which after 1984 became part of an annual published by Locus Press, called simply *Science Fiction, Fantasy, and Horror.* The entire run is available on a CD-ROM titled *The Locus Index to Science Fiction* (1984–1997). The *Index to Science Fiction Anthologies and Collections,* covering short stories published before 1984, is also available on CD-ROM.

Bear, Greg, ed. *New Legends.* Tor, 1995.

Boucher, Anthony, ed. *A Treasury of Great Science Fiction.* Doubleday, 1959. 2 vols. A classic anthology that is still in some libraries.

Bova, Ben, et al. *Future Quartet: Earth in the Year 2042, a Four-Part Invention.* Avon Books, 1994.

Cholfin, Bryan, ed. *The Best of Crank.* Tor, 1998.

Datlow, Ellen, ed. *Omni Visions.* Omni Books, 1993.

Dozois, Gardner. *Modern Classics of Science Fiction.* St. Martin's Press, 1993.

Elliot, Elton. *Nanodreams.* Baen, 1995.

Ellison, Harlan, ed. *Dangerous Visions.* Doubleday, 1967; *Again, Dangerous Visions.* Doubleday, 1972. Groundbreaking anthologies that continue to be read.

Gunn, James, ed. *Road to Science Fiction: Volume 1. From Gilgamesh to Wells.* New American Library, 1979. *Volume 2. From Wells to Heinlein.* New American Library, 1979. *Volume 3. From Heinlein to Here.* New American Library, 1979. *Volume 4. From Here to Forever.* Mentor, 1982. *Volume 5. The British Way.* Borealis, 1998. *Volume 6. Around the World.* White Wolf, 1998. Earlier volumes have been reissued by White Wolf. The first four volumes document the history of science fiction through the short story.

Lapine, Warren, and Stephen Pagel, eds. *Absolute Magnitude.* Tor, 1997.

Le Guin, Ursula K., and Brian Attebery, eds. *The Norton Book of Science Fiction: North American Science Fiction, 1960–1990.* W. W. Norton, 1993.

Mohan, Kim, ed. *More Amazing Stories.* Tor, 1998.

Pringle, David, ed. *The Best of Interzone.* St. Martin's Press, 1997.

Rusch, Kristine Kathryn, ed. *The Best of Pulphouse: The Hardback Magazine.* St. Martin's Press, 1991.

Rusch, Kristine Kathryn, and Edward L. Ferman, eds. *The Best from Fantasy & Science Fiction: A 45th Anniversary Anthology.* St. Martin's Press, 1994.

Serling, Carol, ed. *Journeys to the Twilight Zone.* DAW, 1993.

Shippey, T. A., ed. *The Oxford Book of Science Fiction Stories.* Oxford University Press, 1992.

Turner, Alice K., ed. *The Playboy Book of Science Fiction.* HarperPrism, 1998.

Theme Anthologies

The following anthologies provide an intriguing introduction to the imaginative variety of attitudes on most of the themes explored and to the authors in the genre. Themes are noted in the following list, unless the title is self-explanatory.

Asimov, Isaac, et al., eds. *Machines That Think: The Best Science Fiction Stories About Robots and Computers*. Holt, 1983. Republished as *War with the Robots*. Wings, 1992.

Bujold, Lois McMaster, ed. *Women at War*. Tor, 1997.

Datlow, Ellen, ed. *Alien Sex: 19 Tales by Masters of Science Fiction and Dark Fantasy*. Dutton, 1990.

Drake, David, and Billie Sue Mosiman, eds. *Armageddon*. Baen, 1998.

Greeley, Andrew M., and Michael Cassuth, eds. *Sacred Visions*. Tor, 1991.

Greenberg, Martin Harry, ed. *Dinosaurs*. Donald I. Fine, 1996.

Griffith, Nicola, and Stephen Pagel, eds. *Bending the Landscape: Science Fiction*. Overlook Press, 1998.

Hartwell, David G., ed. *Christmas Stars*. Tor, 1992.

Hartwell, David G., and Kathryn Cramer, eds. *The Ascent of Wonder: The Evolution of Hard SF*. Tor, 1994.

Manson, Cynthia, and Charles Ardai, eds. *Aliens and UFOs: Extraterrestrial Tales from Asimov's Science Fiction and Fact*. Smithmark, 1993.

Preiss, Byron, and Robert Silverberg, eds. *The Ultimate Dinosaur: Past, Present, Future*. Bantam, 1992.

Robinson, Kim Stanley, ed. *Future Primitive: The New Ectopias*. Tor, 1994.

Smith, David Alexander, ed. *Future Boston: The History of a City, 1990–2100*. Tor, 1994.

Turtledove, Harry, Elizabeth Moon, and Roland Green, eds. *Alternate Generals*. Pocket, 1998. (alternate history).

Additional access to reading by theme may be found through the "Checklist of Themes" in *The Science Fiction Encyclopedia,* edited by Peter Nicholls (see "Encyclopedias," p. 336, for a fuller description). For each theme, the encyclopedia article provides definition, history, and criticism of the treatment of the theme in general literature as well as in science fiction, including the key works (both short stories and novels). Most of the themes analyzed in this chapter are listed, and the following is a short selection to indicate the diverse approaches available to the reader: black holes, clones, communications, cosmology, cryonics, discovery and invention, genetic engineering, mathematics, metaphysics, mutants, politics, psychology, reincarnation, terraforming, time paradoxes, war, and weather control. *The Visual Encyclopedia of Science Fiction,* edited by Brian Ash (see "Encyclopedias"), is arranged under themes and has a similar access to both novels and short stories. There are 19 major themes, with further subdivisions under each theme (e.g., under "Warfare and Weaponry" is a subdivision "War with the Aliens"). The major themes are spacecraft and star drives; exploration and colonies; biologies and environments; warfare and weaponry; galactic empires; future and alternative histories; utopias and nightmares; cataclysms and dooms; lost and parallel worlds; time and nth dimensions; technologies and artifacts; cities and cultures; robots and androids; computers and cybernetics; mutants and symbiotes; telepathy, psionics, and ESP; sex and taboos; religion and myths; inner space.

Anthology Series

For decades the anthology series was of major importance in science fiction. Many libraries still have the old anthology series on their shelves, and they continue to be used. Most of the series have now been discontinued for a number of years. For a more comprehensive listing of anthology series, consult earlier editions of *Genreflecting*.

The Best from Fantasy and Science Fiction. The 24th and last series was published in 1982, but there were 40th and 45th anniversary editions published by St. Martin's Press in 1989 and 1994.

Full Spectrum. Number 5 was published in 1995.

L. Ron Hubbard Presents Writers of the Future. Number 12 was published in 1996.

Nebula Award Stories. 1965– . Number 31 was published in 1997.

Starlight. Edited by Patrick Nielsen Hayden. 1996– . Number 2 was published in 1998.

The Year's Best Science Fiction. Edited by Gardner Dozois. Number 14 was published in 1997.

Bibliographies

Most of the following books include authors who write both science fiction and fantasy. Good bio-bibliographical listings are to be found in *The Encyclopedia of Science Fiction* and *The Science Fiction Encyclopedia* (see "Encyclopedias," p. 336). The following annotations indicate whether the books include any considerable historical and critical material as well.

Ash, Brian. *Who's Who in Science Fiction.* Taplinger, 1976. Brief bio-bibliographical listings with critical evaluations of characteristics of a science fiction writer. Prefaced with a "Chronological Guide: 100 Leading Writers and Editors in Their Main Periods of Production," from 1800 to the 1970s.

Barron, Neil, ed. *Anatomy of Wonder: A Critical Guide to Science Fiction.* 4th ed. Bowker, 1994. Critically annotated author listings are grouped by period or type with introductory essays: "The Emergence of Science Fiction: The Beginnings to the 1920s," by Thomas Clareson; "Science Fiction Between the Wars: 1918–1938," by Brian Stablefield; "The

Modern Period: 1938–1980," by Joe De Bolt and John R. Pfeiffer; "Children's Science Fiction," by Francis J. Molson; "Foreign Language Science Fiction," by several authors, covering German, French, Russian, Italian, Japanese, and Chinese. "Research Aids" includes chapters on indexes, bibliographies, history and criticism, author studies, film and television, illustration, classroom aids, magazines, library collections, and a core collection checklist.

Bloom, Harold. *Classic Science Fiction Writers.* Chelsea House, 1995.

Burgess, Michael. *Reference Guide to Science Fiction, Fantasy, and Horror.* Libraries Unlimited, 1992. A comprehensive guide to secondary materials.

Pringle, David. *Science Fiction: The 100 Best Novels.* 2d ed. Carroll & Graf, 1997. The titles are presented chronologically, each with full, and very readable, story analysis and critical evaluation. Michael Moorcock's foreword (to the first edition) suggests that while anyone might quarrel with some of the selections, most readers would agree on at least 50, "an excellent percentage."

————. *The Ultimate Guide to Science Fiction.* Pharos Books/St. Martin's Press, 1990. Science fiction enthusiasts will enjoy paging through Pringle's work. It provides brief synopses of all the major (and some of the minor) science fiction novels and short stories written in English since the term *science fiction* was coined (approximately 1929). In the introduction, Pringle pokes fun at science fiction clichés and outlines the beginnings of science fiction writing. He explains the structure of every entry and evaluates each work. Where appropriate, he includes the names of sequels, related works, film versions, and author pen names. Occasionally he also inserts quotations from other science fiction critics. The A-to-Z list contains nearly 3,000 entries. Works are arranged alphabetically by title. To enable readers to quickly find an entry, Pringle uses two types of cross-references: variant titles for the same books and parent novels of series or related works.

Reginald, R. *Science Fiction and Fantasy Literature: A Checklist, 1700–1974.* Gale, 1979.

Science Fiction and Fantasy Literature, 1975–1991: A Bibliography of Science Fiction, Fantasy, and Horror Fiction Books and Nonfiction Monographs. Gale, 1993. Cites approximately 22,000 monographs. Lists series titles, awards, and other topics of interest to readers.

Watson, Noelle, and Paul E. Schellinger, eds. *Twentieth-Century Science Fiction Writers.* St. James Press, 1991.

Encyclopedias

The following encyclopedias contain extensive bibliographical, historical, and critical material.

Clute, John. *Science Fiction: The Illustrated Encyclopedia.* DK Publishing, 1995. While not exactly an encyclopedia, this lavishly illustrated browsing book does an outstanding job of placing science fiction in a historical context.

Clute, John, and Peter Nicholls. *The Encyclopedia of Science Fiction.* St. Martin's Press, 1995. The essential guide to science fiction lists trends, authors, titles, terminology, and much more in narrative and pictures. It has 4,360 entries. Alphabetical arrangement of themes, biography, and other topics, with many cross-references. Historical and critical, with extensive bibliographical material. Biographical listings for many little-known authors. Many of the articles are extended critical essays.

Gunn, James, ed. *The New Encyclopedia of Science Fiction.* Viking-Penguin, 1988. Summaries, criticism, and bibliographical and historical information on people, books, topics, trends, and films in science fiction.

Dictionaries

Rogow, Roberta. *FutureSpeak: A Fan's Guide to the Language of Science Fiction.* Paragon House, 1991. An overall survey of the world of science fiction, from books to movies to fandom.

Stableford, Brian M., ed. *The Dictionary of Science Fiction Places.* Fireside, 1999. The history, geography, and inhabitants of more than 15,000 imaginary places that were created by 250 authors.

History

Science fiction history may start either in classical literature or in the nineteenth century, depending on an author's definition of the genre. Many of the following books are critical to the point of being controversial. They are written by authors of the genre and by fans, both lay and academic. In addition to the following books, the reader will find historical material in "Encyclopedias" and in "Criticism."

Ackerman, Forrest J. *Forrest J. Ackerman's World of Science Fiction.* General Publishing Group, 1997. A highly personalized view of the history of science fiction written by the fan who coined the term *sci-fi.*

Alkon, Paul K. *Science Fiction Before 1900: Imagination Discovers Technology.* Twayne, 1994.

Landon, Brooks. *Science Fiction After 1900: From the Steam Man to the Stars.* Twayne, 1997.

Perret, Patti. *The Faces of Science Fiction: Photographs.* Bluejay Books, 1984. Introduction by Gene Wolfe. With short essays by the featured authors.

Criticism

The quantity of critical exposition on science fiction is daunting. The quality of it varies from the fan popular to the academic obscurant, with, fortunately, some lively and imaginative discussion in between, by both authors of the genre and fans in the academic world. The following is merely a sampling that demonstrates the wealth of commentary available.

Asimov, Isaac. *Asimov's Galaxy: Reflections on Science Fiction.* Doubleday, 1989. Essays published as editorials in Isaac Asimov's science fiction magazine.

Bleiler, Everett F., ed. *Science Fiction Writers: Critical Studies of the Major Authors from the Early Nineteenth Century to the Present Day.* Scribner's, 1982. Seventy-six authors analyzed in essays by various writers.

Bloom, Harold, ed. *Classic Science Fiction Writers.* Chelsea House. 1995. History, criticism, and bio-bibliography of Edward Bellamy, Edgar Rice Burroughs, Sir Arthur Conan Doyle, Aldous Huxley, C. S. Lewis, Jack London, H. P. Lovecraft, George Orwell, Edgar Allan Poe, Mary Shelley, Olaf Stapledon, and H. G. Wells.

Disch, Thomas M. *The Dreams Our Stuff Is Made Of: How Science Fiction Conquered the World.* Free Press, 1998.

Fletcher, Marilyn P., ed. *Readers' Guide to Twentieth-Century Science Fiction.* American Library Association, 1989.

Hartwell, David G. *Age of Wonders: Exploring the World of Science Fiction.* Tor, 1996.

Hassler, Donald M., and Clyde Wilcox, eds. *Political Science Fiction.* University of South Carolina Press, 1997.

Landon, Brooks. *Science Fiction After 1900: From the Steam Man to the Stars.* Twayne, 1997.

Le Guin, Ursula K. *The Language of the Night: Essays on Fantasy and Science Fiction.* HarperCollins, 1992.

McCaffery, Larry. *Across the Wounded Galaxies: Interviews with Contemporary American Science Fiction Writers.* University of Illinois Press, 1990. Covers Gregory Benford, William S. Burroughs, Octavia E. Butler, Samuel R. Delany, Thomas M. Disch, William Gibson, Ursula K. Le Guin, Joanna Russ, Bruce Sterling, and Gene Wolfe.

Sanders, Joe, ed. *Science Fiction Fandom.* Greenwood, 1994.

Shippey, T. A., ed. *Magill's Guide to Science Fiction and Fantasy.* Salem Press, 1996. 4 vols.

Spinrad, Norman. *Science Fiction in the Real World.* Southern Illinois University Press, 1990.

Writers' Manuals

The following are meant to instruct writers but are also illuminating for the reader of the science fiction genre.

Bova, Ben. *The Craft of Writing Science Fiction That Sells.* Writer's Digest Books, 1994.

Card, Orson Scott. *How to Write Science Fiction and Fantasy.* Writer's Digest Books, 1990.

Costello, Matthew J. *How to Write Science Fiction.* Paragon House, 1992.

Dozois, Gardner, ed. *Writing Science Fiction and Fantasy.* St. Martin's Press, 1991.

Ochoa, George, and Jeffrey Osier. *The Writer's Guide to Creating a Science Fiction Universe.* Writer's Digest Books, 1993.

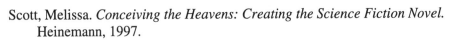

Scott, Melissa. *Conceiving the Heavens: Creating the Science Fiction Novel.* Heinemann, 1997.

Spinrad, Norman. *Staying Alive: A Writer's Guide.* Donning, 1983.

Magazines

Of the hundreds of science fiction and fantasy magazines started since the 1920s, few have survived. The multitude of original paperback anthologies possibly contributed to their demise. However, a few magazines are still successful, serving as an important showcase for new authors. Most contain reviews, critical articles, and scientific explication. (For a full history of the magazines, see "Encyclopedias," p. 336.) The following magazines usually include fantasy; they also provide reviews and often columns or articles on science.

Amazing Stories. 1926– .

Analog. (Astounding Science Fiction). 1930– .

Isaac Asimov's Science Fiction Magazine. 1977– .

Magazine of Fantasy and Science Fiction. 1949– .

Reviews

Most of the magazines and fanzines of science fiction contain reviews. There are, however, a few other outstanding sources of reviews.

Locus
P.O. Box 13305
Oakland, CA 94661

Published monthly, *Locus* lists all SF and fantasy published in English. Seven accomplished reviewers discuss not only book-length fiction but also short stories. Author interviews, news of events and personalities, bibliographies, and the highly respected Locus Poll also make it very useful.

New York Review of Science Fiction
Dragon Press
P.O. Box 570
Pleasantville, NY 10570

http://ebbs.english.vt.edu/olp/nyrsf/nyrsf.html
(accessed 15 November 1999)
Essays and articles in addition to reviews.

Science Fiction Chronicle
P.O. Box 022730
Brooklyn, NY 11202-0056

Monthly publication of reviews and science fiction news. This is also a good source for up-to-date information on awards.

VOYA: Voice of Youth Advocates
Scarecrow Press
4720A Boston Way
Lanham, MD 20706

A bimonthly that reviews books for young adults, and has remarkably good coverage of science fiction, fantasy, and horror paperback originals.

Associations and Conventions

Associations

European Science Fiction Society. Formed in 1972, it has a membership of fans from several European countries and meets at an annual convention.

The National Science Fiction and Fantasy Society. A Canadian organization. Membership consists of science fiction and fantasy professionals, readers, writers, other media artists, and enthusiasts. The Society carries out activities to promote awareness, appreciation, and growth of speculative fiction and other imaginative works in Canada.

Science Fiction and Fantasy Writers of America. The association was founded in 1965. It sponsors the annual "Nebula" awards for several categories of science fiction writing. The group's motto is "The Future Isn't What It Used to Be."

Science Fiction Research Association. Has an academic and research orientation but is open to all.

SF Canada. Formerly called the Speculative Writers' Association of Canada. Open to published authors.

Conventions

Fans and writers form many associations and hold innumerable conventions, usually combining science fiction and fantasy, and often adding horror and the supernatural. "Con" is usually part of the conference name. They are listed in science fiction magazines and on the Internet. The SF Site at http://www.sfsite.com/home.htm (accessed 15 November 1999) does an exceptionally good job of listing "cons."

World Science Fiction Convention ("WorldCon"). The first was held in 1939; the 57th was held in Melbourne, Australia, in 1999.

Awards

Awards are generally reported in the various science fiction magazines as soon as possible after the results are announced. For a comprehensive listing of awards up to 1990, consult *Reginald's Science Fiction and Fantasy Awards: A Comprehensive Guide to the Awards and Their Winners,* by Daryl F. Mallett and R. Reginald (Borgo, 1991). Currently the easiest way to find award information is on the World Wide Web.

ISFDB Award Listings: http://www.sfsite.com/isfdb/award.html (accessed 15 November 1999)

Award Web: http://www.dpsinfo.com/awardweb (accessed 15 November 1999)

Lists of award-winning titles can be found in several of the previously listed bibliographies, histories, and encyclopedias. The following are the best-known major awards for science fiction:

Arthur C. Clarke Award. Awarded for the best British science fiction novel from the previous year.

Compton Crook Award. Awarded by the Baltimore Science Fiction Society for the best first novel of science fiction (including fantasy).

Ditmar. Australian science fiction award.

Hugo. Awarded at World Science Fiction Conventions. Named after Hugo Gernsback, it is voted on by members of the annual WorldCon; in other words, the winner is selected by readers of science fiction. One of the most prestigious awards, it is a reflection of fan opinion.

James Tiptree, Jr. Award. Named for Alice Sheldon, who wrote under this male pseudonym, this award is presented for science fiction and fantasy that looks at gender in a different way. The James Tiptree, Jr. Award is "given to the work of science fiction or fantasy published in one year which best explores or expands gender roles."

Locus. Is awarded as a result of a poll taken among the subscribers to *Locus.*

Nebula. Awarded by the Science Fiction and Fantasy Writers of America. The winners are selected by a vote of the members of the organization. A prerequisite of membership is the publication of a work of science fiction, fantasy, or horror by the candidate. Membership in SFWA is open only to published authors in the field, making this prestigious award a writers' award that reflects high literary merit.

Philip K. Dick Award. Awarded to a science fiction or fantasy book published in paperback. It is administered by the Philadelphia SF Society.

Prix Aurora Award. Given to the best in Canadian science fiction and fantasy.

Sapphire Award for Best SF Romance of the Year. Sponsored by the *SF Romance Newsletter*. http://members.aol.com/sfreditor/bestsfr.htm (accessed 20 January 2000).

The SFWA Hall of Fame (The Grand Masters). The following are winners of the Grand Master award:

- Robert A. Heinlein 1974 (deceased)
- Jack Williamson 1975
- Clifford D. Simak 1976 (deceased)
- L. Sprague de Camp 1978
- Fritz Leiber 1981 (deceased)
- Andre Norton 1983
- Arthur C. Clarke 1985
- Isaac Asimov 1986 (deceased)
- Alfred Bester 1987 (deceased)
- Ray Bradbury 1988
- Lester del Rey 1990 (deceased)
- Frederik Pohl 1992
- Damon Knight 1994
- A. E. van Vogt 1995
- Jack Vance 1996
- Poul Anderson 1997
- Hal Clement 1998

Locus Poll of Best Science Fiction Ever (Compiled in 1987)

The *Locus* polls are a terrific window into what American science fiction readers really like. Voting eligibility does not require publication credits like the Nebula or a large chunk of money to support the annual World Con like the Hugo, although I suspect that many of the voters in the *Locus* poll also vote in one or both of the other major awards. The following list includes the top 42 vote recipients from the last "best ever" poll. It is to be hoped that another will be done in the near future.

Most science fiction aficionados will have already read most of the books in this list.

1. *Dune,* Frank Herbert

2. *The Left Hand of Darkness,* Ursula K. Le Guin

3. *Childhood's End,* Arthur C. Clarke

4. *The Moon Is a Harsh Mistress,* Robert A. Heinlein

5. *Stranger in a Strange Land,* Robert A. Heinlein

6. The Foundation trilogy, Isaac Asimov

7. *A Canticle for Leibowitz,* Walter M. Miller Jr.

8. *Gateway,* Frederik Pohl

9. *Ringworld,* Larry Niven

10. *The Stars My Destination,* Alfred Bester

11. *Lord of Light,* Roger Zelazny

12. *More Than Human,* Theodore Sturgeon

13. *The Mote in God's Eye,* Larry Niven and Jerry Pournelle

14. *The Man in the High Castle,* Philip K. Dick

15. *The Time Machine,* H. G. Wells

16. *Stand on Zanzibar,* John Brunner

17. *The Dispossessed,* Ursula K. Le Guin

18. *The Demolished Man,* Alfred Bester /*The Forever War,* Joe Haldeman (tie)

19. *The Martian Chronicles,* Ray Bradbury

20. *Starship Troopers,* Robert A. Heinlein

21. *Dying Inside,* Robert Silverberg

22. *Dhalgren,* Samuel R. Delany

23. *Time Enough for Love,* Robert A. Heinlein

24. *Rendezvous with Rama,* Arthur C. Clarke/*Way Station,* Clifford D. Simak (tie)

25. *To Your Scattered Bodies Go,* Philip José Farmer

26. *Earth Abides,* George R. Stewart

27. *The Door into Summer,* Robert A. Heinlein

28. *City,* Clifford D. Simak

29. *The Witches of Karres,* James H. Schmitz

30. *The City and the Stars,* Arthur C. Clarke

31. *The Caves of Steel,* Isaac Asimov

32. *1984,* George Orwell

33. *Norstrilia,* Cordwainer Smith

34. *Mission of Gravity,* Hal Clement

35. *Ubik,* Philip K. Dick

36. *2001: A Space Odyssey,* Arthur C. Clarke/*Timescape,* Gregory Benford (tie)

37. *Fahrenheit 451,* Ray Bradbury

38. *Downbelow Station,* C. J. Cherryh

39. *The War of the Worlds,* H. G. Wells

40. *Last and First Men,* Olaf Stapledon

41. *Double Star,* Robert A. Heinlein

42. *Davy,* Edgar Pangborn

Locus Annual Best SF Novel

Following are winners of the "Best SF Novel" poll. The year of each poll is listed first, with the publication year after the author's name.

1971   *Ringworld,* Larry Niven, 1970

1972   *The Lathe of Heaven,* Ursula K. Le Guin, 1971

1973   *The Gods Themselves,* Isaac Asimov, 1972

1974   *Rendezvous with Rama,* Arthur C. Clarke, 1973

1975   *The Dispossessed,* Ursula K. Le Guin, 1974

1976   *The Forever War,* Joe Haldeman, 1974

1977   *Where Late the Sweet Birds Sang,* Kate Wilhelm, 1976

1978   *Gateway,* Frederik Pohl, 1977

1979   *Dreamsnake,* Vonda N. McIntyre, 1978

1980   *Titan,* John Varley, 1979

1981   *The Snow Queen,* Joan D. Vinge, 1980

1982   *The Many-Colored Land,* Julian May, 1981

1983   *Foundation's Edge,* Isaac Asimov, 1982

1984   *Startide Rising,* David Brin, 1983

1985   *The Integral Trees,* Larry Niven, 1984

1986   *The Postman,* David Brin, 1985

1987   *Speaker for the Dead,* Orson Scott Card, 1986

1988   *The Uplift War,* David Brin, 1987

1989   *Cyteen,* C. J. Cherryh, 1988

1990   *Hyperion,* Dan Simmons, 1989

1991   *The Fall of Hyperion,* Dan Simmons, 1990

1992   *Barrayar,* Lois McMaster Bujold, 1991

1993   *Doomsday Book,* Connie Willis, 1992

1994   *Green Mars,* Kim Stanley Robinson, 1993

1995   *Mirror Dance,* Lois McMaster Bujold, 1994

1996   *The Diamond Age,* Neal Stephenson, 1995

1997   *Blue Mars,* Kim Stanley Robinson, 1996

1998   *The Rise of Endymion,* Dan Simmons, 1997

Science Fiction Book Clubs

There are two major SF book clubs, one in the United States and one in Britain. The British club reprints or distributes the publisher's hardcover edition. The U.S. club, owned by Doubleday Direct, publishes hardcover club editions of both hardcover and paperback originals and also original omnibus editions. The clubs issue an extensive number of titles and are an important source of hardcover editions for libraries. The Science Fiction Book Club has a Web site at http://www.sfbc.com/ (accessed 15 November 1999).

Publishers

For years, science fiction was published most extensively in paperback, with a few of the "big" authors and major anthologies coming out in hardcover. As the acceptance (and commercial success) of science fiction has grown, hardcover publication has increased. The advantage to publishing in hardcover is that the books have a better chance of being reviewed and of reaching a mainstream audience. On the other hand, science fiction fans really do seem to like the paperback versions better. It is not uncommon on the Internet to find correspondence from a reader asking if a specific title is so essential to read immediately that it should be purchased in hardcover; the reader will usually wait for the paperback edition. Science fiction readers have also been known to donate hardcover copies of a title when the paperback is released because they can then purchase the size that keeps their collection consistent!

346 Chapter 6—Science Fiction

Anthologies appear widely in both formats. Critical works, which used to be issued largely in hardcover, are now appearing regularly in both formats also. Illustrated science fiction novels (as well as fantasy) are published in both formats but, notably, in greater numbers in paperback originals.

The following publishers issue science fiction, in most cases both originals and reprints. Special series are noted. The list is selective because there are many publishers that issue an occasional science fiction title only.

Ace

Arkham House

Avon Eos

Baen Books

Bantam/Doubleday/Dell

Bluejay Books. Now defunct, they did, however, issue some great titles that have retained popularity with fans.

DAW

Del Rey/Ballantine

Donald M. Grant

Gollancz (London)

Harcourt Brace

HarperCollins Prism

HarperCollins Voyager (UK)

Headline

New American Library

Orbit

Penguin USA

Putnam/Berkley/Ace

Roc

Simon and Schuster/Pocket

Spectra (Bantam)

St. Martin's Press

Tor Books. The publisher most often selected by readers of *Locus* as the best.

Underwood

Warner

White Wolf

Zebra Pinnacle

Online Resources

Ace Books, from Putnam Berkley: http://www.mca.com/putnam/search.html (accessed 15 November 1999). Select Science Fiction/Fantasy from the Category pull-down menu and click on search. It will take you to the listings by title.

Avon Eos: http://www.avonbooks.com/eos (accessed 20 January 2000).

Baen: http://www.baen.com/ (accessed 20 January 2000).

Del Rey: http://www.randomhouse.com/delrey/ (accessed 20 January 2000).

E-Scape: The Digital Journal of Speculative Fiction: http://www.interink.com/current/index.html (accessed 20 January 2000).

Feminist Science Fiction, Fantasy, & Utopia: http://www.wenet.net/~lquilter/femsf/ (accessed 20 January 2000).

Infinity Plus: The Science Fiction and Fantasy Homepage—novel excerpts, short stories, reviews, and interviews with authors: http://www.users.zetnet.co.uk/iplus/ (accessed 20 January 2000).

Internet Speculative Fiction Database: http://www.sfsite.com/isfdb/sfdbase.html (accessed 20 January 2000).

Just Imagine, a bookstore from the Netherlands, listing SF and fantasy: http://www.abc.nl/abc/first/justjan/ (accessed 20 January 2000).

The Locus Index: Science Fiction, Fantasy, & Horror: 1984–1997. Indexes the magazine, including lists of all books received for review. This is probably the most comprehensive listing of science fiction, fantasy, and horror published since 1984: http://www.sff.net/locus/0start.html (accessed 20 January 2000).

NESFA Press: http://www.nesfa.org/press/ (accessed 20 January 2000).

Omni Magazine: SF, Fantasy, Horror: http://www.omnimag.com/fiction/index.html (accessed 20 January 2000).

Orbit: http://www.orbitbooks.co.uk/ (accessed 20 January 2000) (for a view of British SF & fantasy publishing).

Penguin Putnam, including DAW, Ace, and Roc: http://www.penguinputnam.com/catalog/index.htm (accessed 20 January 2000).

Science Fiction Book Club: http://www.sfbc. (accessed 20 January 2000).

Science Fiction Weekly: http://www.scifi.com/sfw/ (accessed 20 January 2000).

SF Site: The Home Page for Science Fiction and Fantasy. Lots of reviews, tons of information, and a nicely designed site: http://www.sfsite.com/ (accessed 20 January 2000).

Spectra: http://www.randomhouse.com/sciencefiction (accessed 20 January 2000).

Tor: http://www.tor.com/ (accessed 20 January 2000).

Tristom Cook's Internet Top 100 Science Fiction and Fantasy List: http://www.clark. net/pub/iz/Books/Top100/top100list.txt (accessed 20 January 2000).

University of Michigan Science Fiction and Fantasy Page: http://www.umich. Edu/~umfandsf/ (accessed 20 January 2000).

Voyager, from HarperCollins UK: http://www.voyager-books.com (accessed 20 January 2000).

White Wolf: http://www.white-wolf.com/Fiction/Fiction.html (accessed 20 January 2000).

Wildside List of SF and Fantasy authors pages: http://www.wildsidepress.com (accessed 20 January 2000).

D's Science Fiction Picks

Asaro, Catherine. *The Last Hawk*.

Bujold, Lois McMaster. *Komarr*.

Gould, Steven. *Helm*.

Stephenson, Neal. *The Diamond Age, or, Young Lady's Illustrated Primer*.

Willis, Connie. *To Say Nothing of the Dog*.

Chapter 7

Fantasy

"Difficult truths can sometimes only be told through the medium of fantasy."
—Lisa Goldstein

"The best fantasy is written in the language of dreams. It is alive as dreams are alive, more real than real."
—George R. R. Martin, *Faces of Fantasy,* Tor, 1996

"Fantasy was my first love, from the day I learned to read. It deals in the inner truth, the hopes and fears common to all humanity. It forces us to confront our archetypes, the core of our own spirits, our hearts and our minds."
—Marion Zimmer Bradley, *Faces of Fantasy,* Tor, 1996

Fantasy may be the most ancient of genres, if all tales of magic combined with adventure are considered such. The oldest of written tales, *Gilgamesh,* the *Odyssey,* and *Beowulf,* could also be considered to be the oldest of fantasy. The fairy tales committed to paper by Charles Perrault in seventeenth-century France and by the Brothers Grimm in nineteenth-century Germany are the stories many think of as the origins of fantasy. The eighteenth-century trend toward sanitizing and Christianizing fairy tales and the twentieth-century Disney and picture-book versions we see have led to the common misconception that fantasy is a children's genre.

The origins of modern fantasy are usually attributed to J. R. R. Tolkien who, along with C. S. Lewis, was a member of a group called the "Inklings" that started in the 1930s.

"Fantasy" began appearing on the spines of paperback books in the late 1960s and early 1970s. It gained professional recognition in 1992 when The Science Fiction Writers of America added "Fantasy" to the title of their organization, recognizing the intimate relationship between the two speculative fiction genres. Many of the following authors also write science fiction or horror.

Fantasy fans are the least "ageist" of all readers. They do not confine themselves to reading "age-appropriate" tales, whether adult or child. While it is common in all genres for teen fans to read books published for adults, fantasy is the only genre where adult readers readily and unashamedly read books published for children and young adults. The Harry Potter series by J. K. Rowling is an obvious example, with three titles appearing in the top 10 on best-seller lists.

Themes and Types

Sword and Sorcery

Sword and sorcery is usually set in an alternate pastoral or nonindustrialized world, sometimes akin to medieval European kingdoms, where magic is manifest and heroic deeds, including swashbuckling feats of derring-do, are commonplace. The protagonist usually starts off as an ordinary soul who is caught up in a chain of events leading to encounters with magic and the need to fight or flee.

As one of the most popular types of fantasy, this subgenre features encounters with magic and the supernatural, often involving some romance and daunting hazards. The heroes, and sometimes heroines, of the sword-and-sorcery, magic-filled adventures usually inhabit a world created for them, and typically appear in trilogies or in lengthy, open-ended series. Quests involving several characters of different backgrounds are a dominant theme. The quintessential sword-and-sorcery tales are of course Tolkien's *The Hobbit* and *The Lord of the Rings*.

Brooks, Terry
The Shannara series.

The Sword of Shannara.

The Elfstones of Shannara.

The Wishsong of Shannara.

The Scions of Shannara.

The Druid of Shannara.

The Elf Queen of Shannara.

The Talismans of Shannara.

The First King of Shannara.

Bujold, Lois McMaster
The Spirit Ring.

Clayton, Jo

Wild Magic series.

    Wild Magic.

    Wildfire.

    Magic Wars.

Drums series.

    Drum Warning.

    Drum Calls.

    Drums of Chaos.

Cole, Allan

    Wizard of the Winds.

Cook, Glen

The Black Company.

    The Black Company.

    Shadows Linger.

    The White Rose.

    The Silver Spike.

    Shadow Games.

    Dreams of Steel.

    Bleak Seasons.

Cook, Hugh

Wizard War series (also called The Chronicles of an Age of Darkness). Many U.S. public libraries have the British editions (with title variations, shown below in parentheses), even though Roc published the series in the United States.

    Wizard War (The Wizards and the Warriors).

    The Questing Hero (The Wordsmiths and the Warguild).

    The Hero's Return (The Women and the Warlords).

    The Oracle (The Walrus and the Warwolf).

    Lords of the Sword.

    The Wicked and the Witless.

    The Wishstone and the Wonderworkers.

    The Wazir and the Witch.

    The Werewolf and the Wormlord.

    The Worshippers and the Way.

    The Witchlord and the Weaponmaster.

    When Heroes Return.

de Camp, L. Sprague, and Fletcher Pratt

Harold Shea series.

The Incompleat Enchanter.

The Castle of Iron.

Wall of Serpents (sometimes titled *The Enchanter Compleated*).

An omnibus edition of the three de Camp–Pratt titles was released as *The Intrepid Enchanter: The Complete Magical Misadventures of Harold Shea* in some editions and *The Complete Compleat Enchanter* in others. The series continued in the 1990s with Christopher Stasheff as co-author replacing the late Pratt.

Sir Harold and the Gnome King.

The Enchanter Reborn.

The Exotic Enchanter.

Drake, David

Lord of the Isles.

Lord of the Isles.

Queen of Demons.

Eddings, David, and Leigh Eddings (Even though Leigh is not listed as co-author of the early books, it has been reported that she was.)

Belgariad series.

Pawn of Prophecy.

Queen of Sorcery.

Magician's Gambit.

Castle of Wizardry.

Enchanter's End Game.

Malloreon series.

Guardians of the West.

King of the Murgos.

Demon Lord of Karanda.

Sorceress of Darshiva.

The Seeress of Kell.

Belgarath the Sorcerer.

Polgara the Sorceress.

Ellenium series.

The Diamond Throne.

The Ruby Knight.

The Sapphire Rose.

Domes of Fire.

The Shining Ones.

The Hidden City.

Farland, David

The Runelords.

Brotherhood of the Wolf.

Feist, Raymond E.

Riftwar series.

Magician. Most frequently available in two volumes as *Magician: Apprentice* and *Magician: Master.*

Silverthorn.

A Darkness at Sethanon.

Prince of the Blood.

The King's Buccaneer.

Serpentwar saga.

Shadow of a Dark Queen.

Rise of a Merchant Prince.

Rage of a Demon King.

Shards of a Broken Crown.

Gemmell, David

Drenai series.

Legend (also published as *Against the Horde*).

Waylander.

The King Beyond the Gate.

Quest for Lost Heroes.

Waylander II: In the Realm of the Wolf.

The First Chronicles of Druss the Legend.

Sipstrassi series.

Wolf in Shadow.

The Jerusalem Man (also published as *The Last Guardian*).

Bloodstone.

Goodkind, Terry

Sword of Truth series.

Wizard's First Rule.

Stone of Tears.

Blood of the Fold.

Temple of the Winds.

Heinlein, Robert A.

Glory Road.

Hobb, Robin

The Farseer series.

> **Assassin's Apprentice.**
>
> **Royal Assassin.**
>
> **Assassin's Quest.**

The Liveship Traders.

> **Ship of Magic.**
>
> **Mad Ship.**

Howard, Robert E.

Conan series.

Jordan, Robert

The Wheel of Time series.

> **The Eye of the World.**
>
> **The Great Hunt.**
>
> **The Dragon Reborn.**
>
> **The Shadow Rising.**
>
> **The Fires of Heaven.**
>
> **Lord of Chaos.**
>
> **Crown of Swords.**
>
> **The Path of Daggers.**

Kerr, Katharine

Deverry series.

> **Daggerspell.**
>
> **Darkspell.**
>
> **The Bristling Wood.**
>
> **The Dragon Revenant.**
>
> **A Time of Exile.**
>
> **A Time of Omens.**
>
> **Days of Blood and Fire.**
>
> **Days of Air and Darkness.**
>
> **The Red Wyvern.**
>
> **The Black Raven.**

Lee, Adam

The Dominions of Irth.

> **The Dark Shore.**
>
> **The Shadow Eater.**

Le Guin, Ursula K.

The Earthsea tetralogy.

      A Wizard of Earthsea.

      The Tombs of Atuan.

      The Farthest Shore.

      Tehanu.

Leiber, Fritz

Fafhrd and the Gray Mouser series. Possibly the greatest sword-and-sorcery series ever, featuring massively heroic barbarian Fafhrd and thief, sorcerer, and swordsman the Gray Mouser. Over the years since the first Fafhrd and the Gray Mouser short story was introduced in 1939, the tales have been released in many different editions and combinations. As of 1998 the following were available:

      Fritz Leiber's Ill Met in Lankhmar.

      Fritz Leiber's Lean Times in Lankhmar.

      Fritz Leiber's Return to Lankhmar.

Martin, George R. R.

Song of Ice and Fire.

      A Game of Thrones.

      A Clash of Kings.

McKiernan, Dennis L.

      The Dragonstone.

      The Eye of the Hunter.

      Voyage of the Fox Rider.

Iron Tower trilogy.

      Dark Tide.

      Shadows of Doom.

      Darkest Day.

Silver Call duology.

7

      Trek to Kraggen-Cor.

      The Brega Path.

McKillip, Patricia A.

The Hed trilogy.

      The Riddle-Master of Hed.

      Heir of Sea and Fire.

      Harpist in the Wind.

Modesitt, L. E., Jr.

Recluce series.

      The Magic of Recluce.

      The Towers of the Sunset.

> The Magic Engineer.
>
> The Order War.
>
> The Death of Chaos.
>
> Fall of Angels.
>
> Chaos Balance.
>
> The White Order.

Moon, Elizabeth

The Deed of Paksenarrion. "Better a soldier's life than a pigfarmer's wife."

> Sheepfarmer's Daughter.
>
> Divided Alliance.
>
> Oath of Gold.

Rawn, Melanie

Exiles series.

> The Ruins of Ambrai.
>
> The Mageborn Traitor.

Reichert, Mickey Zucker

> Legend of Nightfall.

Reimann, Katya

Tielmaran chronicles.

> Wind from a Foreign Sky.
>
> A Tremor in the Bitter Earth.

Roberson, Jennifer

The Sword-Dancers saga (this is what Roberson calls it) is also sometimes referred to as The Tiger and Del series.

> Sword-Dancer.
>
> Sword-Singer.
>
> Sword-Maker.
>
> Sword-Breaker.
>
> Sword-Born.
>
> Sword-Sworn.

Rosenberg, Joel

Guardians of the Flame series.

> The Sleeping Dragon.
>
> The Sword and the Chain.
>
> The Silver Crown.
>
> The Heir Apparent.

      The Warrior Lives.

      The Road to Ehvenor.

      The Road Home.

Rowling, J. K.

Harry Potter series.

      Harry Potter and the Sorcerer's Stone (Harry Potter and the Philosopher's Stone).

      Harry Potter and the Chamber of Secrets.

      Harry Potter and the Prisoner of Azkaban.

Fantasy readers of all ages enjoy these.

Russell, Sean

Moontide and Magic Rise series.

      World Without End.

      Sea Without a Shore.

      Beneath the Vaulted Hills.

Salvatore, R. A.

Demon Awakens series.

      The Demon Awakens.

      The Demon Spirit.

Shinn, Sharon

      The Shape-Changer's Wife.

Tolkien, J. R. R.

      The Hobbit.

The Lord of the Rings trilogy.

      The Fellowship of the Rings.

      The Two Towers.

      The Return of the King.

7

Vance, Jack

The Dying Earth series. In a far future world, magic works, but not too well, in this series made up mostly of linked or related short stories. Published in book form, they are:

      The Dying Earth.

      The Eyes of the Overworld.

      Cugel's Saga.

      Rhialto the Marvelous.

Weis, Margaret, and Tracy Hickman

Death Gate Cycle.

> **Dragon Wing.**
>
> **Elven Star.**
>
> **Fire Sea.**
>
> **Serpent Mage.**
>
> **The Hand of Chaos.**
>
> **Into the Labyrinth.**
>
> **Seventh Gate.**

Williams, Tad

Memory, Sorrow, and Thorn series.

> **The Dragonbone Chair.**
>
> **Stone of Farewell.**
>
> **To Green Angel Tower.**

Wrede, Patricia C.

The Lyra Books.

> **Shadow Magic.**
>
> **Daughter of Witches.**
>
> **The Harp of Imach Thyssel.**
>
> **Caught in Crystal.**
>
> **The Raven Ring.**

An omnibus edition of the first three books is titled *Shadows over Lyra*.

Wurts, Janny

> **The Wars of Light and Shadows.**
>
> **The Curse of the Mistwraith.**
>
> **The Ships of Merior.**
>
> **Warhost of Vastmark.**
>
> **Alliance of Light.**
>
> **Fugitive Prince.**

Zelazny, Roger

Amber series.

> **Nine Princes in Amber.**
>
> **The Guns of Avalon.**
>
> **Sign of the Unicorn.**
>
> **The Hand of Oberon.**
>
> **The Courts of Chaos.**
>
> **Trumps of Doom.**
>
> **Blood of Amber.**

Sign of Chaos.

Night of Shadows.

Prince of Chaos.

Saga, Myth, and Legend

Many readers come to fantasy through a love of the tales that some consider a precursor of fantasy and others a subset. Here the reader will find tales based on the familiar myths and legends. Many of the following are sword-and-sorcery adventures set against a backdrop made familiar because of its basis in a myth, legend, or saga.

Arthurian Legend

The most enchanting of the legendary backgrounds is the Arthurian, set in medieval England, with Merlin often the dominating figure. The fact that for nearly 1,000 years writers have been exploring this epoch attests to its universal and lasting appeal. Since Marion Zimmer Bradley's groundbreaking *The Mists of Avalon* (1982), women have been playing a larger role in these stories.

Cochran, Molly, and Warren Murphy

The Forever King.

The Broken Sword.

Crompton, Anne Eliot

Merlin's Harp.

Gemmell, David

The Stones of Power sequence is part of Gemmell's Sipstrassi series, in that Maedhlyn or Merlin owes his power to the Sipstrassi meteor.

Ghost King.

Last Sword of Power.

Jones, Courtway

Dragon's Heirs trilogy.

In the Shadow of the Oak King.

Witch of the North.

A Prince in Camelot.

Kennealy-Morrison, Patricia

The Keltiad series. The titles originally issued under the name Patricia Kennealy now are printed with the Kennealy-Morrison name. The widow of rocker Jim Morrison sets her Arthurian tales on a distant planet.

The Copper Crown.

The Throne of Stone.

> The Silver Branch.
>
> The Hawk's Gray Feather.
>
> The Oak Above the Kings.
>
> The Hedge of Mist.

Lawhead, Stephen R.

Pendragon series. This is a Christian take on the legend, full of spirituality.

> Taliesin.
>
> Merlin.
>
> Arthur.

Newman, Sharan

Told from Guinevere's viewpoint, this gently humorous series contains more fantasy elements than many Arthurian tales, including a unicorn.

> Guinevere.
>
> The Chessboard Queen.
>
> Guinevere Evermore.

Norton, Andre

> Merlin's Mirror. Merlin and Arthur are aliens in possession of advanced scientific knowledge.

Saberhagen, Fred

> Merlin's Bones.

Springer, Nancy

> I Am Mordred.

Stewart, Mary

The Merlin Sequence.

> The Crystal Cave.
>
> The Hollow Hills.
>
> The Last Enchantment.
>
> The Wicked Day.

White, T. H.

The Once and Future King. The collective title for:

> The Sword in the Stone.
>
> The Witch in the Wood (The Queen of Air and Darkness).
>
> The Ill-Made Knight.
>
> The Candle in the Wind.
>
> The Book of Merlyn.

Wolfe, Gene

Castleview.

Woolley, Persia

Child of the Northern Spring.

Queen of the Summer Stars.

Guinevere: The Legend in Autumn.

Robin Hood and Sherwood Forest

Cadnum, Michael

The Wild Wood. This take on the Robin Hood tale portrays a sympathetic sheriff who likes and respects Robin. There is No Maid Marion in this very adult-
feeling version published as a young adult title.

Godwin, Parke

Sherwood. The Robin Hood legend set in the time of the Norman Conquest,
with Robin upholding the Saxon traditions.

Robin and the King. A middle-aged Robin continues to fight for what he thinks
is right.

McKinley, Robin

Outlaws of Sherwood. A feminist version of Robin Hood.

Morpurgo, Michael

Robin.

Roberson, Jennifer

Lady of the Forest. A prequel, this story tells about the assemblage of the well-
known characters of the Robin Hood legend.

Ancient Civilizations

The setting could be ancient Greece or Rome or even the lost world of Atlantis or Mu.

Bradley, Marion Zimmer

The Firebrand. Kassandra, a princess of Troy, is at the center of cataclysmic
events.

Fall of Atlantis.

Lindskold, Jane

The Pipes of Orpheus. The Pied-Piper's true identity is discovered by his child
prisoners in a book from his library.

Norton, Andre, and Susan Shwartz

Empire of the Eagle. Quintus, a member of a defeated Roman legion, is sent
east with the Golden Eagle into the mists of legend to see wonders previously
unknown to any Roman.

Saberhagen, Fred

Book of the Gods series.

> **The Face of Apollo.** Young Jeremy Redthorn and the world he inhabits will never be the same since the ancient gods are back.

Silverberg, Robert

> **Letters from Atlantis.** Correspondence between two time travelers, one of whom is in Atlantis.

Wolfe, Gene

> **Soldier of the Mist.** After a soldier, possibly a Roman legionnaire, suffers a grievous head wound, he wakes each day to amnesia and his journal. The journal is how he knows what happened, as he has no memories.

Celtic

Alexander, Lloyd

The Prydain chronicles. Although for the young, these are also read by adults. Based on the Mabinogion of Welsh legend.

> **The Book of Three.**
>
> **The Black Cauldron.**
>
> **The Castle of Llyr.**
>
> **Taran Wanderer.**
>
> **The High King.**

Bradley, Marion Zimmer

> **The Forest House.**

Chant, Joy

Vandarei series. Celtic, pre-Arthurian. Three children oppose the Dark Lord.

> **Red Moon and Black Mountain.**
>
> **The Grey Mane of Morning.**
>
> **When Voiha Wakes.**
>
> **The High Kings.**

Cooper, Susan

The Dark Is Rising Sequence.

> **Over Sea, Under Stone.**
>
> **The Dark Is Rising.**
>
> **Greenwitch.**
>
> **The Grey King.**
>
> **Silver on the Tree.**

Flint, Kenneth C.

Finn MacCumhal series. The heroic Finn MacCumhal rallies forces to defend Ireland.

     Challenge of the Clans.

     Storm Shield.

     The Dark Druid.

Sidhe series. Features the legend of Tuath De Danann.

     Riders of the Sidhe.

     Champions of the Sidhe.

     Master of the Sidhe.

Godwin, Parke

     The Tower of Beowulf. Beowulf and Grendel.

Lawhead, Stephen R.

Song of Albion series.

     The Paradise War.

     The Silver Hand.

     The Endless Knot.

Llywelyn, Morgan

     Red Branch. The hero Cuchulain.

     Finn MacCool.

McAvoy, R. A.

     Grey Horse.

     Book of Kells.

Morris, Kenneth

Morris, who died in 1937, is credited with creating the modern genre of Celtic fantasy.

     The Fates of the Princes of Dyfed.

     Book of the Three Dragons.

Vance, Jack

Lyonesse series.

     Suldrun's Garden.

     The Green Pearl.

     Madouc.

Walton, Evangeline
The Mabinogion series.

> **The Prince of Annwn.**
>
> **The Children of Llyr.**
>
> **The Song of Rhiannon.**
>
> **The Virgin and the Swine.**

The Americas

Bruchac, Joseph
Dawn Land.

de Lint, Charles
Someplace to Be Flying.

Morris, Kenneth
The Chalchiuhite Dragon.

Europe

Cherryh, C. J.
Rusalka sequence.

> **Rusalka.**
>
> **Chernevog.**
>
> **Yvgenie.**

Grundy, Stephan
Rhinegold.

King, Bernard
Lambisson series.

> **Starkadder.**
>
> **Vagr-Moon.**
>
> **Death-Blinder.**

Milan, Victor, and Melinda Snodgrass
Runespear.

Paxson, Diana L.
The Wolf and the Raven.

The Dragons on the Rhine. Based on the Nibelungen, the Nordic myth that inspired Wagner's *Ring Cycle* of operas.

Reichert, Mickey Zucker

The Renshai trilogy.

The Last of the Renshai.

The Western Wizard.

Child of Thunder.

The Renshai Chronicle is a sequel series.

Beyond Ragnarok.

Prince of Demons.

The Children of Wrath.

Schaefer, Frank

Whose Song Is Sung.

Africa and the Middle East

When we think of myths and legends of the Middle East, genies, djinn, flying carpets, and other denizens of "1,001 Arabian Nights" come to mind. We think of Aladdin and his magical lamp and even Sidney Sheldon's TV series *I Dream of Jeannie.*

Friesner, Esther

Wishing Season.

Myers, Walter Dean

The Legend of Tarik.

Fairy Tales

Retelling of fairy tales and old folktales, often with a new twist, is a growing trend. Some of the stories told in the following novels will be familiar, while others will seem to be new but with an underlying feeling that they have been told before. Definitely not for children only, Tor Books' Fairy Tale Series, created by Terri Windling, was written for adults. Readers who enjoy fantasy with the flavor of fairy tales and folktales may also want to check out collections and compilations of the original stories. They are often shelved in the nonfiction sections in the children's and adult areas of libraries, places that fantasy readers may not think to visit without the suggestion of a readers' advisor.

An overview of the last 150 years of the short form of fairy tale can be found in *The Oxford Book of Modern Fairy Tales,* edited by Alison Lurie (Oxford University Press, 1993).

The Familiar

Sometimes the classic fairy tale is elaborated upon, with the characters developed beyond stereotype and given backgrounds and motivation. Other familiar fairy tales are used as jumping-off points: The original premise is there but is used as a springboard into something entirely different, taking the hero or heroine into another century or situation.

Dean, Pamela

Juniper, Gentian, and Rosemary. Inspired by the traditional ballad.

de Lint, Charles

Jack of Kinrowan. A contemporary, feminist "Jack the Giant Killer."

Lackey, Mercedes

Fire Rose. A Beauty and the Beast tale.

Firebird. Based on the Russian tale.

Levine, Gail Carson

Ella Enchanted. Although published for children or young adults, this down-to-earth yet filled-with-magic take on the Cinderella story delights adult readers.

Maguire, Gregory

Wicked: The Life and Times of the Wicked Witch of the West.

McKinley, Robin

Beauty. A retelling of "Beauty and the Beast."

The Rose Daughter. Most unusual in that McKinley had previously and in a very different way retold the same story years ago in *Beauty*.

Deerskin. This tale unveils the horrors of incest in a tale of a beautiful princess and her dog, based on the fairy tale "Donkeyskin."

Napoli, Donna Jo

The Magic Circle. A retelling of "Hansel and Gretel."

Zel. The motivations of the characters from "Rapunzel" are brought to life in this tale of an adopted daughter living in a remote cottage.

Scarborough, Elizabeth Ann

Godmother. In a fractured fairy tale sort of way, Scarborough sets her tales of a Fairy Godmother in contemporary Seattle.

Godmother's Apprentice.

Springer, Nancy

Fair Peril. A plump, middle-aged storyteller refuses to kiss a frog who wants to be returned to his princely form.

Tepper, Sheri S.

Beauty. Beauty pricks her finger on her 16th birthday, but instead of sleeping for 100 years she travels to the twenty-first century.

Wrede, Patricia C.

Snow White and Rose Red.

The Enchanted Forest chronicles. Written for teens, this series is always sneaking in elements of fairy tales, including magic carpets, giants, and beanstalks.

Dealing with Dragons.

Searching for Dragons.

Calling on Dragons.

Talking to Dragons.

Yolen, Jane

Briar Rose. When her dying grandmother says "I am Briar Rose; find the castle," a young journalist sets off on a journey of discovery that combines the tale of "Sleeping Beauty" with the horrors of the Holocaust's death camps.

Originals

The following stories seem very much like fairy tales but are not built on the foundation of previous tales, even though some of the same devices and conventions will be found in them.

Barnes, John

One for the Morning Glory.

Furlong, Monica

Wise Child.

Juniper.

Goldman, William

The Princess Bride: S. Morgenstern's Classic Tale of True Love and High Adventure, The "Good Parts" Version. Basis of the movie *The Princess Bride.*

Jones, Diana Wynne

Howl's Moving Castle.

Castle in the Air.

McKillip, Patricia A.

The Book of Atrix Wolfe.

Pyle, Howard

Garden Behind the Moon: The Real Story of the Moon Angel.

Wolfe, Gene

The Devil in a Forest.

Yolen, Jane

The Books of Great Alta. A two-in-one volume that contains *Sister Light, Sister Dark* and *White Jenna.*

The One-Armed Queen. Continues the tale.

Fairy Tale Short Stories

Fairy tales and folktales seem to be particularly well suited to the short story form. Many outstanding writers have turned their hand to this genre of short story, giving readers a chance to sample a great variety of talents. Fans of the following should be reminded of the pleasures to be found in the Dewey decimal system's 398s.

Datlow, Ellen, and Terri Windling, eds.

Black Swan, White Raven.

Black Thorn, White Rose.

Snow White, Blood Red.

Ruby Slippers, Golden Tears.

Kerr, Katharine, ed.

Enchanted Forests.

McKinley, Robin

The Door in the Hedge.

Vande Velde, Vivian

Tales from the Brothers Grimm and the Sisters Weird.

Humorous

Humor plays a major role in fantasy. Often full of topical "in jokes," such books present more humor to the well-read.

Anthony, Piers

Xanth series. Books in this series are full of puns and plays on words.

A Spell for Chameleon.

The Source of Magic.

Castle Roogna.

(And on and on and on for many more volumes.)

Asprin, Robert Lynn

The M. Y. T. H. series.

Another Fine Myth.

Myth Conceptions.

Myth Directions.

Hit or Myth.

Myth-ing Persons.

Little Myth Marker.

M. Y. T. H. Inc. Link.

Myth-Nomers and Im-Perfections.

M. Y. T. H. Inc. in Action.

Sweet Myth-tery of Life.

Brooks, Terry

Magic Kingdom of Landover series.

Cook, Rick

Mall Purchase Night.

Wiz Zumwalt series.

Wizard Compiled.

Wizard's Bane.

Wizardry Consulted.

Wizardry Cursed.

Wizardry Quested.

DeChancie, John

Castle Perilous series.

Castle Perilous.

Castle for Rent.

Castle Kidnapped.

Castle War!

Castle Murders.

Castle Dream.

Castle Spellbound.

Bride of the Castle.

Readers may also enjoy Zelazny's Amber series, described in the "Alternate Worlds" section.

Gaiman, Neil, and Terry Pratchett

Good Omens: The Nice and Accurate Prophecies of Agnes Nutter, Witch. A demon and an angel try to stop the apocalypse because they are having too good a time in this world to see it all end.

Gardner, Craig Shaw

The Cineverse Cycle. Roger cruises the various alternate worlds of a universe based on movie genres using his Captain Crusader decoder ring.

Slaves of the Volcano God.

Bride of the Slime Monster.

Revenge of the Fluffy Bunnies.

Gentle, Mary

Grunts. Some editions have the subtitle *A Fantasy with Attitude,* which says it all. Orc marines obtain modern weapons in a hilarious but earthy and, to some, obscene tale of fantasy warfare told from the "bad guy's" point of view.

Jones, Diana Wynne

Howl's Moving Castle.

Castle in the Air.

Pratchett, Terry

Discworld series.

Eric: A Discworld Novel.

Lords and Ladies.

The Light Fantastic.

Guards! Guards!

Small Gods.

Men at Arms.

Wyrd Sisters.

Moving Pictures.

Pyramids: The Book of Going Forth.

Witches Abroad.

Strata.

Interesting Times.

Feet of Clay.

Maskerade.

Jingo.

Hogfather.

Rogers, Mark E.

Samurai Cat series.

The Adventures of Samurai Cat.

More Adventures of Samurai Cat.

Samurai Cat in the Real World.

The Sword of the Samurai Cat.

Samurai Cat Goes to the Movies.

Samurai Cat Goes to Hell.

Turtledove, Harry

The Case of the Toxic Spell Dump.

Watt-Evans, Lawrence, and Esther Friesner

Split Heirs.

Zelazny, Roger, and Robert Sheckly

> **Bring Me the Head of Prince Charming.**
>
> **If at Faust You Don't Succeed.**

A Bestiary

Animals play a large role in fantasy. It seems that every fantasy has some kind of nonhuman creature in it, whether it is a major character with a speaking role or mere window dressing in the form of a cat soaking up some sunshine. Fantasy with the emphasis on animals ranges from animal fables in which humans play no role and the characters are sentient beasts, to books where the emphasis is on the relationship between humans and animals. The preponderance of magic workers in fantasy brings with it animal familiars, who may facilitate the magic of humans or even work magic of their own. Communication between humans and animals is a frequently occurring theme.

Anthologies

Animals are a popular topic for fantasy in its short form. Both fantastical beasts and everyday animals are popular subjects. Cats often play a major role.

Beagle, Peter S., and Janet Berliner

> **Immortal Unicorn.**

Greenberg, Martin H., ed.

> **Christmas Bestiary.**
>
> **Dinosaur Fantastic.**
>
> **Dragon Fantastic.**
>
> **Horse Fantastic.**

Norton, Andre, and Martin H. Greenberg, eds.

> **Catfantastic.** This anthology has been so popular that it was turned into a series, with four volumes out by 1998.

Unicorns

Often portrayed as one-horned horses, unicorns in the following books are viewed in different ways. They are generally good creatures that possess magic.

Beagle, Peter S.

> **The Last Unicorn.** A unicorn, fearing she is the last of her kind, embarks on a quest to see if others survive. Basis of the animated film.

Bishop, Michael

> **Unicorn Mountain.** The problems of unicorns in another dimension dying off and the AIDS epidemic in our world intersect.

Coville, Bruce

Written for children.

Unicorn Chronicles.

Into the Land of Unicorns.

A Glory of Unicorns.

Lee, John

Unicorn Quest series. Filled with political intrigue.

The Unicorn Quest.

The Unicorn Dilemma.

The Unicorn Solution.

The Unicorn Peace.

The Unicorn War.

Lee, Tanith

Unicorn series. Tanaquil's mother is a sorceress and her sister is an empress, making her own life as a mender difficult, in this series written for teens but enjoyed by adults too.

The Black Unicorn.

The Gold Unicorn.

The Red Unicorn.

Pierce, Meredith Ann

Firebringer series. A young unicorn saves his clan by bringing them fire.

Birth of the Firebringer.

Dark Moon.

The Son of Summer Stars.

Dragons

Dragons, who have been depicted in many different ways throughout history, are often portrayed as telepathic creatures in fantasy fiction.

Bradshaw, Gillian

Dragon and the Thief.

The Land of Gold.

Brown, Mary

Master of Many Treasures.

Callander, Don

Dragon Companion.

Dragon Rescue.

Dickson, Gordon R.

The Dragon and the George series.

The Dragon and the George.

The Dragon Knight.

The Dragon on the Border.

The Dragon at War.

The Dragon, the Earl, and the Troll.

Dragon and the Gnarly King.

Fletcher, Susan

Dragonsayer series.

Dragon's Milk.

Flight of the Dragon Kyn.

Sign of the Dove.

Hambly, Barbara

Dragonsbane. Jenny, a witch, has conflicting feelings about slaying dragons.

Kellogg, Marjorie B.

The Dragon quartet. As of 1998 only two of the books in the series had been published.

The Book of Earth.

The Book of Water.

 7

Kerner, Elizabeth

Song in the Silence.

McCaffrey, Anne

Pern series. Even though McCaffrey contends, and even presents evidence to prove, that her works are science fiction, dragon-loving fantasy fans claim the books set on the planet Pern as their own.

Murphy, Shirley Rousseau

Dragonbards series.

Nightpool.

The Ivory Lyre.

Dragonbards.

Norton, Andre, and Mercedes Lackey

Halfblood chronicles.

The Elvenbane.

Elvenblood.

Radford, Irene

Dragon Nimbus.

Glass Dragon.

The Perfect Princess.

The Loneliest Magician.

The Dragon Nimbus History.

The Dragon's Touchstone.

Rowley, Christopher

Bazil Broketail series. Battledragons and their dragoneers.

Bazil Broketail.

A Sword for a Dragon.

Dragons of War.

Battledragon.

A Dragon at World's End.

Dragons of Argonath.

Stasheff, Christopher, ed.

Dragon's Eye.

Vande Velde, Vivian

Dragon's Bait.

Yolen, Jane

Pit Dragons series. For kids but read by adults.

Dragon's Blood.

Heart's Blood.

A Sending of Dragons.

Uncommon Common Animals

Animals from our world—ordinary creatures such as rabbits, ants, dogs, cats, skunks, and horses—may not seem to fit the fabric of fantasy, but in these stories they do. The animals can range from the mundane and ordinary to sentient members of complex societies.

Adams, Richard

Watership Down. A modern classic about rabbits heroically seeking a new home.

Bell, Clare

The Named, a clan of intelligent, catlike creatures living in prehistoric times, are featured in this unnamed series.

Ratha's Creature.

Clan Ground.

      Ratha and Thistle-Chaser.

      Ratha's Challenge.

Brown, Mary

      Pigs Don't Fly.

Greeno, Gayle

Ghatti's Tale series. Telepathic, catlike creatures.

      Finder's Keepers.

      Mind-Speaker's Call.

      Exile's Return.

Hawdon, Robin

A Rustle in the Grass. Their world in peril, a colony of ants takes on a devastating army of killer red ants.

Horwood, William

Duncton chronicles. Series about romance and adventure in a neighborhood of moles.

      Duncton Wood.

      Duncton Quest.

      Duncton Found.

      Duncton Tales.

      Duncton Rising.

      Duncton Stone.

Jacques, Brian

The Redwall series. Woodland creatures battle evil in fantasy adventure; popular with all ages.

      Redwall. In 1998 a 10th anniversary edition with new illustrations was published.

      Mossflower.

      Mattimeo.

      Mariel of Redwall.

      Salamandastron.

      Martin the Warrior.

      The Bellmaker.

      Pearls of Lutra.

      The Long Patrol.

      Marlfox.

King, Gabriel

      The Wild Road.

      The Golden Cat.

Lackey, Mercedes
Valdemar series.

Murphy, Shirley Rousseau
Catswold Portal.

Joe Grey, Cat Detective series.

> **Cat on the Edge.**
>
> **Cat Under Fire.**
>
> **Cat Raise the Dead.**

Tolkien, J. R. R.
Roverandom. A dog, transformed into a toy, searches for the wizard who cursed him.

Wangerin, Walter
The Book of the Dun Cow. Barnyard animals.

The Book of Sorrows.

Williams, Tad
Tailchaser's Song.

World of Faerie

While not a large subgenre, the world of Faerie has influenced much of fantasy, and its conventions frequently pop up in many types of literature and popular media. This is not a world inhabited by Tinkerbell-like creatures but rather one where dwells a strange and mysterious race with powers that seem magical to mere humans. Plots in this subgenre almost always involve the conflict between humans and the elven inhabitants of Faerie, who seem to have a proclivity for falling in love with each other. Tales of changelings also abound.

Readers may also enjoy urban fantasy in which the worlds of Faerie and humans collide, the idea of a place existing side by side with our world that has different rules of nature and where time passing at a different rate has surely played a role in the development of fantasy dealing with parallel worlds.

Dean, Pamela
Tam Lin. Set in a Vietnam-era midwest college town; a young woman rescues her love from the Queen of Faerie.

de Lint, Charles
Greenmantle.

The Wild Wood.

Jack of Kinrowan. An omnibus edition containing *Jack the Giant Killer* and *Drink Down the Moon.*

The Ivory and the Horn.

Dietz, Tom

Featuring David Sullivan, who has a kind of second sight that allows him to see into the Faerie realm.

Windmaster's Bane.

Fireshaper's Doom.

Darkthunder's Way.

Sunshaker's War.

Stoneskin's Revenge.

Ghostcountry's Wrath.

Dreamseeker's Road.

Landslayer's Law.

Dunsany, Lord

The King of Elfland's Daughter (1924). A classic that has influenced many of the later works set in Faerie.

Edghill, Rosemary

Sword of Maiden's Tears.

Cup of Morning Shadows.

Goldstein, Lisa

Strange Devices of the Sun and Moon.

Holdstock, Robert

Mythago Cycle. Ryhope Wood is an enchanted world where mythic images come to life.

Mythago Wood.

Gate of Ivory, Gate of Horn.

Kushner, Ellen

Thomas the Rhymer.

MacDonald, George

Phantastes: A Faerie Romance for Men and Women (1858).

McKillip, Patricia A.

Something Rich and Strange.

Sherman, Josepha

A Strange and Ancient Name.

Windleaf.

Prince of the Sidhe.

The Shattered Oath.

Forging the Runes.

Snyder, Midori

The Flight of Michael McBride. A unique blend of Faerie and the Old West; could almost be considered a historical urban fantasy.

Windling, Terri
The Wood Wife.

Contemporary

The cornerstone of contemporary fantasy is a setting that is readily recognizable to us. While some of the following titles exhibit the more extreme features of fantasy, there are always parts that are identifiable in our world. Sometimes stories set in our mundane world are called "low fantasy" or "realistic fantasy" (an oxymoron, much like "jumbo shrimp"). For some, the recognizable settings make this fantasy more accessible, while for others the settings detract from the escapism of a totally made-up world.

Urban Fantasy

Drugs, racism, gangs, and other scourges of modern life are evident in the cyberpunk subgenre of fantasy, where a rift between our world and the world of Faerie has occurred. Magic and technology share a place in gritty, dangerous cities. Readers of urban fantasy should also check the "Shared World Series" section later in this chapter for the Borderlands and Serrated Edge series.

Brust, Steven, and Megan Lindholm
The Gypsy.

Bull, Emma
War for the Oaks.

Finder.

Charnas, Suzy McKee

The Sorcery Hill trilogy. Valentine Marsh fights evil from another universe in this young adult trilogy.

> **The Bronze King.**
>
> **The Silver Glove.**
>
> **The Golden Thread.**

Dalkey, Kara
Steel Rose. Gritty.

de Lint, Charles
Dreams Underfoot.

Memory and Dream.

Moonheart.

Jack the Giant-Killer.

Drink down the Moon.

Gaiman, Neil

Neverwhere. Gritty London setting.

Huff, Tanya

Gate of Darkness, Circle of Light. Unicorns in Toronto.

Lackey, Mercedes, and Ellen Guon

A Knight of Ghosts and Shadows.

Summoned to Tourney.

Bedlam's Bard. Combines *A Knight of Ghosts and Shadows* and *Summoned to Tourney* in one volume.

Lindskold, Jane

Brother to Dragons, Companion to Owls. Sarah, who hears inanimate objects and can speak only in literary quotes, is forced out of the asylum and rescued from the streets by Abalone, who uses his computer skills to delve into her past.

Shetterly, Will

Elsewhere. Runaway Ron ends up in Bordertown.

NeverNever. Ron, now transformed into a wolf-boy, comes of age as he discovers what life is really about.

Springer, Nancy

Argue on the Wing.

Windling, Terri, and Delia Sherman, eds.

The Essential Borderland. Shared-world short stories set in Bordertown.

The Human Condition

The triumphs, trials, and tribulations of being human are examined in the following books in which fantasy highlights the problems and sometimes shows solutions.

Anthony, Piers

The Incarnations of Immortality series.

On a Pale Horse.

Bearing an Hourglass.

With a Tangled Skein.

Wielding a Red Sword.

Being a Green Mother.

For Love of Evil.

And Eternity.

Bishop, Michael

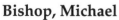

Brittle Innings. Rural Georgia in 1943 is the setting (not exactly contemporary, but this century at least) for a story of redemption when a brutalized young baseball player discovers friendship with Hank Clervall, Frankenstein's gentle monster.

Bisson, Terry
Talking Man.

Blaylock, James P.
All the Bells on Earth. Humans try to beat the forces of evil after the devil tries to claim three souls brokered by a bogus minister.

de Lint, Charles
Trader. Max Trader awakes one morning to find that he has been dreamed into the body and life of deadbeat scumbag Johnny Devlin.

Gaiman, Neil
Neverwhere. A girl named Door leads Richard Mayhew into the weird subterranean world that exists under London.

Heinlein, Robert A.
Job: A Comedy of Justice.

Nylund, Eric S.
Dry Water. An author with some precognitive abilities flees his life in the city for a New Mexico filled with magical battles.

Reed, Robert
Exaltation of Larks. A tale of strange goings-on at a 1970s college. Long out of print, it was reissued in 1998.

Resnick, Mike
A Miracle of Rare Design.

Springer, Nancy
Larque on the Wing. Larque, who can create doppelgangers, sometimes even without doing it consciously, finds herself in the body of a young man but with her woman's heart intact.

Stewart, Sean
Mockingbird. When her mother dies, Toni finds herself inhabited by six gods, who take possession of her at various times.

Tepper, Sheri S.
A Plague of Angels.

Willard, Nancy
Things Invisible to See. Ben enters into a "deal with the devil" and must play a baseball game against death.

Magic Realism

Magic realism features an ordinary workaday setting in which magic and mythology are an integral part of the spiritual makeup. The contemporary settings are similar to those of urban fantasy but with more spirituality and less emphasis on urban problems such as gangs and drugs. For years the name has been applied only to Latin American literary works, but readers apply the term to the following works as well.

Blaylock, James P.

The Paper Grail. Many are in on the hunt in California for a nineteenth-century woodcut sketch that is imbued with magical powers.

Block, Francesca Lia

Dangerous Angels: The Weetzie Bat Books. An omnibus title for the five rollicking, surrealist punk fairy tales about a teen family made of love, not blood, in modern-day Venice Beach. While published as young adult books, they have a huge following among hip 20-something readers as well as older teens.

> **Weetzie Bat.**
>
> **Witch Baby.**
>
> **Cherokee Bat and the Goat Guys.**
>
> **Missing Angel Juan.**
>
> **Baby Be-Bop.**

de Lint, Charles

Someplace to Be Flying.

Goldstein, Lisa

Walking the Labyrinth.

Kindl, Patrice

The Woman in the Wall. Anna, "small and thin, with a face like water," fades into the walls of her family's dilapidated Victorian home, her shyness making her invisible to her family, in this young adult title.

Scarborough, Elizabeth Ann

The Healer's War. A military nurse serving in Vietnam during the war is given a powerful talisman in this Nebula award winner.

Shetterly, Will

Dogland. Is the fountain of youth to be found near a 1950s Florida theme park?

Windling, Terri

The Wood Wife. In the desert, poet Maggie Black begins to see things that don't jibe with her sense of reality.

Alternate and Parallel Worlds

Other fully developed worlds, whether our own transformed by a difference in history or one that can be traveled to from our world, are featured in this subgenre. Sometimes the alternate world is a fully fleshed-out one that has no relation to our own but rather has its own fully developed history and rules.

Alternate History

Due to a divergence someplace in time, the worlds presented are very different from the world we know. Alternate history is an area that is most frequently claimed by science fiction, but many titles fit into the fantasy arena as well as or better than into science fiction.

Anthony, Piers

Geodyssey.

> **Isle of Woman.**
>
> **Shame of Man.**
>
> **Hope of Earth.**

Ball, Margaret

Tamai series. In an alternate nineteenth century, Tamai uses her magic to protect her people, keeping Chin an isolated country by refusing contact with the British.

> **Flameweaver.**
>
> **Changeweaver.**

Bear, Greg

> **Dinosaur Summer.**

Blaylock, James P.

> **The Paper Grail.**

Brust, Steven, and Emma Bull

> **Freedom and Necessity.** A magical, mysterious romp through mid-nineteenth-century England.

Card, Orson Scott

Chronicles of Alvin Maker. In this alternate nineteenth-century North America, hexes and spells work and the states never became a union. It is American history with a twist and echoes of the life of Joseph Smith, the founder of Mormonism.

> **Seventh Son.**
>
> **Red Prophet.**
>
> **Prentice Alvin.**
>
> **Alvin Journeyman.**
>
> **Heartfire.**

Ciencin, Scott

The Elven Ways. When elves deserted a dying Faerie in the fifteenth century, they passed themselves off as angels in our world, taking control and changing the destiny of humankind.

> **The Ways of Magic.**
>
> **Ancient Games.**

Conner, Mike

Archangel. An alternate 1920s Minneapolis is the sight of a viral epidemic that is draining its victims of blood.

Dalkey, Kara

Blood of the Goddess. Sixteenth-century India.

Goa.

Bijapur.

Bhagavati.

Dreyfuss, Richard, and Harry Turtledove

The Two Georges. Our world would be very different if George Washington had reconciled the rebellious colonies with King George.

Edgerton, Teresa

Goblin sequence. The harmony of an alternate Europe is shattered when an inept alchemist awakens a malign force.

Goblin Moon.

Gnome's Engine.

Gemmell, David

Dark Prince. Four-year-old Alexander is kidnapped by an evil King Philip of Macedon from a parallel universe. Sequel to *Lion of Macedon*.

Gentle, Mary

Rats and Gargoyles.

The Architecture of Desire. Politics and magic in an alternate seventeenth-century London.

Goldstein, Lisa

The Red Magician. "Turns the hidden world of Eastern European Jews during the 1940s into a world of wonders, then transcends the Holocaust with magical optimism."—*The New York Times*.

Harrison, Harry

Hammer and the Cross trilogy. Shef, a Norseman, leads the Viking army to victory over England.

The Hammer and the Cross.

One King's Way.

King and Emperor.

MacAvoy, R. A.

Trio for Lute. Renaissance Italy. Damiano Delstrego, a witch boy, and his dog familiar meet the angel Raphael.

Damiano.

Damiano's Lute.

Raphael.

McIntyre, Vonda N.
The Moon and the Sun.

Roessner, Michaela
The Stars Dispose.

Rohan, Michael Scott
The Lord of Middle Air.

Rohan, Michael Scott, and Allan Scott
The Spell of Empire: The Horns of Tartarus. A conflict arises between Scandinavian and Mediterranean cultures in Europe.

Sargent, Pamela
Climb the Wind: A Novel of Another America.

Snyder, Midori
The Innamorati. Set in an alternate Renaissance Venice.

Turtledove, Harry
Between the Rivers. At the dawn of history, Sharur lives in the thriving city-state of Gibil, a city that is in danger from the gods of other cities, who do not like the burgeoning creativity of the townspeople.

Parallel Worlds

The following works all present characters who travel from one world to another. The conflict in the story often arises from being a stranger in a strange land.

Anderson, Poul
Three Hearts and Three Lions. A classic.

Anthony, Piers
The Apprentice Adept series.

> **Split Infinity.**
>
> **Blue Adept.**
>
> **Juxtaposition.**
>
> **Out of Phaze.**
>
> **Robot Adept.**
>
> **Unicorn Point.**
>
> **Phaze Doubt.**

Anthony, Piers, and Robert Kornwise
Through the Ice. The most remarkable thing about this book is that it was started by a teenage fan of Anthony's who was killed in an accident and was then finished by the prolific author.

Ball, Margare
Lost in Translation.

Bear, Greg
Songs of Earth and Power.

Bradley, Marion Zimmer
House Between Worlds.

Bradley, Marion Zimmer, and Holly Lisle
Glenraven series.

Glenraven.

In the Rift.

Brooks, Terry
Magic Kingdom of Landover series.

Magic Kingdom for Sale—Sold.

The Black Unicorn.

Wizard at Large.

The Tangle Box.

Witches' Brew.

Carroll, Jerry Jay
Top Dog. A vicious Wall Street executive finds himself suddenly in a medieval fantasy world in the form of a dog. For a kinder, gentler take on life as a dog, readers may enjoy *Dogsbody*, by Diana Wynne Jones, which is also great for younger readers.

Chalker, Jack L.
Changewinds. Originally published as *When the Changewinds Blow, Riders of the Winds*, and *War of the Maelstrom*.

Donaldson, Stephen R.
Mordant's Need duology.

The Mirror of Her Dreams.

A Man Rides Through.

The Chronicles of Thomas Covenant, the *Unbeliever*.

First Chronicle:
Lord Foul's Bane.

The Illearth War.

The Power That Preserves.

Second Chronicle:
The Wounded Land.

The One Tree.

White Gold Wielder.

Duncan, Dave
Great Game series.

Past Imperative: Round One of the Great Game.

Present Tense: Round Two of the Great Game.

Future Indefinite: Round Three of the Great Game.

Foster, Alan Dean

The Spellsinger series.

>> **Spellsinger.**

>> **The Hour of the Gate.**

>> **The Day of the Dissonance.**

>> **The Moment of the Magician.**

>> **The Paths of the Perambulator.**

>> **Son of the Spellsinger.**

Gardner, Craig Shaw

Dragon Circle series.

>> **Dragon Sleeping.**

>> **Dragon Waking.**

>> **Dragon Burning.**

Hambly, Barbara

Darwath series.

>> **The Time of the Dark.**

>> **The Walls of Air.**

>> **The Armies of Daylight.**

>> **Mother of Winter.**

Heinlein, Robert A.

> **Glory Road.**

Jones, Diana Wynne

> **A Sudden Wild Magic.**

> **Hexwood.**

Jones, J. V.

> **The Barbed Coil.**

King, Stephen

The Dark Tower series.

>> **The Gunslinger.**

>> **The Drawing of the Three.**

>> **The Waste Lands.**

>> **Wizard and Glass.**

Le Guin, Ursula K.

> **The Lathe of Heaven.** George Orr's dreams become reality. A classic.

L'Engle, Madeleine

Time Quartet.

Modesitt, L. E., Jr.
The Spellsong Cycle.

The Soprano Sorceress.

The Spellsong War.

Moorcock, Michael
Blood: A Southern Fantasy.

O'Donohue, Nick
Crossroads.

The Magic and the Healing.

Under the Healing Sign.

The Healing of Crossroads.

Pullman, Philip
His Dark Materials.

The Golden Compass.

The Subtle Knife.

Rawn, Melanie, Jennifer Roberson, and Kate Elliott
The Golden Key.

Reichert, Mickey Zucker
The Bifrost Guardians.

Godslayer.

Shadow Climber.

Dragonrank Master.

Shadow's Realm.

By Chaos Cursed.

Rohan, Michael Scott

The Anvil of Ice.

The Forge in the Forest.

The Hammer of the Sun.

Rosenberg, Joel
Keepers of the Hidden Ways series.

The Fire Duke.

The Silver Stone.

Rusch, Kristine Kathryn
The Fey.

The Sacrifice.

The Changeling.

        The Rival.

        The Resistance.

        Victory.

Sarti, Ron

Chronicles of Scar.

        Chronicles of Scar.

        Legacy of the Ancients.

Savage, Felicity

Ever series.

        The War in the Waste.

        The Daemon in the Machine.

        A Trickster in the Ashes.

Stasheff, Christopher

Rod Gallowglass series.

        The Warlock in Spite of Himself.

        King Kobold Revived.

        The Warlock Unlocked.

        Escape Velocity.

        The Warlock Enraged.

        The Warlock Wandering.

        The Warlock Is Missing.

        The Warlock Heretical.

        The Warlock's Companion.

        The Warlock Insane.

        The Warlock Rock.

        Warlock and Son.

Rogue Wizard series.

        A Wizard in Mind.

        A Wizard in Bedlam.

        A Wizard in War.

        A Wizard in Peace.

The Warlock's Heirs.

        A Wizard in Absentia.

        M'Lady Witch.

        Quicksilver's Knight.

        A Wizard in Midgard.

Wizard in Rhyme series.

> **Her Majesty's Wizard.**
> **The Oathbound Wizard.**
> **The Witch Doctor.**
> **The Secular Wizard.**

Turtledove, Harry

Videssos cycle.

> **Misplaced Legion.**
> **An Emperor for the Legion.**
> **Legion of Videssos.**
> **Swords of the Legion.**

Zelazny, Roger

Amber series.

Alternate Worlds

Fully realized worlds with their own histories of politics and culture are found in much of fantasy. While many of the books in this section would be just as comfortable in sword and sorcery, some of them are of a more distinctive nature. All the following have an emphasis on building worlds of complexity.

Anderson, Poul

A Midsummer Tempest. The worlds of Shakespeare come to life in the era of Roundheads and Cavaliers.

Bradley, Marion Zimmer

Darkover series.

Brust, Steven

Vlad Taltos series.

> **Taltos.**
> **Jhereg.**
> **Teckla.**
> **Phoenix.**

Clayton, Jo

Drums of Chaos series.

> **Drum Warning.**
> **Drum Calls.**

Coney, Michael Greatrex

> **Fang, the Gnome.**
> **King of the Scepter'd Isle.**

Cross, Ronald Anthony
The Eternal Guardians.

> **The Fourth Guardian.**
>
> **The Lost Guardian.**
>
> **The White Guardian.**

Delany, Samuel R.
They Fly at Ciron.

Dorsey, Candas Jane
Black Wine.

Eddison, E. R.
The Worm Ouroboros. Strong elements of myth and legend in this challenging read from early in the century (1922).

The Zimiamvian trilogy.

> **Mezentian Gate.**
>
> **A Fish Dinner in Memison.**
>
> **Mistress of Mistresses.**

Elliott, Kate
Crown of Stars series.

> **Kings Dragon.**
>
> **Prince of Dogs.**
>
> **The Burning Stone.**

Haggard, H. Rider
The She series. Some of the titles are still in print over a century after they were first published. They take place in a lost-world, alternate African setting.

> **She** (1887).
>
> **Ayesha** (1905).
>
> **She and Allen** (1921).
>
> **Wisdom's Daughter** (1923).

Hodgell, P. C.
Kencyrath series.

> **God Stalk.**
>
> **Dark of the Moon.**
>
> **Seeker's Mask.**

Huff, Tanya
> **No Quarter.**
>
> **Sing the Four Quarters.**
>
> **Fifth Quarter.**

Kay, Guy Gavriel
Tigana.

King, Stephen, and Peter Straub
The Talisman.

Kurtz, Katherine
The Deryni Saga encompasses several trilogies. The Chronicles of the Deryni.

Deryni Rising.

Deryni Checkmate.

High Deryni.

The Legends of Camber of Culdi series.

Camber of Culdi.

Saint Camber.

Camber the Heretic.

The Heirs of Saint Camber series.

The Harrowing of Gwynedd.

King Javan's Year.

The Bastard Prince.

The Histories of King Kelson series.

The Bishop's Heir.

The King's Justice.

The Quest for Saint Camber.

Moorcock, Michael
Gloriana; or, The Unfulfill'd Queen. Elizabeth in Albion, a Faerie world.

Nix, Garth
Sabriel. Winner of both the Best Fantasy Novel and Best Young Adult Novel in the 1995 Australian Aurealis Awards.

Nye, Jody Lynn
Waking in Dreamland.

O'Leary, Patrick
The Gift.

Peake, Mervyn
The Gormenghast trilogy.

Titus Groan (1946).

Gormenghast (1950).

Titus Alone (1959).

Scott, Melissa, and Lisa Barnett
Point of Hopes.

Volsky, Paula
The Wolf of Winter.

Wells, Angus
Lords of the Sky.

Willey, Elizabeth
Prospero series. Rich in language and characterization, this may be too slow-moving for aficionados of swashbuckling adventure fantasy.

The Well-Favored Man.

A Sorcerer and a Gentleman.

The Price of Blood and Honor.

Williamson, Jack
Demon Moon.

Wolfe, Gene
The Book of the New Sun. A science fantasy tetralogy featuring some of the best world building ever seen.

The Book of the Long Sun series, while set in the same world, is more science fiction than fantasy.

The Shadow of the Torturer.

The Claw of the Conciliator. These two are combined in *Shadow and Claw.*

The Sword of the Lictor.

The Citadel of the Autarch. These two are combined in *Sword and Citadel.*

Time Travel

The "how" of time travel dictates whether a title is fantasy or science fiction. Inexplicable travel to another time is usually fantasy, whereas time travel using a machine or other scientific premise falls into science fiction.

Curiously enough, time travel is one of the subgenres in fantasy where adult and teen readers' interests don't have much overlap.

Cherryh, C. J.
Morgaine series.

Gate of Ivrel.

Well of Shiuan.

Fires of Azeroth.

Gabaldon, Diana
Outlander series also features romantic time travel.

Matheson, Richard
Bid Time Return. Also published as *Somewhere in Time*.

Millhiser, Marlys
The Mirror.

Tepper, Sheri S.
Beauty.

Willis, Connie
Lincoln's Dreams. Annie experiences the Civil War by dreaming Robert E. Lee's dreams, making it real and immediate for the reader.

YA Time Travel

The following are at the younger end of the young adult range.

Bond, Nancy
Another Shore.

Cooney, Caroline B.
Both Sides of Time.
Other Side of Time.
Prisoner of Time.

Griffin, Peni R.
Switching Well.

L'Engle, Madeleine
An Acceptable Time.

Lindbergh, Anne
Nick of Time.

Parks, Ruth
Playing Beatie Bow.

Vande Velde, Vivian
A Well-Timed Enchantment.

Yolen, Jane
The Devil's Arithmetic.

Paranormal Powers

Telepathy, telekinesis, precognition, shapeshifting, and immortality are just some of the paranormal abilities that crop up in fantasy.

Psionic Powers

Psionic powers include the abilities to communicate telepathically with other beings, to see into another's thoughts, to see the future, and to move objects or oneself through space. A telepathic bond between a human and an animal or animal-like companion is common in fantasy fiction.

Bradley, Marion Zimmer
Darkover series.

Fancher, Jane S.
Dance of the Rings series.

Gould, Steven
Jumper. Contemporary setting.

Greeno, Gayle
Ghatti's Tale series.

Harper, Tara K.
Tales of the Wolves series.

Huff, Tanya
Quarter series.

King, Stephen
Firestarter. Readers will also like *The Hollow Man,* by Dan Simmons.

Lackey, Mercedes
Several series.

Lackey, Mercedes, and Larry Dixon
The Mage Wars series.

McCaffrey, Anne
Pern series.

Murphy, Pat
The Falling Woman. High literary quality.

Norton, Andre
Witch World series.

Pierce, Tamora
The Immortals series.

Simmons, Dan
The Hollow Man. Very dark.

Springer, Nancy
The Hex Witch of Seldom.

West, Michelle
Hunter's Oath.
Hunter's Death.

Wieler, Diana
Ranvan series. Contemporary setting; young adult.

Shapeshifters

Shapeshifters have the ability to take on a different form, usually that of an animal. Shapeshifting tales seem to have a preponderance of southwestern settings but can be set anywhere. In addition to simply shifting into the form of an animal, or from animal to human, some shapeshifters are "were-animals" having aspects of both species. Werewolves are common in romantic fantasy and dark fantasy.

Bertin, Joanne
The Last Dragonlord.
Dragon and Phoenix.

Kindl, Patrice
Owl in Love.

Murphy, Pat
Nadya.

Murphy, Shirley Rousseau
Catswold Portal.

Roberson, Jennifer
Cheysuli series.

Immortality

The prospect of living forever is a theme that is considered more frequently in science fiction, but occasionally there is a book that puts immortality in the fantasy realm. The Highlander series is a shared world series dealing with immortality. Many vampire dark fantasy and horror novels also involve immortality.

Babbitt, Natalie
Tuck Everlasting. Written for children but enjoyed by adults.

Duncan, Lois
Locked in Time. Young adult.

Eddings, David, and Leigh Eddings
Belgarath the Sorcerer.

Grimwood, Ken
Replay.

Supernatural Beings

The supernatural plays a large part in fantasy. Many of the beings are more commonly found in horror novels, but the elements of scariness and terror aren't present. The paranormal beings can be the embodiment of good or evil or very ordinary. Examples of supernatural beings are angels, vampires, werewolves, and fairy tale–like fairies.

Crowther, Peter, ed.
Heaven Sent: 18 Glorious Tales of the Angels.

Dedman, Stephen
The Art of Arrow Cutting. A photographer becomes the target of three supernatural beings out of Japanese mythology when he receives a key from a woman who later is found dead.

Scarborough, Elizabeth Ann
The Godmother.

Godmother's Apprentice.

Shinn, Sharon
Samaria series.

Archangel.

Jovah's Angel.

The Alleluia Files.

Graphic Novels

Sometimes described as overgrown comics, graphic novels feature stories set to artwork. Usually the violence is also graphic. Fortunately there are now bibliographic guides to these books. In *Graphic Novels,* by D. Aviva Rothschild (Libraries Unlimited, 1995), a self-proclaimed graphic novel evangelist offers an enthusiastic look at this subgenre, providing astute reviews and important bibliographic information. Her chapter on fantasy lists 49 titles, some of which are series, with detailed reviews. Steve Weiner's *100 Graphic Novels for Public Libraries* was published in 1996 by Kitchen Sink Press. Kat Kan writes a graphic novel column for *VOYA* that often features fantasy-themed graphic novels.

Barr, Mike W., and Brian Bolland
Camelot 3000.

Gaiman, Neil

Sandman series. The cream of the crop of original graphic novels.

McCaffrey, Anne

Dragonflight. Illustrated by Lela Dowling, Cynthia Martin, and Fred Von Tobel.

Moore, Alan, and Dave Gibbons

Watchmen.

Nocenti, Ann

Someplace Strange. Illustrated by John Bolton.

Pini, Wendy, and Richard Pini

Elfquest series.

Spiegelman, Art

Maus: A Survivor's Tale, Volumes I & II. The Holocaust as animal fantasy.

Talbot, Bryan

Tale of One Bad Rat.

Tolkien, J. R. R.
The Hobbit. Illustrated by David Wenzel.

Celebrity Characters

Real and imaginary people are alive and well in the pages of fantasy literature. The characters of fiction and other forms of literature take on historical reality in a fantasy world rich in literary allusion. Some creators join their characters. The following books make the reader draw on whatever allusions his or her lifetime's worth of reading has provided.

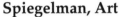

Anderson, Poul
A Midsummer Tempest.

Bova, Ben

Triumph. Featuring Joseph Stalin and Franklin Delano Roosevelt.

Davidson, Avram
The Phoenix and the Mirror. Virgil as a wizard.

de Camp, L. Sprague, and Fletcher Pratt
The Compleat Enchanter: The Magical Misadventures of Harold Shea.
Collective title for *The Incompleat Enchanter, The Castle of Iron: A Science Fantasy Adventure*, and *The Wall of Serpents*. Adventures in the worlds created in literature, including Spenser's *Faerie Queene*.

Farmer, Philip José
Riverworld series.

Gemmell, David
Dark Prince. In a parallel universe, the evil King Philip of Macedon kidnaps four-year-old Alexander into his reality.

Kerr, Katharine, ed.
Weird Tales from Shakespeare.

Maguire, Gregory
Wicked: The Life and Times of the Wicked Witch of the West. Could it be that Elphaba has been given a bum rap in Oz?

Myers, John Myers
Silverlock. The picaresque hero's adventures are in the worlds of great Western literature.

Powers, Tim
The Anubis Gates. Samuel Coleridge pops up in this tale of a modern-day scholar's time-travel foray into the seventeenth century.

Rucker, Rudy
The Hollow Earth.

Swanwick, Michael
Jack Faust. Yet again *Faustus* is reworked, this time giving him access to twentieth-century knowledge in exchange for his soul.

Weis, Margaret, ed.
Fantastic Alice. Several fantasy authors present short stories featuring Lewis Carroll's Alice.

Williams, Tad
Caliban's Hour. Twenty years after the events that unfolded in Shakespeare's *The Tempest*, Caliban seeks his revenge on Miranda.

Shared Worlds

Shared world novels are those that are written by various authors, set in a world conceived and developed by another individual or group. Sometimes they arise organically from a novel or series so beloved that it achieves a life of its own, such as Norton's Witch World and Bradley's Darkover. Some shared worlds are created when a group of like-minded authors want to work together, as in the case of the Trillium series, in which Andre Norton, Julian May, and Mary Zimmer Bradley co-authored the first volume, then built on it with individual titles. Shared worlds do not necessarily evolve from other books. They can have their genesis in television or movies or in games, either computerized or not.

The introduction of shared world stories, in which an imaginary world is created by an editor, author, or group and is then used as a background by several authors, has resulted in the publication of several series. As in any set of works created by committee, there is bound to be some variation in quality, but the following series have been popular.

The shared worlds seem to be particularly popular in series based on role-playing games, movies, television shows, and even computer games. A growing trend in shared world universes has been for the setting and characters to appear in several different venues: novels, graphic novels, comics, games, and the Internet.

Shared World Series

Bordertown

This quintessential shared world series basically created the urban fantasy. *Locus* called it "the finest of all shared worlds."

Bull, Emma
Finder.

Shetterly, Will
Elsewhere.
NeverNever.

Windling, Terri, and Delia Sherman, eds.
The Essential Borderland.

Bard's Tale

Based on the computer game.

Lackey, Mercedes, and Mark Shepherd
Prison of Souls.

Lackey, Mercedes, and Josepha Sherman
Castle of Deception.

Lackey, Mercedes, and Ru Emerson
Fortress of Frost and Fire.

Lisle, Holly, and Aaron Allston
Wrath of the Princes.
Thunder of the Captains.

Shepherd, Mark
Escape from Roksamur.

Sherman, Josepha
The Chaos Gate.

Conan Series

The world created by Robert E. Howard for his heroic barbarian sword-and-sorcery hero Conan has turned into a shared world universe, with books written by L. Sprague de Camp, Lin Carter, Poul Anderson, Robert Jordan, Ronald Green, John C. Hocking, and others.

Darkover

Marion Zimmer Bradley's Darkover has proven to be popular enough to work its way into a shared world universe. She has edited the following anthologies of stories set in the world she created.

Domains of Darkover.

Four Moons of Darkover.

Free Amazons of Darkover.

The Keeper's Price.

Leroni of Darkover.

Marion Zimmer Bradley's Darkover.

The Other Side of the Mirror.

Red Sun of Darkover.

Renunciates of Darkover.

Snows of Darkover.

Sword of Chaos.

Towers of Darkover.

Brian Froud's Faerielands

In a unique twist on shared worlds, artist and illustrator Brian Froud created over 50 drawings and paintings that were divided among Charles de Lint, Patricia A. McKillip, Midori Snyder, and Terri Windling. They were all to write their own stories based on the premise that the current ecological crisis caused by humans also threatens the natural world of Faerie.

de Lint, Charles
The Wild Wood.

McKillip, Patricia A.
Something Rich and Strange.

Highlander

A movie series, a television series, and a book series.

Henderson, Jason
The Element of Fire.

Holder, Nancy
Measure of a Man.

Lettow, Donna
Zealot: A Novel.

McConnell, Ashley
Scimitar.

Neason, Rebecca
The Path: A Novel.

Roberson, Jennifer
Scotland the Brave.

Magic Series

A universe of magic created by Larry Niven in his *The Magic Goes Away*. Niven then edited two illustrated volumes. Originally published in the late 1970s and early 1980s, they were reprinted in 1993.

The Magic May Return.

More Magic.

Magic in Ithkar Series

Edited by Andre Norton and Robert Adams, 4 volumes. Stories by Lin Carter, George Alec Effinger, Linda Haldeman, R. A. Lafferty, and others.

Magic, the Gathering

At the root of this series is the role-playing game, but novels and anthologies have taken off from it much as the DragonLance books have taken off from Dungeons and Dragons. Here the setting is the magical world of Dominica, where Minotaur and Elf are embroiled in a bloody conflict involving foul magic and dirty politics. The following is not a comprehensive list, just examples of titles and authors.

Braddock, Hanovi
Ashes of the Sun.

Emery, Clayton
Final Sacrifice.

Forstchen, William R.
Arena.

Ice, Kathy, ed.
Distant Planes: An Anthology.

McLaren, Teri
The Cursed Land.
Song of Time.

Vardeman, Robert E.
Dark Legacy.

Merovingen Nights

Created by C. J. Cherryh in the novel *Angel with the Sword*, the following are anthologies featuring stories by Cherryh, Janet Morris, and Chris Morris.

Festival Moon.

Fever Season.

Endgame.

Serrated Edge

Created by Mercedes Lackey, Serrated Edge is a shared world urban fantasy involving elves who have formed SERRA, the South Eastern Road Racing Association.

Lackey, Mercedes, and Holly Lisle
When the Bough Breaks. A girl with psi powers could wreak havoc on Faerie if her pain is not relieved.

Lackey, Mercedes, and Larry Dixon
Born to Run. Mixes hot cars, rock and roll, abused youths, and elves.
Chrome Circle. Mixes Celtic rock, elves and dragons, and romance.

Lackey, Mercedes, and Mark Shepherd
Wheels of Fire. A parental kidnapping, a racing car, and an elf to the rescue.

Shepherd, Mark
Spiritride. Set in Albuquerque, featuring motorcycles and skateboards.
Elvendude. Features a prince of Faerie who is raised in our world so he can grow to adulthood and take on the dark elves.

Shadowrun

Not only a shared world series, Shadowrun was originally a popular role-playing game from FASA Corporation. It combines urban and dark fantasy in a dangerous future. The following is merely a sampling of stories based on it.

Charrette, Robert N.
> **Never Deal with a Dragon.**
> **Choose Your Enemies Carefully.**
> **Find Your Own Truth.**
> **Just Compensation.**
> **Into the Shadows.**

Dowd, Tom
> **Night's Pawn.**
> **Burning Bright.**

Findley, Nigel D.
> **House of the Sun.**
> **Lone Wolf.**
> **2XS.**
> **Shadow Play.**

Kenson, Stephen
> **Technobabel.**

Koke, Jak
> **Dead Air.**
> *Dragon Heart saga.*
> > **Stranger Souls.**
> > **Clockwork Asylum.**
> > **Beyond the Pale.**

Kubasik, Christopher
> **The Changeling.**

 7

Odom, Mel
> **Preying for Keeps.**
> **Headhunters.**

Pollotta, Nicholas
> **Shadowboxer.**

Sargent, Carl, and Marc Gascoigne
> **Streets of Blood.**
> **Noseferatu.**
> **Black Madonna.**

Smedman, Lisa

The Lucifer Deck.

Blood Sport.

Smith, Nyx

Who Hunts the Hunter.

Striper Assassin.

Fade to Black.

Steel Rain.

Spector, Caroline

Words Without End.

Starshield

Created by Margaret Weis and Tracy Hickman. The first book of the series is *The Mantle of Kendis-Dai*, originally published with the title *Starshield: Sentinels*. Book two is *The Nightsword*. It survives as an online role-playing game.

Sword of Knowledge Series

Created by C. J. Cherryh, each novel has a different co-author (listed after the titles).

A Dirge for Sabis (Leslie Fish).

Wizard Spawn (Nancy Asire).

Reap the Whirlwind (Mercedes Lackey).

Thieves' World-Sanctuary Series

The creation of Robert Lynn Asprin and Lynn Abbey in 1978. All books were published between 1979 and 1990. While many shared world series are based on games, a game was created based on the Thieves' World series. A graphic novel series was also created. Among the contributing authors were Lynn Abbey, Poul Anderson, Robert Lynn Asprin, Robin Wayne Bailey, Marion Zimmer Bradley, John Brunner, C. J. Cherryh, Christine DeWeese, David Drake, Diane Duane, Philip José Farmer, Joe Haldeman, Vonda N. McIntyre, Chris Morris, Janet Morris (who has done separate novels on Thieves' World: *Beyond Sanctuary, Beyond Wizard-Wall,* and *Beyond the Veil*), Andrew Offutt, Diana L. Paxson, and A. E. van Vogt. The first six volumes (original paperbacks) were gathered into two volumes by Science Fiction Books in *Sanctuary: Thieves' World, Tales from the Vulgar Unicorn, Shadows of Sanctuary,* and *Cross Currents: Storm Season, The Face of Chaos, Wing of Omen.*

Book 7: *The Dead of Winter.*

Book 8: *Soul of the City.*

Book 9: *Blood Ties.*

Book 10: *Aftermath.*

Book 11: *Uneasy Alliances.*

Book 12: *Stealer's Sky.*

Trillium

Bradley, Marion Zimmer, Julian May, and Andre Norton
Black Trillium.

A tale cowritten by three grand dames of fantasy writing, with three princesses, three quests, and three magical talismans, was not enough, so Andre Norton followed up with *Golden Trillium*, Julian May with *Blood Trillium* and *Sky Trillium,* and Marion Zimmer Bradley with *Lady of the Trillium.*

Valdemar

Mercedes Lackey created the world of Valdemar so fully developed and enticing that others wanted to write stories set there. *Sword of Ice: And Other Tales of Valdemar,* edited by Mercedes Lackey and John Yezeguielian, includes 18 stories by Mickey Zucker Reichert, Larry Dixon, Tanya Huff, Michelle Sagara, and others.

Witch World

Andre Norton's Witch World books are another example of a beloved series being taken up by others, turning its setting into a shared world.

Tales of the Witch World

Tales of the Witch World 1.

Tales of the Witch World 2.

Tales of the Witch World 3.

Four from the Witch World.

Witch World: The Turning

Norton has also cowritten some books in a sub-series called Witch World: The Turning, set after the Witches of Estcarp caused a massive cataclysm that moved mountains to block an invasion. This crippled their powers and brought chaos and destruction to all of Witch World.

Storms of Victory. Written with P. M. Griffin.

Flight of Vengeance. Written with P. M. Griffin and Mary H. Schaub.

On Wings of Magic. Written with Patricia Mathews and Sasha Miller.

Secrets of the Witch World

The Key of the Keplian. Written with Lyn McConchie.

Dungeons and Dragons and Other Role-Playing Game Worlds

The game of Dungeons and Dragons (role-playing in a sword-and-sorcery setting) has fostered a considerable body of original paperback publications, too numerous to list here. TSR, now Wizards of the Coast, has had great success marketing books based on their various fantasy role-playing games. The most popular authors are the duo of Margaret Weis and Tracy Hickman. Also extremely popular in hardcover with users of public libraries is R. A. Salvatore. Many of these fantasy novels, based on a game, verge on horror, with vampires, werewolves, and other types of shapeshifters playing important roles.

The following authors have written books that have a fantasy role-playing setting. While not shared world tales, they share a background with them.

Cushman, Carolyn

Witch and Wombat. The world is losing its magic, so a witch takes a crew of fantasy virtual-reality gamers on a quest to help bring back the magic, in this tongue-in-cheek tale.

McKiernan, Dennis L.

Caverns of Socrates. A group of tournament-winning gamers must win through on their quest or never be able to break free of the supercomputer that now holds them.

Rosenberg, Joel

Guardians of the Flame series.

The Sleeping Dragon.

The Sword and the Chain.

The Silver Crown.

Dark Fantasy

Defining dark fantasy is as difficult as defining fantasy itself. It is very strongly linked to horror. Both genres scare or terrify, but in dark fantasy the emphasis is on the magic and often on the conflict between good and evil, while in horror the emphasis is on terrifying the reader. Many titles included in this section appear on horror lists. Many authors who are known for writing horror have been recipients of major fantasy awards because of their dark fantasy titles.

Beagle, Peter S.
The Innkeeper's Song.

Giant Bones. Six novellas set in the world of *The Innkeeper's Song*.

Bischoff, David
Quoth the Crow.

Blaylock, James P.
All the Bells on Earth.

Bradbury, Ray
The October Country.

Something Wicked This Way Comes. A chilling classic.

Brooks, Terry
Running with the Demon.

Knight of the Word.

Card, Orson Scott
Lost Boys.

de Lint, Charles
The Dreaming Place.

Friedman, C. S.
Cold Fire trilogy.

Black Sun Rising.

When True Night Falls.

Crown of Shadows.

Joyce, Graham
Requiem. A very literary dark fantasy set in Jerusalem that won the August Derleth Award.

The Tooth Fairy. Not a pleasant fairy tale.

Klause, Annette Curtis
Blood and Chocolate.

The Silver Kiss.

Lackey, Mercedes
Diana Tregarde series.

Burning Water.

Children of the Night.

Jinx High.

Lee, Tanith

Blood Opera series.

> **Dark Dance.**
>
> **Personal Darkness.**
>
> **Darkness, I.**

The Secret Books of Paradys series.

> **The Book of the Damned.**
>
> **The Book of the Beast.**
>
> **The Book of the Dead.**
>
> **The Book of the Mad.**

Leiber, Fritz

Conjure Wife.

Our Lady of Darkness.

The Dealings of Daniel Kesserich: A Study of the Mass-Insanity at Smithville.

MacIntyre, F. Gwynplaine

The Woman Between the Worlds.

Murphy, Pat

Nadya.

Pierce, Meredith Ann

Darkangel trilogy. Written for children and young adults, this is a dark tale of romance and vampires. Long out of print, this beloved series was reissued in 1998.

> **The Dark Angel.**
>
> **A Gathering of Gargoyles.**
>
> **The Pearl at the Heart of the World.**

Powers, Tim

Expiration Date.

Last Call.

Yarbro, Chelsea Quinn

Saint-Germain series.

> **Hotel Transylvania: A Novel of Forbidden Love.**
>
> **The Palace.**
>
> **Blood Games.**
>
> **Path of the Eclipse.**
>
> **Tempting Fate.**
>
> **The Saint-Germain Chronicles.** Linked stories.
>
> **Out of the House of Life.**
>
> **The Spider Glass.**

Darker Jewels.

Better in the Dark.

Vampire Stories of Chelsea Quinn Yarbro.

Mansions of Darkness. Incan Peru.

Writ in Blood.

A Flame in Byzantium. Featuring Saint-Germain's lover, Atta Olivia Clemens.

Crusader's Torch.

A Candle for D'Artagnan.

Fantasy Featuring Detection

As the lines between the genres increasingly waver and fade, some of the genres combine, to delightful result. The clever and witty Lord Darcy series is the archetype of this type of combination. Frequently creatures of dark fantasy, vampires, werewolves, mummies, and witches are featured in conjunction with detection.

Bacon-Smith, Camille

Eye of the Daemon.

Bowker, David

Featuring Yorkshire police detective Vernon Lavergne.

The Death Prayer.

The Butcher of Glastonbury.

Cook, Glen

Garrett, P.I. series.

Sweet Silver Blues.

Bitter Gold Hearts.

Cold Copper Tears.

Old Tin Sorrows.

Dread Brass Shadows.

Red Pewter Gods.

Davis, Brett

Hair of the Dog. An ex-cop and a reporter are on the hunt for whoever tore out the throats of the researchers who had just announced a cure for lycanthropy.

Garrett, Randall

Lord Darcy series.

Lord Darcy. Title of omnibus edition containing *Too Many Magicians*, *Murder and Magic*, and *Lord Darcy Investigates*.

Like Ian Fleming's James Bond, Lord Darcy refused to die with his creator and the series was continued by Michael Kurland with *Ten Little Wizards* and *A Study in Sorcery*.

Goulart, Ron

The Prisoner of Blackwood Castle. A detective of the Challenge International Detective Agency in a land of magic.

Green, Simon R.

Hawk and Fisher series.

Hamilton, Laurell K.

Featuring Anita Blake, Vampire Hunter.

Guilty Pleasures.

The Laughing Corpse.

Circus of the Damned.

The Lunatic Cafe.

Bloody Bones.

Killing Dance.

Burnt Offerings.

Hood, Daniel

Featuring sleuthing sorcerer Liam Rhenford and his dragon familiar.

Fanuilh.

Wizard's Heir.

Beggar's Banquet.

Scales of Justice.

Huff, Tanya

Featuring Vicki Nelson, former Toronto cop, now a PI.

Blood Price.

Blood Trail.

Blood Lines.

Blood Pact.

Blood Debt.

Hughart, Barry

Master Li series. Eighth-century China.

Bridge of Birds: A Novel of Ancient China That Never Was.

The Story of the Stone.

Eight Skilled Gentlemen.

Killough, Lee

Featuring Garreth Mikaelian, vampire and cop.

Blood Hunt.

Bloodlinks.

Kilworth, Garry D.

Angel. A pair of San Francisco detectives are out to find and stop a pyromaniac angel.

Lackey, Mercedes

Sacred Ground. Featuring Jennifer Talldeer, P. I. and shaman.

Four & Twenty Blackbirds. Featuring Constable Tal Rufen.

Diana Tregarde series.

Burning Water.

Children of the Night.

Jinx High.

Lethem, Jonathan

Gun, with Occasional Music. A noirish Crawford-Award winner.

MacAvoy, R. A.

Tea with the Black Dragon.

Twisting the Rope.

Murphy, Shirley Rousseau

Featuring Joe Grey, cat detective.

Cat on the Edge.

Cat Under Fire.

Cat Raise the Dead.

Rosenberg, Joel

D'Shai series.

D'Shai.

Hour of the Octopus.

Scott, Melissa, and Lisa Barnett

Point of Hopes. Astrology may help a couple of detectives find the many children who have recently gone missing in a medieval-like city.

Wolfe, Gene

Free Live Free.

Pandora by Holly Hollander.

Wrede, Patricia C.

Mairelon the Magician.

Magician's Ward.

Zambreno, Mary Frances

A Plague of Sorcerers.

Journeyman Wizard. A young adult series enjoyed by adult readers.

Romantic Fantasy

A major trend in the romance genre in the 1990s has been the infusion of fantasy. Time travel, supernatural beings, Faerie, and other fantasy tropes have been appearing liberally in romance novels. The combination of the genres is a delight to those who love both. This type is so popular that it has its own award, the Sapphire Award; a bibliography, *Enchanted Journeys Beyond the Imagination,* by Susan W. Bontly and Carol J. Sheridan (Blue Diamond Publications, 1996); and even a monthly print newsletter, *The Alternative Reality Romance Connection*, and a monthly online newsletter, *Science Fiction Romance,* at http://members.aol.com/sfreditor/index.htm (accessed 15 November 1999). Readers who delight in this combination of genres will find them listed in the romance chapter (Chapter 5).

Topics

The resources listed here are intended to broaden the reader's knowledge of the genre.

Anthologies

Anthologies are of particular importance because they showcase a broad range of styles and types. Many of the anthologies offer insightful essays, historical information, and informative commentary on trends and authors. The following is merely a taste of what is available. A more extensive list of anthologies is included in *Fluent in Fantasy* (Libraries Unlimited, 1999), which also lists selected short story collections by individual authors.

The short form of fiction has a long and rich tradition in the fantasy genre. The major awards have categories for short fiction, and qualification for membership in the Science Fiction and Fantasy Writers of America can be earned by publication of short stories. Many anthologies include science fiction stories as well as fantasy. Readers are advised to also check the anthologies listed in the science fiction chapter, Chapter 6.

Dziemianowicz, Stefan, Robert E. Weinberg, and Martin H. Greenberg, eds. *Famous Fantastic Mysteries: 30 Great Tales of Fantasy and Horror from the Classic Pulp Magazines "Famous Fantastic Mysteries" & "Fantastic Novels."* Grammercy, 1991.

Friesner, Esther, ed. *Chicks in Chainmail.* Pocket, 1995. A wildly popular, humorous anthology featuring swordswomen and other formidable females.

————. *Did You Say Chicks?* Baen, 1998. Short stories of sword-wielding warrior women by Elizabeth Moon, Jody Lynn Nye, Margaret Ball, Harry Turtledove, Esther Friesner, and others.

Gilliam, Richard, Martin H. Greenberg, and Edward E. Kramer, ed. *Grails: Quests, Visitations and Other Occurrences*. New American Library, 1994. Stories by Andre Norton, Jane Yolen, Gene Wolfe, Marion Zimmer Bradley, Alan Dean Foster, Orson Scott Card, Mercedes Lackey, Neil Gaiman, Gene Wolfe, Janny Wurts, Diana L. Paxson, and others explore the past and the future of legendary grails.

Griffith, Nicola, and Stephen Pagel, eds. *Bending the Landscape: Fantasy*. White Wolf Publishing, 1997. Gay and lesbian fantasy by Mark Shepherd, Holly Wade Matter, Kim Antieau, Mark W. Tiedemann, Simon Sheppard, J. A. Salmonson, Don Bassingthwaite, Ellen Kushner, Tanya Huff, Robin Wayne Bailey, and others.

Kushner, Ellen, Donald G. Keller, and Delia Sherman, eds. *The Horns of Elfland*. New American Library, 1997. Stories with a musical theme.

Lurie, Alison, ed. *The Book of Modern Fairy Tales*. Oxford University Press, 1993. One hundred and fifty years of fairy tales.

Scarborough, Elizabeth Ann, and Martin H. Greenberg. *Warrior Princesses*. DAW, 1998. Stories by Anne McCaffrey, Jane Yolen, Elizabeth Moon, and more.

Silverberg, Robert, ed. *The Fantasy Hall of Fame: The Definitive Collection of the Best Modern Fantasy Chosen by the Members of the Science Fiction and Fantasy Writers of America*. HarperPrism, 1998. Thirty stories first published between 1939 and 1990, selected by the membership of the Science Fiction and Fantasy Writers of America, offer a sampling of classic fantasy. The voting criteria are explained and the ranking of the stories is listed. The 15 stories receiving the most votes were "The Lottery," Shirley Jackson; "Jeffty Is Five," Harlan Ellison; "Unicorn Variations," Roger Zelazny; "Bears Discover Fire," Terry Bisson; "That Hell-Bound Train," Robert Bloch; "Come Lady Death," Peter S. Beagle; "Basileus," Robert Silverberg; "The Golem," Avram Davidson; "Buffalo Gals, Won't You Come Out Tonight," Ursula K. Le Guin; "Her Smoke Rose up Forever," James Tiptree, Jr. (not included in the anthology); "The Loom of Darkness," Jack Vance; "The Drowned Giant," J. G. Ballard; "The Detective of Dreams," Gene Wolfe; "The Jaguar Hunter," Lucius Shepard; and "The Compleat Werewolf," Anthony Boucher. The collection also includes 16 runners-up.

————. *Legends: Short Novels by the Masters of Modern Fantasy*. Tor, 1998. Stories by Stephen King, Terry Pratchett, Terry Goodkind, Orson Scott Card, Robert Silverberg, Ursula K. Le Guin, Tad Williams, George R. R. Martin, Anne McCaffrey, Raymond E. Feist, and Robert Jordan are a great introduction to current popular fantasy novelists.

Williams, A. Susan, and Richard Glyn Jones, eds. *The Penguin Book of Modern Fantasy by Women.* Penguin USA, 1997. World Fantasy Award. Thirty-eight stories written since 1941. Introduction by Joanna Russ. Authors included are Elizabeth Bowen, Shirley Jackson, Leigh Brackett, Daphne du Maurier, Leonora Carrington, Zenna Henderson, Muriel Spark, Anna Kavan, Anne McCaffrey, Joan Aiken, Hilary Bailey, Kit Reed, Josephine Saxton, Christine Brooke-Rose, Kate Wilhelm, Joanna Russ, P. D. James, James Tiptree, Jr., Margaret Atwood, Fay Weldon, Joyce Carol Oates, Vonda N. McIntyre, Lisa Tuttle, Tanith Lee, Ursula K. Le Guin, Angela Carter, Mary Gentle, Janet Frame, Zoe Fairbairns, Octavia E. Butler, Candas Jane Dorsey, Suniti Namjoshi, Suzy McKee Charnas, Carol Emshwiller, Lynda Rajan, L. A. Hall, Ann Oakley, and Lucy Sussex.

Anthology Series

The Best of Marion Zimmer Bradley's Fantasy Magazine. Nos. 1–2. 1994–1995. Warner Books. Edited by Marion Zimmer Bradley.

Catfantastic. Nos. 1–4. 1991– . DAW. Edited by Andre Norton and Martin H. Greenberg.

Full Spectrum. Nos. 1–5. Bantam. Editors have included Lou Aronica, Amy Stout, Betsy Mitchell, Shawna McCarthy, Tom Dupree, Janna Silverstein, and Jennifer Hershey. Fantasy, science fiction, and horror stories are included.

Nebula Awards: SFWA's Choices for the Best Science Fiction and Fantasy of the Year. 1966– . Harcourt Brace. No. 33. 1999. The annual anthology includes short pieces and excerpts of nominations for the year as well as essays. Editors have included Connie Willis, Pamela Sargent, James Morrow, George Zebrowski, Michael Bishop, Jack Dann, Poul Anderson, Ursula K. Le Guin, James Blish, Lloyd Biggle, Jr., James Gunn, Kate Wilhelm, Joe Haldeman, Brian Aldiss, Roger Zelazny, Clifford D. Simak, Isaac Asimov, Jerry Pournelle, Marta Randall, Robert Silverberg, Samuel R. Delany, Gordon R. Dickson, Frederik Pohl, Frank Herbert, and Damon Knight.

Starlight. Tor. Edited by Patrick Nielsen Hayden. The initial volume was the 1996 winner of the World Fantasy Award for Best Anthology. The second volume was published in 1998.

Sword and Sorceress. 1984– . DAW. Edited by Marion Zimmer Bradley. The 15th annual volume was published in 1998. Features women in heroic fantasy.

Xanadu. Nos. 1–3. 1994–1998. Tor. Original fantasy stories. Edited by Jane Yolen.

Year's Best Fantasy. 1988–1989. St. Martin's Press. Edited by Ellen Datlow and Terri Windling. Name changed to *Year's Best Fantasy and Horror.*

Year's Best Fantasy and Horror. 1990– . St. Martin's Press. Edited by Ellen Datlow and Terri Windling. The 12th annual collection was published in 1999, the numbering continuing from the previous title, *Year's Best Fantasy.*

Year's Best Fantasy Stories. 1974–1988. DAW. Lin Carter edited the first six volumes and Arthur W. Saha the last eight.

Bibliographies and Biographies

Ashley, Michael, and William Contento. *The Supernatural Index: A Listing of Fantasy, Supernatural, Occult, Weird, and Horror Anthologies.* Greenwood, 1995. More than 21,000 stories by over 7,700 authors in more than 2,100 anthologies are indexed.

Barron, Neil. *Fantasy Literature.* Garland, 1990. A scholarly historical treatment of the genre.

Barron, Neil, ed. *What Fantastic Fiction Do I Read Next? A Reader's Guide to Recent Fantasy, Horror and Science Fiction.* Gale, 1998. Non-critical, it lists books released in the specified time span of 1989–1997. Characters, settings, and key worlds are indexed.

Bloom, Harold, ed. *Classic Fantasy Writers.* Chelsea House, 1994.

———. *Modern Fantasy Writers.* Chelsea House, 1995.

Bontly, Susan W., and Carol J. Sheridan. *Enchanted Journeys Beyond the Imagination, Vols. 1 and 2: An Annotated Bibliography of Fantasy Futuristic Supernatural and Time Travel Romances.* Blue Diamond, 1996.

Burgess, Michael. *Reference Guide to Science Fiction, Fantasy, and Horror.* Libraries Unlimited, 1992.

Cawthorn, James, and Michael Moorcock. *Fantasy: The 100 Best Books.* Carroll & Graf, 1991.

Hall, Hal W., ed. *Science Fiction and Fantasy Reference Index, 1985–1991: An International Author and Subject Index to History and Criticism.* Libraries Unlimited, 1993. Definitive listings of secondary materials.

———. *Science Fiction and Fantasy Reference Index, 1992–1995: An International Subject and Author Index to History and Criticism.* Libraries Unlimited, 1997. Definitive listings of secondary materials.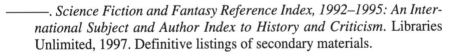

Herald, Diana Tixier. *Fluent in Fantasy: A Guide to Reading Interests.* Libraries Unlimited, 1999. The first readers' advisory tool focusing solely on fantasy, this is the definitive guide to the genre. The book describes thousands of fantasy titles and categorizes them into 15 subgenres (e.g., sword and sorcery, humor, shared world, dark fantasy). It also includes a historical background of the genre, tips for readers' advisors, a recommended core list for libraries, and lists of resources. Award winners and titles that appeal to teens are noted and there are author/title and subject indexes.

Perret, Patti. *The Faces of Fantasy.* Tor, 1996. Renowned photographer Perret offers fantasy lovers a treat in this visual feast of beloved authors. Photographed in various locales and settings, each portrait searches for an inner vision of the over 100 writers featured. Terri Windling provides a fascinating historical overview of fantasy fiction in the introduction.

Pringle, David. *Modern Fantasy: The Hundred Best Novels. An English Language Selection, 1946-1987*. Peter Bedrick Books, 1989.

Pringle, David, ed. *St. James Guide to Fantasy Writers*. St. James Press, 1996.

Waggoner, Diana. *The Hills of Faraway: A Guide to Fantasy*. Atheneum, 1978. An eclectic selection of 996 titles, critically annotated.

Encyclopedias

Clute, John, and John Grant. *The Encyclopedia of Fantasy*. St. Martin's Press, 1997. The first, only, and definitive encyclopedia of fantasy. This is a must-have for every serious fantasy collection. It has over a million words in 4,000 entries. Everything you ever wanted to know about fantasy from the dawn of time to 1995 is included. Not only covering the written word, it also takes on movies, television, art, and live performances that are fantasy based. Awards and conventions are listed, as are themes and motifs.

Guides and Atlases

These delightful books will enchant all fans of fantasy, and many of science fiction, for they describe and map the lands that readers' imaginations have made real.

Anthony, Piers, and Jody Lynn Nye. *Piers Anthony's Visual Guide to Xanth*. Avon Books, 1989. A look at the geography, locations, flora, and fauna of the magical land of Xanth.

Barlowe, Wayne Douglas. *Barlowe's Guide to Fantasy*. HarperPrism, 1996. Fifty fantasy creatures and characters brought to life by illustrator Wayne Barlowe. Very much as in a study by a naturalist, essential facts are given about each creature, including language, weaponry, dietary customs, and if applicable, favorite prey.

Jordan, Robert, and Teresa Patterson. *The World of Robert Jordan's The Wheel of Time*. Tor, 1997. A guide to the popular best-selling series. It serves as an atlas, with maps of the world, the Seanchan Empire, the nations of the Covenant of the Ten Nations, and historical maps of the nations as they were when Artur Paendrag Tanreall began his rise to legend. It also includes illustrations of landscapes, objects of power, and portraits of the central characters.

Manguel, Alberto, and Gianni Guadalupi. *The Dictionary of Imaginary Places*. Updated edition. Harcourt Brace, 1999. A tour of more than 1,200 fantasy realms.

Nye, Jody Lynn. *The Dragonlover's Guide to Pern*. 2d ed. Del Rey, 1997. A guide to the people, places, and creatures of Pern.

Post, J. B., comp. *An Atlas of Fantasy*. Rev. ed. Ballantine, 1979. Many of the maps are for works cited in this guide.

History and Criticism

In addition to the following works, material on fantasy can be found in some histories and criticisms of science fiction.

Hall, Hal W., ed. *Science Fiction and Fantasy Reference Index, 1985–1991: An International Author and Subject Index to History and Criticism.* Libraries Unlimited, 1993.

Le Guin, Ursula K. *The Language of the Night: Essays on Fantasy and Science Fiction.* HarperCollins, 1992. On the writing and reading of fantasy and science fiction—an eloquent statement.

MacRae, Cathi Dunn. *Presenting Young Adult Fantasy Fiction.* Twayne, 1998. Discusses what young adults really read and why, but because in fantasy young adults and adults read the same things, this is a book for all serious fantasy collections. Biographies of Terry Brooks, Jane Yolen, Barbara Hambly, and Meredith Ann Pierce provide more in-depth fantasy analysis.

Magill, Frank N., ed. *Survey of Modern Fantasy Literature.* Salem Press, 1983. 5 vols.

Sobczak, A. J., and T. A. Shippey, eds. *Magill's Guide to Science Fiction and Fantasy Literature.* Salem Press, 1996. 4 vols. *Volume 1. The Absolute at Large—Dragonsbane; Volume 2. Dream—The Lensman Series; Volume 3. Lest Darkness Fall—So Love Returns; Volume 4. Software and Wetware—Zotz!*

Journals

Fantasy is most commonly discussed with science fiction and often with horror. For more journals covering fantasy fiction, consult the science fiction chapter, Chapter 6. The following deal specifically with fantasy.

Marion Zimmer Bradley's Fantasy Magazine. P.O. Box 249, Berkeley, CA 94701. Published quarterly, it features short stories, artwork, and author interviews.

Realms of Fantasy. 11305 Sunset Hills Rd., Reston, VA 20190. Published bimonthly, it features reviews of books, television, and games. Features include discussions of the genre by esteemed authors of fantasy, including Terri Windling and Jane Yolen. Many of its readers purchase it for the short stories by new and established authors.

Online Resources

Online resources specific to fantasy are listed here. Additional listings of sites that group fantasy with science fiction are listed in the science fiction chapter (Chapter 6).

Fantasy Finder, http://www.hoh.se/fantasyfinder/ (accessed 20 January 2000)

Feminist Science Fiction, Fantasy, & Utopia, http://www.wenet.net/~lquilter/femsf/ (accessed 20 January 2000)

Fluent in Fantasy, http://www.sff.net/people/dherald/ (accessed 20 January 2000), features hyperlinks to all sites listed in the book of the same title as well as listing new sites of interest to fantasy readers.

Future Fantasy Bookstore includes lists and links to sample chapters: http://futfan.com/ (accessed 20 January 2000)

International Association for the Fantastic in the Arts, http://ebbs.english.vt.edu/iafa/iafa.home.html (accessed 20 January 2000)

Los Angeles Public Library Readers Advisory Fantasy Lists, http://www.colapublib.org/services/advisory/fantasy/fantasy.html (accessed 20 January 2000)

Reader's Robot Fantasy Page, http://www.tnrdlib.bc.ca/fa-menu.html (accessed 20 January 2000)

Recommended Fantasy Author List, http://www.sff.net/people/Amy.Sheldon/listcont.htm (accessed 20 January 2000)

Sidewise Awards for Alternate History, http://www.skatecity.com/ah/sidewise/ (accessed 20 January 2000)

Publishers

Ace is one of the three science fiction and fantasy imprints of Penguin Putnam.

Arbor House is known for its fine anthologies.

Avon Eos is the new imprint for science fiction and fantasy, replacing Avon's defunct Aspect imprint. They do list whether a title is science fiction or fantasy on their Web site.

Baen is a leader in publishing science fiction and fantasy.

Ballantine is the venerable granddaddy of fantasy publishing and is closely linked with the development of the genre. Ballantine now publishes fantasy under the Del Rey imprint.

Carroll & Graf publishes the occasional fantasy title.

DAW was started by Donald A. Wolheim and is now a fantasy and science fiction imprint of Penguin Putnam.

Del Rey is an imprint of Random House that publishes fantasy and science fiction.

Gollancz is the British publisher that publishes Terry Pratchett and others.

HarperCollins publishes a great deal of fantasy in Great Britain, including the authors J. R. R. Tolkien, David Eddings, and R. A. Salvatore.

HarperPrism is the fantasy and science fiction imprint of HarperCollins in America.

Headline is a British publisher of fantasy and science fiction.

Knopf published the Philip Pullman series His Dark Materials.

Morrow publishes an occasional fantasy title.

NESFA Press. The New England Science Fiction Association publishes a small number of out-of-print classics and also works by guests honored at the Boskone convention.

Orb. An imprint of Tor, it publishes fantasy and science fiction in trade paperback editions.

Orbit is a British imprint of Little, Brown that publishes L. E. Modesitt, Alan Dean Foster, and others.

Penguin publishes fantasy under the Ace, DAW, and Roc imprints.

Roc is one of the imprints of Penguin Putnam that publishes several fantasy novels a year.

Science Fiction Book Club is where many fans get their information about new titles. They often publish omnibus editions and are also a source for paperback originals in hardcover.

Simon and Schuster publishes the occasional fantasy title.

Spectra is a fantasy and science fiction imprint of Random House.

St. Martin's Press is affiliated with Tor and publishes a limited number of fantasy titles.

Tor. Selected 11 years in a row as favorite publisher in the Locus Poll, Tor publishes more fantasy and science fiction than any other publisher. Looking at the Tor catalog is a must for good collection development in fantasy.

TSR is the game company that made a big splash with DragonLance and is now an imprint of Wizards of the Coast.

Underwood-Miller is a small publisher that has published Jack Vance and others.

Viking has published fantasy in the past, but currently Ace, DAW, and Roc, sister imprints in the Penguin Putnam family, are publishing fantasy.

White Wolf publishes cutting-edge fantasy; it is a game company.

Wizards of the Coast is the new owner of TSR and their best-selling DragonLance series.

Mark V. Ziesing is a bookseller who also sometimes publishes. He has been nominated to the Locus Poll in his capacity as a publisher.

Organizations and Conventions

The British Fantasy Society. Established in 1971 and sponsors the annual FantasyCon. They have a Web site at http://www.herebedragons.co.uk/bfs/index.htm (accessed 20 January 2000). FantasyCon XXIII was held in 1998 in Birmingham. BFS also provides a list of recommended books consisting of novels and anthologies nominated for the British Fantasy Awards.

The Mythopoeic Society. Devoted to the study, discussion, and enjoyment of myth and fantasy literature. They hold an annual conference called Mythcon. The 30th annual conference was held in Milwaukee, Wisconsin, in 1999. The Mythopoeic Society maintains a Web site at http://www.mythsoc.org/ (accessed 20 January 2000). The address of the corresponding secretary as of 1999 is:

> Edith Crowe, Corresponding Secretary
> The Mythopoeic Society
> P.O. Box 320486
> San Francisco, CA 94132-0486
> E-mail: ecrowe@email.sjsu.edu

Science Fiction & Fantasy Writers of America. Founded in 1965 by Damon Knight, who also served as the first president. Originally the Science Fiction Writers of America, the name was changed to include fantasy in 1992, better reflecting the intertwined relationship of the two genres. Membership is open only to writers of published science fiction or fantasy.

The Tolkien Society. Maintains a Web site at http://www.tolkiensociety.org/ (accessed 20 January 2000). The society was founded in 1969 to further interest in the works of J. R. R. Tolkien.

World Fantasy Convention. Maintains a Web site at http://www.worldfantasy.org/index.html (accessed 20 January 2000). It lists upcoming conventions. The 25th World Fantasy Convention was held in Providence, Rhode Island, in 1999. It is slated for Corpus Christi, Texas, in 2000 and Montreal, Quebec, in 2001.

> World Fantasy Convention 2000
> P.O. Box 27277
> Austin, TX 78755

Attendance at the convention is limited to 1,000 people, but supporting memberships are also available. Members nominate for the World Fantasy Awards but a panel of judges makes the final decisions.

Awards

The most up-to-date information on awards can be found on the World Wide Web at:

http://www.sfsite.com/isfdb/award.html (accessed 20 January 2000)

http://www.dpsinfo.com/awardweb (accessed 20 January 2000)

Both sites list awards of particular interest to fantasy readers.

Fantasy Awards

The following is a listing of fantasy awards that continue to be given. The winners are listed in *Fluent in Fantasy* (Libraries Unlimited, 1999), as are the winners of now-defunct awards.

August Derleth Award. The British Fantasy Award, often referred to as the August Derleth Award, is selected by members of the British Fantasy Society and attendees of the annual FantasyCon. The close relationship between fantasy and horror is indicated by the number of horror novels awarded this fantasy prize. Several of the books that have received this award are covered in the horror chapter (Chapter 8).

Locus Awards. Readers of *Locus* are annually given a chance to select their favorites in a magazine poll. Because *Locus* is to science fiction, fantasy, and horror what *Billboard* is to music and *Variety* to acting, the poll really reflects what serious readers of fantasy like. The poll has been taken annually since 1971. Ballots are only accepted from subscribers, and results are published in the July or August issue. An online resource listing nominees, winners, and results is at http://www.sff.net/locus/poll/index.html (accessed 15 November 1999). Poll results are given in the categories of SF novel, fantasy novel, horror/dark fantasy novel, first novel, novella, novelette, short story, collection, anthology, nonfiction, art book, editor, magazine, book publisher, and artist. In 1994 and 1990, dark fantasy was not listed as a category even though horror was. Although the poll has been conducted since 1971, the best fantasy novel category first appeared in 1980. Prior to that, fantasy was included in the novel category.

Mythopoeic Award. The Mythopoeic Award is given at the annual Mythcon. The winner is chosen by a committee of Mythopoeic Society members. In 1992 the society divided the fantasy award into categories of fantasy for children and for adults.

Sidewise Awards. "The Sidewise Awards for Alternate History were conceived in late 1995 to honor the best 'genre' publications of the year. The award takes its name from Murray Leinster's 1934 short story 'Sidewise in Time,' in which a strange storm causes portions of Earth to swap places with their analogs from other timelines."—Sidewise award Web site. http://www.skatecity.com/ah/sidewise/ (accessed 20 January 2000).

William L. Crawford Memorial Award. A panel of judges awards this prize at the International Association for the Fantastic in the Arts annual convention for the best first fantasy published during the previous 18 months.

World Fantasy Award. Members of the annual World Fantasy Convention may nominate, but the winners are selected by a panel. The panel also awards the World Fantasy Life Achievement Award to an individual.

D's Fantasy Picks

Bertin, Joanne. *The Last Dragonlord.*

Rowling, J. K. Harry Potter series.

Springer, Nancy. *Fair Peril.*

Windling, Terri. *The Wood Wife.*

Wrede, Patricia C. *Magician's Ward.*

Chapter 8

Horror

"Where there is no imagination there is no horror."

—Sherlock Holmes, in Sir Arthur Conan Doyle, "A Study in Scarlet" (1887)

"you want to know whether I believe in ghosts
of course I do not believe in them if you had known as many of them as I have
you would not believe in them either"

—Don Marquis, *Ghosts in Archy and Mehitabel* (1927)

That which haunts our nightmares is the stuff of horror. Filled with monsters, ghouls, vampires, and hellish creatures, horror creates places where werewolves and psychotic killers lurk in the shadows. It is a journey into the unknown and the forbidden. Call it morbid fascination, call it forbidden pleasures, or call it the power of our dark side, but whatever it's called, horror's appeal cannot be denied. Stephen King's works continue to top best-seller lists and young adults now show an avid interest in the genre, which will likely ensure its longevity. The immense popularity of such horror films as *The Blair Witch Project* and *The Sixth Sense* with young and old audiences alike evidences the pervasiveness and strength of the genre in our culture.

Part of horror's appeal is that it piques the fascination and curiosity of its readers. The reader embarks on a quest to discover how the protagonist overcomes the demons that bedevil him. Like adventure, horror has the ability to provoke an adrenaline rush, much like riding a roller coaster or jumping from an airplane. Why people read horror has been endlessly debated; theories have been posed that range from the suggestion that these readers are atypical individuals who enjoy experiencing fear and disgust, to the idea that the reader is fascinated by the anomaly of the monstrous events and reads despite the fear and disgust. This writer suggests that readers who choose horror do so because they enjoy the thrill of unknown dangers (from a safe vantage point, safely ensconced with a book) and because many horror stories are compellingly well told. In fact, the paragon of horror writers, Stephen King, is arguably the best storyteller of our time.

Horror has close links with many of the other genres. In works of literary history and criticism as well as early anthologies, it is often grouped with mysteries and gothic tales. Often the horrific elements in horror are scientifically derived (e.g., the monster created from science gone astray), linking it with science fiction.

Mary Wollstoncraft Shelley has been called the mother of science fiction because the creation of Frankenstein's monster is definitely a tale of science gone wrong, but it is also the original man-made monster tale, and many readers consider it a tale of horror rather than science fiction. Bram Stoker's *Dracula* has sometimes been called the first horror novel; in fact, when the Horror Writers Association was looking for a name for their awards, they selected Bram Stoker's name.

The horror novels dealing with the supernatural and paranormal have a close link with fantasy. Much of the background and scholarly material on horror is found in articles and monographs dealing with fantasy. Horror novels even frequently win the top fantasy awards. The British Fantasy Award is called the August Derleth Award, after a writer who was known for his weird tales or dark fantasy that can easily be labeled horror. Romance and historical fiction also can be linked to horror. Gothic tales appear in both romance and horror, and at the end of the 1990s, one of the hottest trends in romance fiction was the paranormal romance, often featuring vampires or werewolves, heretofore denizens of horror fiction. Some atmospherically creepy horror novels have fully realized and meticulously detailed historical settings, thus giving them a relationship to historical fiction.

While horror has always been present in literature, it wasn't considered a separate genre until recently (relative to the other genres). In November 1985 the first meeting of what was to become the Horror Writers Association was held. Some contend that the first horror author was Charles Brockden Brown, who wrote *Wieland, or the Transformation* (1798), in which religious mania incites murder, disembodied voices speak, and a man spontaneously combusts. H. P. Lovecraft, who died in 1937, has often been considered the father of modern horror fiction with his weird tales of the old gods and the Cthulhu mythos.

When advising the reader it is important, as always, to come to an understanding of the individual's personal definition of horror. Some readers consider only fiction involving the paranormal to be horror, while others enjoy reading about human monsters such as Hannibal "the cannibal" Lector. It is helpful to keep in mind that many of the qualities readers like in horror may also be found in the other genres mentioned above.

Many of the horror stories currently being published focus on psychological horror, with the terrors often having an explicable cause, however deranged the mind from which the horror emanates. For the much-imitated Lovecraft school of horror, see "Cosmic Paranoia" (p. 431). The possibilities for inexplicable acts are limited only by the author's dark imagination.

Themes and Types

Classic Authors

Brown, Charles Brockden
    Wieland, or the Transformation (1798).

Hawthorne, Nathaniel
    The House of the Seven Gables (1851).

Hodgson, William Hope
    The House of the Borderland (1908).

Irving, Washington
    "The Legend of Sleepy Hollow" (1819).

Kipling, Rudyard
    Phantoms and Fantasies.

Lovecraft, H. P.
    The Shadow over Innsmouth (1936).
    At the Mountains of Madness.
    The Dunwich Horror.
    The Lurking Fear.
    The Shuttered Room.
    The Tomb.

Machen, Arthur
    Tales of Horror and the Supernatural.

O'Brien, Fitz-James
    The Supernatural Tales of Fitz-James O'Brien.

Poe, Edgar Allan
    Tales of the Grotesque and Arabesque (1840).
    The Pit and the Pendulum (1842).
    18 Best Stories by Edgar Allan Poe.

Saki
    Classic horror short stories:
        "The Interlopers."
        "The Open Window."

Shelley, Mary Wollstonecraft
    Frankenstein; or, The Modern Prometheus (1818).

Stoker, Bram
>**Dracula** (1897).

Wells, H. G.
>**The Invisible Man** (1897).
>**"The Truth About Pyecraft."**

Wilde, Oscar
>**The Picture of Dorian Gray** (1891).

The Occult and Supernatural

In this category are stories of the unseen and malevolent, the macabre and ghostly: poltergeists; girls transformed by night into bats, cats, monkeys, or snakes; souls being stolen or sold to the devil; minds being read or invaded.

The occult embraces all mysterious things beyond human understanding. The term is also used to describe those sciences, often appearing in horror literature, that involve knowledge and use of the supernatural. The supernatural encompasses all things existing or occurring outside humanity's normal experience. A supernatural event cannot be explained by any known force of nature. Accompanying a belief in supernatural forces is the belief that these forces intervene to control nature and the universe and that these forces are above ordinary nature. Naturally, then, it follows that supernatural beings and powers exist that are active in the ordinary world. A person sensitive to such forces beyond the physical world is called a psychic or medium. The term *psychic* refers to happenings beyond natural (or known) physical processes; that is, a psychic phenomenon supersedes the physical laws of nature and, therefore, must be caused by spiritual or supernatural agencies.

The following list includes a miscellany of themes and presents authors important in this subgenre.

Aiken, Joan
>**The Windcreep Weepers.**
>**The Green Flash.**

Anderson, Michael Falconer
>**The Covenant.**

Andrews, V. C.
>**Flowers in the Attic.**
>**Petals in the Wind.**
>**Seeds of Yesterday.**

All are macabre, gothic soap operas.

Anthony, Piers
>**Shade of the Tree.** Supernatural.

Barker, Clive
    Weaveworld.

Bloch, Robert
    Psycho.

Block, Lawrence
    Ariel. Evil child.

Bradbury, Ray
    The October Country.
    Something Wicked This Way Comes.

Bradley, Marion Zimmer
    The Inheritor. Poltergeist.

Campbell, Ramsey
    Incarnate.
    Hungry Moon.
    Midnight Sun.

Coyne, John
    Hobgoblin. Features a fantasy role-playing game akin to Dungeons and Dragons.

Due, Tananarive
    My Soul to Keep. Immortality.

Farris, John
    Fiends.

Feist, Raymond E.
    Faerie Tale.

Gannett, Lewis
    The Living One.

Grant, Charles L.
    The Sound of Midnight.
    In a Dark Dream. Children with supernatural powers.

Herbert, James
    The Dark.
    The Spear.

King, Francis
>**Voices in an Empty Room.** Paranormal communication.

Koontz, Dean R.
>**Darkfall.** Voodoo.

Laski, Marghanita
>**The Victorian Chaise Longue.** Nightmare.

Leiber, Fritz
>**Our Lady of Darkness.**

Little, Bentley
>**The Ignored.**

Masterton, Graham
>**The Manitou.**
>**Revenge of the Manitou.**
>**Burial.**

McCammon, Robert R.
>**Usher's Passing.** Descendants of Poe's Usher family.

Mills, James
>**The Power.**

Raucher, Herman
>**Maynard's House.**

Saul, John
>**Shadows.**

Sherman, Nick
>**The Surrogate.**

Slade, Michael
>**Ghoul.**

Slater, Philip
>**How I Saved the World.** Psychic.

Straub, Peter
>**Floating Dragon.**

Strieber, Whitley
>**Black Magic.** Telepathy.

Woods, Stuart
>**Under the Lake.**

Ghosts

The ghost, often haunting a house or a person, is a pervasive presence in the horror genre. Most ghosts are malevolent, but some are sad or plaintive. The crux of these tales may be the answer to the question, Why can't the dead rest?

Ansa, Tina McElroy
  Baby of the Family.
  The Hand I Fan With.

Ashe, Rosalind
  Moths.

Brody, Jean
  A Coven of Women.

Disch, Thomas M.
  The Businessman: A Tale of Terror.

Fraser, Anthea
  Whistler's Lane.

Herbert, James
  Haunted.
  Ghosts of Sleath.

Hynd, Noel
  A Room for the Dead.

Jackson, Shirley
  The Haunting of Hill House.

James, Henry
  The Turn of the Screw.

James, Peter
  Possession.

Lofts, Norah
  Gad's Hall.
  The Haunting of Gad's Hall.

Michaels, Barbara
  Here I Stay.
  The Walker in the Shadows.
  Ammie Come Home.

Ghosts haunt these novels of romantic suspense.

Saul, John
The Unloved.

Ghost Short Stories

Ghosts have long been popular in the short form.

Blackwood, Algernon
Best Ghost Stories.

Bowen, Elizabeth
The Demon Lover and Other Stories.

Coppard, A. E.
Fearful Pleasures.

Cox, Michael, and R. A. Gilbert, eds.
Victorian Ghost Stories: An Oxford Anthology.
12 Victorian Ghost Stories.
The Oxford Book of Twentieth-Century Ghost Stories.
The Oxford Book of English Ghost Stories.

Dalby, Richard, ed.
The Mammoth Book of Ghost Stories.
Modern Ghost Stories by Eminent Women Writers.

Davies, Robertson
High Spirits.

De La Mare, Walter
The Wind Blows Over.

Dickens, Charles
Charles Dickens' Christmas Ghost Stories.

Dunsany, Lord
God, Men and Ghosts.

Greenberg, Martin H., ed.
Civil War Ghosts.

James, M. R.
Ghost Stories of an Antiquary.

LeFanu, J. S.
Ghost Stories and Mysteries.
Best Ghost Stories of J. S. LeFanu.

Leithauser, Brad, ed.
    The Norton Book of Ghost Stories.

Lindley, Charles
    The Ghost Book of Charles Lindley, Viscount Halifax.

McSherry, Frank D.
    Great American Ghost Stories.

Munby, A. N. L.
    The Alabaster Hand and Other Ghost Stories.

Onions, Oliver
    The First Book of Ghost Stories: Widdershins. Includes "The Beckoning Fair One," *the* classic ghost story.

Wakefield, H. Russell
    The Best Ghost Stories of H. Russell Wakefield. The author required that a ghost story should "bring upon you the odd, insinuating little sensation that a number of small creatures are simultaneously camping on your scalp and sprinkling ice-water down your back-bone" (Genreflecting, 2d ed., 1986).

Walter, Elizabeth
    Dead Woman and Other Haunting Experiences.
    In the Mist and Other Uncanny Encounters.
    The Sin-Eater and Other Scientific Impossibilities.

Young, Richard Alan, and Judy Dockrey Young, eds.
    Ghost Stories from the American Southwest.

Cosmic Paranoia

Sometimes called weird tales and categorized as fantasy, the mythology created by H. P. Lovecraft, with its malevolent life-force, nightmares, monsters, and "The Great Old Ones," has had an important influence on horror literature. This list includes the works of Lovecraft and some of his followers.

Berglund, Edward P., ed. *The Disciples of Cthulhu,* 2d rev. ed. Wizards Attic, 1996. An anthology of stories by followers of Lovecraft. The editor describes the Cthulhu Mythos as "a malign pantheon, including the octopoid Cthulhu, that lurk practically everywhere, and that any mortal mixing with them is going to end up dead, mad or worse."

Bloch, Robert
    Strange Eons.

Campbell, Ramsey, ed. *New Tales of the Cthulhu Mythos*. Arkham, 1980. Includes tales written in the manner of Lovecraft.

Koontz, Dean R.
Phantoms.

Lovecraft, H. P.
At the Mountains of Madness.

The Dunwich Horror.

The Lurking Fear.

The Shuttered Room.

The Tomb.

"All my tales are based on the fundamental premise that common human laws and emotions have no validity or significance in the cosmos-at-large." Lovecraft created an entire mythology, the Cthulhu Mythos, and defined it as "the fundamental lore or legend that this world was inhabited at one time by another race who, in practicing black magic, lost their foothold and were expelled, yet live on outside, ever ready to take possession of this earth again" (Genreflecting, 2d ed., 1986). The publisher Arkham House is named for Lovecraft's fantasy land (for a map, see Post's *An Atlas of Fantasy*).

Lumley, Brian
Demogorgon.

Titus Crow series.

The Burrowers Beneath.

The Transition of Titus Crow.

The Clock of Dreams.

Spawn of the Winds.

In the Moons of Borea.

Elysia.

The Coming of Cthulhu.

Dreamlands series.

Hero of Dreams.

Ship of Dreams.

Mad Moon of Dreams.

Iced on Aran.

Schreffler, Philip A. *The H. P. Lovecraft Companion*. Greenwood, 1977. Summaries of stories and an "Encyclopedia of Characters and Monsters" of the Cthulhu Mythos.

Turner, Jim, ed. *Cthulhu 2000: A Lovecraftian Anthology*. Arkham, 1995. Includes, among others, "The Barrens," by F. Paul Wilson; "Pickman's Modem," by Lawrence Watt-Evans; "Shaft Number 247," by Basil Copper; "The Adder," by Fred Chappell; "Fat Face," by Michael Shea; "The Big Fish," by Kim Newman;

"H.P.L.," by Gahan Wilson; "The Shadow on the Doorstep," by James P. Blaylock; "Lord of the Land," by Gene Wolfe; "The Faces at Pine Dunes," by Ramsey Campbell; "On the Slab," by Harlan Ellison; and "Views of Mt. Fuji, by Hokusai," by Roger Zelazny.

————. *Eternal Lovecraft: The Persistence of HPL in Popular Culture.* Golden Gryphon Press, 1998. Eighteen short stories by Stephen King, Robert Charles Wilson, Fritz Lieber, Gene Wolfe, Harlan Ellison, Nancy A. Collins, and others.

Weinberg, Robert E., and Martin H. Greenberg, eds. *Lovecraft's Legacy.* Tor, 1990. Original horror tales in honor of Lovecraft's centennial.

Stephen King

Stephen King's first novel was published in 1973, and he quickly became *the* modern name defining the horror genre. Books he wrote under the name Richard Bachman are now published under his own name. His horror novels are best sellers and generate long reserve lists in libraries. They have been made into movies and television miniseries, and many of them are also available in audio format on cassette tapes. Other authors whom readers of King like include Dean Koontz and Robert R. McCammon.

Demonic Possession and Exorcism

The taking over of an innocent mind by a demon or ghost, sometimes through domination by a psychotic living person, is one of the most terrifying themes in folklore. Belief in possession is widespread and many religions have rituals for exorcising the evil spirits. The following listing is selective, as several very popular modern prototypes have led to seemingly endless imitations. (See also "Mind Control.")

Blatty, William
The Exorcist.

Bloch, Robert
Lori.

Campbell, Ramsey
The Parasite.

Coyne, John
The Piercing.
The Searing.

De Felitta, Frank
Golgatha Falls.

Farris, John
Son of the Endless Night.

Household, Geoffrey
The Sending.

Levin, Ira
Rosemary's Baby.
Son of Rosemary.

Mitchell, Mary Ann
Drawn to the Grave.

Ross, Clarissa
Satan Whispers.

Strieber, Whitley
Unholy Fire.

Thompson, Gene
Lupe.

Walton, Evangeline
Witch House.

Haunted Houses

A house possessed is only a tiny bit less terrifying than a mind possessed. Haunted houses have long been a staple in the horror genre. What town does not feature a haunted house as a Halloween fund-raising project? The following tales tell of dealings with homes or lodgings that display malevolence.

Amis, Kingsley
The Green Man.

Brite, Poppy Z.
Drawing Blood.

Campbell, Ramsey
Nazareth Hill. A haunted apartment complex. "It is said that the truth shall set you free. In Nazareth Hill, the truth brings captivity and death."—publisher's comments in catalog

Herbert, James
Haunted.

The Magic Cottage.

Jackson, Shirley
The Haunting of Hill House. Four people and a haunted mansion.

King, Stephen

The Shining. In an isolated Rocky Mountain hotel, a writer, the father of a psychic son, is being driven insane by forces of evil.

Wilde, Oscar

The Centerville Ghost.

Satanism, Demonology, and Black Magic

Worshipping the devil, pacts with the devil, raising the devil, hauntings by demons, transmigration of souls, magicians, and black magic: The diversity of topics in this category is frightening.

Bester, Alfred

Golem 100.

Blish, James

Black Easter. Demons are released from hell to prey on the world.

Bontly, Thomas

Celestial Chess.

Campbell, Ramsey

Obsession.

Collier, John

Of Demons and Darkness.

Garton, Roy

Crucifax Autumn.

Herbert, James

Moon. A psychic computer expert shares a mind link with a monstrously evil killer.

King, Stephen, and Peter Straub

The Talisman.

Levin, Ira

Rosemary's Baby. A young woman's dream apartment turns into a nightmare when she is raped and impregnated by Satan.

Masterton, Graham

The Hell Candidate.

Spellman, Cathy Cash

Bless the Child.

Stewart, Fred Mustard
  The Mephisto Waltz.

Straczynski, J. Michael
  Demon Light.

Straub, Peter
  Shadowland.

Talbot, Michael
  The Bog.

Thompson, Gene
  Lupe.

Wellman, Manly Wade
  The School of Darkness.
  The Old Gods Waken.

Wheatley, Dennis
  The Devil Rides Out.
  The Satanist.
  Strange Conflict.
  To the Devil a Daughter.
  Gateway to Hell.
  They Used Dark Forces.

Witches and Warlocks

Witches often appear in the historical romance, but usually as secondary characters. In the following books, the witch and the warlock are persons of reality, in the present as well as in the past, and they may be practitioners of either white or black witchcraft.

Buchan, John
  Witch Wood.

Copper, Basil
  Not After Nightfall.

Curtis, Peter (pseudonym of Norah Lofts)
  The Devil's Own.

Gunn, David
  The Magicians. A private investigator, Casey, takes on a case involving black magicians, witches, and warlocks.

Hamilton, Jessica
Elizabeth.

Harris, Marilyn
The Conjurers.

Heidish, Marcy
The Torching.

Leiber, Fritz
Conjure Wife. Behind every great man is a witch.

Rice, Anne
The Witching Hour.

Lasher.

Updike, John
The Witches of Eastwick. Three small-town New England witches in the 1960s. "A wicked entertainment with lots (and lots) of sex."—*The New Republic*

Warner, Sylvia Townsend
Lolly Willowes. A genteel classic. Witchcraft without horror; a witch's coven in an English village in this century.

Monsters

Monstrous creations by a freakish nature—taking unnatural form from any of the elements (water, earth, air), plants, or animals—abound in horror fiction.

Clegg, Douglas
The Halloween Man.

Herbert, James
The Rats.

Domain. Mutant animals in London after a nuclear attack.

Joyce, Graham
The Tooth Fairy.

Koontz, Dean
Watchers. A genetically engineered monster escapes from a secret laboratory.

Shelley, Mary Wollstonecraft
Frankenstein; or, The Modern Prometheus. First published in 1818. May be considered as part of science fiction (e.g., androids, mad scientist). *Forrest J. Ackerman's World of Science Fiction* (General Publishing Group, 1997) devotes 30 pages to discussion of the 250 editions of this book and to the countless spinoffs, from movies to toys.

Stevenson, Robert Louis

The Strange Case of Dr. Jekyll and Mr. Hyde. First published in 1886. The drug and psychological aspects were also influential in science fiction.

Wiesel, Elie

The Golem: The Story of a Legend.

Vampires

Those restless undead who escape their graves at night to drink the blood of innocent sleepers are stock folklore figures, now largely identified with Bram Stoker's Count Dracula. Although there has been a recent trend toward making the vampire legend humorous, most examples are macabre if not horrifying. Some vampires, instead of going after the blood of their victims, covet their minds or souls. Lichtenberg's vampires come from another planet. Some vampires are quite romantic, so readers of this subgenre may also enjoy paranormal romance in Chapter 5.

Brite, Poppy Z.

Lost Souls.

Collins, Nancy A.

Midnight Blue: The Sonja Blue Collection: *Sunglasses After Dark*, *In the Blood*, and *Paint it Black*. In this collection of three titles originally published separately, Sonja is not only a vampire but a vampire slayer, too.

Daniels, Lee

The Black Castle.

The Silver Skull.

Geare, Michael, and Michael Corby

Dracula's Diary. Tongue-in-cheek.

Greenburg, Dan

The Nanny.

Guigonnat, Henri

Daemon in Lithuania.

Hambly, Barbara

Those Who Hunt the Night.

Hamilton, Laurell K.

Anita Blake series.

Hays, Clark, and Kathleen McFall

The Cowboy and the Vampire: A Very Unusual Romance. A contemporary Wyoming cowboy must fight for the woman he loves, who just may be the next queen of the vampires, as good and evil vampires battle to win her over to their respective sides.

Huff, Tanya

Blood Lines.

Blood Pact.

Blood Price.

Blood Trail.

Kalogridis, Jeanne

Covenant with the Vampire.

Children of the Vampire.

Lord of the Vampires.

King, Stephen

Salem's Lot.

Lee, Tanith

Sabella; or, The Blood Stone.

Lichtenberg, Jacqueline

Those of My Blood.

Linssen, John

Tabitha Fffoulkes: A Love Story About a Reformed Vampire and His Favorite Lady.

Martin, George R. R.

Fevre Dream.

Matheson, Richard

I Am Legend.

Newman, Kim

Anno-Dracula.

The Bloody Red Baron.

Raven, Simon

Doctors Wear Scarlet.

Rice, Anne

Interview with the Vampire.

The Vampire Lestat.

Queen of the Damned.

Tale of the Body Thief.

Memnoc the Devil.

Pandora.

The Vampire Armand.

Saberhagen, Fred

The Dracula Tapes.

A Matter of Taste.

A Sharpness on the Neck.

Simmons, Dan

Carrion Comfort.

Children of the Night. Joshua, adopted as an infant from Romania, is kidnapped by the vampiric srigoi after his mother, a hematologist, discovers that his blood may hold the cure for AIDS and cancer.

Stoker, Bram

Dracula. First published in 1897, the novel, like its hero, has never died and has produced bloodthirsty progeny in novels, stage plays, and motion pictures.

Strieber, Whitley

The Hunger.

Sturgeon, Theodore

Some of Your Blood.

Tremayne, Peter

Bloodright: A Memoir of Mircea, Son of Vlad Tepes, Prince of Wallachia, Also Known as Dracula ... Born on This Earth in the Year of Christ 1431, Who Died in 1476 but Remained Undead.

The Revenge of Dracula.

The Palace: A Historical Horror Novel.

Yarbro, Chelsea Quinn

Hotel Transylvania.

The Palace.

Blood Games.

Path of the Eclipse.

Tempting Fate.

A Flame in Byzantium.

Crusader's Torch.

Darker Jewels.

Animals Run Rampant, Werewolves

One of humans' primal fears is of being attacked by monstrous types of animals, but another fear is of being attacked by ordinary animals turned horrifying. One of the most fearsome animals in folklore is the wolf. More fearsome is the magic transformation of a man into a wolf (lycanthropy) or werewolf. (In Oriental folklore, a common motif is the dual nature of woman as fox or cat.)

Bakis, Kirsten

Lives of the Monster Dogs. "Augustus Rank created the 'monster dogs' during the latter part of the 19th century. The dogs—Rottweilers and Dobermans—have been enhanced with surgery and prosthetics, allowing them to walk and talk and think like humans."—Amazon.com

Boucher, Anthony

The Compleat Werewolf.

Copper, Basil

House of the Wolf.

DiSilvestro, Roger L.

Ursula's Gift.

Du Maurier, Daphne

The Birds.

Dvorkin, David

Ursus.

Endore, Guy

The Werewolf of Paris.

Gregory, Stephen

The Cormorant.

King, Stephen

Cujo.

Koontz, Dean

Watchers.

Prantera, Amanda

Strange Loop.

Rouché, Berton

The Cats.

Smith, Wayne

Thor. Only Thor, the family German shepherd, may be able to save his human pack from a werewolf.

Stableford, Brian

The Werewolves of London.

The Angel of Pain.

The Carnival of Destruction.

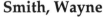

Strieber, Whitley
The Wolfen.

Tessier, Thomas
The Nightwalker.

Yarbro, Chelsea Quinn
The Godforsaken.

Mind Control

The domination of another's mind by the living or the dead, by humans or demons, is a strong theme in folklore and horror literature. It appears in several religions and is related to the rite of exorcism (see "Demonic Possession and Exorcism," p. 433). Sometimes a person loses control of his or her mind to a cult.

Brookes, Owen
Deadly Communion.

Chesbro, George C.
Veil.

David, James F.
Fragments.

Hallahan, William H.
The Keeper of the Children.

Koontz, Dean
Strangers. Several strangers are lured, through their nightmares, to the Tranquility Motel, where terror awaits them.

Masterton, Graham
The Burning.

Simmons, Dan
Carrion Comfort. Vampires of the mind wrest mental control from their victims.

Siodmak, Curt
Donovan's Brain.

Medical Horror and Evil Science

Doctors, sometimes mad, and hospitals in which unnatural medicine is practiced exist in a horrifying subgenre. Readers may also find similar titles in Chapter 4, "Adventure," in the "Biothrillers" section.

Cook, Robin
Brain.

Coma.

Fever.

Godplayer.

Harmful Intent.

Vital Signs.

Mutation.

Mindbend.

Chromosome 6.

David, James F.

Fragments. A psychologist melds together the minds of five idiot-savants, but a sixth mind, the spirit of a woman raped and murdered, joins them and takes over.

Gerritsen, Tess
Gravity.

Bloodstream. A doctor and mother must find out what is the cause of strange episodes of violence that periodically crop up in the peaceful small town she has moved to, before her son is destroyed.

Jordan, B. B.
Principal Investigation.

Katz, William
Facemaker.

Klein, Daniel
Embryo.

Wavelengths.

Palmer, Michael

Natural Causes. Dr. Sarah Baldwin suddenly loses several patients who have been taking an herbal supplement she had prescribed.

Pearson, Ridley
The Angel Maker. Street kids are found dead, with missing organs (kidneys, livers, and lungs).

Perry, Stephani D.
Resident Evil series. Based on the electronic game.

Ravin, Neil
Seven North.

Saul, John

Creature.

The God Project. Healthy babies in their Eastbury, Massachusetts, cribs suddenly turn cold.

The Presence. Why would healthy 17-year-old boys suddenly drop dead?

Shobin, David

The Obsession.

The Seeding.

The Unborn.

Slattery, Jesse

The Juliet Effect.

Spruill, Steven G.

My Soul to Take.

Zimmerman, R. D.

Mindscream.

Dark Fantasy

A hint of evil, a touch of magic, and a dark look at the world combine to create fantasy with a surrealistic feeling that shades into horror. Readers may also enjoy titles listed in Chapter 7, "Fantasy."

Berliner, Janet, and George Guthridge

Madagascar Manifesto.

Child of the Light.

Child of the Journey.

Children of the Dusk. Stoker Award winner.

Brooks, Terry

Running with the Demon.

Knight of the Word.

Dedman, Stephen

The Art of Arrow Cutting.

King, Stephen

The Dark Tower series.

The Gunslinger.

The Drawing of the Three.

The Waste Lands.

Wizard and Glass.

Powers, Tim

    Expiration Date.

    Earthquake Weather.

    Last Call. In a bizarre poker game involving Tarot cards, Scott Crane must face down his father, the Fisher King.

Apocalypse

A horror is unleashed that is so terrible the world could be destroyed.

Grant, Charles L.

Millennium quartet. The Four Horsemen of the Apocalypse sweep the planet.

    Symphony.

    In the Mood.

Herbert, James

    Portent.

    The Fog.

Masterton, Graham

    Burial.

Psychological Horror

Many of the horror stories currently being published are about psychological horror, and the terrors often do have an explicable cause, however deranged the mind from which the horror emanates. Serial killer stories fall into this category.

Bloch, Robert

    Psycho.

Campbell, Ramsey

    The Count of Eleven.

    Nazareth Hill.

Coyne, John

    Fury.

Craig, Kit

    Twice Burned.

Dobyns, Stephen

    The Church of Dead Girls. A town spins out of control as a series of girls are murdered in a literary tale of terror.

Harris, Thomas
    Red Dragon.
    Silence of the Lambs.
    Hannibal. Erudite cannibal Hannibal Lector goes up against FBI Agent Clarice Starling.

Hoffman, Barry
    Hungry Eyes.

King, Stephen
    Misery.

Klavan, Andrew
    Animal Hour.

Krabbé, Tim
    The Vanishing.

Massie, Elizabeth
    Sineater.

McCammon, Robert R.
    Mine.

Monninger, Joseph
    Incident at Potter's Ridge.

Reeves-Stevens, Garfield
    Dark Matter.

Stirling, Blake
    Chiller.

Splatterpunk

Graphic violence, gore, sex, and a dismal outlook are attributes of horror's cutting edge. *Splatterpunks: Extreme Horror*, edited by Paul M. Sammon (St. Martin's Press, 1990), offers a selection of stories from the best-known writers of this type. A sampling of authors who write in this subgenre are:

    Barker, Clive

    Brite, Poppy Z.

    Lansdale, Joe R.

    Masterton, Graham

    Schow, David J.

    Shirley, John

    Skipp, John, and Craig Spector

    Slade, Michael

Detectives and Horror

A detective is sometimes engaged in cases involving the supernatural, with the detection plot often secondary to the eerie background.

Ackroyd, Peter
Hawksmoor.

Blatty, William Peter
The Exorcist.

Legion.

Clements, Mark A.
Children of the End.

Copper, Basil
Necropolis.

Hamilton, Laurell K.
Anita Blake Vampire Slayer series. A charming combination of detection, horror, and romance.

Huff, Tanya
The Victory Nelson series. Another combination of detection, horror, and romance.

> **Blood Price.** Ancient forces of chaos have been loosed on Toronto.
>
> **Blood Trail.** Innocent Canadian werewolves are being killed.
>
> **Blood Lines.** A mummy feeds on the unwary.
>
> **Blood Pact.** Vicki's mom's body disappears from a funeral home.
>
> **Blood Debt.** Wraiths play a deadly nightly game.

Koontz, Dean
Whispers.

Morgan, Robert
Things That Are Not There.

Slade, Michael
Goul.

Reaper.

Primal Scream.

Straub, Peter
Koko.

Mystery.

Strieber, Whitley
    The Wolfen.

Comic Horror

Surprisingly enough, horror—the most uncomedic of genres—can sometimes be combined with comedy.

Hamilton, Laurell K.

The Anita Blake series. Combines humor, romance, and detection.

Guilty Pleasures.

The Laughing Corpse. A murderous zombie is on the loose.

Circus of the Damned.

The Lunatic Cafe. Just how is one to choose between a werewolf and a vampire as a romantic interest?

Bloody Bones.

Killing Dance.

Burnt Offerings. An arsonist is targeting vampires.

Moore, Christopher
    Practical Demonkeeping: A Comedy of Horrors.

Topics

Horror Grand Masters

Forrest J. Ackerman

Robert Bloch

Ray Bradbury

Hugh B. Cave

Ronald Chetwynd-Hayes

Harlan Ellison

Christopher Lee

Fritz Leiber

Ira Levin

Frank Belknap Long

Richard Matheson

Joyce Carol Oates

Ray Russell

Clifford D. Simak

Gahan Wilson

Short Stories

The short story has been popular in horror from the beginning. It wasn't until Stephen King roared onto the scene that it was surpassed by the novel form.

Anthologies

The large number of horror anthologies indicates both the popularity of such collections and the significance of the short story in the genre. There are several inveterate anthologists; the listings here are but a selection from their volumes. Other horror stories can be found in anthologies listed for science fiction (see p. 332) and fantasy (see p. 371), and some authors from those fields appear in the following anthologies. One of the interesting facts about horror anthologies is that libraries seem to hang onto them forever. Even when they are not reprinted, anthologies published long ago can still be found on library shelves.

Annual Anthologies

Datlow, Ellen, and Terri Windling, eds. *The Year's Best Fantasy and Horror.* St. Martin's Press. The 11th annual collection was published in 1998.

Grant, Charles L., ed. *Shadows.* Doubleday, 1978–1991.

Jones, Stephen ed. *The Mammoth Book of Best New Horror.* Carroll & Graf. The ninth annual edition was published in 1999.

The Year's Best Horror Stories. Daw. 1972–1990. Annual.

General Anthologies

Bloch, Robert. *Robert Bloch's Psychos.* Pocket, 1998.

Gorman, Ed, and Martin H. Greenberg, eds. *Night Screams: Twenty-Two Stories of Terror.* New American Library, 1996.

Grant, Charles L., ed. *Gallery of Horror.* New American Library, 1997. A reprint edition of the 1983 *Dodd Mead Gallery of Horror.*

Hartwell, David G., ed. *The Dark Descent.* Tor, 1987. Reprinted in paperback in 1997.

Pelan, John, ed. *Darkside: Horror for the Next Millennium.* New American Library, 1998.

Wagner, Phyllis Cerf, and Herbert Wise, eds. *Great Tales of Terror and the Supernatural.* Modern Library, 1994.

Weinberg, Robert E., Stefan Dziemianowicz, and Martin H. Greenberg, eds. *Between Time and Terror.* New American Library, 1995.

Theme Anthologies

Brite, Poppy Z., ed. *Love in Vein: Twenty Original Tales of Vampiric Erotica.* Harper-Prism, 1994.

———. *Love in Vein II: 18 More Tales of Vampiric Erotica.* HarperPrism, 1997.

The Darkest Thirst: A Vampire Anthology. Design Image Group, 1998.

Datlow, Ellen, and Terri Windling, eds. *Sirens and Other Daemon Lovers.* Harper-Prism, 1998.

Dziemianowicz, Stefan R., Robert E. Weinberg, and Martin H. Greenberg, eds. *Weird Tales: 32 Unearthed Terrors.* Bonanza Books, 1988.

Elrod, P. N., and Martin H. Greenberg, eds. *The Time of the Vampires.* Daw, 1996.

Gorman, Ed, and Martin H. Greenberg, eds. *Night Screams: Twenty-Two Stories of Terror.* New American Library, 1996.

———. *Predators.* Roc, 1993.

Greenberg, Martin H., ed. *Haunted Houses: The Greatest Stories.* Fine Communications, 1997.

———. *Vampire Detectives.* New American Library, 1995.

Hambly, Barbara, and Martin H. Greenberg, eds. *Sisters of the Night.* Warner, 1995.

Jones, Stephen, ed. *The Mammoth Book of Terror.* Carroll & Graf, 1993.

———. *The Mammoth Book of Vampires.* Carroll & Graf, 1993.

———. *The Mammoth Book of Zombies.* Carroll & Graf, 1993.

Masterton, Graham, ed. *Scare Care.* Tor, 1989. Severn House, 1990.

Pelan, John, ed. *Darkside: Horror for the Next Millennium.* New American Library, 1998.

Slung, Michele B. *I Shudder at Your Touch: 22 Tales of Sex and Horror.* Roc, 1991.

Weinberg, Robert E., Stefan Dziemianowicz, and Martin H. Greenberg, eds. *Between Time and Terror.* New American Library, 1995.

Winter, Douglas E., ed. *Revelations.* HarperPrism, 1997. Includes "Men and Sin," by Clive Barker; "The Big Blow," by Joe R. Lansdale; "If I Should Die Before I Wake," by David Morrell; "Aryans and Absinthe," by F. Paul Wilson; "Triads," by Poppy Z. Brite and Christa Faust; "Riding the Black," by Charles L. Grant; "The Open Doors," by Whitley Strieber; "Fixtures of Matchstick Men and Joo," by Elizabeth Massie; "Whatever," by Richard Christian Matheson; "Dismantling Fortress Architecture," by David J. Schow and Craig Spector; "The Word," by Ramsey Campbell; and "A Moment at the River's Heart," by Clive Barker.

Wolf, Leonard, ed. *Blood Thirst: 100 Years of Vampire Fiction.* Oxford University Press, 1997.

Short Story Collections: Individual Authors

Before Stephen King's impact on the genre in the 1970s, the horror tale was probably best known in the form of the short story. Most of the classic and modern authors are available in published collections. They and others are readily found in the many anthologies listed in this chapter. Most of the following collections contain a variety of the types of horror tale.

Aickman, Robert
Cold Hand in Mine.

Night Voices: Strange Stories.

The Wine Dark Sea.

Barker, Clive
The Books of Blood.

Cabal.

Bierce, Ambrose
Ghost and Horror Stories.

Blackwood, Algernon
Tales of the Mysterious and the Macabre.

Tales of the Uncanny and Supernatural.

Bloch, Robert
Out of the Mouths of Graves.

Chills.

Bowen, Elizabeth
The Cat Jumps and Other Stories.

Braunbeck, Gary A.
Things Left Behind.

Collier, John
Fancies and Goodnights.

Collins, Wilkie
Tales of Terror and the Supernatural.

Copper, Basil
Here Be Daemons: Tales of Horror and the Uneasy.

Voices of Doom: Tales of Terror and the Uncanny.

Derleth, August
Dwellers in Darkness.

Dinesen, Isak
Seven Gothic Tales.
Winter's Tales.

Doyle, Arthur Conan, Sir
The Best Supernatural Tales. Edited by E. F. Bleiler.

Du Maurier, Daphne
Echoes from the Macabre: Selected Stories.

Etchison, Dennis
The Dark Country.
The Blood Kiss.

Hartley, L. P.
The Traveling Grave, and Other Stories.

Harvey, W. F.
Midnight Tales.

Leiber, Fritz
Heroes and Horrors.

Long, Frank Belknap
The Hounds of Tindalos.

Lumley, Brian
Fruiting Bodies and Other Fungi.

McNaughton, Brian
The Throne of Bones.

Oates, Joyce Carol
Night-Side.

Poe, Edgar Allan
The Collected Tales and Poems of Edgar Allan Poe.

The Complete Stories.

The Fall of the House of Usher and Other Tales.

18 Best Stories by Edgar Allen Poe. Includes "The Black Cat;" "The Fall of the House of Usher;" "The Masque of the Red Death;" "The Facts in the Case of M. Valdemar;" "The Premature Burial;" "Ms. Found in a Bottle;" "A Tale of the Ragged Mountains;" "The Sphinx;" "The Murders in the Morgue;" "The Tell-Tale Heart;" "The Gold-Bug;" "The System of Dr. Tarr and Prof. Fether;" "The Man That Was Used Up;" "The Balloon Hoax;" "A Descent into the Maelstrom;" "The Purloined Letter;" "The Pit and the Pendulum;" "The Cask of Amontillado."

Ryan, Alan
   The Bones Wizard.

Wagner, Karl Edward
   Exorcisms and Ecstasies.

Wellman, Manly Wade
   Who Fears the Devil.
   Worse Things Waiting.

Bibliographies

Ashley, Michael, and William Contento. *Supernatural Index: A Listing of Fantasy, Supernatural, Occult, Weird, Horror Anthologies.* Greenwood, 1995. Indexes over 2,100 anthologies containing more than 21,000 stories by over 7,700 authors, published between 1813 and 1994.

Barron, Neil, ed. *Horror Literature.* Garland, 1990. Includes historical/critical essays.

Fonseca, Anthony J., and June Michele Pulliam. *Hooked on Horror: A Guide to Reading Interests in Horror Fiction.* Libraries Unlimited, 1999. The ultimate guide to advising the horror reader classifies approximately 1,000 works into 13 subgenres (e.g., psychological horror, technohorror, splatterpunk). Award winners are listed and a comprehensive guide to bibliographies, history, criticism, organizations, and conferences important in the genre is included. There is also a thorough index to horror short stories.

Encyclopedias

In addition to the following encyclopedia, *The Encyclopedia of Fantasy* (see p. 416) covers a great deal of horror, in particular dark fantasy.

Sullivan, Jack, ed. *The Penguin Encyclopedia of Horror and the Supernatural.* With an introduction by Jacques Barzun. Viking, 1986. An exemplary encyclopedia of awesome text and abundant fearful illustrations that covers literature, art, film, radio, television, music, and illustration. "The main criteria for coverage are that the evocation of fear, whether supernatural or psychological, be the main or at least the major part of the artist's interest and that the work be either historically important or of enduring quality."—*Genreflecting* 2d ed., 1986. There are 54 theme essays listed alphabetically, with names (authors, artists, composers, actors, film directors) and film titles. All entries are signed, and the list of contributors is impressive. All of the theme essays (and, indeed, all the entries) are engrossing reading. A few of the theme essays indicate specific significance to genre fiction, although the whole work is, of course, relevant: "Definitions: Horror, Supernatural, and Science Fiction"; "Detection and Ghosts"; "The Devil, Devils, Demons"; "Frankenstein: The Myth"; "Ghosts"; "Horror and Science Fiction"; "Mad Doctors"; "Occult Fiction"; "Poltergeists"; "Possession"; "Vampires"; "Werewolves"; "Zombies." The work is invaluable for readers' advisors as a critical guide to authors, their works, and types of fiction within the genre. Of particular use is the lengthy essay "Writers of Today," a critical roundup of current authors, each listed with a cross-reference within the main alphabet. Jacques Barzun's introduction, "The Art and Appeal of the Ghostly and Ghastly," undoubtedly will become a classic in the literature.

History and Criticism

The definitive history and criticism of the horror genre are yet to be written. Until they are, the following books may be used for background on various aspects of the genre.

Bleiler, E. F., ed. *Supernatural Fiction Writers: Fantasy and Horror.* Scribner's, 1985. 2 vols. Brief biography and criticism of 148 authors.

Bloom, Clive, ed. *Gothic Horror: A Reader's Guide from Poe to King and Beyond.* St. Martin's Press, 1998.

Bloom, Harold. *Classic Horror Writers.* Chelsea House Publishers, 1994. Biographical, bibliographical, and critical analysis of a dozen early writers of horror, including Ann Radcliffe, Edgar Allan Poe, Ambrose Bierce, Robert Louis Stevenson, and Bram Stoker.

Cox, Greg. *Transylvanian Library: A Consumer's Guide to Vampire Fiction.* Borgo, 1993. Includes chapters such as "History of the Vampire," "In the Wake of Dracula," "The Vampire Meets the Atomic Age," "Return of the Heroic Vampire," and "The Heroic Vampire Triumphs." It also contains author, title, subject, publisher, and character indexes.

Joshi, S. T. *The Weird Tale.* University of Texas, 1990. The fantastic writings of Arthur Machen, Lord Dunsany, Algernon Blackwood, M. R. James, Ambrose Bierce, and H. P. Lovecraft are surveyed.

King, Stephen. *Danse Macabre.* Everest House, 1979. These essays in history and criticism of the horror novel and film are personal and often anecdotal, albeit at the same time sharply critical and interpretative. Recommended reading for those who are *not* fans of the genre.

Lovecraft, Howard Phillips. *Supernatural Horror in Literature.* With a new introduction by E. F. Bleiler. Dover, 1973. Essential reading as definition, history, and criticism. "The one test of the truly weird is simply this—whether or not there be excited in the reader a profound sense of dread, and of contact with unknown spheres and powers; a subtle attitude of awed listening, as if for the beating of black wings or the scratching of outside shapes and entities on the known universe's utmost rim." —*Genreflecting*, 2d ed., 1986

Conventions

World Horror Convention. The first (annual) was held in Nashville, Tennessee, in 1991. The 1999 convention was held in Atlanta, Georgia, in March.

Organizations

The Horror Writers Association. Formerly the Horror Writers of America; has awarded the Bram Stoker Awards annually since 1987. In 1998 it had 732 members. Presidents of the association have been elected from the brightest lights of the horror community: Dean Koontz, 1986–1987; Charles L. Grant, 1987–1988; Chelsea Quinn Yarbro, 1988–1990; Craig Shaw Gardner, 1990–1992; Dennis Etchison, 1992–1994; Lawrence Watt-Evans, 1994–1996; Brian Lumley, 1996–1997; Janet Berliner, 1997–present. Web site: http://www.horror.org/ (accessed 20 January 2000).

The International Horror Guild. Founded in 1995 by Nancy A. Collins. It awards the International Horror Guild Award annually in several categories. The gargoyle-shaped statuettes are awarded at the World Horror Convention. Web site: http://slaughter.net/worldhorror.org/ihg/ (accessed 20 January 2000).

Awards

Many of the titles that are nominated for and frequently winners of the World Fantasy Award fall into the horror genre. The Horror Writers of America presents the Bram Stoker Awards annually.

1987: *Misery* by Stephen King
  Swan Song by Robert R. McCammon
1988: *The Silence of the Lambs* by Thomas Harris
1989: *Carrion Comfort* by Dan Simmons
1990: *Mine* by Robert R. McCammon
1991: *Boy's Life* by Robert R. McCammon
1992: *Blood of the Lamb* by Thomas F. Monteleone
1993: *The Throat* by Peter Straub
1994: *Dead in the Water* by Nancy Holder
1995: *Zombie* by Joyce Carol Oates
1996: *The Green Mile* by Stephen King
1997: *Children of the Dusk* by Janet Berliner & George Guthridge
1998: *Bag of Bones* by Stephen King

Publishers

Arkham House was founded in 1939 to preserve the writings of H. P. Lovecraft and now publishes horror, fantasy, and science fiction. Dover Books, the reprinter of Lovecraft's *Supernatural Horror in Literature,* has a strong line of trade quality paperback reprints of the classics, listed in its catalog as the "Dover Library of Ghost Stories." Carroll & Graf have brought out several huge horror anthologies in their Mammoth line of trade paperbacks, including *The Mammoth Book of Zombies.* Severn House reprints genre titles in hardcover, often from original paperback releases. The Abyss line, from the conglomerate that includes Dell and Delacorte, is dedicated solely to publishing horror. Publishers of horror novels include the following:

Abyss (Dell and Delacorte)
Arkham House
Bantam
Carroll & Graf
Daw Books
Gollancz
HarperCollins
Headline
Knopf
Little, Brown
Putnam
Simon and Schuster
St. Martin's Press
Tor
Warner Books
White Wolf
Mark V. Zeisling

Review Journals

Horror is most often reviewed with science fiction and fantasy (see both "Critical Journals," and "Journals"). *Necrofile*, started in 1991, is a quarterly review source devoted to reviewing horror. It attempts to list all horror fiction currently being published in the United States and Great Britain.

Writers' Manuals

Wiater, Stanley. *Dark Thoughts on Writing.* Underwood, 1997. Not just a "how to write and get published" book, this is much more, as can be seen from the table of contents: "Basic Influences"; "Working in the Dark"; "Short Story, Novel, or Script?"; "Regarding Fame and Fortune"; "Going to the Movies"; "Sex and Death and Other Unspeakable Concerns"; "Censored"; "Personal Fears and Practical Philosophies"; "Shocking Advice"; "The Function and Importance of Unpleasant Truths"; "Where Do You Get Your Ideas?"; "A Reader's Guide to Writing Horror"; "Modern Horror Fiction: A Selection of 113 Best Books"; and "The Best in Short Fiction: Anthologies."

Williamson, J. N. *How to Write Tales of Horror, Fantasy and Science Fiction.* F&W, 1991.

Online Resources

Classic Horror and Fantasy Page, http://www.geocities.com/Area51/Corridor/5582/ (accessed 20 January 2000).

Horror Writers Association, http://www.horror.org/ (accessed 20 January 2000).

Masters of Terror and Horror Fiction, http://pluto.spaceports.com/~mot (accessed 20 January 2000). Provides bibliographic information on over 400 authors, reviews, a top 100 listing, and links to other horror-related Web sites.

D's Horror Picks

Hamilton, Laurell K. Anita Blake Vampire Slayer series.

Harris, Thomas. *Hannibal.*

Hays, Clark, and Kathleen McFall. *The Cowboy and the Vampire: A Very Unusual Romance.*

Saul, John. *The Presence.*

Author/Title Index

Subject Index

Character Index